CW00938674

Examining Gun Regulations, Warning Behaviors, and Policies to Prevent Mass Shootings

Selina E.M. Kerr
Independent Researcher, UK

A volume in the Advances in Human Services and
Public Health (AHSPH) Book Series

Published in the United States of America by
IGI Global
Information Science Reference (an imprint of IGI Global)
701 E. Chocolate Avenue
Hershey PA, USA 17033
Tel: 717-533-8845
Fax: 717-533-8661
E-mail: cust@igi-global.com
Web site: http://www.igi-global.com

Library of Congress Cataloging-in-Publication Data

Names: Kerr, Selina E. M., author.
Title: Examining gun regulations, warning behaviors, and policies to
   prevent mass shootings / by Selina E.M. Kerr.
Description: Hershey, PA : Information Science Reference, [2021] | Includes
   bibliographical references and index. | Summary: "This book investigates
   and analyzes the debates around and responses to mass shootings,
   covering the prevention, preparation, response and recovery of mass
   shootings as well as gun proposals introduced and raised following each
   incident"-- Provided by publisher.
Identifiers: LCCN 2020028646 (print) | LCCN 2020028647 (ebook) | ISBN
   9781799839163 (hardcover) | ISBN 9781799867678 (paperback) | ISBN
   9781799839170 (ebook)
Subjects: LCSH: Gun control--United States. | Mass shootings--United
   States--Prevention. | Firearms and crime--United States. | Firearms
   ownership--United States. | Firearms--Law and legislation--United
   States.
Classification: LCC HV7436 .K47 2021 (print) | LCC HV7436 (ebook) | DDC
   364.4--dc23
LC record available at https://lccn.loc.gov/2020028646
LC ebook record available at https://lccn.loc.gov/2020028647

This book is published in the IGI Global book series Advances in Human Services and Public Health (AHSPH) (ISSN: 2475-6571; eISSN: 2475-658X)

British Cataloguing in Publication Data
A Cataloguing in Publication record for this book is available from the British Library.

For electronic access to this publication, please contact: eresources@igi-global.com.

Advances in Human Services and Public Health (AHSPH) Book Series

Jennifer Martin
RMIT University, Australia

ISSN:2475-6571
EISSN:2475-658X

Mission

The well-being of the general public should be a primary concern for any modern civilization. Ongoing research in the field of human services and public healthcare is necessary to evaluate, manage, and respond to the health and social needs of the global population.

The **Advances in Human Services and Public Health (AHSPH)** book series aims to publish high-quality reference publications focused on the latest methodologies, tools, issues, and strategies for managing the health and social welfare of the public. The AHSPH book series will be especially relevant for healthcare professionals, policy makers, government officials, and students seeking the latest research in this field.

Coverage

- Healthcare Reform
- Social Welfare Policy
- Youth Development
- Health Policy
- Poverty
- Assistance Programs
- Social Work
- Public Funding
- Domestic Violence
- Medicare and Medicaid

IGI Global is currently accepting manuscripts for publication within this series. To submit a proposal for a volume in this series, please contact our Acquisition Editors at acquisitions@igi-global.com or visit: https://www.igi-global.com/publish/.

Titles in this Series

701 East Chocolate Avenue, Hershey, PA 17033, USA
Tel: 717-533-8845 x100 • Fax: 717-533-8661
E-Mail: cust@igi-global.com • www.igi-global.com

Table of Contents

Section 1
Understandings of Mass Shootings

Section 2
Assessing the Risk of Mass Shootings

Preface

As I write this, the world is dealing with the COVID-19 epidemic. Countries are in lockdown, economies have shut down and millions have been directly affected by the coronavirus. A rather surprising consequence of the global pandemic has been a decline in mass shootings in the United States. For the first time in almost twenty years, there were no school shootings during the month of March in 2020. This may be linked to the United States going into lockdown on the 16th of March 2020 in response to the threat from the coronavirus. Schools have been closed down and students are being home-schooled (Vallejo, 2020). Mass shootings as a whole declined whilst the country was in quarantine, with this being attributed to the closure of businesses, entertainment venues, schools and religious places. With the United States re-emerging from lockdown status, fears have been expressed that this could result in an increase in mass shootings (Klemko, 2020).

This goes some way to indicating the scale of the problem of mass shootings in the United States. Although these are only a small fraction of the gun-related deaths every year, mass shootings still occur at a higher rate there than in other developed countries (BBC News, 2019). It was a mass shooting at a school in my home country of the United Kingdom that first got me interested in the issue. The Dunblane Primary School incident in Scotland in 1996 was a landmark moment for gun laws in Great Britain, with this incident leading to some of the tightest handgun restrictions in the world. A previous mass shooting in 1989 in England had resulted in a ban on semi-automatic rifles. The response of my own country in comparison to that of the United States has always been a subject of interest for me. Whilst the United States has suffered from hundreds of mass shootings over the years, policy change relating to guns has been limited in scope. Recognizing that the United States has a written constitution, as well as a different history and culture to the United Kingdom, its response should not be the same. What did interest me was the debate about guns that seems to unfold after mass shootings. Unfortunately, it seems to be just that, a debate with a distinct lack of action. Another aspect of interest to me was the mind-set of preparedness the United States has to deal with mass shootings, with emergency management planning and threat assessment procedures all becoming commonplace strategies to avert and negate potential threats.

Considering this, the rationale of this book is to analyze the debates around and responses to mass shootings. The focus is two-fold in nature: the prevention, preparation, response and recovery of mass shootings; the gun proposals raised following these incidents. With regards to the first part, threat assessment, emergency management and leakage are discussed. Interviews with experts in these areas contribute to guidance about how to try to prevent, prepare for, respond to and recover from mass shootings. Another focus of the book is on policy debates pertaining to guns. This involves scrutinizing the news media coverage following the current worst mass shooting incident in Las Vegas (2017) documenting its role in policy discussions. Using the same case study, also examined in the book are news media constructions of mass shootings and how they pertain to categorization, definitions, risk perceptions and fear. The voices of those involved in gun violence prevention are also captured to detail which policy responses may reduce harm in mass shootings and the likelihood of these gaining traction. This book should be of interest to scholars working on research relating to policymaking, news media, framing, US politics, mass violence, firearms, emergency management, threat assessment and the culture of fear. Those working in policymaking and practical procedures relating to guns, threat assessment and emergency management may also find the book of interest. Students undertaking courses in sociology, criminology, politics and policymaking should also find this work useful.

The Introduction, as well as the Understandings of Mass Shootings and Methodological Approach chapters, set up the context of the book. The Introduction details the rationale of the book, previous studies in this area and the roadmap of the book. Chapter 1 focuses on the understandings of mass shootings, examining definitions, current trends and categorizations of these incidents. The Methodological Approach documents the methodologies adopted, the samples of news media content and interviewees selected for analysis purposes. The next two chapters focus on the Las Vegas mass shooting, using results from news media analysis and findings from interviews with gun violence prevention activists. The third chapter centers on perceptions of risk and fear in relation to mass shootings. Chapter 4 examines gun policy reform (and lack thereof) after the Las Vegas incident. The next three chapters move on to look at the prevention of mass shootings. The fifth chapter examines leakage and other warning behaviors displayed prior to attack in a selection of mass shooting incidents. Chapter 6 looks at ways to assess the risk of mass shootings. Building upon this, Chapter 7 details the most appropriate means to assess threats relating to mass shootings. Changing topic, Chapter 8 documents advances in emergency management planning and training to prepare for mass shootings. The ninth chapter then looks at ways to respond to and recover with these incidents when they transpire. The final three chapters focus on gun policies, particularly how these might develop in future. Chapter 10 details the policy proposals advanced by gun violence prevention (GVP) interviewees. It also surmises which of these have the greatest chances of gaining traction in future. Chapter 11 then looks at framing approaches that could be used to mobilize the GVP movement. The twelfth and final chapter of the book projects into the future, considering elements like the results of the 2020 presidential election and levels of public support. An Appendix provides further details of the interviewees involved in the study.

REFERENCES

BBC News. (2019, December 29). *U.S. saw highest number of mass killings on record in 2019, database reveals.* https://www.bbc.co.uk/news/world-us-canada-50936575?SThisFB&fbclid=IwAR05I7b7PFrG ypjs3CDxoqBxKhsO_1aFHtY4paidxsw8iI84S_HSrEdik7U

Klemko, R. (2020, May 28). *Gatherings as states reopen could spell return of another dark American phenomenon: mass shootings.* Washington Post. https://www.washingtonpost.com/national/coronavirus-reopening-mass-shootings/2020/05/28/8b8ea396-a02e-11ea-81bb-c2f70f01034b_story.html

Vallejo, J. (2020, April 15). *US has first March without school shooting in 18 years: 'It shouldn't have taken a pandemic to make this possible.'* The Independent. https://www.independent.co.uk/news/world/americas/us-school-shooting-stats-gun-laws-hillary-clinton-coronavirus-a9465406.html

Acknowledgment

I am grateful to all my research participants for taking part in this work. Working in this interesting, albeit emotionally challenging, topic for over a decade has afforded me opportunities to meet a number of inspirational people. The interviewees who have become involved in school safety or gun violence prevention efforts after losing or almost losing a child to gun violence have been particularly inspiring to me: Andy, Ellen, John-Michael, Mick and Tom. They also happen to be some of the nicest people I have been fortunate enough to meet.

My gratitude is also extended to those who proofread my work: my friends, Billie and Sharon; my sister, husband, mum, and stepdad; David Tierney and Jennifer Young. I am also grateful for all other assistance and support I have received whilst writing this book.

I would like to dedicate this book to my daughter who came into the world in 2020.

Introduction

"I never thought it could happen here." This is the phrase often used by communities who have experienced a mass killing. These incidents tend to take place in everyday locations, such as movie theaters, restaurants, schools and so forth. The focus of this book will be on those incidents where a firearm is used to enact a mass killing spree, defined as "mass shootings." Out of the forty-one mass killings in the United States in 2019, thirty-three were perpetrated using firearms (BBC News, 2019a). This was the highest number of mass killings in a year since the inception of record-keeping by the AP/USA Today and Northeastern database in the 1970s (Pane, 2019).

Despite a recent increase in incidents, mass shootings only constitute a tiny fraction of gun violence deaths in the United States (BBC News, 2019b). In spite of this, these incidents tend to provoke policy debates in relation to guns (see Fleming, 2012; Fleming et al., 2016; Goss, 2006; Kerr, 2018a; Rood, 2019). Other policies generally discussed after a mass shooting center on ways to prevent, prepare for and respond to such incidents. Risk assessment and threat assessment procedures are ways to try to prevent mass shootings. In terms of preparing for and responding to incidents emergency management and communication strategies are the methods used (see Doran, 2014; Drysdale, Modzeleski & Simons, 2010; Erikson, 2001; Kerr, 2018b; Vossekuil, Fein, Reddy, Borum & Modzeleski, 2002). This book encompasses all of those policy areas: debates about guns; threat and risk assessment processes; and strategies in emergency management and communication.

News media content in terms of the amount of coverage and how issues are covered, first of all, have the potential to affect how media audiences interpret and understand mass shootings (see Delli Carpini, 2005; Fowler, 1991). Secondly, the gun debate following these incidents plays out in a number of public arenas, such as the political sphere, news media and citizen discussions. The news media covers the arguments advanced by politicians following these incidents; whilst media content may shape how readers think about the gun issue (Callaghan & Schnell, 2005; Jacobs & Shapiro, 2000). Based on this, the decision was reached to choose news media articles as units of analysis. The methodological approach for this analysis was informed by the literature on framing (Callaghan & Schnell, 2005; Chong & Druckman, 2007; Woodly, 2015). Also captured within this book are the views of activists in the gun violence prevention movement to gauge their thoughts on which policies would reduce mass shootings and what may happen with this debate in future. Threat assessment and emergency management and communication are not discussed much in the news media; thus, interviews with experts in threat and risk assessment and/or emergency management were chosen as the method to research these issues. This allowed for a discussion of the different techniques in terms of benefits and potential pitfalls.

This chapter starts off by defining mass shootings, going through the particulars of this type of violence. It will be demonstrated that even though they are rare, these events can have a notable impact in terms of provoking debate. It then documents previous research relating to the key issues of interest in this book: understandings and interpretations of mass shootings; gun debates surrounding these incidents; threat assessment used to prevent mass shootings; emergency management and communication policies utilized in these situations. A roadmap to the rest of the book is then provided.

MASS SHOOTINGS: A SPECIFIC TYPE OF VIOLENCE

It may be questioned what actually constitutes a mass shooting. Scholars have tended to define a "mass shooting" as an incident in which four or more victims are murdered with a firearm at one or multiple locations that are geographically close within a short period of time (Follman, Aronsen & Pan, 2016; Krouse & Richardson, 2015; Silver, Horgan & Gill, 2018). Markedly, this definition excludes the perpetrator(s) of the attack from the death toll (Silver, Horgan & Gill, 2018). It has been said that mass shootings are a "distinctly American problem" (Rood, 2019, p. 4). Trends of mass shootings in the United States have been documented in a number of reports. Examples of these are available in Table 1.

Table 1. Mass Shooting Trends

Study	Time Period	Number of Mass Shootings
Blair & Schweit (2014)	2000-2013	160
Capellan & Lewanowski (2018)	1966-2016	278
Krouse & Richardson (2015)	1999-2013	317
Silva & Capella (2019)	1966-2016	314
Silver, Horgan & Gill (2018)	1990-2014	115

It may be noted that the number of incidents recorded vary widely across the different studies. This is because there are areas of contention around the definition, which can cause problems in correctly estimating the trends (Mears, Moon & Thielo, 2017, p. 944). For example, in their 2018 study, Capellan and Lewanowski included attacks where the perpetrator(s) has attempted to kill four or more people in a public location within a twenty-four hour time period. The authors advanced the argument that these incidents were just as significant as those where four or more people were actually killed. To narrow the variables, however, this study will not include these types of incidents in its definition of a mass shooting. The definition adopted in this book will instead follow the line of thinking advanced by Silver, Horgan and Gill (2018, p. 95) that mass murders that occur in the home and tend to be motivated by intimate partner violence are distinct from the attacks which take place in public spaces such as businesses, leisure locations, sites of worship and schools. Further to this, mass shootings motivated by organized crime/ gangs are also excluded from the definition. Those incidents that take place in public places and are motivated by ideological reasons, e.g. radical or far-right beliefs, are included in the definition.

The varying definitions can also make it difficult to estimate trends relating to mass shootings. Blair and Schweit's (2014) review of mass shootings from 2000 through to 2013 recorded four hundred and eight-six deaths and five hundred and eighty-six injured across a hundred and sixty incidents. Moreover, the first half of that time period saw on average 6.4 incidents a year; the last seven years yielded an average of 16.4 incidents annually (Blair & Schweit, 2014, p. 8). Another study looking at mass shootings found that thirteen out of three hundred and seventeen incidents resulted in double digit death tolls (Krouse & Richardson, 2015, pp. 2, 22). Another study looking just at trends in 2019 found that two hundred and twenty one victims were recorded in 41 incidents and all but eight of them involved firearms. In terms of states, California was found to have the greatest number of incidents, recording eight that year (Pane, 2019). Furthermore, the majority of perpetrators were found to be male (96.5%) and White (60.6%) in a study of 314 mass shootings in public places (Silva & Capella, 2019, p. 87). In terms of location, a National Threat Assessment Center (2019) report looking at attacks in public spaces found that 70% occurred at places of business, 14% in open spaces, 11% in schools and 4% in places of worship.

WHY STUDY MASS SHOOTINGS

To put mass shooting trends into the wider context of gun violence in the United States, there were 38,658 gun-related deaths in 2016. Seventy-one deaths were caused by mass shootings in the same year (BBC News, 2019b). Mass shootings in public spaces, therefore, only account for a small percentage of the overall gun violence toll. Given the relative rarity of mass shootings within the wider spectrum of gun violence, one may question why the author chose to research these incidents. The main reason is that the emergence of a problem or crisis known as a "focusing event" may act as a catalyst to shift particular issues onto the policy agenda and its set of alternatives. The policy agenda is defined as the "list of subjects or problems to which government officials are paying serious attention to at any given time" (Kingdon, 1994/2003, pp. 3, 16). A focusing event is one which happens suddenly with little or no warning, is quite rare and unpredictable in nature (Birkland, 1997, p. 22). An event like a mass shooting with its infrequent and shocking nature meets those criteria; hence, can provoke debates about regulatory gun policies. Of key importance here is the term *debate*, where gun violence issues are discussed; yet, it tends to be the case that very little legislation is actually passed. This was the case after several high-profile mass shootings, including Columbine (1999), Virginia Tech (2007) and Sandy Hook (2012). An alternative reaction following mass shootings is increased calls for more gun ownership or to expand the places where guns can be carried, e.g. in schools (see Goss, 2006; Kerr, 2018a; Kupchik, Brent & Mowen, 2015, Rood, 2019).

What this book is interested in exploring are the ways in which debates about both tightening gun restrictions and loosening them unfold after mass shooting incidents. This is a macro-level approach, examining how political actors and institutions like the media, interest groups, Congress and so forth set the parameters on issues for political debate (Callaghan & Schnell, 2005, pp. xii-xiii). Of key importance in this book is the news media portrayal of mass shootings and related policy issues and how this can affect debates. It is worth noting that not all mass shootings gain national attention in the news media nor do they provoke policy debates. Factors such as the age and presumed vulnerability and innocence of victims play a role in whether a mass shooting garners attention. Moreover, when the location is more "shocking," i.e. occurring in a place thought to be safe like a church and/or occurring in a community with little criminal activity, a mass shooting is more likely to be covered in the news media and prompt debates (Rood, 2019, p. 79). Once the news media has selected the incidents to cover, there are a number of techniques influencing how they are covered. "Priming" is where the news media ascribes higher importance to certain issues in coverage. Moreover, the media also sets the agenda by covering set issues within its coverage. Agenda-setting and priming can, therefore, have some influence on how citizens think about certain issues and how they evaluate policymakers discussing these issues (Callaghan & Schnell, 2005, p. 2). Also important to the process of giving an issue policy traction are the organizations referred to as "advocacy or interest groups," a collection of people with shared attitudes seeking to affect change in a particular social or policy issue (Grossman, 2012, p. 24; Truman, 1951/1993, p. 213).

This book has similar limitations to Spitzer's (2004) work about the politics of gun control. Although there is some discussion of policies passed at the state-level in this book, the focus is mainly on national-level policy-making (and lack thereof). Given how much there is to talk about in relation to the United States and gun violence, there is also little comparative analysis of policies in the United States with those from other countries. The only exception to this is the comparison of statistics of gun violence within the United States with other developed countries in Chapter One. Moreover, there are a few mentions of gun-related legislation in Great Britain in Chapters One and Eleven, documented to highlight the differences between that country and the United States following mass shootings. Another limitation is that only activists from one "side" of the gun debate are included in the research sample: those involved in campaigning for "gun violence prevention" (what was previously known as "gun control"). The reason for focusing solely on gun violence prevention advocates is this group is under-researched in the current literature about the politics of guns in the United States. In contrast, there has been work on gun owners (Carlson, 2015; Kohn, 2004; Stroud, 2015) and gun-rights groups like the NRA (Brown & Abel, 2003; Patterson, 1998; Wilson, 1981). This book also builds upon the previous work by the author, which has focused on GVP interest groups (see Kerr, 2018a, 2018b; Kerr, 2020).

The way an issue is "framed" functions to organize thinking around an issue and guide action on it (Snow, Burke Rochford Jr., Worden & Benford, 1986). Haider-Markel and Josyln's (2001) study highlighted the partisan response to attributing blame to either weak gun laws or violence in the media based on citizens voting Democrat or Republican respectively. Their conclusion was that frames advanced by politicians during periods of extensive public attention may serve to reinforce or stimulate pre-existing beliefs of citizens. For something like gun violence, mass shootings give temporary salience to the issue. Interest groups, thus, have a limited window of opportunity in which to mobilize support from members of the public and politicians, something which is needed to enact policy changes (Birkland, 1997; Fleming, 2012; Fleming et al., 2016; Kingdon, 1994/2003). Framing the issue in a particular way can influence public attitudes and opinions and potentially assist with this process of attempting to obtain support (see Callaghan & Schnell, 2005; Chong & Druckman, 2007; Entman, 2010). This book seeks to document ideas about ways to potentially frame the issue of gun violence in order to successfully pass gun legislation debated after mass shootings.

This book will also focus on some of the other policy areas specific to mass shootings: emergency management and communication processes; risk and threat assessment methods. Whilst gun policies tend not to gain traction after mass shootings, change often does occur in these other policy areas. Emergency management and communication improvements were made both nationwide and in specific states following high-profile shootings at Columbine High School (1999) and Virginia Tech University (2007) (Doran, 2014; Kerr, 2018b). Threat assessment improvements were also implemented (see, for instance, Drysdale, Modzeleski & Simons, 2010; Erikson, 2001; Vossekuil, Fein, Reddy, Borum & Modzeleski, 2002). What this book intends to do is to explore the changes made following mass shootings and to outline on-going developments in these areas.

PREVIOUS RESEARCH

Scholars have been exploring the phenomenon of mass shootings and its related issues for years. For the purposes of this book, there are generally three areas of interest. The first is how the news media discuss mass shootings. These incidents, particularly those with a higher death toll, tend to receive saturated and sensationalized coverage (see Chyi & McCombs, 2004; Kerr, 2018a; Lombardi, 2018; Muschert, 2009; Schildkraut, 2014; Silva & Capella, 2014). Duwe (2005) argued that this coverage affects how the phenomenon is portrayed. For instance, there is a tendency to conflate mass shootings with mental health issues within the news media (McGinty, Webster, Jarlenski & Barry, 2014; Metzl & MacLeigh, 2015).

The second area of interest is gun legislation, which news media discussions in national papers also tend to focus on (Hawdon, Agnich, Wood & Ryan, 2015). Accordingly, public support for gun-related policies is found to have increased after mass shootings (Barry, McGinty, Vernick & Webster, 2015). In line with this, more restrictive gun legislation is introduced by policymakers after mass shootings (Fleming, 2012; Fleming et al., 2016). Despite this, the gun debate tends to just be a debate and there is little in the way of policy traction (see Kerr, 2018a; Schildkraut & Coz Hernanckez, 2014).

The final area of interest is how to prevent, prepare for and respond to mass shootings. The first part of prevention draws upon the work of scholars in the fields of risk and threat assessment, allowing for threats and risk factors to be assessed and judged on the basis of their perceived viability (see Cornell, 2013; Meloy & O'Toole, 2011; O'Toole, 1999; Spearman, 2019). Although studies have indicated there is no profile of a mass shooter, there are some warning signs that can help inform the threat assessment process (Fein & Vossekuil, 1998; Vossekuil et al., 2002; Pollack, Modzeleski & Rooney, 2008). The second part of preparation and response examines emergency management and communication procedures, drawing upon the advice of national government guides (see U.S. Department of Education, 2013; U.S. Department of Health and Human Services, 2014).

News Media Coverage

The way mass murder is portrayed by the news media has previously been the focus of research in this field. Looking at news media coverage of nine hundred and nine mass killings taking place from 1990 to 1999, Duwe (2005) discovered that the most high-profile incidents were covered. Consequently, it was maintained the news media's tendency to cover the most sensational cases of mass murder affects how the phenomenon is socially constructed. The cases used as typifying examples involved larger body counts, stranger victims, public locations, the use of assault weapons and offenders who were older, suicidal and White. Similar results were found by Silva and Capella (2018) in their examination of how the *New York Times* covered mass shootings over the time period of 1966 to 2016. Findings showed that incidents with higher death and injury tolls were indicative of more news coverage. Interestingly, Silva and Capella's (2018) findings differed from Duwe (2005) in that their study showed that the offenders more likely to be considered newsworthy were young, Middle Eastern and ideologically motivated. The main findings from both of these studies is that the way the news media covers mass shootings is not accurately representative of the phenomenon, with the most high-profile cases being covered and the majority receiving little or no coverage (Duwe, 2005; Silva & Capella, 2018).

Research has also found that the news media coverage pertaining to mass shootings tends to be saturated over a short period of time. The agenda-setting model prescribes that the salience of an issue featured in the media is relative to the amount and time period of coverage it receives (Chyi & McComb,

2004, p. 1). Since news is defined as information about recent events, time and space constrain what is on the media's agenda (Delli Carpini, 2005, pp. 28-29). A hundred and seventy articles from the New York Times covering the Columbine (1999) school shooting up to thirteen months after the incident were analyzed by Chyi and McComb (2004). Findings showed that the newspaper increased the salience of the story by mixing media coverage frames to keep the story novel. Another study examined media frames in 683 print and broadcast news items covering the Columbine incident. The most prevalent theme in the coverage, present in 72.1% of items, was causal explanations for the shooting. Actual coverage of the actors, actions and consequences of Columbine only accounted for 40.2% of examples. It was suggested that the media frame was reshaped into an analysis of the shooting and similar crimes to increase the salience of the story (Muschert, 2009). Mirroring the other studies, Schildkraut (2014) found that whilst most of the articles were published in the first five days after an event and then dissipated over the next five days, the Columbine shooting had more gradual coverage that expanded the "shelf-life" of this incident. An explanation for the findings from these studies that Columbine had a longer than anticipated salience in the news media could be the fact that this incident was found to be the most newsworthy mass public shooting in the fifty year period since the Texas Sniper (1966) attack (Silva & Capella, 2018). Other studies have also highlighted the infamous nature of the Columbine incident (Doran, 2014; Kerr, 2018a; Larkin 2009). Moreover, Kupchik and Bracy's (2009, p. 148) study found that out of the 157 articles in their sample referencing Columbine, only 33 of them were directly related to that shooting. Extrapolating from this, it appears that Columbine is referenced as a comparative incident when other mass shootings occur.

Some recent dissertations have focused specifically on news media coverage of the 2018 shooting at Douglas Stoneman High School (more commonly known as the "Parkland" shooting). In her Masters dissertation, Lombardi (2018) assessed the language used in fifty online news headlines relating to this shooting. Emotion-laden words like "deadliest," "panic," "massacre" and "maniac" were used. All headlines referred to the incident as a "campus shooting" or a "school shooting," demonstrating how these terms have become familiar and recognizable to the media audience. Also present in all headlines was the location of the shooting, providing the city, county or state in which it took place. Possibly to add to the sensationalism the number of victims of the shooting also tended to be included in headlines. Three of the headlines further dramatized the event by using sentences such as "the worst of humanity," "deadliest in U.S. history" and "worse than Columbine" (Lombardi, 2018, pp.34-35). This mirrors results from another study which found that Columbine was used as a benchmark for other incidents of school violence, exemplified in phrases like "Columbine-like," "before Columbine" and "worst since Columbine" (Kupchik &Brady, 2009, p. 149). Another dissertation looked at the audience reaction to the Parkland (2018) shooting via the amount of emotional ranges of the Tweets about it. The majority of these were found to convey fear, particularly in the first couple of days after the incident. This emotional response then shifted to empathy and advocacy, most likely as a result of the gun violence prevention activism work by survivors that took place after this shooting. Moreover, the advocacy tweets yielded the most engagement with other Twitter users (Fiore, 2018).

Researchers have also focused on the main social issues discussed in the aftermath of mass shootings: mental illness and gun policies. Turning firstly to mental illness, a study by Metzl and MacLeigh (2015) explored the linkage between this and mass shootings as portrayed in the media, literature and historical sources. Four assumptions commonly advanced after mass shootings were explored: mental illness causes gun violence; psychiatric diagnoses can predict gun crime before it happens; mass shootings teach citizens to fear mentally ill loners; gun control cannot prevent mass shootings due to the complex psychiatric histories of mass shooters. As a result of these assumptions, mass shootings come to represent gun crime; despite only being a small percentage of it. Moreover, "mentally ill" becomes synonymous with a violent threat. These assumptions are unrealistic and inaccurate, particularly since there is little evidence that persons with mental illnesses are more likely to commit gun crimes. A research study by McGinty, Webster, Jarlenski and Barry (2014) further explored the link between serious mental illness and gun violence as portrayed in news media framing. A random news media sample of stories from 1997 to 2012 was used. Findings indicated that in the two weeks following mass shootings, 33% of stories identified "dangerous people with serious mental illness" as a cause of gun violence; whereas 25% mentioned "dangerous weapons." Moreover, the majority of news stories did not acknowledge that most people with serious mental illnesses are not violent. The implication from this is that the news media coverage may contribute to negative public perceptions about persons with serious mental illnesses.

Guns

Unsurprisingly, perhaps, mass shootings provoke debates about gun usage, ownership and policies in the United States. Research has focused on how mass shooters have procured firearms prior to attacks. In 2019, Lankford, Adkins, Grace and Madfis examined the fifteen deadliest mass shootings in the United States and found that the attackers were more likely to display warning signs and be reported to law enforcement than other active shooters. In spite of this, the perpetrators were still able to access firearms. Consequently, it is recommended that firearm access should be limited for those who have displayed suicidal or homicidal ideation, particularly if they have referenced the desire to carry out a mass shooting. By contrast, Lott (2016) looked at forty-seven mass shootings and came to the conclusion that additional background checks on private transfers would not have prevented any of those incidents. Furthermore, it is reported that there was a higher rate of killings and injuries from mass shootings in states that adopted additional background checks on private transfers.

Studies have also focused on how the news media and public have reacted to the gun discussions that follow mass shootings. Hawdon, Agnich, Wood and Ryan (2015) examined news media coverage after the 2012 Sandy Hook shooting, comparing and contrasting local and national newspapers. Findings indicated that local papers avoided discussion of causal factors such as handgun legislation and instead focused on frames of community solidarity. National newspaper discussions, by contrast, had more issue-focused stories looking at potential causal factors such as gun legislation. After the Columbine school shooting, Haider-Market and Joslyn (2001) looked at whether alternative information frames centering on either blaming media violence or blaming gun laws would affect citizens' opinions about these issues and which factor they blamed for the incident. Mirroring the frames used by Republicans in Congressional debates, Republican voting citizens were more responsive to the blame media violence frame. On the contrary, citizens who were likely to vote Democrat mirrored the sentiments of Democratic politicians by being more likely to favor the weak gun laws frame. Barry, McGinty, Vernick and Webster (2015) carried out a survey to follow-up on previous research carried out in the aftermath of the 2012 Sandy Hook school shooting. It was discovered that similar to their earlier study, the most recent survey indicated most citizens supported policies offering strong gun regulations in states and federal law. In a different study, support and opposition to gun regulations were explored by analyzing gun-related tweets in the period after the Sandy Hook (2012) incident. Hashtags were categorized as being in support or opposition of gun control. Tweets in favor of gun control were found to be very salient at the earliest stages after the shooting, when gun policies were being discussed by the Obama administration. These then fade away later on; although they did spike again when Connecticut passed gun regulations and the federal proposals were defeated in the Senate. Gun rights tweets were more prevalent later on in the discussion and were particularly prominent when the debates centered on universal background checks and the assault weapons ban, as well as the Senate filibuster that resulted in the federal proposals being defeated (Benton, Hancock, Coopersmith, Ayers & Dredze, 2016).

The other facet of gun-related research has explored the policy debates following mass shootings themselves. Fleming (2012) described incidents like mass shootings as "focusing events" which tend to result in guns becoming part of the policy agenda. Looking at bills over a lengthy period of time (1960s to 2000s), it was found that gun control policy is not a salient issue at times when there are no focusing events. At those times, more lenient gun restrictions are proposed. By contrast, following five major focusing events — most of which were mass shootings — there was found to be a larger number of restrictive bills raised in Congress, particularly in the House (Fleming, 2012, pp. 63-69). This was followed up in later research looking at twelve focusing events from 1947 to 2010. Interestingly, findings indicated that there were more restrictive, punitive and lenient bills introduced in the House following a focusing event; whilst the Senate had an increase in punitive and lenient but not restrictive bills. This difference is attributed to the make-up of the Senate which is more diverse with Senators representing entire states; whereas the House is more likely to be homogenous, with representatives from constituencies within states (Fleming, Rutledge, Dixon & Peralton, 2016, p. 4).

After three of the most high-profile school shootings, it was found that both lenient and restrictive bills were introduced. There was some progress at the state level for the passage of gun restrictions in addition to lenient gun laws; yet, federally there was a distinct lack of laws passed (Kerr, 2018a). Concurrently, Schildkraut and Cox Hernanckez (2014) found there were myriad legislative responses to school shootings; in spite of this, few of these bills actually passed. To deal with this, it is suggested that future research explore whether members of the public perceive the legislative responses as effective in preventing school shootings or simply to be reactive, "feel good legislation." Providing some explanation for this may be the results of Haider-Markel and Joslyn's study (2001), which found that responses to mass shootings were influenced by pre-existing partisan attitudes: those who support Democrats blamed weak gun control; whilst citizens voting Republican insisted it was violence in the media. Inferring from this, it may be the case that frames are unlikely to influence citizens who do not already believe in them; thus, frames may be likely to reinforce or trigger partisan beliefs. It will be interesting to see whether this pattern continues with future mass shooting events.

Preventing, Preparing for and Responding to Mass Shootings

The other research strand of interest in this book is preventing, preparing for and responding to mass shootings. Firstly, the prevention of such attacks has been discussed by scholars. In their examination of the fifteen deadliest mass shootings, Lankford, Adkins and Madfis (2019) found that most of these incidents were preventable. Specifically, these mass shooters showed warning signs that included leakage of violent thoughts and intentions, concerning behaviors and a specific interest in mass killings. This resulted in some of these perpetrators being reported to law enforcement prior to their attack. It is advised that prevention efforts should focus on educating, encouraging and pressuring members of the public to report warning signs; as well as training law enforcement to thoroughly investigate potential threats. Assisting the prevention process, researchers have defined what constitutes a threat (an expression of intent to enact harm) and how these may be expressed (orally, visually, in person, electronically and in writings) (Cornell, 2013; Meloy & O'Toole, 2011; O'Toole, 1999; Spearman, 2019). Practical guides have been drafted prescribing how to carry out effective threat assessment (see, for example, Drysdale, Modzeleski & Simons, 2010; Goodrum & Woodward, 2019; Spearman, 2019).

There have been studies examining commonalities between attackers. In 1998, Fein and Vossekuil examined assassins of public figures such as politicians. Their overall conclusion was that there was no "profile" of who was likely to commit such an attack and mental illness rarely plays a role. Of particular importance was the finding that those who pose a threat do not often make *direct* threats; rather, they allude to their attack. Another notable result was that these perpetrators plan their attacks over a long period of time. Nearer the time of the attack, their lives become consumed with planning activities (Fein & Vossekuil, 1998, pp. 12-16). Similarly, Vossekuil and colleagues (2002) reviewed acts of gun violence in schools. In 73% of these, the attacker killed one or more student, faculty members or others (e.g. security) at the school; whilst in 24% a gun was used to injure at least one person. An interesting finding was that in 81% of those attacks at least one person had prior knowledge that the attacker was planning or at least thinking about perpetrating an attack. Moreover, more than one person had knowledge of it in 59% of cases. For the majority of cases, the people with prior knowledge were friends, schoolmates or siblings. A study by Pollack, Modzeleski and Rooney (2008) yielded similar findings about bystanders in school shootings, with the majority of them being friends or schoolmates with the attacker. Following interviews with the bystanders, the reasons given for not reporting the potential attack was disbelief that it would occur or thinking it was a joke. Additionally, a lot of the time the information shared did not provide specifics about the imminence of an attack so bystanders did not know how long they had to act on their knowledge.

Another issue identified in previous mass shootings in schools was the failure of schools to take threats seriously and the disjointed sharing of information. Using two case studies of school shootings in Westside Middle School (1998) and Heath High School (1997), Fox and Harding's (2005) study applied qualitative methodologies of interviews and participant observations to trace information flow throughout the schools. It was discovered that the bureaucratic rules and procedures, as well as the structure and culture of the schools led to a disruption in information flow which potentially could have prevented the shootings. It is further argued that only receiving fragmented pieces of the "information puzzle" is problematic because it dilutes the seriousness of the issue. This is further illustrated in their finding that school staff, for the most part, were unaware of the perpetrators' problems and were shocked at their violent actions. For instance, a student reported that one of the perpetrators of the Westside Middle School incident, Andrew Graham, had threatened to harm other students; yet the school claimed he only posed a threat to himself. Similarly, the Heath High School shooting perpetrator wrote violent stories in school, but because these did not fall into prescribed categories they were not flagged as an "alert paper" (Fox & Harding, 2005, pp. 78-80, 86-88). In a similar vein, Elliott (2009) highlighted that this was also the case at Columbine High School where there was no information flow between relevant parties (law enforcers, school, parents, mental health agencies and so forth). If there had been a more connected picture of information built up, the signs may have been spotted and dealt with earlier. Concurrently, Woodward and Goodrum (2016) carried out a report into what happened in the Arapahoe High School (2013) attack and concluded there were failures in information sharing. Only five out of the twenty-five possible risk factors on the threat assessment model were used, resulting in safety planning and follow-up that was inadequate.

The other component of relevance in this section is how to prepare for and respond to mass shootings. Following high-profile shootings at Columbine High School (1999) and Virginia Tech University

(2007), there were numerous internal and external investigations about how the institutions could have been better prepared and responded in a more effective way. Columbine High School had not prepared for an active shooter incident, with its planning only covering fire drills. Conversely, Virginia Tech University was prepared for an active shooting, a result of a post-9/11 focus on security. There were gaps in the institution's plan, however, and some serious flaws with its emergency communication system. As well as critiquing the responses to previous incidents, suggestions were made for ways to better prepare for future ones, e.g. hiring more school resource officers to provide security (see, for example, Brooks, Schiraldi & Ziedenberg, 2000; O' Leavitt, Spellings & Gonzales, 2007; Rasmussen & Johnson, 2008; U.S Fire Administration, 2001; Virginia Tech Review Panel, 2007/2009). This book will describe ways to effectively prepare for and respond to mass shootings using federal guides (e.g. U.S. Department of Education, 2013; U.S. Department of Health and Human Services, 2014) and recommendations from experts in this area.

ROADMAP

This book is structured by topic area. Section One contains four chapters outlining the concept of mass shootings, the methodologies used in this book and utilizing a case study to provide an illustrative example. Chapter One goes into further detail about mass shooting definitions, trends and comparisons with other countries. The second chapter discusses the methodological approach used in this book. Further details are provided about the samples of interviewees and media content. Also detailed in the chapter are the research methodologies used: content analysis, critical discourse analysis, visual discourse analysis and qualitative interviews. The next two chapters focus on a case study of the high-profile 2017 Las Vegas mass shooting. This incident was chosen for its prominence in recent policy debates, its infamous nature and its occurrence during the Trump Presidency (2017-2021). Chapter Three looks at the potential of the Las Vegas shooting to create a culture of fear and distorted risk perceptions. The following chapter outlines gun-related policy reform debates after Las Vegas. Findings from the news media sample and interviews are used to inform the discussion in these chapters.

Section Two contains three chapters focusing on preventing the risk of mass shootings. Chapter Five uses case studies of the eleven worst[1] mass shootings in the United States to document what "leakage" (communication of an intention to do harm) occurred prior to the attacks. The following chapter builds upon this by discussing the warning signs and perceived motivations for the shootings in these case studies; in addition to interrogating whether risk assessment and profiling can be used to manage risk of mass shootings. Chapter Seven uses findings from interviews to provide details about threat assessment and how this can be used to deal with threats pertaining to mass shootings.

Section Three shifts focus onto the preparation, response and recovery procedures should a mass shooting transpire. Chapter Eight looks at ways to prepare for a mass shooting attack, in terms of emergency management planning and training. The next chapter documents how to respond efficiently and recover from trauma when a mass shooting incident does occur. Results from interviews inform the discussion, alongside federal guidance on how to effectively manage crises.

Section Four contains three chapters looking at gun legislation and the future direction of the gun violence prevention movement. Chapter Ten documents the policy proposals said to reduce harm caused in mass shootings, as well as lower levels of gun violence generally. Chapter Eleven details some potential framing approaches that could be used to make gun violence a salient issue in American society.

Discussed in the final chapter conclusion are recent trends in United States politics, including the 2018 midterm and 2020 presidential election results. These are then discussed within the wider context of what they could mean for gun violence prevention in future. Interview findings are utilized throughout this final section.

CONCLUSION

This chapter sets up the context for the entire book. The main focus of this book is on mass shootings, a specific type of gun violence. This phenomenon was defined by explaining what separates it from all other forms of violence perpetrated with a gun. Mass shootings involve a perpetrator(s) trying to kill as many people as possible within a short period of time. The motivations for these attacks can vary from revenge against a particular institution, a desire for infamy or ideological reasons (e.g. misogyny, racial bias). Mass shootings tend to receive attention, likely due to the news media coverage being saturated with a focus on those incidents with the highest death tolls (Duwe, 2005; Schildkraut, 2014; Silva & Capella, 2018).

Whilst a small portion of gun violence in the United States, mass shootings do tend to have a noticeable impact on gun debates (Fleming, 2012; Fleming et al., 2016; Kerr, 2018a). News media coverage tends to center on gun legislation (Hawdon, Agnich, Wood & Ryan, 2015) and public support increases following a mass shooting (Barry, McGinty, Vernick & Webster, 2015). The impact on the gun debate is one of the facets explored within this book in relation to a recent high-profile shooting, as well as what might happen with gun debates in future.

Another area of debate provoked by mass shootings is how to prevent these, as well as how to effectively manage them when they do occur. Scholars have found that most mass attackers displayed warning signs prior to attacks (Fein & Vossekuil, 1998; Lankford, Adkins & Madfis, 2019; Pollack, Modzeleski & Rooney 2008; Vossekuil et al., 2002). Developing robust processes of assessing threats can assist with trying to prevent attacks before they occur (Cornell, 2013; Meloy & O'Toole, 2011; O'Toole, 1999; Spearman, 2019). In cases where attacks cannot be prevented, there needs to be a system in place to deal with them. Reviews after high-profile mass shootings highlighted problems with the emergency management response and suggested ways to improve (Brooks, Schiraldi & Ziedenberg, 2000; O' Leavitt, Spellings & Gonzales, 2007; Rasmussen & Johnson, 2008; U.S Fire Administration, 2001; Virginia Tech Review Panel, 2007/2009). This book draws upon the insights of experts to discuss how to conduct threat assessment and devise emergency management procedures to reduce the harm caused by mass shooters.

REFERENCES

Barry, C. L., McGinty, E. E., Vernick J. S., & Webster, D. W. (2015). Two years after Newtown – public opinion on gun policy revisited. *Preventive Medicine, 79*, 55-58.

BBC News. (2019a, December 29). *U.S. saw highest number of mass killings on record in 2019, database reveals.* https://www.bbc.co.uk/news/world-us-canada-50936575?SThisFB&fbclid=IwAR05I7b7PFrG ypjs3CDxoqBxKhsO_1aFHtY4paidxsw8iI84S_HSrEdik7U

BBC News. (2019b, August 5). *America's gun culture in charts*. https://www.bbc.co.uk/news/world-us-canada-41488081

Benton, A., Hancock, B., Coopersmith, G., Ayers, J. W., & Dredze, M. (2016). *After Sandy Hook Elementary: A Year in the Gun Control Debate on Twitter*. Bloomberg Data for Good Exchange Conference, New York, NY.

Birkland Thomas, A. (1997). *After Disaster: Agenda Setting, Public Policy and Focusing Events*. Georgetown University Press.

Blair, J. P., & Schweit, K. W. (2014). *A Study of Active Shooter Incidents, 2000-2013*. Texas State University and Federal Bureau of Investigations, U.S. Department of Justice.

Brooks, K., Schiraldi, V., & Ziedenberg, J. (2000). *School House Hype: Two Years Later*. Justice Policy Institute.

Brown, P. H., & Abel, D. G. (2003). *Outgunned: Up Against the NRA. The First Complete Insider Account of the Battle Over Gun Control*. The Free Press.

Callaghan, K., & Schnell, F. (2005). *Framing American Politics*. University of Pittsburgh Press. doi:10.2307/j.ctt6wrbqk

Capellan, J. A., & Lewanowski, C. (2018). Can threat assessment help police prevent mass shootings? Testing an intelligence-led policing tool. *Policing, 42*(1), 16–30. doi:10.1108/PIJPSM-07-2018-0089

Chong, D., & Druckman, J. N. (2007). Framing Theory. *Annual Review of Political Science, 10*(1), 103–126. doi:10.1146/annurev.polisci.10.072805.103054

Chyi, H., & McCombs, M. (2004). Media Salience and the Process of Framing: Coverage of the Columbine School Shootings. *Journalism & Mass Communication Quarterly, 81*(1), 22–35. doi:10.1177/107769900408100103

Cornell, D. (2013). The Virginia Student Threat Assessment Guidelines: An Empirically Supported Violence Prevention Strategy. In N. Boeckler, T. Seeger & P. Sitzer, Peter (Eds.), School Shootings: International Research, Case Studies and Concepts for Prevention, (pp. 379-400). New York: Springer Science-Business Media.

Davis, J. (2020). *American School Shooting: The Growing Problem of Mass Shooting for Homeland Security*. James Davis.

Delli Carpini, M. X. (2005). News from somewhere: Journalistic frames and the debate over 'public journalism. In K. Callaghan & F. Schnell (Eds.), *Framing American Politics* (pp. 21–53). University of Pittsburgh Press. doi:10.2307/j.ctt6wrbqk.6

Doran, S. E. M. (2014). *News Media Constructions and Policy Implications of School Shootings in the United States* (Doctoral thesis). Glasgow, UK: University of Glasgow.

Drysdale, D. A., Modzeleski, W., & Simons, A. B. (2010). *Campus Attacks: Targeted Violence Affecting Institutions of Higher Education*. U.S. Secret Service, U.S. Department of Homeland Security, Office of Safe and Drug-Free Schools, U.S. Department of Education, and Federal Bureau of Investigation, U.S. Department of Justice.

Duwe, G. (2005). A Circle of Distortion: The Social Construction of Mass Murder in the United States. *Western Criminology Review*, 6(1), 59–78.

Elliott, D. (2009). Lessons from Columbine: Effective school-based violence prevention strategies and programmes. *Journal of Children's Services*, 4(4), 53–62. doi:10.5042/jcs.2010.0021

Entman, R. M. (2010). Media framing biases and political power: Explaining slant in news of campaign 2008. *Journalism*, 11(4), 389–408. doi:10.1177/1464884910367587

Erikson, W. H. (2001). *The report of Governor Bill Owens' Columbine Review Commission*. State of Colorado Governor's Office.

Fein, R. A., & Vossekuil, B. (1998). *Protective Intelligence and Threat Assessment Investigations: A Guide for State and Local Law Enforcement Officials*. National Institute of Justice, U.S. Department of Justice.

Fein, R. A., Vossekuil, B., Pollock, W. S., Borum, R., Modzeleski, W., & Reddy, M. (2002). *Threat Assessment in Schools: A Guide to Managing Threatening Situations and to Creating Safe School Climate*. United States Secret Service and United States Department of Education.

Fiore, G. J., III. (2018). *Emotional Tweeters: What Causes Individuals to React During a Crisis? A Mixed Methodological Analysis Examining Crisis Response Tweets to the 2018 Stoneman Douglas High School Shooting* (Masters dissertation). South Orange, NJ: Seton Hall University Dissertations and Theses. (ETDS 2612)

Fleming, A. K. (2012). *Gun Policy in the United States and Canada: The Impact of Mass Murders and Assassinations on Gun Control*. Continuum International Publishing Group.

Fleming, A. K., Rutledge, P. E., Dixon, G. C., & Peralta, J. S. (2016). When the smoke clears: Focusing events, issue definition, strategic framing and the politics of gun control. *Social Science Quarterly*, 97(5), 1–13. doi:10.1111squ.12269

Follman, M., Aronsen, G., & Pan, D. (2016, July 18). *A Guide to Mass Shootings in America*. Mother Jones. https://www.motherjones.com/politics/2012/07/mass-shootings-map/

Fox, C., & Harding, D. J. (2005). School Shootings as Organisational Deviance. *Sociology of Education*, 78(1), 69–97. doi:10.1177/003804070507800104

Goodrum, S., & Woodward, W. (2019). *Colorado School Safety Guide*. Attorney General's Office.

Goss, K. A. (2006). *Disarmed: The Missing Movement for Gun Control in America*. Princeton University Press.

Grossman, M. (2012). *The Not-So-Special Interests: Interest Groups, Public Representation and American Governance*. Stanford University Press. doi:10.1515/9780804781343

Haider-Markel, D. P., & Joslyn, M. R. (2001). Gun policy, Opinion, Tragedy, and Blame Attribution: The Conditional Influence of Issue Frames. *The Journal of Politics, 63*(2), 520–543. doi:10.1111/0022-3816.00077

Hawdon, J., Agnich, L., Wood, R., & Ryan, J. (2015). Framing Mass Gun Violence: A Content Analysis of Print Media Coverage of the VT and Sandy Hook Elementary School Tragedies. In L. Eargle & A. Esmail (Eds.), *Gun Violence in American Society: Crime, Justice and Public Policy* (pp. 214–232). University Press of America.

Kerr, S. E. M. (2018a). *Gun Violence Prevention? The Politics Behind Policy Responses to School Shootings in the United States*. Palgrave MacMillan.

Kerr, S. E. M. (2018b). Emergency Management and Communication Improvements: Changing the Landscape of School Safety. In G. Crews (Ed.), *School Violence in K-12 American Education* (pp. 474–493). IGI Global.

Kingdon, J. W. (1994/2003). *Agendas, Alternatives and Public Policies* (2nd ed.). Longman.

Krouse, W. J., & Richardson, D. J. (2015). *Mass Murder with Firearms: Incidents and Victims, 1999-2013*. Congressional Research Service.

Kupchik, A., & Bracy, N. L. (2009). The News Media on School Crime and Violence: Constructing Dangerousness and Fueling Fear. *Youth Violence and Juvenile Justice, 7*(2), 136–156. doi:10.1177/1541204008328800

Kupchik, A., Brent, J. J. & Mowen, T. J. (2015). The Aftermath of Newtown: more of the same. *British Journal of Criminology,* 1-16.

Lankford, A., Adkins, K. G., & Madfis, E. (2019). Are the Deadliest Mass Shootings Preventable? An Assessment of Leakage Information Reported to Law Enforcement and Firearms Acquisition Prior to Attacks in the United States. *Journal of Contemporary Criminal Justice, 35*(3), 315–341. doi:10.1177/1043986219840231

Larkin, R. W. (2009). The Columbine Legacy: Rampage Shootings as Political Acts. *The American Behavioral Scientist, 52*(9), 1309–1326. doi:10.1177/0002764209332548

McGinty, E. E., Webster, D. W., Jarlenski, M., & Barry, C. L. (2014, March). News media framing of serious mental illness and gun violence in the United States, 1997-2012. *American Journal of Public Health, 104*(3), 406–413. doi:10.2105/AJPH.2013.301557 PMID:24432874

Mears, D. P., Moon, M., & Thielo, A. J. (2017). Columbine Revisited: Myths and Realities about the Bullying-School Shootings Connection. *Victims & Offenders, 12*(6), 939–955. doi:10.1080/15564886.2017.1307295

Metzl, J. M., & MacLeigh, K. T. (2015). Mental Illness, Mass shootings and the Politics of American Firearms. *American Journal of Public Health, 105*(2), 240–249. doi:10.2105/AJPH.2014.302242 PMID:25496006

Muschert, G. W. (2009). Frame-Changing in the Media Coverage of a School Shooting: The Rise of Columbine as a National Concern. *The Social Science Journal, 46*(1), 164–170. doi:10.1016/j.soscij.2008.12.014

National Threat Assessment Center. (2019). *Attacks in Public Spaces – 2018*. U.S. Secret Service, Department of Homeland Security.

O'Leavitt, M., Spellings, M., & Gonzales, A. R. (2007). *Report to the President on Issues Raised by the Virginia Tech Tragedy*. U.S. Department of Justice.

Pane, L. M. (2019, December 23). *US mass killings hit new high in 2019, most were shootings*. AP News. https://apnews.com/4441ae68d14e61b64110db44f906af92

Pollack, W. S., Modzeleski, W., & Rooney, G. (2008). *Prior Knowledge of Potential School-Based Violence: Information Students Learn May Prevent a Targeted Attack*. U.S. Secret Service and U.S. Department of Education.

Rasmussen, C., & Johnson, G. (2008). *The Ripple Effect of Virginia Tech: Assessing the Nationwide Impact on Campus Safety and Security Policy and Practice*. Midwestern Higher Education Compact.

Rood, C. (2019). *After Gun Violence: Deliberation and Memory in an Age of Political Gridlock*. The Pennsylvania State University Press. doi:10.5325/j.ctv14gp5h1

Schildkraut, J., & Cox Hernanckez, T. (2014). Laws that Bit the Bullet: A Review of legislation responses to school shootings. *American Journal of Criminal Justice, 39*(2), 358–374. doi:10.100712103-013-9214-6

Schildkraut, J. V. (2014). *Mass Murder and the Mass Media: An Examination of the Media Discourse on U.S. rampage shootings, 2000-2012* (Ph.D dissertation). San Marcos, TX: Texas State University.

Silva, J. R., & Capella, J. A. (2018). The media's coverage of mass public shootings in America: Fifty years of newsworthiness. *International Journal of Comparative and Applied Criminal Justice, 43*(1), 77–97. doi:10.1080/01924036.2018.1437458

Silver, J., Horgan, J., & Gill, P. (2018). Foreshadowing targeted violence; Assessing leakage of intent by public mass murderers. *Aggression and Violent Behavior, 38*(Jan-Feb), 94–100. doi:10.1016/j.avb.2017.12.002

Snow, D. A., Rochford, E. B. Jr, Worden, S. K., & Benford, R. D. (1986). Frame Alignment Process: Micromobilization and movement participation. *American Sociological Review, 51*(4), 461–481. doi:10.2307/2095581

Spearman, M. M. (2019). *School Based Behavioural Threat Assessment and Management: Best Practices Guide for South Carolina*. Department of Education, States of South Carolina.

Spitzer, R. J. (2004). The Politics of Gun Control (3rd ed.). Washington, DC: Congressional Quarterly (CQ) Press.

U.S. Department of Education. (2013). *Guide for Developing High-Quality School Emergency Operations Plans*. Office of Elementary and Secondary Education, Office of Safe and Healthy Students, U.S. Department of Education.

U.S. Department of Health and Human Services. (2014). *Incorporating Active Shooter Incident Planning into Healthcare Facility Emergency Operations Plans.* U.S. Office of the Assistant Secretary for Preparedness and Response, Department of Health and Human Services.

U.S. Fire Administration. (2001). *Wanton Violence at Columbine High School.* Department of Homeland Security.

Virginia Tech Review Panel. (2009). *Mass shootings at Virginia Tech April 16, 2007: Report of the Virginia Tech Review Panel presented to Timothy M. Kaine, Governor, Commonwealth of Virginia* (updated ed.). https://www.vtreviewpanel.org/report/index.html

Vossekuil, B., Fein, R. A., Reddy, M., Borum, R., & Modzeleski, W. (2002). *Final report and findings of the Safe School Initiative: Implications for the prevention of school attacks in the United States.* U.S. Department of Education, Office of Elementary and Secondary Education, Safe and Drug-Free Schools Program and the U.S. Secret Service, National Threat Assessment Center.

Wintemute, G. J. (2015). The Epidemiology of Firearms Violence in the Twenty-First Century United States. *Annual Review of Public Health*, *36*(1), 5–19. doi:10.1146/annurev-publhealth-031914-122535 PMID:25533263

ENDNOTE

[1] Worst in this context refers to those with the highest death toll.

Section 1
Understandings of Mass Shootings

The theme of this section is to introduce the reader to mass shootings, with the use of a case study to provide an illustrative example.

Chapter 1
Defining Mass Shootings

ABSTRACT

This chapter interrogates public understandings of mass shootings. First of all, gun violence statistics for the United States are compared with those in other developed countries. The varying definitions and trends of mass shooting are shown to be problematic in trying to gain an accurate understanding of the phenomenon. Discussed is the history of mass shootings in the United States from "going postal" attacks occurring in post offices and workplace massacres through to school shootings and mass shootings in public places. Possible reasons why the United States has the highest number of mass shootings are deliberated. Hofstede's often-quoted cultural model is used to discuss two national characteristics: high levels of individualism and low power distance between social groups. Other factors highlighted relate to Harding, Fox, and Mehta's model about influencers of school shootings, as well as notions of extreme masculinity which are often expressed via misogynistic behavior.

INTRODUCTION

The purpose of this chapter is to explore understandings, definitions and trends pertaining to mass shootings. The first part looks at the trends around violence involving guns more generally in the United States and mass shootings. The United States is found to have a higher rate of gun violence than other Western countries (Grinshteyn & Hemenway, 2016; Naghavi et al., 2018). Out of the total number of gun deaths, mass shootings only represent a small fraction. In spite of this, gun violence prevention (GVP) interviewees noted that there seems to be the perception that these mass shootings have increased in recent years, likely due to news media coverage of high-profile incidents. The Las Vegas and Parkland shootings were said by interviewees to have had a noticeable positive effect on the GVP movement, showing how these atypical but high-profile events can have a wider influence.

The second part of this chapter reviews definitions, understandings and possible reasons for mass shootings. It is shown that there are conflicts about how to define mass shootings, making it difficult to determine trends. The history of mass shootings in modern day America is documented. Starting with the "going postal" attacks taking place in post offices in the 1980s (Ames, 2007; Baron, 2000), the discussion explores how shootings then progressed onto workplaces, schools and other locations. The

DOI: 10.4018/978-1-7998-3916-3.ch001

final section explores some of the reasons why the United States may have the highest number of mass shootings in the world. A model by Harding, Fox and Mehta (2002) about five possible factors influencing school shootings is applied to mass shootings more generally. Hofstede's (2001) cultural model is utilized to show the macro-level factors that could be influencing this trend. Lastly, extreme notions of masculinity are discussed in terms of their potential to be expressed in misogynistic behaviors seen in some mass shooters such as stalking and domestic violence.

GUN VIOLENCE TRENDS

How Do Gun Deaths in the United States Compare to Other Countries?

The most recent available figures from the Gun Violence Archives (2020) indicate there were 39,221 deaths in the United States from firearms in 2018. Examining gun-related deaths worldwide finds the United States ranks highly. To put this into perspective, the United States represented 4.3% of the global population; yet had 35.3% of global firearm suicides and 9% of global firearm homicides. Looking at the countries with the highest number of firearm-related deaths (combining accidental injuries, homicides and suicides) in 2016 finds the United States ranks second in terms of overall total number of deaths, as documented in Table 1 (Naghavi et al., 2018).

Table 1. Aggregate Firearm-Related Deaths in 2016

Country	Total Number of Deaths	Deaths per 10,000 Population
Brazil	43,200	21.9
United States	37,200	12.21
India	26,500	0.28
Mexico	15,400	7.64
Colombia	13,300	18.65

Looking at the United States in comparison to other developed, high-income countries finds a similar pattern. When compared to twenty-six countries (e.g. Australia, most European countries, and New Zealand) that provide data to the World Health Organization, it was found that the United States had greater than 80% of the combined number of firearm deaths. The gun-related homicide and suicide rates were found to be twenty-five times and eight times higher respectively in the United States than other high-income countries. Further to this, the unintentional gun death rate was found to be more than six times higher in the United States (Grinshteyn & Hemenway, 2016).

In contrast, the five countries with the lowest rates of gun deaths are documented in Table 2 (Naghavi et al., 2018). Interestingly, Iceland has the lowest rate of deaths in spite of having relatively high rates of private firearm ownership at 31.7 per 100 residents. This is in direct opposition to the United States which has high rates of firearm-related deaths coupled with the highest estimated rates of private firearm ownership at a rate of 120.5 per 100 residents (BBC News, 2019a). Extrapolating from this, there must be key differences in the way firearms are owned and wider cultural factors to cause a disparity

Table 2. Aggregate Firearm-Related Deaths in 2016

Country	Total Number of Deaths	Deaths per 10,000 Population
Iceland	0	0.07
Singapore	1	0.025
Hong Kong	2	0.03
Qatar	4	0.15
Azerbaijan	7	0.07

Figure 1. Firearm Suicides in the United States 2014-2018

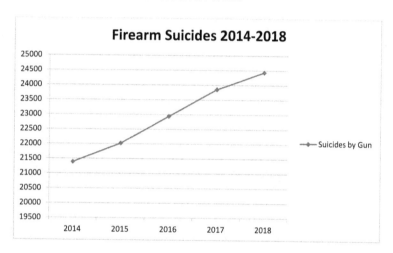

between Iceland being the country with the fewest number of gun deaths and the United States being the second highest one.

The most prevalent type of gun death in the United States is suicide, with figures ranking at 24,432, which accounted for 63% of all firearm-related deaths in 2018. Figure 1 shows that the rate of firearm suicides has been steadily increasing in the United States in recent years (Gun Violence Archives, 2020).

Similarly, when looking at global rates, the United States was found to be the highest ranking in terms of firearm-related suicide deaths (Naghavi et al., 2018) as detailed in Table 3.

Of the remainder of gun-related deaths in the United States, 1305 were ranked as other (including accidental shootings) and 14,451 were related to homicides (BBC News, 2019a). This gives a firearm-

Table 3. Firearm-Related Suicide Deaths

Country	Firearm-Related Suicides Per 10,000 Population
United States	7.32
Montenegro	6.49
Uruguay	4.68
Finland	2.94
Switzerland	2.74

related homicide rate of 4.46 per 100,000 of the population per year. In terms of global rankings, the United States ranks 17th for its firearm-related homicide rate behind countries such as Brazil, South Africa and Mexico (Naghavi et al., 2018). Looking at the percentages of homicides across countries find that those involving firearms stand at 73% for the United States compared to 38% for Canada, 13% for Australia and 3% for the United Kingdom (excluding Scotland and Northern Ireland) (BBC News, 2019a). Putting that into perspective of the annual rates per 100,000 of the population gives rates of 0.61 for Canada, 0.18 for Australia and 0.06 for the United Kingdom (Naghavi et al., 2018). Similar to Iceland, Canada has a high number of firearms located within private ownership at 34.7 per 100 residents (BBC News, 2019a). This suggests that it is other factors aside from owning guns that give the United States a relatively high homicide rate in comparison to other high-income countries — possible reasons will be discussed later on in this chapter.

How Prevalent Are Mass Shootings?

Out of the 38,658 gun-related deaths in the United States recorded by the Center for Disease Control in 2016, only 71 of these were the result of mass shootings (BBC News, 2019a). Within the wider spectrum of gun violence in the United States, mass shootings which take place in public places are, therefore, actually quite rare. Speaking to interviewees finds similar results, with the general consensus being that mass shootings are only a tiny portion of gun violence in the United States. To that end, eradicating mass shootings would not solve the problem as it were: "We'd still have [firearm-related] domestic violence, suicide and other types of gun violence."-Heather Ross (TGS).

In spite of this, it is mass shootings that receive media attention. Jonathan Perloe (CAGV) compared the coverage of two mass shootings in one weekend to more "commonplace" community gun violence: "In the same weekend as Dayton and El Paso, there were just as many people killed in Chicago and that doesn't make the headlines." This is akin to something like international terrorism, which on average kills twenty-three American citizens every year. Despite the chances of dying from a gunshot being much higher than being killed in a terrorist-related attack, terrorism garners all the attention in the media and public discussions (Abu-Lughool, 2015, pp. 177-178). Brian Malte's group, H&HF, have funded Berkeley Media Group to research the way the news media cover mass shootings. This report found that mass shootings dominate media narratives; whilst other more common types of gun violence remain invisible. Even when news coverage spikes after a mass shooting, there is no increase in articles relating to guns and domestic violence, suicide or community violence. It is maintained that this is counterproductive, for the public and policymakers require an understanding of "what every-day, all-too-common gun violence looks like, where it happens and how it harms people" (Berkley Media Group, 2018). It could be more fruitful perhaps for the media to use a mass shooting as the "hook" to gain people's attention and then put it into context by discussing the wider trends relating to gun violence. This would involve drawing upon both episodic and thematic framing respectively, whereby an individual story is used to elicit a response and then this is put into a wider context using evidence like statistics (Aaroe, 2011; Gross, 2008; Iyengar, 1991).

Whilst rare in the overall spectrum of gun violence in the United States, mass shootings have increased in frequency over recent years. Appropriating the definition of a total of at least four people being killed and/or harmed, the Gun Violence Archive (2020) found that 2019 had the highest rate of mass shootings since its inception in 2014. Figure 2 below shows the trajectory of mass shooting incidents from 2014 through to 2019

Figure 2. Mass Shooting Incidents 2014-2019

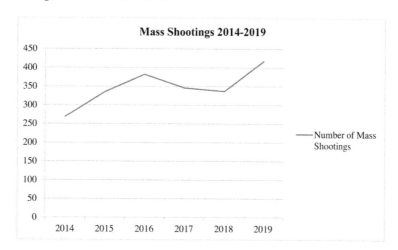

As can be seen in the graph, in spite of a slight dip in incidents from 2017 and 2018, the trajectory of mass shootings appears to have increased over the past five years (Gun Violence Archive, 2020). Out of the top ten shooting incidents with the highest number of casualties, eight of those have occurred in the past ten years (BBC News, 2019a). Interviewees claimed that members of the public have noticed this trend and are becoming increasingly upset about it:

I think these horrific mass shootings are happening more frequently and with higher death tolls. As those numbers go up in amongst the media coverage, the public is getting upset. – Adam Skaggs (GLCPGV).

There is a general perception that the incidents are coming thicker and faster. – Andrew Goddard (VCPS).

Further to this, some of the recent mass shootings were said to be "tipping points" for members of the public. The 2017 Las Vegas mass shooting was described as one of those incidents:

The Las Vegas incident was so egregious — so many people were hit that they had to do something. – Andrew Goddard (VCPS).

Las Vegas in terms of the sheer number of people killed and injuries obviously got people's attention. – Jonathan Perloe (CAGV).

The Las Vegas mass shooting is considered to be the "worst" in modern United States history based on its death toll and high number of injuries (BBC News, 2019a, 2019b). The perpetrator fired at attendees of a country music festival from a hotel window. A "bump stock" measure was used to increase the rate of gunfire able to be fired. It was explained by Jonathan Perloe (CAGV) that this shooting was perhaps the first mass shooting to affect people from all over the country, since there had been mass travel from outside states to Las Vegas for the purposes of attending the festival. Moreover, the bump stock law passed by Executive Order was said to have been attributable to Las Vegas: "President [Donald] Trump wouldn't have enacted this law without this shooting."-Marvin Lim (KGOC). For those reasons, Las

Vegas was selected as the main case study for this book. Chapter 3 and 4 focuses more on the news media coverage and firearm policies following this incident. It should be cautioned, however, that Las Vegas did not seem to change opinions nation-wide: "That actually did not seem to happen in terms of getting people in conservative states to think differently."-Jonathan Perloe (CAGV). In contrast, the shooting which probably shifted opinions more so than Las Vegas was the 2018 Parkland school shooting.

The Parkland attack was a shooting at a high school perpetrated by an expelled student. It is ranked as the eightieth worst mass shooting in the United States based on its death toll (BBC News, 2019a). Despite this, it was said that "the entire GVP movement became more intense after Parkland."-Eileen McCarron (CC). One of the reasons for this could be the attention it gained with graphic footage from the shooting being posted by one of the survivors via mobile internet application SnapChat. Students used this alongside Twitter to organize protests, marches and walkouts, with the message that gun reform was needed in the United States. Some of the survivors launched campaigns using Twitter as their outlet to call for companies to boycott the NRA (Wright, Molloyo & Lockharto, 2018). Interviewees highlighted that this incident resulted in the greater involvement of youth in the GVP movement, companies distancing themselves from the NRA and more attention to the issue of gun violence. Rukmani Bhatia (formerly CAP) explained it in the following way: "I think it [Parkland] took a narrative that no one really wanted to talk about and made it essentially impossible for people to stop thinking about it for months."

The momentum created by Parkland and, to a lesser degree, Las Vegas was said to be assisted by the traction provided by the Sandy Hook (2012) school shooting, where twenty young children and six educators were killed at an elementary school in Connecticut. Interviewees suggested this incident pointed to this incident that acted as a catalyst for action:

I think Sandy Hook was the starting point. That definitely got people to go 'oh, wow' and help get more people involved. – Heather Ross (TGS).

For many people I know, Sandy Hook was the defining moment. – Shaun Dakin (PAASD).

Previous work has highlighted the importance of the Sandy Hook incident in the GVP movement, resulting in greater involvement of activists, more funding and the passage of some comprehensive gun legislation in a number of states (Kerr, 2018a). It was highlighted by interviewees that it also created the foundation for a shift in the conversation about GVP. Po Murray, NAA, explained that the movement has been very successful in changing the dialogue since this incident. Moreover, Adam Skaggs (GLCPGV) explained that the years following the Sandy Hook (2012) incident paved the way for the youth movement resulting from Parkland: "So there's a lot of hard work that went in in those intervening years without an amount of success, but I think that created policy space where young people could survive and could make a real difference."

UNDERSTANDING MASS SHOOTINGS

Varying Definitions

One of the reasons perceptions about mass shootings are skewed is the various definitions used within public discussions. The definition used can affect the number of incidents recorded. As mentioned earlier, the Gun Violence Archive (2020) recorded hundreds of incidents based on a definition whereby a minimum number of people were harmed. In contrast, Mother Jones (2020) recorded 118 incidents in total from 1982 through to early 2020 by utilizing the definitions appropriated by the Federal Bureau of Investigation. Until 2012, the Federal Bureau of Investigation used the definition of four or more killed in recording official statistics of mass shootings. This was then changed in 2013 via a mandate issued by former President Barack Obama to encompass a death toll of three or more.

Explicating this point, a study looking at the recording of mass shooting incidents across various databases found these vary widely depending on which definition was used. The Gun Violence Archive recorded 346 incidents in 2017 based on a definition of incidents where four or more people are shot, regardless of whether they were killed or not. Moreover, it appeared that some of the shooters included the perpetrator in the injury count. By contrast, Mother Jones documented 11 cases in 2017, using the definition appropriated by the FBI of three or more individuals killed in a single attack. When the definition was adjusted across all databases to the strictest definition of four or more people killed, the number of incidents decreased: for instance, the Gun Violence Archive and Mothers Jones recorded 24 and 5 such incidents in 2017. Despite this, there were still variations in which incidents were included in databases due to differences like whether these took place in a public place or were indiscriminate in nature (Booty, O'Dwyer, Webster, McCourt & Crifasi, 2019, pp. 3-4, 6). Similarly, Fox (2020) found that Everytown for Gun Safety reported school shootings incidents where there was only one fatality or none at all, resulting in a high number of incidents being recorded. The danger of this, he argued, is that it overestimates the extent of the problem.

Research studies in this area have appropriated varying definitions of mass shootings. Some researchers define mass shootings by the death toll, whereby it is an incident in which four or more victims are murdered with a firearm by one or more perpetrators in a single event lasting a short period of time (e.g. minutes to hours). Importantly, even if the perpetrator(s) of the shooting dies as a result of the shooting they are not included in the death toll of four (Follman, Aronsen & Pan, 2016; Fox & Levin, 2003; Krouse & Richardson, 2015; Lankford, 2016a; Silver, Horgan & Gill, 2018). Fox and Levin (2003) argued that having a minimum body count of four or more victims differentiates mass murder from homicides more generally. Moreover, by defining these acts to those committed by one or a few perpetrators means incidents involving large-scale organized crime rings and terrorist cells are not included in the definition.

Other studies, by contrast, define mass shootings as ones in which a minimum number of people were *injured* rather than killed. The National Threat Assessment Center (2019a) defined "mass attacks" as incidents taking place in a public location in which three or more people excluding the attacker were harmed. This is also the definition used by the United States Secret Service to assess targeted violence in various locations, e.g. workplaces, schools and public spaces (National Threat Assessment Center, 2019b, p. 1). Similarly, Silva and Capella (2018, p. 83) define a mass shooting as an incident in which a perpetrator kills or attempts to kill four or more victims. Other qualifications include the main weapon being a firearm, the attack not being related to criminal activity and it taking place at multiple locations within a twenty-four hour time period. Andrew Goddard (VCPS) advocated using definitions that include harm rather than deaths when calculating the number of mass shootings in the United States: "The problem with the government's definition of four dead is what if twenty-seven people are shot and wounded — are they going to say that's *not* a mass shooting?" The point of this, he argued, is that the term shooting involves someone being shot, regardless of whether that is fatal or not. Moreover, when someone is shot, Andrew Goddard (VCPS), explained, their lives are unalterably changed — this is something he has lived experience of, given his son was wounded in the 2007 Virginia Tech attack. A similar point was made by Booty and colleagues (2019, p. 7) that those who are injured but survive these incidents will likely suffer trauma for the rest of their lives. They, therefore, advocate that mass shooting definitions should include four or more causalities to avoid discounting those who were shot non-fatally.

The other facet of the definition is whether to include those incidents that take in intimate contexts like the home. Booty and colleagues (2019, p. 7) advocate the inclusion of mass shootings taking place in non-public locations like the home within the definition. In those cases, the perpetrator will shoot their intimate partner and other victims, e.g. friends, colleagues and family members. These attacks tend to occur following separation from their intimate partners (Zedi, 2018, pp. 2, 6). Complicating matters further, in some mass shootings involving public spaces, there is domestic abuse in the perpetrator's history, e.g. the Pulse Nightclub (2016), Sutherland Springs (2017) and Ohio (2019) mass shootings (see Bosman, Taylor & Arango, 2019; Kerr, 2018b; Kerr & Markey, 2020). Interviewee, Rachel Graber (NCADV), ascribed this link to the threat of a mass shooting being a tactic of power and control: "It's said 'If you leave me, I will go out to the mall and shoot everybody.'" In spite of this, most definitions of mass shootings only include those taking place in public locations.

History of Mass Shootings

In the 1970s, researchers distinguished between serial murders, mass murders and spree murders. The first refers to a series of homicides in which at least three people are killed with there being a "cooling off" period between the murders. Mass murders or killings were described as incidents in which a number of victims are killed over a short duration of time (minutes or hours). The final type refers to multiple murders that are committed over a longer time span of a few days or weeks (Duwe, 2005, p. 64). It was thought the lexicon changed with the 1984 San Ysidro McDonald's mass shooting, with this being referred to as a mass murder rather than a serial murder (Davis, 2020). The trend then continued with "going postal" attacks in the 1980s, which provided the "cultural script where ultimate vengeance is carried out by showy, public violence." These then translated into "rampage reconstructions" carried out by workplace shooters and later school shooters (Kroll-Smith & Hunnicutt, 2008, p. 112).

The phenomenon of "going postal" began in 1986, when Patrick Sherrill killed fourteen people and injured six others in a postal office in the United States. The 1986 postal office massacre was said to have "provided a kind of script that had never existed before, a language of direct vengeance" that henceforth became compelling to others (Ames, 2007, pp. 14-15). Mass shootings incidents were confined to postal offices until 1989, when Joseph Wesbecker carried out a workplace massacre at the printing press Standard Gravure killing seven colleagues and wounding twenty. Unsurprisingly, perhaps, it is said that Joseph Wesbecker was fascinated by Patrick Sherrill. This incident, thus, became "the bridge between the post office massacres and office massacres" (Ames, 2007, pp. 14-15 Baron, 2000, p. 73).

It may be questioned what motivated people to carry out these "going postal" incidents in the first place. In his aptly named book "Going Postal," Ames (2007) theorizes that these massacres can be attributed to the ruling of Ronald Reagan, the fortieth president of the United States, in the 1980s. The "Reagan Revolution" was said to be "a return to old-fashioned Republicanism," resulting in decreased governmental assistance for the poor, less emphasis on civil rights, less controls on industry, an emphasis on competition profit-making, and larger tax breaks for those with wealth (Dallek, 1984, p. vii). These neo-liberal economic policies transformed corporate culture by "giving executives the opportunity to squeeze as much profit as possible for as little expenditure as possible" (Ames, 2007, p. 39). Furthermore, Reaganism was also seen as "an ideology expressing strong feelings about how Americans should order their lives" (Dallek, 1984, p. viii). Trade unions were seen as "inherently working against American values" and thereafter collapsed leading to poorer working conditions for employees (Ames, 2007, p. 130). It can be concurred that this was certainly the case for both Patrick Sherrill and Joseph Wesbecker. Sherill felt bullied by his superiors and decide "I gotta do something, right now [about the problem]" (Baron, 2000, p. 70). Similarly, Wesbecker requested time off from Standard Gravure because he felt the fumes from solvents were harming him. Even though Wesbecker had a doctor's letter to verify his claims, the company still refused to grant him leave. This is what brings Ames (2007, p. 133) to his conclusion that the "rampage murderer who attacks his workplace seeks to kill the abstract company by killing its literal assets and splattering the image in blood, thereby killing both employees and the company." This argument certainly seems convincing when it is considered that both Sherrill and Wesbecker were mistreated by their company and the notion of "killing" the company both literally with its employees and figuratively if the incident results in the company's closure, as it did with Standard Gravure, would offer them some semblance of vengeance. It could be said, however, that Ames is too focused on attributing the blame to Reagan himself, as barely any other possible causal factors of the "going postal" phenomenon are addressed. Additionally Ames' anger towards him is evident throughout the book. In the postscript, for instance, Ames bemoans the fact that Reagan died peacefully in his sleep whilst modern-day America still feels the effects of his corporate culture. There is also the fact to consider that "[whilst] Reagan gave that movement focus and leadership" the Reagan Revolution "went far beyond one man" (Anderson, 1988, pp. 6-7).

Mass shootings shifted from post offices and workplaces in the 1980s and early 1990s to educational institutions. Global trends pertaining to school shootings found that the United States had the highest number totaling 76 school shootings compared to the combined total for incidents around the world being 44 (Böckler, Seeger, Sitzer & Heitmeyer, 2013, p. 10). School shootings became particularly prolific in the United States in the latter half of the 1990s, with the occurrence of high-profile incidents such as Pearl High School (1997), Heath High School (1997), Westside Middle School (1997), Thurston High School (1998) and Columbine High School (1999). These incidents provoked former President Bill Clinton to convene an expert committee in the White House to provide advice on school safety (Fox, 2020). Although the first recorded incident in modern-day America at a school was in 1966 with the University of Texas shooting, mapping out incidents over the years shows a steady increase from the 1980s onwards. Seven occurred in the 1980s, causing 12 deaths; thirteen incidents in the 1990s, resulting in 36 deaths. This is based on the definition of a situation in which a perpetrator plans to kill or injure four of more people using guns at a school or school-related event. The definition of school refers only to K-12 education here; thus, excludes universities. Incidents declined slightly in the 2000s to five shootings resulting in 14 deaths and increased again in the 2010s to eight shootings causing 51 deaths. Similar to the increase in mass shootings generally, the school shootings that have occurred after 2000 have resulted in a greater number of deaths totaling 66 than the 55 that occurred in the whole of the 20th Century. It is postulated that this may be attributable to a greater access to high-power firearms in the 21st Century school shootings (Katsiyannis, Whitford & Ennis, 2018).

Why Does the United States Have the Most Mass Shootings?

Scholars have conducted research to address the question of why the United States has the greatest number of mass shootings, including those taking place at schools (see, for example, Böckler, Seeger, Sitzer & Heitmeyer, 2013; Lankford, 2016a, 2016b). Conducting research on the causal factors of school shootings is subject to what Harding, Fox and Mehta (2002) call the "degrees of freedom" problem. This methodological issue is explained as having many potential causal factors influencing school shootings and too few incidents to properly determine a significant variable as being the direct cause. Claiming that one factor is solely or mainly responsible for causing mass shootings is problematic. For instance, the shooting at Columbine High School led to debates about violence in films and video games (Moore, 2002). In spite of this, a Federal Bureau of Investigation (2000) study about school shootings found that only a quarter of perpetrators were interested in violent movies and an eighth in video games. Through their in-depth qualitative research using case studies of several school shooting incidents, Harding, Fox and Mehta (2002) were able to construct five potential factors, in order of tangibility, for school shootings: gun availability; adherence to a particular cultural script; the shooter's perception of their social world; individual problems; failure of social support system.

This model may also be applied to mass shootings more generally. Going through each of these factors finds that gun availability is perhaps the most obvious potential factor. Lankford (2016b) found that the United States and other nations with high levels of firearm ownership may be particularly susceptible to mass shootings. Behind the United States, the countries with the highest number of school shootings are Canada and Germany (Böckler, Seeger, Sitzer & Heitmeyer, 2013, p. 10). Looking at the levels of civilian gun ownership in those countries finds the United States has the highest rate worldwide with 120.5 per 100, 000 population. Canada and Germany are eight and twenty-ninth respectively with rates of 34.7 and 19.6 per 100, 000 population (World Population Review, 2020). Three mass shootings have taken place in the United Kingdom (see Kerr, 2018a). Moreover, the country has a very low civilian gun ownership rate of 4.3 per 100, 000 population, putting it outside the top hundred countries with civilians owning guns (World Population Review, 2020). Further to this, ideals about masculinity are entrenched in gun usage in the United States (Carlson, 2015).

Although gun ownership clearly is a contributory factor, it is problematic to ascribe one factor as the sole cause of mass shootings. The second factor in Harding and colleague's (2002) model is the "cultural script" set by previous shooting incidents. Future mass shooters may use this ascribed plan of action as a means to "resolve" their problems (see, for instance, Kennedy-Kollar & Charles, 2013; Klein, 2005, 2006; Lankford, 2013, 2015). This could explain the increase in copycat attacks and threats following a high-profile incident (Coleman, 2004; Lankford & Madfis, 2017; Lankford & Tomek, 2017; Towers, 2015). The remaining three factors of the shooter's perception of the world, individual struggles and a lack of support from others (Harding et al., 2002) have also been evidenced in studies of mass shooters more generally (see, for example, Doran & O'Grady, 2015; Fox & Fridel, 2016; Kerr & Markey, 2020). More details will be given in this book regarding individual examples in Chapters 5 and 6 which focus on the eleven worst mass shootings in the United States.

It may be questioned, however, how these factors apply to the United States when other countries also have citizens struggling with personal problems and a lack of support. Utilizing Hofstede's (2001) cultural model, it can be seen that nations whose ideology resonates with the following have the highest number of incidents: high individualism, predicated on a sense of self-importance, personal privacy and a need for individual gratification; and lower power distance, where the unequal distribution of power between social groups is rarely challenged. Looking at the U.S. suggests the explanation may partially lie in cultural expectations. It is an individualistic society, meaning there are fewer tendencies to talk through problems (Esposito & Finley, 2014; Kennedy-Kollar & Charles, 2013). Moreover, the individualistic nature of the United States and the importance placed on achievement could explain the tendency for mass shootings in that country to center on workplaces and schools; whilst incidents in other countries tend to focus on military sites (Lankford, 2016a). This was supported by an investigation of mass shootings in the United States by Mother Jones (2020), which found more than half of the cases involved school or workplace shootings. That is not to over-state the reliability of Hofstede's cultural model, however, by presuming that values are universal throughout each nation and that culture is transferable. In reality, nations are heterogeneous in nature; albeit united by commonalities in cultural beliefs. For something like mass shootings, a shift in cultural preconceptions is needed to reduce the prevalence of these within the United States.

Another factor could be notions of masculinity, with the majority of mass shooters being male (Mother Jones, 2020). It is said that cultural notions of masculinity "identify aggression as a means of earning and maintaining respect" (Harding, Fox & Mehta, 2002, pp. 196-197). Ideals of masculinity may play a role in the use of guns (Carlson, 2015; Lankford, 2016b). Moreover, a violent boy culture is said to exist in the United States and have been a contributory factor in previous school shootings (Kimmel & Mahler, 2003; Klein & Chancer, 2000). Taking this even further, a link has also been identified between mass shooters and misogyny. The shooter of the Isla Vista Campus (2014) shooting spoke about an "Incel" rebellion. This is defined as "involuntary celibates," which is an online subculture of males who display rage at females, fantasize about violence (particularly sexual violence) and express fandom for mass shooters (Bosman, Taylor & Arango, 2019). Rachel Graber (NCADV) explained it in the following way for the Isla Vista perpetrator: "He felt himself entitled to sex and he wasn't getting it so he killed a bunch of people."

Another commonality in mass shootings is stalking: for instance, the Virginia Tech (2007) attacker stalked several females at his university (Kerr, 2018b). As a topic, stalking is said to be not well understood: "I think there's a lot of misperceptions about stalking versus harassment. Stalking is not just being annoying and repeated text messages. Stalking often involves surveillance that would cause a person to fear a material harm."-Rachel Graber (NCADV). In addition to this, stalking is not discussed in public discussions and there are no large advocacy groups focusing specifically on this issue. Due to this, there are still gaps in the law whereby those convicted of stalking are still able to own and purchase firearms in some states (Kerr, 2018b). An example of this was a mass shooting committed by a man who had a history of stalking women; yet was still able to own and purchase firearms. As it transpired, he shot his former girlfriend and her three children in a mass shooting attack (New York Times, 2017).

Considering all of this, further research is needed into the potential warning signs of all types of mass shooters. This includes those who perpetrate harm in public places, as well as those who carry out more intimate attacks. Whilst this book utilizes the first definition of a mass shooting in its discussion of attackers and policy proposals, this is not to undermine the importance of research into mass shootings involving intimate partner violence. As mentioned earlier, a history of intimate partner violence and/or stalking can be a characteristic of perpetrators who carry out mass shootings in public places anyway. From that perspective, policy solutions could extend to appropriate treatment for mental illness. Heather Ross (TGS) suggested therapy for everyone on a regular basis, with depression being treated as a mental illness. A similar point was advanced by Sheila Islong (Giffords) who maintained that priority should be given to how mental health spaces can be organized to hopefully prevent the use of guns. Improving mental health screening and treatment was supported by 89% of all adults and 86% of those aged 13-17 as a means of preventing school shootings (Graf, 2018). Focusing on mental health should assist with reducing the rate of firearm-related suicides. Another solution would be to raise awareness of the signs of mass shootings and explain when to take threats seriously: "People need to be more cognizant of things like that. It's hard to know if things are just a joke."-Heather Ross (TGS).

Attempting to address the underlying causes of behaviors like stalking and domestic violence would also be helpful. Heather Ross (TGS) focuses on sex education on her radio show "The Sex Ed Show" on KOOP (https://www.koop.org/programs/sex-ed-show), with the intention of helping to reduce sexual assault, domestic violence and challenge stigma and stereotypes. "I feel it indirectly impacts gun violence because a lot of gun violence stems from domestic violence, assault, and suicide." Another step could involve undertaking more education with young people in order to "invest more in shaping the culture."-Rachel Graber (NCADV). This would try to address the sense of entitlement which is entrenched within "Incel" subculture, as can be seen from Rachel Graber (NCADV)'s explanation that the Isla Vista shooter believed he was entitled to access women's bodies for sexual activity and resorting to violence when this was not fulfilled.

CONCLUSION

This chapter offered an investigation into trends and understandings relating to gun violence and mass shootings in the United States. A review of data relating to gun violence in the United States found it has a very high level of deaths in comparison to other countries (Grinshteyn & Hemenway, 2016; Naghavi et al., 2018). The majority of these deaths are actually caused by firearm-related suicide (BBC News, 2019a; Gun Violence Archives, 2020; Naghavi et al., 2018). Although they generate attention, mass shootings are only a tiny fraction of the gun violence rates. In spite of this, the number of mass shootings has increased over recent years (BBC News, 2019a; Gun Violence Archives, 2020; Silverstein, 2020). Interviewees postulated that some of the recent mass shootings were "tipping points" for citizens. The Las Vegas incident was notable for the bump stock law passed by Executive Order — more will be said on this in Chapter 4 — and the Parkland (2018) school shooting resulted in the greater involvement of young people in the GVP movement.

A difficulty in discussing and measuring the rate of mass shootings is the various definitions appropriated. The typical definition is an incident where four of more victims (not the shooter(s)) are killed with a firearm in a single location or multiple locations in close proximity (Follman, Aronsen & Pan, 2016; Fox & Levin, 2003; Krouse & Richardson, 2015; Lankford, 2016; Silver, Horgan & Gill, 2018). Other studies use the definition where there is the *attempt* (whether successful or not) to kill four or more people (Silva & Capella, 2018) or three or more people are harmed in an incident taking place in a public location (National Threat Assessment Center, 2019a, 2019b). Another issue is whether to include incidents taking place in non-public locations like the home. There are a number of incidents where an intimate partner violence attack involves killing the partner and multiple other family members (Zedi, 2018). Additionally, for a number of the mass shootings taking place in public locations, the perpetrator has a history of domestic abuse (Bosman, Taylor & Arango, 2019; Kerr, 2018b; Kerr & Markey, 2020). The variations in defining mass shootings can skew the trends recorded, so it is something that requires further research to determine the most appropriate definition(s) to use.

Looking at the history of mass shootings finds the lexicon generally changed in the 1980s from serial murder in which there are "cooling off" periods between murders to mass murder where all the killing takes place over a short period of time (Davis, 2020; Duwe, 2005). Attacks in postal offices became more prevalent in the 1980s, leading to the phrase "going postal." The change in working conditions said to have been caused by Reaganism (Ames, 2007; Anderson, 1988; Dallek, 1984) is said to have prompted mass shootings to then shift locations to the workplace (Ames, 2007; Baron, 2000; Kroll-Smith

& Hunnicutt, 2008). In the late 1990s, mass shootings in schools then began to increase (Fox, 2020; Katsiyannis, Whitford & Ennis, 2018).

Although relatively rare in the overall spectrum of gun violence (BBC News, 2019a), the United States does have the highest number of mass shootings globally (Böckler, Seeger, Sitzer & Heitmeyer, 2013; Lankford, 2016a, 2016b). To determine the reasons why, Harding, Fox and Mehta's (2002) model of five potential influencers was used. The first of those is gun availability, with the United States having the highest levels of firearm ownership in the world (World Population Review, 2020). Another factor is the "cultural script" created by previous mass shootings (Kennedy-Kollar & Charles, 2013; Klein, 2005, 2006; Lankford, 2013, 2015). The other three factors in the model are the shooter's perception of the world, individual struggles and a lack of support from others, which have been seen in previous studies of mass shooters (Doran & O'Grady, 2015; Fox & Fridel, 2016; Kerr & Markey, 2020). Utilizing Hofstede's (2001) cultural model finds that the high individualism and unequal power distribution between social groups present in the United States could be another contributing factor (Esposito & Finley, 2014; Kennedy-Kollar & Charles, 2013). Extreme notions of masculinity may also be a factor, with violent boy culture (Kimmel & Mahler, 2003; Klein & Chancer, 2000) and conflating maleness with gun usage (Carlson, 2015; Lankford, 2016b) possibly playing a role in past mass shootings. Reviewing previous mass shootings finds that other misogynistic aspects like stalking and "involuntary celibates" subculture are prevalent in previous mass shooters (Bosman, Taylor & Arango, 2019; Kerr, 2018b). Interviewees suggested methods to try to deal with mass shooters, such as educating them about appropriate sexual behavior, mental health treatment and training on warning signs.

REFERENCES

Aaroe, L. (2011). Investigating Frame Strength: The Case of Episodic and Thematic Frames. *Political Communication, 28*(2), 207–226. doi:10.1080/10584609.2011.568041

Abu-Lughool, R. (2015). Gun Violence in the U.S.: A Muted Type of Terrorism? In L. Eargle & A. Esmail (Eds.), *Gun Violence in American Society: Crime, Justice and Public Policy* (pp. 162–181). University Press of America.

Ames, M. (2007). *Going Postal: Rage, Murder and Rebellion in America.* Snowbooks Ltd.

Anderson, M. (1988). *Revolution: The Reagan Legacy.* Harcourt Brace Jovanovich Publishers.

Baron, S. A. (2000). *Violence in the Workplace: A Prevention and Management Guide for Businesses* (2nd ed.). Pathfinder Publishing of California.

BBC News. (2019a, August 5). *America's gun culture in charts.* https://www.bbc.co.uk/news/world-us-canada-41488081

BBC News. (2019b, December 29). *U.S. saw highest number of mass killings on record in 2019, database reveals.* https://www.bbc.co.uk/news/world-us-canada-50936575?SThisFB&fbclid=IwAR05I7b7PFrG ypjs3CDxoqBxKhsO_1aFHtY4paidxsw8iI84S_HSrEdik7U

Berkley Media Studies Group. (2018, June 18). *Issue 25: More than mass shootings: Gun violence narratives in California news.* http://www.bmsg.org/resources/publications/gun-suicide-community-domestic-violence-news-narratives-california/

Böckler, N., Seeger, T., Sitzer, P., & Heitmeyer, W. (2013). School Shootings: International Research, Case Studies and Concepts for Prevention. New York: Springer Science + Business Media. doi:10.1007/978-1-4614-5526-4

Booty, M., O'Dwyer, J., Webster, D., McCourt, A., & Crifasi, C. (2019). Describing a "mass shooting": The role of databases in understanding burden. *Injury Epidemiology, 6*(4), 1–8. doi:10.118640621-019-0226-7 PMID:31828004

Bosman, J., Taylor, K., & Arango, T. (2019, August 10). A Common Trait Among Mass Killers: Hatred Toward Women. *The New York Times.* https://www.nytimes.com/2019/08/10/us/mass-shootings-misogyny-dayton.html

Coleman, L. (2004). *The Copycat Effect: How the Media and Popular Culture Trigger the Mayhem in Tomorrow's Headlines.* Paraview Pocket Books.

Dallek, R. (1984). *Ronald Reagan: The Politics of Symbolism.* Harvard University Press.

Davis, J. (2020). *American School Shooting: The Growing Problem of Mass Shooting for Homeland Security.* James Davis.

Doran, S. E. M., & O'Grady, M. A. (2015). Shattered Self-Images: School Shooters, Narcissism and Egotistical Suicide. In L. Eargle & A. Esmail (Eds.), *Gun Violence in American Society: Crime, Justice and Public Policy* (pp. 19–48). University Press of America.

Duwe, G. (2005). A Circle of Distortion: The Social Construction of Mass Murder in the United States. *Western Criminology Review, 6*(1), 59–78.

Esposito, L., & Finley, L. L. (2014). Beyond Gun Control: Examining Neoliberalism, Pro-gun politics and Gun Violence in the United States. *Theory in Action, 7*(2), 74–103. doi:10.3798/tia.1937-0237.14011

Follman, M., Aronsen, G., & Pan, D. (2016, July 18) *A Guide to Mass Shootings in America.* Mother Jones. https://www.motherjones.com/politics/2012/07/mass-shootings-map/

Fox, J. A. (2020, February 19). *School shootings are not the new normal, despite statistics that stretch the truth.* USA Today. https://eu.usatoday.com/story/opinion/2018/02/19/parkland-school-shootings-not-new-normal-despite-statistics-stretching-truth-fox-column/349380002/

Fox, J. A., & Levin, J. (2003). Mass Murder: An Analysis of Extreme Violence. *Journal of Applied Psychoanalytic Studies, 5*(1), 47–64. doi:10.1023/A:1021051002020

Graf, N. (2018, April 18). *A majority of U.S. teens fear a shooting could happen at their school, and most parents share their concern.* Pew Research Center. https://www.pewresearch.org/fact-tank/2018/04/18/a-majority-of-u-s-teens-fear-a-shooting-could-happen-at-their-school-and-most-parents-share-their-concern/

Grinshteyn, E., & Hemenway, D. (2016). Violent Death Rates: The U.S. Compared with Other High-Income OECD Countries, 2010. *The American Journal of Medicine, 129*(3), 266–273. doi:10.1016/j.amjmed.2015.10.025 PMID:26551975

Gross, K. (2008). Framing Persuasive Appeals: Episodic and Thematic Framing, Emotional Response and Policy Opinion. *Political Psychology, 29*(2), 169–192. doi:10.1111/j.1467-9221.2008.00622.x

Gun Violence Archive. (2020). *Home Page.* https://www.gunviolencearchive.org/

Hofstede, G. (2001). *Culture's consequences: Comparing values, behaviors, institutions, and organizations across nations* (2nd ed.). Sage.

Iyengar, S. (1991). *Is anyone responsible? How television frames political issues.* University of Chicago Press. doi:10.7208/chicago/9780226388533.001.0001

Katsiyannis, A., Whitford, D. K., & Ennis, R. P. (2018). Historical Examination of United States Intentional Mass School Shootings in the 20th and 21st Centuries: Implications for Students, Schools, and Society. *Journal of Child and Family Studies, 27*(8), 2562–2573. doi:10.100710826-018-1096-2

Kennedy-Kollar, D., & Charles, C. (2013). Hegemonic Masculinity and Mass Murderers in the United States. *Southwest Journal of Criminal Justice, 8*(2), 62–74.

Kerr, S. E. M. (2018a). *Gun Violence Prevention? The Politics Behind Policy Responses to School Shootings in the United States.* Palgrave MacMillan.

Kerr, S. E. M. (2018b). The Gendered Nature of Intimate Partner Gun Violence. In A. Trier-Bieniek (Ed.), *The Politics of Gender* (pp. 127–144). Brill.

Kerr, S. E. M., & Markey, M. A. (2020). Exploring the Phenomenon of Mass Shootings in Public Locations. In G. Crews (Ed.), *Handbook of Research on Mass Shootings and Multiple Victim Violence* (pp. 122–155). IGI Global. doi:10.4018/978-1-7998-0113-9.ch008

Kimmel, M. S., & Mahler, M. (2003). Adolescent Masculinity, Homophobia, and Violence: Random School Shootings, 1982-2001. *The American Behavioral Scientist, 46*(10), 1439–1458. doi:10.1177/0002764203046010010

Klein, J. (2005). Teaching her a lesson: Media misses boys' rage relating to girls in school shootings. *Crime, Media, Culture, 1*(1), 90–97. doi:10.1177/1741659005050245

Klein, J. (2006). Cultural Capital and High School Bullies: How Social Inequality Impacts School Violence. *Men and Masculinities, 9*(1), 53–75. doi:10.1177/1097184X04271387

Klein, J., & Chancer, L. S. (2000). Masculinity Matters: the omission of gender from high-profile school violence cases. In S. U. Spina (Ed.), *Smoke and Mirrors: the hidden context of violence in schools and society* (pp. 129–162). Rowman and Littlefield Publishers.

Kroll-Smith, S., & Hunnicutt, G. (2008). Satire, Guns and Humans: Lessons from the Nacirema. In B. Agger & T. W. Luke (Eds.), *There is a gunman on campus: tragedy and terror at Virginia Tech* (pp. 105–117). Rowman and Littlefield.

Lankford, A. (2013). A Comparative Analysis of Suicide Terrorists and Rampage, Workplace, and School Shooters in the United States From 1990 to 2010. *Homicide Studies, 17*(3), 255–274. doi:10.1177/1088767912462033

Lankford, A. (2015). Mass Shooters in the USA, 1966–2010: Differences Between Attackers Who Live and Die. *Justice Quarterly, 32*(2), 360–379. doi:10.1080/07418825.2013.806675

Lankford, A. (2016a). Are America's public mass shooters unique? A comparative analysis of offenders in the United States and other countries. *International Journal of Comparative and Applied Criminal Justice, 40*(2), 171–183. doi:10.1080/01924036.2015.1105144

Lankford, A. (2016b). Public Mass Shooters and Firearms: A Cross-National Study of 171 Countries. *Violence and Victims, 31*(2), 187–199. doi:10.1891/0886-6708.VV-D-15-00093 PMID:26822013

Lankford, A., & Madfis, E. (2017). Don't Name Them, Don't Show Them, But Report Everything Else: A Pragmatic Proposal for Denying Mass Killers the Attention They Seek and Deterring Future Offenders. *The American Behavioral Scientist, 62*(2), 260–279. doi:10.1177/0002764217730854

Lankford, A., & Tomek, S. (2017). Mass Killings in the United States from 2006 to 2013: Social Contagion or Random Clusters? *Suicide & Life-Threatening Behavior, 48*(4), 459–467. doi:10.1111ltb.12366 PMID:28726336

Naghavi, M., Marczak, L. B., Kutz, M., Shackelford, K. A., Arora, M., Miller-Petrie, M., Aichour, M. T. E., Akseer, N., Al-Raddadi, R. M., Alam, K., Alghnam, S. A., Antonio, C. A. T., Aremu, O., Arora, A., Asadi-Lari, M., Assadi, R., Atey, T. M., Avila-Burgos, L., Awasthi, A., ... Murray, C. J. L. (2018). Global Mortality from Firearms, 1990-2016. *Journal of the American Medical Association, 320*(8), 792–814. doi:10.1001/jama.2018.10060 PMID:30167700

National Threat Assessment Center. (2019a). *Attacks in Public Spaces – 2018*. U.S. Secret Service, Department of Homeland Security.

National Threat Assessment Center. (2019b). *Protecting America's Schools: A U.S. Secret Service Analysis of Targeted School Violence*. U.S. Secret Service, Department of Homeland Security.

Silva, J. R., & Capella, J. A. (2018). The media's coverage of mass public shootings in America: Fifty years of newsworthiness. *International Journal of Comparative and Applied Criminal Justice, 43*(1), 77–97.

Silver, J., Horgan, J., & Gill, P. (2018). Foreshadowing targeted violence; Assessing leakage of intent by public mass murderers. *Aggression and Violent Behavior, 38*(Jan-Feb), 94–100. doi:10.1016/j.avb.2017.12.002

The New York Times. (2017, December 19). *Boyfriends Can Kill, Too*. https://www.nytimes.com/interactive/2017/12/19/opinion/boyfriend-loophole-guns.html

Towers, S., Gomez-Lievano, A., Khan, M., Mubayi, A., & Castillo-Chavez, C. (2015). Contagion in Mass Killings and School Shootings. *PLoS One, 10*(7), e0117259. doi:10.1371/journal.pone.0117259 PMID:26135941

World Population Review. (2020). *Gun Ownership by Country 2020*. https://worldpopulationreview.com/country-rankings/gun-ownership-by-country

Wright, M., Molloyo, M., & Lockharto, K. (2018, February 26). *Parkland students vs the NRA: Has the powerful US gun lobby met its match in Generation Snapchat.* The Telegraph, https://www.telegraph.co.uk/news/2018/02/26/parkland-students-vs-nra-has-powerful-us-gun-lobby-met-match/

Zedi, A. M. (2018). *Multiple victim homicides, mass murders and homicide-suicides as domestic violence events.* The Battered Women's Justice Project.

ADDITIONAL READING

Ames, M. (2007). *Going Postal: Rage, Murder and Rebellion in America.* Snowbooks Ltd.

Grinshteyn, E., & Hemenway, D. (2016). Violent Death Rates: The U.S. Compared with Other High-Income OECD Countries, 2010. *The American Journal of Medicine, 129*(3), 266–273. doi:10.1016/j.amjmed.2015.10.025 PMID:26551975

Hofstede, G. (2001). *Culture's consequences: Comparing values, behaviors, institutions, and organizations across nations* (2nd ed.). Sage.

Lankford, A. (2016b). Public Mass Shooters and Firearms: A Cross-National Study of 171 Countries. *Violence and Victims, 31*(2), 187–199. doi:10.1891/0886-6708.VV-D-15-00093 PMID:26822013

Naghavi, M., Marczak, L. B., Kutz, M., Shackelford, K. A., Arora, M., Miller-Petrie, M., Aichour, M. T. E., Akseer, N., Al-Raddadi, R. M., Alam, K., Alghnam, S. A., Antonio, C. A. T., Aremu, O., Arora, A., Asadi-Lari, M., Assadi, R., Atey, T. M., Avila-Burgos, L., Awasthi, A., ... Murray, C. J. L. (2018). Global Mortality from Firearms, 1990-2016. *Journal of the American Medical Association, 320*(8), 792–814. doi:10.1001/jama.2018.10060 PMID:30167700

KEY TERMS AND DEFINITIONS

Cultural Script: This prescribes a particular course of action infiltrated into society through mass media reporting of previous mass shooting incidents.

Going Postal: This phrase refers to an individual becoming extremely angry and committing violence. It originated from mass shooting attacks in post offices in the United States in the 1980s.

Gun Violence: The term used to refer to the trend of gun-related deaths and injuries.

High Individualism: Taken from Hofstede's cultural model this refers to a national characteristic predicated on a sense of self-importance, as well as gratification and privacy for individuals.

Incels: This refers to a subculture of those who are involuntary celibate. Common features are expressing rage at women, having violent sexual fantasies and admiration for previous mass shooters.

Low Power Distance: A characteristic from Hofstede's cultural model referring to an unequal distribution of power between social groups which is rarely challenged.

Mass Shootings: An incident in which a perpetrator(s) uses a firearm(s) to enact harm against others. Definitions vary from at least four people (aside from the shooter) being killed to three or four other people being harmed.

Serial Murders: A series of homicides in which at least three murders are committed in different periods of time.

Spree Murders: Multiple murders committed over the time span of a few days or weeks.

Chapter 2
Methodological Approach

ABSTRACT

This chapter continues to set the context of the book by describing the methodological approach adopted. The importance of framing in policy debates is highlighted, justifying why feature articles, letters to the editor, and videos were selected as the units for analyses. Described is the process undertaken to retrieve a news media sample from a number of sources. Detailed are the methodologies adopted to assess the news media sample: content analysis, critical discourse analysis, and visual discourse analysis. The qualitative research undertaken for this book is documented, outlining the methodological approach of interviews and the sample of interviewees chosen. The overall purpose of this chapter is to inform the reader about the methodologies, samples, and approaches utilized.

INTRODUCTION

This chapter justifies the approach and methodologies chosen for this book. Selecting a media sample for analysis is a key part of research design to examine how issues are framed (Chong & Druckman, 2007, p. 106). Detailed here are the three news media sources chosen for analysis: New York Times, TIME and Washington Post. The sample selected from each of these sources is documented. In order to get behind the portrayal of gun-related issues in the news media, feature articles and letters to the editor were selected. With their evaluative and emotive nature, these types of sources give an indication of opinions around a certain issue (Ericson, Baranek & Chan, 1989; Fowler, 1991). Chong and Druckman (2007) recommended including feature articles in studies about framing. Letters to the editor have been used in other studies researching public opinions about gun control (Goss, 2006; Kerr, 2018a). Also selected were videos and images published by the news media sources. A set time period corresponding to the date of the Las Vegas (2017) shooting up until a year afterwards was chosen for selecting sources.

Content analysis was the methodology appropriated to determine the themes emerging from news media content (Altheide, 1996; Bryman, 2008; Holsti, 1969). Analyses were taken even further by utilizing critical discourse analysis, an approach critiquing the language used (Fairclough 1995; Krippendorff, 2004; Mayr & Machin, 2012; van Dijk 1998b). For the news media sample, lexical techniques, such as tone, rhythm, use of signifiers and so forth were assessed (Fowler, 1991; Garland, 1985; Mayr &

DOI: 10.4018/978-1-7998-3916-3.ch002

Machin, 2012; Parlmer, 1976/1981; van Leeuwen, 1996). Visual discourse analysis was used to analyse the videos and images included in the sample (Mayr & Machin, 2012; Müller, 2011; Van Dijk, 1998).

The qualitative research conducted is then detailed. Qualitative interviews allow for opinions, ideas and experiences to be examined by affording the interviewer a greater depth of questioning (Arksey & Knight, 1999, p. 96; Bloor & Wood, 2006, Laggard, Keegan & Ward, 2003). Nineteen semi-structured qualitative interviews were conducted to find out more about the themes of interest in this book: how mass shootings are understood in society; gun debates following these and the gun violence prevention movement in general; threat assessment to try to detect and prevent mass shootings; emergency management and communication procedures. Taking part in these interviews were twenty-one participants, with two of the interviews involving two interviewees at a time. Participants were purposefully selected to fulfil a particular function (Newborn, 2007). Some were involved in the gun violence prevention movement and/or gun-related research and policymaking. Others specialized in threat assessment and/or emergency management and communication. Interestingly, a number of interviewees were found to have direct links to gun violence, having relatives who had been killed or injured. The sample of interviewees is provided in Table 1. Also detailed is the process adopted to analyze findings from interviews in the form of open and axial coding to interrogate the emerging themes (Boeijjie, 2010).

This chapter is structured as above. The opening section goes into more detail about framing debates and explains why the case study of the 2017 Las Vegas incident was selected. The discussion then details the news media sample and how this was selected. The methodologies of content analysis, critical discourse analysis and visual discourse analysis are documented, explaining why each of these was used. The chapter then discusses the qualitative research carried out, detailing the interviewees selected and the process of interviewing them.

NEWS MEDIA –FRAMING AND POLICY DEBATES

This book analyzes news media content in order to explore debates about policies in the aftermath of mass shootings. As a research methodology, analyzing news media articles affords a number of benefits. In addition to offering plentiful data to be assessed, it gives an insight into the content consumed by media audiences and how it may be shaping their thinking. By deciding which issues to cover and to what extent, the news media can influence which issues citizens think about based on the amount of information available to them to form judgments (Delli Carpini, 2005, p. 35). The words and phrases utilized by journalists who produce the news can denote value judgments and ideological meanings (Lombardi, 2018, p.5; Schildkraut, 2014, p. 7; van Dijk, 1998b, 31-32). Consumers engage in an active process of "reading in" media content in order to make sense of the world (Fowler, 1991, p. 46).

Described as "arguments that co-occur together repeatedly" (Woodly, 2015, p. 11), frames are another element of interest when studying news media content. Frames can be "thematic" or "episodic" in nature. A thematic frame places an issue or event into context; whilst an episodic one centers on a specific event or person (Callaghan & Schnell, 2005, p. 4). These may affect attitudes and interpretations of a political issue. An experiment found that media frames were more likely to influence beliefs when they interacted with the pre-existing cognitive elements of individuals (Shen, 2004). Further to this, there appears to be a symbiotic relationship between the news media and policy-making. Developments in the political sphere involving elected officials, political parties, interest groups and citizens influence media coverage; whilst news content may influence how politicians and other policy-making figures are perceived (Callaghan & Schnell, 2005, p. 5; Jacobs & Shapiro, 2000, p. 217).

This book studies the news media coverage following the 2017 Las Vegas incident. This was a shooting at an open-air outdoor concert in October 2017, whereby the perpetrator fired from an open window at a nearby hotel. Since the conclusion in the author's previous book (Kerr, 2018a) featured deliberations about what a Trump presidency might look like for the gun prevention violence movement, covering a mass shooting that occurred during this time period provides an opportunity to critique this. The reason for selecting this incident is its infamous nature. Las Vegas is considered the "worst" mass shooting in United States history with its death toll of fifty-eight and over eight hundred people injured. Studies have found that news media coverage of mass shootings tends to focus on the most violent incidents and be saturated for up to a month afterwards (e.g. Maguire, Weatherby & Mathers, 2002; Robinson, 2011). As the media sample selects articles up until a year after the incident, there are also mentions of other mass shootings that occurred during this time period: the 2017 Sutherland Springs shooting at a Baptist Church in Texas; the 2018 Parkland school shooting in Florida. Both of these also feature in the top ten worst mass shootings in modern American history (CNN, 2020). The eleven worst mass shootings are covered in more detail in Chapter 5 which looks at leakage prior to attacks.

By focusing on the Las Vegas incident in Chapters 3 and 4 and eleven of the worst incidents in Chapters 5 and 6, this book utilizes a case study approach. This is a frame to determine the parameters of information gathering (Stoecker, 2006, p. 150). A well-designed case study builds up a picture of the case through an examination of information gleaned from different levels (De Vaus, 2006, p. 7). This gives the research richness and "realness" (Stoecker, 2006, p. 160). The Las Vegas incident is examined in-depth through the news media analyses carried out. The other case studies discussed in Chapters 5 and 6 are researched via reading about each incident to build up a picture of what motivated perpetrators and indicators of warning signs prior to attacks.

Media Sample

To collect the news media sample, articles were retrieved from the following news media sources: the Washington Post and New York Times, both of which are national newspapers; in addition to the newsweekly magazine, TIME. The New York Times has been described as the "gold standard" of newspaper data in the United States, due to its capacity for setting the policy agenda (Schildkraut, 2014, p. 190; Steidley & Cohen, 2016, p. 7). Additionally, the New York Times and Washington Post are national newspapers with high levels of readership. These sources have also been utilized in numerous other research studies around policy framing (e.g. Hawdon, Agnich, Wood & Ryan, 2015; Kupchik & Bracy, 2009; Woodly, 2015). TIME magazine was chosen for its in-depth, feature-style reporting, which affects how issues are portrayed. It has previously been utilized in studies by the author (e.g. Doran, 2014; Kerr, 2018a).

It should be noted that there are limitations with using these sources. The New York Times was found to be more likely to cover gun-control groups like the Brady Campaign in its coverage, as opposed to gun rights organizations like the National Rifle Association (Steidley & Cohen, 2016, p. 17). Furthermore, both the Washington Post and New York Times are deemed to have a center-left bias. This is something that will have affected the slant and tone of articles relating to gun debates. TIME magazine is also denoted as being centrist/liberal, so similar perspectives can be expected from its content (Media Bias Fact Checker, n.d.). Similar to Kupchik and Bracy (2009, p. 141) who used the New York Times in their sample, another limitation is the bias towards readers in the North-East of the United States with the New

York Times and Washington Post covering that part of the country. Moreover, since only three sources were used in the news media sample for this book, it can only be seen as representing a *snapshot* of the coverage (Holsti, 1969, p. 128).

Once those three news media sources were decided upon, articles were sampled across a number of time periods to capture the debates and developments relating to gun policy. Coverage of a tragic event like a mass shooting tends to result in saturated coverage for the first two weeks (Hawdon, Agnich, Wood & Ryan, 2015, p. 218; McGinty, Webster, Jarlenski & Barry, 2014, p. 406). Within this time period, the news media attempts to work through the tragedy looking at factors such as: the perpetrator's life and any warning signs displayed; if any failings led to this event (e.g. police not following up a tip); the impact on the lives of those directly affected and the wider community; policy proposals that may prevent future tragedies. Considering this, it can be expected that following an incident like a mass shooting policy proposals to reduce gun violence are likely to be discussed. After the "emergency phase" of the first two weeks, policy change takes place over a substantial period of time (Entman, 2010; Woodly, 2015). Considering this, the news media sample goes up to one year after the shooting incident, taking it up to the 1st of October 2018. Interestingly, other high-profile mass shootings (e.g. Sutherland Springs, Parkland) occurred in the one year period after Las Vegas; hence, multiple incidents are, at times, discussed concurrently. Research into framing can commonly make the mistake of treating time as linear in nature (Entman, 2010; Woodly, 2015). This book addresses this issue by noting that there are overlaps and breaks in framing debates as they pertain to the Las Vegas shooting and other subsequent incidents.

Once articles had been retrieved for the time period of the 1st October 2017 through to the 1st of October 2018, the sample was then narrowed down to its final form. Firstly, any irrelevant articles not relating to gun debates or understandings of mass shootings were removed from the potential sample. A similar procedure was adopted by Kupchik and Brady (2009) to ensure all relevant content was included in their media sample. Once a potential sample of articles was available, all feature or editorial articles were selected. These types of articles tend to be argumentative in nature and capture an editorial voice (Fowler, 1991, p. 211). It was, therefore, believed it would be beneficial to include such articles in the sample to gauge media perspectives on guns at that moment in time (Chong & Druckman, 2007; van Dijk 1998b). The final sample consisted of one hundred and forty feature articles across the three news sources.

Also selected for inclusion were letters to the editor from the Washington Post and New York Times. Letters submitted to the editor provide a forum for the airing of public opinion. They are generally published in the editorial pages and accompanied by the name of the author; henceforth, contextualizing these as a form of personal opinion. Since letters provide a snapshot into public opinion, they may entrench, challenge or reshape understandings of the topic (Ericson, Baranek & Chan, 1989, pp. 6, 32, 334, 341, 375). Analyzing letters to the editor to examine reaction to gun policies is a technique that has been utilized in other research studies (e.g. Doran, 2014; Goss, 2006; Kerr, 2018a). It should be noted, however, that letters to the editor also go through an editorial process and are selected for "newsworthiness" influencing what letters say and which ones are accepted for publication. Moreover, the letters accepted for publication are usually in response to an agenda already covered in news stories within the publication (Ericson, Baranek & Chan, 1989, pp. 334, 339, 341). This means that the letters published can give an indication of the scope of policy options being raised in debates (Woodly, 2015, p. 25). All letters in the potential media sample were included in the sample for analysis, giving a total of thirty-seven. Table 1 gives an indication of all the feature articles and letters to the editor included in the final sample.

Table 1. Sample of feature articles and letters

Source	Number of Feature Articles	Number of Letters to the Editor
New York Times	33	24
TIME	31	0
Washington Post	76	13
Total	140	37

All images (including two political cartoons) and videos from the news media sample were also included to add an angle of visual news discourse to the analysis. Political cartoons enable media consumers to classify, organize and interpret social issues (Greenberg, 2002). Images and videos are able to capture emotional reactions from victims' families and survivors, something which is a bit more challenging in print news stories (Chermak, 1995, pp. 123-125). The use of images in the media coverage of mass shootings has been discussed in other studies in this field, indicating that pictures tend to focus on the perpetrators more than victims (e.g Dahmen, 2018; Müller, Seizov, Wiencek & Pinar, 2009; Parks 2008). This book sought to determine whether this was still the case for the news media sources in the sample. Videos posted on the news sources' websites gave an insight into how mass shootings are represented in visual and audible formats. Figures for images, videos and cartoons are all detailed in Table 2.

Content Analysis

The methodological approach of content analysis was utilized to explore themes emerging from the full media sample. Content analysis started to become widely used as a research method in the 1930s, mainly with American newspapers as the sample. Notably, it was employed during the 1940s to make inferences from Nazi propaganda — this is most commonly associated with the work of Harold Lasswell (Holsti, 1969, p. 22). Since then, it has grown in popularity amongst researchers and has extended to other "texts'" such as films, television news and so forth. The process of content analysis involves counting the occurrences of subjects/themes, words/phrases, actors or dispositions (Krippendorff, 1980, p. 15). Qualitative content analysts, however, have questioned whether the frequency of occurrence alone is actually enough to signify its importance (Holsti, 1969, p. 10). In order to understand their significance and meaning, the occurrences counted thus need to be placed within a theoretical, qualitative-based framework (Anders, 1998, p. 96). To take this argument further, content analysis should examine both the "manifest" (those which are palpable) and "latent" (those which are more ambiguous) meaning of texts by analyzing its semantic style and persuasion techniques (Bryman, 2008, p. 275; Holsti, 1969, p. 26). This is achieved

Table 2. Sample of videos, images and cartoons

Source	Number of Videos	Number of Images/Cartoons
New York Times	14	0
TIME	0	0
Washington Post	30	40
Total	44	40

by assessing the "themes" (recurring ideas throughout the report) and "frames" (the parameters of what will be discussed about an event) of documentation (Altheide, 1996, p. 31).

Of key importance to content analysis being methodologically sound is taking steps to ensure reliability and validity of results. Reliability of findings is evident when other analysts could replicate the research in the sample and obtain similar findings. This may be achieved by ensuring the coding is employed in a systematic manner, i.e. according to predefined guidelines to instill some degree of objectivity into the process. There should also be transparency in coding procedures and the formation of categories (Holsti, 1969, pp. 3-4, 135). The other feature of viable research is validity relating to whether the technique measured what it intended to. To achieve validity in content analyses, the following steps should be taken: comparing data with external criterion; ensuring the sample is representative of the larger body of work; making sure categories are exhaustive (i.e. each item can be placed into a category) and units with relevant meanings/connotations are grouped together; coding procedures are precise enough to guide the analysis (Holsti, 1969, pp. 93, 99, 142-143; Weber, 1990/2004, pp. 119, 121).

Considering all of this, the process employed for this book was systematic in nature. The qualitative content analysis procedure specified by Altheide (1996) was followed: formulation of categories and creation of a data collection sheet (protocol); testing of protocol using a few examples; revision of and adding to protocol if necessary; collection of data; coding of data and highlighting concepts; comparing and contrasting each category with brief summaries; combining these summaries and then illustrating the conclusion with examples of "typical" and "extreme" cases. Following a process like this means that coding is ultimately quite fluid in nature and thus constantly being revised. This can mean coding results in too many categories of data; however, this problem can be solved by using axial coding to assess the usefulness of the current categories and determine which ones could be combined or deleted (Bryman, 2001, p. 392).

Critical Discourse Analysis

Discourse has the power to reinforce ideologies, which are defined as representations of social reality shared by members of groups (Blackledge, 2012, p. 617; van Dijk, 1988, p. 8). In order to understand how this exists within news media content, critical discourse analysis was adopted. This allows for a fuller understanding of the language used in news media content and how this may potentially influence how people "read" texts (see Fairclough 1995; Krippendorff, 2004; van Dijk 1998b). For instance, Mayr and Machin (2012) found that a critical approach was useful for revealing more subtle nuances — which may have far-reaching implications — within discourse. Due to their detailed and opinionated nature, letters to the editor and feature articles were considered the most appropriate media content to analyze in this book. Evincing strong opinions and feelings, the vocabulary in them tends to be emotive making use of evaluative adverbs and adjectives, e.g. evil, innocent and so forth. The "voice" in feature articles refutes the ideas of others and advances its own arguments (Fowler, 1991, pp. 210-211). It has been said that letters to the editor buttress the arguments of feature articles in that they are purposefully chosen by editors to sustain a new story or to counter another source (Ericson, Baranek & Chan, `989, p. 338).

To carry out critical discourse analysis, a number of lexical techniques employed by the news media were examined. Words/phrases used were examined, for vocabulary can signify value judgments. These were put in the wider context of the sentence, paragraph and letter/article in which they occurred to derive their meaning (Parlmer, 1976/1981, pp. 17, 37; van Dijk, 1998b, pp. 31-32). Moreover, when analyzing the feature articles, headlines were included as a unit of analysis. Since "headlines not only globally define or summarise an event, they also evaluate it" (van Dijk, 1991, p.53), their lexical style can have ideological implications. Lexical techniques appropriated from key theorists in this area were examined within the letters and articles (Fowler, 1991; Garland, 1985; Mayr & Machin, 2012; Parlmer, 1976/1981; van Leeuwen, 1996):

- Hyperbole, representing exaggerated statements;
- Paralinguistic features in the form of stress, intonation and rhythm;
- An ironic or sarcastic tone conveying a difference between what is said and the latent meaning;
- Metaphors and signifiers, conveying emotive or evaluative meanings;
- Deriding an argument through hedging, which involves phrases like "sort of" and "kind of";
- Connotations of words, referring to their emotive or evaluative meanings;
- Substitutions, where details can be replaced by abstract terms or generalizations;
- Additions, adding legitimations and reactions;
- Evaluations, drawing conclusions about issues;
- Contrastive stress, indicated by using italics or underlining;
- Social actor analysis, examining the visual and written portrayals and classifications of key actors.

Visual Discourse Analysis

Given graphics and sound are usually categorized as "observable" expressions of discourse (Van Dijk, 1998, p. 203), analyzing videos and images from the sample required a different process from the one outlined above. Images tend to differ from language in that their meaning is less fixed; hence, they are able to signify discourses in more understated ways (Mayr & Machin, 2012, p. 29). To analyze the subtle signifiers within images, iconographical analysis was employed (refer to Mayr & Machin 2012; Müller, 2011; Panofsky, 1982 for more information). Iconography has been described as "a qualitative method of visual content analysis and interpretation" (Müller, 2011, p. 285). Originally used in 16th Century art collecting to categorize visual motifs, it is now a method and approach to study the content and meaning of visuals. Utilized in the approach to iconographical analysis was Panofsky's (1982) approach to iconographical analysis consisting of three steps. The first is to devise a description that sharpens the attention to visual detail. The second stage is to formulate categories for images in the sample. The third step is to compare and contrast differences and similarities of images and then locate within the wider social, political and cultural context (Müller, 2011, pp. 283, 290).

To examine videos within the sample, visual analysis of decoding texts was adopted. The goal of this was to "break down signifying components and structures [of the videos] without breaking up the object of study as a meaningful whole" (Newbold, 1998, p. 131). This involved looking at technical elements (editing and production) and visual constructions (i.e. what the audience "sees"). More specifically, this process requires an examination of the following signifiers: technical camera angles, camera movement, shot duration, lighting, depth of field, costume, sound effects, objects, performance, setting, location (Newbold, 1998, pp. 133-138) Also assessed were the components of sound (pitch, volume and intonation), which may also reveal certain emphases of semantic and ideological importance (Van Dijk, 1998, p. 202).

QUALITATIVE RESEARCH

Sample

Nineteen interviews were conducted with twenty-one interviewees. Two of the interviews were group ones, where two people were interviewed at the same time. An overview of all interviewees is detailed in Table 3 below, organized alphabetically by the surnames of participants. To sample interviewees, a purposive sampling strategy intended to fulfil a particular purpose was used (Newburn, 2007, p. 912). In the case of this book, campaign groups were selected for their prominence in a particular cause. In this case, working to eradicate school or gun violence or to negate the effects of such violence (e.g. through school safety measures). The importance of these groups to the policy-making process in the U.S. should not be underestimated, for "with enough public support and media exposure, they can influence members of Congress" (McKay, 2009, p. 307). The majority of interviewees were recruited through pre-existing contacts of the author. A handful of participants were referred to the author via snowball sampling in which an existing interviewee referred them on; others were recruited through a notice posted in a nationwide gun violence prevention mailing list.

One type of campaign group included in the sample was "interest groups" — sometimes known as a pressure group. Their sole purpose is to influence the decisions made by government (Loomis, 1998, p. 3). There have been a number of studies focusing on interest groups (see, for example, Anderson & Loomis, 1998; Grossman, 2012; Hrebenar & Scott, 1982; Wilson, 1981). National interest groups tend to focus on decisions made by federal government; whilst coordinating with regional, state or local counterparts to pass policies on a state-by-state basis. State groups tend to focus exclusively on state policy issues and have their own members and budget (Anderson & Loomis, 1998, pp. 84, 88). Both types of interest groups specializing in gun violence prevention were included in the final research sample: five national groups (four of these were based in the United States; one in the United Kingdom); seven state groups based in California, Connecticut, Colorado, Texas and Virginia. Also included in the sample was a national grassroots organization focusing on domestic violence policy, some of which relates to guns.

Another type of political group recruited to this book was "political action committees" (PACs). They are more focused on government influence, providing campaign endorsements, funds and assistance to candidates. Interest groups can establish PACs to complement their lobbying efforts (Hrebenar & Scott, 1982, p. 135; Holyoke, 2014, p. 248). Also included in the sample was a "think tank." These organizations have access to policymakers and tend to convey their ideas via research and writing in news media pieces (Rich & Weaver, 1998, p. 248). Included in the final sample were one state-based PAC (Colorado) and one national-level think tank.

The one type of organization that was not included in the research sample was gun rights interest groups. The most prominent one is probably the National Rifle Association, whose reputation and goals focus on promoting gun usage and the rights of gun owners (Patterson, 1998, p. 120). Although not always the case, the group tends to oppose new gun restrictions. When the Obama administration tried to pass a suite of measures after the Sandy Hook shooting in 2012, the NRA were some of the most vocal opposition against the proposals. Subsequently, Obama blamed the NRA when the measures failed to pass (Grossman, 2012, p. 529; Noel, 2013, p. 203). The reason for not including gun rights groups like the NRA in this research sample was to exclusively focus on gun violence prevention. Since most of the policies raised after mass shootings focus on gun restrictions, it makes sense to find out more about the process involved in lobbying for these measures and why these tend to stall. Moreover, although there

Table 3. Final List of Interviewees

Interviewee	Role	Group	Type of Group
Adelyn Allchin	Senior Director of Public Health and Policy	Coalition to Stop Gun Violence	National GVP interest group
Rukmani Bhatia	Senior Policy Analyst	Center for American Progress (at time of interview)	National GVP interest group
Heilit Biehl	Threat Assessment Coordinator	Adams 12 Five Star Schools	Educational institution
Stephen Brock	Professor & School Psychology Program Coordinator	California State University	Educational institution
Shaun Dakin	Founder	Parents Against School Shooter Drills	State GVP interest group (Virginia)
Andrew Goddard	Legislative Director & Treasurer	Virginia Center for Public Safety	State GVP interest group (Virginia)
Rachel Graber	Director of Public Policy	National Coalition Against Domestic Violence	National grassroots organization – domestic violence
Sheila Islong	Engagement Director	Giffords: Courage to Fight Gun Violence	National GVP interest group
Jim Kessler	Vice-President for Policy	Third Way	National think tank – variety of issues
John-Michael Keyes	Executive Director	I Love U Guys	National non-profit foundation - school safety and emergency management
Marvin Lim	Legal Director	Keep Guns Off Campus	National GVP interest group
Brian Malte	Executive Director	Hope and Heal Fund: The Fund to Stop Gun Violence in California	State GVP non-profit foundation (California)
Tom Mauser	Spokesperson	Colorado Ceasefire	State GVP interest group (Colorado)
Eileen McCarron	President & Treasurer	Colorado Ceasefire Legislative Action & Colorado Ceasefire PAC	State GVP political action committee and advocacy branch (Colorado)
Po Murray	Chairman	Newtown Action Alliance	National GVP Advocacy group
John Nicoletti	Co-Founder	Nicoletti-Flater Associates	State service organization – violence prevention, threat assessment and emergency management (Colorado)
Mick North	Activist	Gun Control Network	National GVP interest group (United Kingdom)
Jonathan Perloe	Director of Communications	CT Against Gun Violence	GVP state interest group (Connecticut)
Melissa Reeves	Senior Consultant	SIGMA Threat Management Associates	National service organization -threat assessment and management
Heather Ross	Activist	Texas Gun Sense	State GVP interest group (Texas)
Adam Skaggs	Chief Counsel & Policy Director	Giffords Law Center to Prevent Gun Violence	National GVP interest group
Ellen Stoddard-Keyes	Operations Director	I Love U Guys	National non-profit foundation - school safety and emergency management

have been a few studies in this area (Doran, 2014; Kerr 2018a; Kerr 2018b), there is still a considerable gap in the research for these types of interest groups. Capturing their voices in this book gives an insight into the challenges involved in gun violence prevention.

The other types of interviewees included in the research sample were those focused on emergency management, threat assessment or school safety. The Executive Director and Operations Director of a non-profit foundation that trains schools and workplaces in emergency management procedures were included. Also included in the sample were two interviewees who authored a crisis prevention guide and were panel members on the National Association of School Psychologists. One of the co-founders of an organization that advises on threat assessment and emergency management was also included. A threat assessment coordinator for a school district in Colorado was also in the final sample.

Interviewees and Gun Violence

A number of interviewees were found to have been motivated to enter GVP activism or school safety efforts due to either a mass shooting and/or a personal connection with gun violence. The only British representative in the sample, Dr. Mick North (GCN), became involved after losing his daughter, Sophie, in a school shooting in Dunblane, Scotland in 1996. He was involved in the Snowdrop Campaign, which helped to pass a handgun ban in Great Britain shortly after the Dunblane shooting, and is now a member of the Gun Control Network, an activist group in the United Kingdom. He has helped efforts in the United States by supporting families of Sandy Hook victims and speaking at events. The last event he spoke at was at John Hopkins University in 2014. The intention was to speak at another one in 2020; however, this was curtailed by the COVID-19 pandemic and the nation-wide lockdown enforced in the United Kingdom to deal with this. Additionally, he wrote an open letter to the Parkland students that resulted in some interaction.

There are also a number of American interest group representatives with personal connections. Tom Mauser (CC) lost his son, Daniel, at the school shooting at Columbine High School in 1999. He led on efforts to close the gun show loophole in Colorado via a citizen ballot shortly after the shooting (see Kerr, 2018) and has since been a spokesperson for Colorado Ceasefire, a state-based interest group. The Legislative Director and Treasurer of state interest group, Virginia Center for Public Safety, Andrew Goddard, got involved in GVP efforts after his son, Colin, was shot and wounded in the 2007 Virginia Tech incident. Whilst Po Murray (NAA) did not lose a child in the Sandy Hook (2012) school shooting, her four children attended this school and the perpetrator was her neighbor. This motivated Po Murray to help form the Newtown Action Alliance to advocate for gun violence prevention laws in Connecticut and federally. The efforts in Connecticut resulted in the state passing the "second strongest gun laws in the nation, including background checks, assault weapons ban, eligibility certificate for ammunition purchases and limits on large capacity magazines."-Po Murray (NAA). Interviewees Jonathan Perloe (CAGV), Shaun Dakin (PASSD) and Heather Ross (TGS) also got involved in the GVP movement following the Sandy Hook School shooting. Jonathan Perloe (CAGV) lives in Connecticut so this incident resonated with him. In a similar vein, Shaun Dakin (PASSD) got involved after Sandy Hook because he has a son who was about the same age as the victims when the attack happened. Heather Ross (TGS) explained that it was the nature of the Sandy Hook shooting that motivated her to get involved: "Mass shootings are messed up anyway but when it was small children – what has a small child done? Kids are innocent." In terms of a personal connection, another motivating factor was losing some of her relatives to firearm suicide.

Another set of interviewees were John-Michael Keyes and Ellen Stoddard-Keyes, the founders of a non-profit school safety organization, I Love U Guys. They set this group up after losing their daughter, Emily, in a hostage situation in a school in Colorado. Although guns were used in the Platte Canyon incident (2006), John-Michael and Ellen have chosen to direct their efforts to improving school safety through emergency management training rather than activism relating to firearms.

Interviews

In order to capture voices from activists involved in gun violence prevention, qualitative interviews were utilized. Interviewing has been defined as "the elicitation of research data through the questioning of respondents" (Bloor & Wood, 2006, p. 104). Interviews that are qualitative in nature have a greater depth of questioning; thus, allowing for the examination of opinions, ideas and experiences of interviewees. This gives qualitative interviews a higher degree of validity than other types (Arksey & Knight, 1999, p. 96; Bloor & Wood, 2006, p. 104). "Content-mapping" questions were used in qualitative interviews for this book. These take three forms: "ground-mapping" to start a new interview topic; "dimension-mapping" to focus interview on a particular subject; "perspective-widening" to get interviewees to look at something from different angles (Laggard, Keegan & Ward, 2003, pp. 148-152).

Two of the interviews took place in a face-to-face context. One involved two Americans visiting the United Kingdom for a conference prior to the COVID-19 pandemic. The other was with an activist who lives in Scotland. The remainder of the interviews took place on Skype or on the telephone. Audio recordings were taken during interviews and thereafter transcribed, a process which "captures" the spoken discourse of the interview (Bloor & Wood, 2006, p. 166). The interview transcripts were then analyzed using a process of "open coding," where similar fragments of data are grouped together into categories and assigned codes which serve as descriptors for the meaning of that piece of text. This was continuously revised via "axial coding" to check whether any categories need to be merged and new codes added (Boeijjie, 2010, pp. 96-98, 108).

Grossman (2012, p. 9) has argued that interest group research has too much of a focus of the micro-level context of organizations, e.g. their history and strategies; thus, meaning the macro-level concerns are not properly explored. Considering this, interviews examined macro-level factors such as the political climate at the moment in time and public support for policy proposals. Findings from interviews were bolstered by the analyses of news media articles and letters to the editor.

CONCLUSION

This chapter detailed the methodological approach, research design and samples utilized in this book. Guiding the design of the research was literature on framing (Callaghan & Schnell, 2005; Chong & Druckman, 2007; Woodly, 2015). Analysis of news media content was thought to be an appropriate methodology to explore how mass shootings are discussed and the subsequent debates about gun regulations. The news media can promote or refute arguments put forward by politicians at this time. Additionally, the amount of coverage and the way an issue is covered has the ability to shape understandings of it (Callaghan & Schnell, 2005; Delli Carpini, 2005; Fowler, 1991; Jacobs & Shapiro, 2000). Letters to the editor and feature articles have an even greater potential to do this, given they are written in an evaluative and emotive way (Chong & Druckman, 2007; Ericson, Baranek & Chan, 1989; Fowler, 1991). Based on this, letters and feature articles were chosen from three news media sources: New York Times, TIME and Washington Post. Videos and images were also included to add another dimension onto analysis. The sampling procedure for selecting these was detailed in this chapter.

The chapter then covered all research methodologies appropriated for this book. Content analysis was used to explore the significance of themes within the news media sample (Altheide, 1996; Bryman, 2008; Holsti, 1969). Critical discourse analysis (Fairclough 1995; Krippendorff, 2004; Mayr & Machin, 2012; van Dijk 1998b) was utilized on the letters and feature articles to explore the language used, for this has the potential to shape understandings of mass shootings and the gun debate. Visual discourse analysis (Mayr & Machin, 2012; Müller, 2011; Van Dijk, 1998) was used to explore the meanings behind the images and videos in the news media sample. The final methodology used is qualitative interviewing, allowing for a deeper exploration of the ideas and experiences of interviewees (Arksey & Knight, 1999, p. 96; Bloor & Wood, 2006, Laggard, Keegan & Ward, 2003). The interview sample is outlined, with details provided why each interviewee was chosen, i.e. experience in gun violence prevention or gun-related research and policymaking; experience and knowledge in threat assessment and/or emergency management and communication procedures.

REFERENCES

Altheide, D. L. (1996). *Qualitative Media Analysis*. Sage Publications. doi:10.4135/9781412985536

Anders, H. (1998). Content Analysis. In H. Anders, S. Cottle, R. Negrine, & C. Newbold (Eds.), *Mass Communication Research Methods* (pp. 91–129). Palgrave.

Anderson, B., & Loomis, B. A. (1998). Taking organization seriously: the structure of interest group influence. In A. J. Cigler & B. A. Loomis (Eds.), *Interest Group Politics* (5th ed., pp. 83–96). Congressional Quarterly Inc.

Arskey, H., & Knight, P. T. (1999). *Interviewing for Social Scientists*. Sage.

Bloor, M., & Wood, F. (2006). *Keywords in Qualitative Methods: A Vocabulary of Research Concepts*. Sage. doi:10.4135/9781849209403

Boeijie, H. R. (2010). *Analysis in Qualitative Research*. Sage.

Bottoms, A. E. (2000). The relationship between theory and research in criminology. In R. King & E. Wincup (Eds.), *Doing Research on Crime and Justice* (pp. 75–116). Oxford University Press.

Bryman, A. (2001). *Social Research Methods*. Oxford University Press.

Bryman, A. (2008). *Social Research Methods* (3rd ed.). Oxford University Press.

Callaghan, K., & Schnell, F. (2005). *Framing American Politics*. University of Pittsburgh Press. doi:10.2307/j.ctt6wrbqk

Chermak, S. M. (1995). *Victims in the News: Crime and the American News Media*. Westview Press.

Chong, D., & Druckman, J. N. (2007). Framing Theory. *Annual Review of Political Science*, *10*(1), 103–126. doi:10.1146/annurev.polisci.10.072805.103054

CNN. (2020, May 3). *Mass Shootings in the US: Fast Facts*. https://edition.cnn.com/2019/08/19/us/mass-shootings-fast-facts/index.html

Dahmen, N. S. (2018). Visually Reporting Mass Shootings: U.S. Newspaper Photographic Coverage of Three Mass School Shootings. *The American Behavioral Scientist, 62*(2), 163–180. doi:10.1177/0002764218756921

De Vaus, D. (2006). Case Study Design. In D. De Vaus (Ed.), *Research Design* (Vol. 4, pp. 5–20). Sage Benchmarks in Social Research Methods.

Doran, S. E. M. (2014). *News Media Constructions and Policy Implications of School Shootings in the United States* (Doctoral thesis). Glasgow, UK: University of Glasgow.

Doran, S. E. M. (2016). *Creating a Market? The Entrepreneurialism of Fear in the United States.* Conference presentation. 20 September. Fear and Anxieties in the 21st Century: 3rd Global Conference. Oxford, UK: Interdisciplinary.Net.

Entman, R. M. (2010). Media framing biases and political power: Explaining slant in news of Campaign 2007. *Journalism, 11*(4), 389–408. doi:10.1177/1464884910367587

Ericson, R., Baranek, P., & Chan, J. (1989). *Negotiating Control: A Study of New Sources.* Open University Press.

Fairclough, N. (1995). *Critical Discourse Analysis: The Critical Study of Language.* Pearson Education Limited.

Fowler, R. (1991). *Language in the News: Discourse and Ideology in the Press.* Routledge.

Garland, D. (1985). Politics and Policy in Criminological Discourse: A Study of Tendentious Reasoning and Rhetoric. *International Journal of the Sociology of Law, 13*, 1–33.

Goss, K. A. (2006). *Disarmed: The Missing Movement for Gun Control in America.* Princeton University Press.

Graham, K. W. (1981). *Interest ~Groups in the United States.* Oxford University Press.

Greenberg, J. (2002). Framing and temporality in political cartoons: A critical analysis of visual news discourse. *The Canadian Review of Sociology and Anthropology. La Revue Canadienne de Sociologie et d'Anthropologie, 39*(2), 181–198. doi:10.1111/j.1755-618X.2002.tb00616.x

Grossman, M. (2012). *The Not-So-Special Interests: Interest Groups, Public Representation and American Governance.* Stanford University Press. doi:10.1515/9780804781343

Halliday, M. A. K. (1994). *An Introduction to Functional Grammar* (2nd ed.). Edward Arnold.

Hawdon, J., Agnich, L., Wood, R., & Ryan, J. (2015). Framing Mass Gun Violence: A Content Analysis of Print Media Coverage of the VT and Sandy Hook Elementary School Tragedies. In L. Eargle & A. Esmail (Eds.), *Gun Violence in American Society: Crime, Justice and Public Policy* (pp. 214–232). University Press of America.

Holsti, O. R. (1969). *Content analysis for the social sciences and humanities.* Addison-Wesley Publishing Company.

Holyoke, T. T. (2014). *Interest Groups and Lobbying: pursuing Political Interests.* Westview Press.

Hrebenar, R. J., & Scott, R. K. (1982). *Interest Group Politics in America*. Prentice-Hall Inc.

Jacobs, L. R., & Shapiro, R. Y. (2000). *Politicians don't pander: political manipulation and the loss of Democratic responsiveness*. University of Chicago Press.

Kerr, S. E. M. (2018a). *Gun Violence Prevention? The Politics Behind Policy Responses to School Shootings in the United States*. Palgrave MacMillan.

Kerr, S. E. M. (2018b). Emergency Management and Communication Improvements: Changing the Landscape of School Safety. In G. Crews (Ed.), *School Violence in K-12 American Education* (pp. 474–493). IGI Global.

Kupchik, A., & Bracy, N. L. (2009). The News Media on School Crime and Violence: Constructing Dangerousness and Fueling Fear. *Youth Violence and Juvenile Justice, 7*(2), 136–156. doi:10.1177/1541204008328800

Lombardi, D. (2018). *Critical Discourse Analysis of Online News Headlines: A Case of the Stoneman Douglas High School Shooting* (Masters dissertation). Malmö, Sweden: Malmö University.

Loomis, B. A. (1998). Introduction: The Changing Nature of Interest Group Politics. In A. J. Cigler & B. A. Loomis (Eds.), *Interest Group Politics* (5th ed., pp. 1–32). Congressional Quarterly Inc.

Maguire, B., Weatherby, G. A., & Mathers, R. A. (2002). Network news coverage of school shootings. *The Social Science Journal, 39*(3), 465–470. doi:10.1016/S0362-3319(02)00201-X

Mayr, A., & Machin, D. (2012). *The language of crime and deviance: an introduction to critical linguistics analysis in media and popular culture*. Continuum Publishing Group.

McKay, D. (2009). *American Politics and Society* (7th ed.). Wiley-Blackwell.

Media Bias Fact Check. (n.d.). *Left/Center Bias*. https://mediabiasfactcheck.com/leftcenter/

Müller, M. G., Seizov, O., Wiencek, Fl., & Yildiz, P. U. (2009). Visualising Victims and Victimizers. An Iconological Approach to Analyzing Media Coverage of School Shootings. *Violence and Network Society-School Shootings and Social Violence in Contemporary Public Life Conference*.

Newbold, C. (1998). Analysing the Moving Image: Narrative. In H. Anders, S. Cottle, R. Negrine, & C. Newbold (Eds.), *Mass Communication Research Methods* (pp. 130–162). Palgrave.

Newburn, T. (2007). *Criminology*. Willan Publishing.

Noel, H. (2008). Political parties and ideology: interest groups in context. In M. Grossmann (Ed.), *New Directions in Interest Group Politics* (pp. 196–229). Routledge.

Panofsky, E. (1982). *Meaning in the Visual Arts*. University of Chicago Press.

Park, A. (2008). *The right to know about violent images? The Virginia Tech Killer's Gun Points at the Viewer*. Paper presented at the International Communication Association annual conference, Montreal, Canada.

Parlmer, F. R. (1976/1981). *Semantics* (2nd ed.). Cambridge: Cambridge University Press.

Patterson, K. (1998). The Political Firepower of the NRA. In A. J. Cigler & B. A. Loomis (Eds.), *Interest Group Politics* (5th ed., pp. 119–142). Congressional Quarterly Inc.

Rich, A., & Weaver, R. K. (1998). Advocates and analysts: think tanks and the politicization of expertise. In A. J. Cigler & B. A. Loomis (Eds.), *Interest Group Politics* (5th ed., pp. 235–253). Congressional Quarterly Inc.

Robinson, M. B. (2011). *Media Coverage of Crime and Criminal Justice*. Carolina Academic Press.

Schildkraut, J. V. (2014). *Mass Murder and the Mass Media: An Examination of the Media Discourse on U.S. rampage shootings, 2000-2012* (PhD dissertation). San Marcos, TX: Texas State University.

Shen, F. (2004). Effects of news frames and schemas on individuals' issue interpretations and attitudes. *J & MC Quarterly, 81*(2), 400-416.

Steidley, T., & Cohen, C. G. (2016). Framing the Gun Control Debate: Press releases and Framing Strategies of the National Rifle Association and the Brady Campaign. *Social Science Quarterly, 98*(2), 608–627. doi:10.1111squ.12323

Stoecker, R. (2006). Evaluating and Rethinking the Case Study. In D. De Vaus (Ed.), *Research Design* (Vol. 4, pp. 141–164). Sage Benchmarks in Social Research Methods.

Truman, D. (1951/1993). *The Governmental Process: Political Interests and Public Opinion* (2nd ed.). University of California.

van Dijk, T. A. (1991). *Racism and the Press*. Routledge.

van Dijk, T. A. (1998). *Ideology: a multidisciplinary approach*. Sage.

van Leeuwen, T. (1996). The representation of social actors. In C. R. Caldas-Coulthard & M. Coulthard (Eds.), *Readings in Critical Discourse Analysis* (pp. 32–70). Routledge.

Weber, R. P. (1990/2004). Content Analysis. In C. Seale (Ed.), *Social Research Methods: A Reader* (pp. 117–123). Routledge.

Woodly, D. R. (2015). *The Politics of Common Sense: How Social Movements Use Public Discourse to Change Politics and Win Acceptance*. Oxford University Press. doi:10.1093/acprof:oso/9780190203986.001.0001

ADDITIONAL READING

Bloor, M., & Wood, F. (2006). *Keywords in Qualitative Methods: A Vocabulary of Research Concepts*. Sage. doi:10.4135/9781849209403

Callaghan, K., & Schnell, F. (2005). *Framing American Politics*. University of Pittsburgh Press. doi:10.2307/j.ctt6wrbqk

Fairclough, N. (1995). *Critical Discourse Analysis: The Critical Study of Language*. Pearson Education Limited.

Fowler, R. (1991). *Language in the News: Discourse and Ideology in the Press*. Routledge.

Krippendorff, K. (1980). *Content Analysis: an introduction to its methodology*. Sage.

KEY TERMS AND DEFINITIONS

Case Study: A frame to determine the parameters of information gathering.

Content Analysis: This is a method examining the themes (ideas that keep reoccurring) and frames (how an issue is discussed) inherent within a text.

Critical Discourse Analysis: A more critical approach to analyzing a text, looking at the language used and how this may influence how people "read" it.

Frames: Parameters set around how an issue is discussed.

Qualitative Interviewing: A technique focusing on eliciting findings by questioning participants.

Sample: The selection of sources chosen for analytical purposes.

Visual Discourse Analysis: The process involved in analyzing still and moving images.

Chapter 3
Creating a Climate of Fear:
The Case of Las Vegas

ABSTRACT

This chapter looks at the news media articles relating to the 2017 Las Vegas shooting incident. It is shown that this incident is categorized by death toll in media coverage. Mass shootings generally are portrayed as an "ongoing trend" and are "normalized" to the extent that it appears they will occur again in the future. The news media also debates whether the incident should be defined as terrorism, deliberating about the criteria needed for an attack to be viewed as a terrorist act. Moreover, a sense of fear is conveyed and then amplified in news media coverage through accounts from eyewitnesses, descriptions of the shooting, and visualizations of the attack. This ultimately creates a culture of fear, whereby the risk of becoming victimized by a mass shooting is disproportionate to the actual threat faced.

Deviance amplification

INTRODUCTION

This chapter focuses on news media coverage relating to the 2017 Las Vegas incident, chosen as the main case study for this book. Feature articles, letters to the editor, images and videos are analyzed to explore how this incident is portrayed. Examined are the ways this portrayal could affect understandings of mass shootings more generally. Mirroring Schildkraut's (2014) study, news media analyses indicate that the incident is categorized based on death toll and is also compared to other incidents; this serves to portray the idea of mass shootings as a trend. The news media's focus on death toll has some possible implications for copycat attacks (Coleman, 2004; Lankford & Madfis, 2017; Lankford & Tomek, 2017; Towers, 2015). The media also continues the story by focusing on other frames pertaining to the incident (Callaghan & Schnell, 2005; Delli Carpini 2005). Additionally, there is a prominent theme around whether the Las Vegas incident should be defined as "terrorism," referring to acts of ideological violence against a particular person, group or institution (Meloy, 2016).

Whilst the previous chapter showed how rare mass shootings are within the wider spectrum of gun violence, there is still the potential for them to generate high levels of fear due to an overestimation of risk. The risk perceptions associated with a threat are more likely to be distorted when they relate to incidents

DOI: 10.4018/978-1-7998-3916-3.ch003

that are salient, unexpected and shocking (Slovic, 1987; Sunstein, 2005). This chapter documents that the news media coverage of Las Vegas contributes to this via several techniques: portraying mass shootings as an ongoing trend; normalizing the phenomenon to the extent that it appears inevitable another attack will occur in future; documenting what it was like to be victimized by the Las Vegas incident with descriptions from eyewitnesses and visualizations of the attack and its aftermath. The argument is advanced that these themes create a perception that these incidents are continuous and inevitable, which serves to make individuals feel that they are at greater risk of being victimized (Alheide, 2002; Furedi, 1997; Garland, 2001) than is actually the case.

The chapter also explores how the news media coverage of Las Vegas feeds into a climate of fear (Altheide 1997, 2002; Furedi 1997, 2006, 2007; Glassner 1999, 2004) and "fear of crime" (Ferraro & LaGrange, 1987; Gabriel & Greve, 2003; Lee, 2007) pertaining to mass shootings. Results from opinion polls suggest there is fear amongst the public about the potential of becoming victimized in a future mass shooting attack. It is also found that news media coverage of the Las Vegas incident contributes to a wider climate of fear around mass shootings in which feelings of fear and anxiety percolate throughout society (Altheide 1997, 2002; Furedi 1997, 2006, 2007; Glassner 1999, 2004).

THE CASE OF LAS VEGAS: DEFINING THE WORST MASS SHOOTING

Categorizing Las Vegas

With Las Vegas being one in a series of mass shootings, there is a need to define it in relation to previous incidents. Given its high death and injury toll, Las Vegas is categorized as the "worst" mass shooting. Until this point, the Pulse Nightclub (2016) incident was considered to be the worst one based on its death toll. References to Las Vegas as the "deadliest," "largest" or "worst" mass shooting in modern United States history were evident throughout news media coverage.

Exemplifying this, feature articles commonly cite the death and injury toll. This mirrors Schildkraut's (2014, p. 188) findings that the media coverage of mass shootings emphasizes the sensational characteristics of the event, such as the victim counts. In the immediate aftermath of the shooting when the exact death figures are known the caveats of "more than" and "at least" are used. For example, a TIME article (3ʳᵈ October 2017) written the day after the shooting describes it in the following way: "More than 500 people had been injured and at least 59 were killed, making it the deadliest mass shooting in recent U.S. history." This sentiment is echoed in the press release video by the Las Vegas Metropolitan Police Department shortly after the incident, where it is noted that whilst the deaths are currently fifty-eight and injuries are 515 people the numbers continue to rise (Washington Post, 2ⁿᵈ October 2017). As it stands, the final number of deaths were fifty-eight (excluding the shooter) and more than seven hundred were injured (Las Vegas Metropolitan Police Department, 2018, p. 8).

Another facet of categorizing the Las Vegas incident is to compare it with other incidents. Within the news media sample, there are a number of articles and videos listing the five or ten deadliest mass shootings. For instance, there is a TIME (3ʳᵈ October 2017) article entitled "The 10 Deadliest Mass Shootings in Modern United States History," which proceeds to list these on the basis of which ones have the highest death tolls. Similarly, there is a video with the caption "The 5 deadliest modern mass shootings" showing clips from each of these incidents (Washington Post, 2ⁿᵈ October 2017). In some cases, the names of the places are just listed with the death toll in brackets: "There was Orlando (49 killed) and before that Charleston (9) and Roseburg (9) and San Bernardino (14) and Aurora (12) and Newtown (27)" (Washington Post, 2ⁿᵈ October 2017). The use of shorthand to describe the incidents shows how these incidents have become so well-known they have become incorporated into the lexicon. Placing a particular incident within the larger history of mass shootings is significant, precisely because it portrays it as a pattern rather than an aberration and suggests that potential solutions should be sought. To that end, it is "extending the memory" of an incident by showing it is part of a larger trend (Rood, 2019, pp. 84-86).

There are also direct references made to incidents, usually in articles advocating the need for stricter gun regulations. Sandy Hook is cited often, because of the failed action on gun control following this incident (see Kerr, 2018a). Writers of articles generally use Sandy Hook as a comparative point to maintain that given there was nothing significant after this incident, there would be no action on gun laws after the Las Vegas shooting. For instance, a Washington Post (24ᵗʰ October 2017) article made the following claim:

If a measure that has the support of 90 percent of the public — universal background checks — can't pass in the wake of 20 elementary school children being slaughtered, what hope is there for any new gun law?

Previous studies have cited constant references to the 1999 Columbine shooting, with it being used as a reference point or benchmark to compare other incidents against (Doran, 2014; Kupchik & Bracy, 2009; Schildkraut, 2014). In contrast to this, a surprising finding from the media analyses in this book was that there were only sporadic references to the Columbine incident. The reason for this may be the fact that Columbine no longer makes it onto top ten lists of mass shootings, with subsequent incidents having significantly higher death tolls. Moreover, since the media sample spans a year after the Las Vegas incident, there are also references to other mass shootings that occur during that time period. The most notable ones are the Parkland (2018) school shooting and the Sutherland Springs (2017) attack, both of which generated a fair amount of attention.

The conflation between the title of the "worst mass shooting" and the death toll is indicative of a larger media issue relating to these types of incidents. It has been postulated that media coverage of mass shooters increases the sense of competition with future ones, driving them to maximize victim fatalities. To that end, "many fame-seeking offenders deliberately kill and wound in numbers of victims because they know it will help them garner more media attention" (Lankford & Madfis, 2017, p. 263). In a similar vein, studies have examined whether there are copycat attacks after high-profile mass shootings (Coleman, 2004; Lankford & Madfis, 2017; Lankford & Tomek, 2017; Towers, 2015). After examining media coverage on mass shootings throughout the 1990s and early 2000s, Coleman (2004) found that the numbers of incidents increased. The only exception to this was between 2001 and 2002, which is attributed to the "media blackout" on any other violent events with 9/11 taking all the attention during that time period. Lankford and Madfis (2017, p. 265) postulated that media coverage of mass shootings can act as a "social contagion" inflicting the risk to others, particularly for suicidal ideation. The idea of contagion was explored in more detail in a study by Towers and colleagues (2015) who applied a contagion model to recent datasets of mass shootings. Findings indicated that mass shootings tend to occur in clusters, with each incident inciting at least 0.30 new ones. This probability lasts thirteen days, going some way to explain why mass shootings were found to occur every two weeks in the United States. A similar study utilized the same dataset and also added a second dataset of 500 randomly generated dates to simulate 232 mass killings. Data was retrieved from Google Trends to measure how much attention each incident received. Although findings indicate that there was not a significant short-term contagion effect, it is cautioned that the frequency and lethality of these incidents may be having longer-term copycat effects (Lankford & Tomek, 2017).

Considering all of this, it could be the case that continual references to the death and injury toll in mass shootings could be acting as an incentive for future mass shooters. Certainly, in the case of the Las Vegas shooter, it appears that achieving infamy was the main motivation for his attack; although this is ultimately unknown. It should be cautioned, however, that with most mass shooters committing suicide at the end of their attacks it is difficult to know exactly where this ideation came from (Towers, Gomez-Lievano, Khan, Mubayi & Castillo-Chavez, 2015). Moreover, news media audiences are not passive recipients of its content; rather, they have an *active* role in interpreting media texts based on their own social values and beliefs (Fowler, 1991, pp. 41, 46). This stance is supported by Roshier (1973) who states that passive recipient models "grossly underestimates" the abilities of the media audience. What the news media could do, however, is change the way it reports on mass shootings. A set of guidelines have been drafted for media organizations covering mass shootings: do not name the perpetrator or use photos/likenesses of them; adopt the same approach for past perpetrators; report everything else about the incident in as much detail as required. The only exception to this would be in cases where it is in the public's interest to know (i.e. if the perpetrator is still at large). It is acknowledged that there will be challenges with this, particularly around media resistance to change (Lankford & Madfis, 2017, p. 265, 271-272). It could be the case that adopting these guidelines could reduce the sense of fear following mass shootings. An additional guideline could also be for the media to stop adding the death of the perpetrator(s) onto the overall toll to increase the severity, since the deaths of the victims and the perpetrator(s) occurred in very different circumstances.

Defining Terrorism

Following on from this, if the incident had been categorized as a terrorist act this would have negated the need to search for a motive. The act of terrorism is the showcasing of violence against a particular person, group or institution (Meloy, 2016). The distinction between terrorist incidents and mass shootings tends to be the targeted nature of the killing: terrorists are driven by an ideological motive; whilst mass shooters are targeting a particular site for the intended purpose of causing high casualties (Davis, 2020). Further to this, it is claimed that labels such as "terrorist" dehumanizes perpetrators (Rood, 2019, p. 116).

In line with this, the final theme in the news media coverage of how Las Vegas should be understood is that of "terrorism." In the immediate aftermath of the attack, there is a TIME (2nd October 2017) article with the title "'Call This What It Is. Terrorism.' Ariana Grande Shares Powerful Message After Las Vegas Shooting." The article notes that the pop star, Ariana Grande — who survived a terrorist attack at one of her concerts in the United Kingdom earlier that year — classifies the incident in this way. Further articles in the sample debate the differences between mass shootings and terrorism. Some articles accused Trump of being hypocritical for saying he would take stronger action on terrorism; yet not implementing policy change after Las Vegas. For example, one article accuses Trump of deflecting the debate away from guns to mental health precisely because it does not fit his notion of terrorism: "Do we, as President Trump, chalk up the murders to a 'mental health problem' — that is, if the shooter isn't someone of a darker hue named Mohammed?" (The Washington Post, 17th November 2017). The tone here is scathing in nature, with the use of scare quotes indicating that the writer is not convinced by this argument. This irony requires the reader to distinguish that there is a mismatch between the apparent meaning and the situational context, based on the ironic tone of voice adopted by the writer (Fairclough, 1992, p. 123).

Unsurprisingly, the issue of race features in these debates. Another Washington Post (5th October 2017) has the headline "I was devastated about Las Vegas — but quietly relieved that the shooter was White." The writer goes on to explain that minority groups "know there will be a fallout if a shooter is Black, Hispanic or Muslim." The use of the word "know" in this context is an example of a "truth comment," whereby the writer is indicating a commitment to the proposition they have made (Fowler, 1991, p. 85). The article goes on to argue that if the shooter had been Hispanic, it would have been an excuse to pass immigration laws. Rood (2019, p. 112) made similar points about the role of "Whiteness" in discourse relating to gun violence, whereby it is rarely discussed when the perpetrator(s) is White. In the same article, the lack of action after a mass shooting is contrasted with that after a terrorist attack: "We don't militarize airports and ban entire populations from U.S. entry the way we do after even a whiff of "Islamic terrorism." We don't enact preventive measures. We don't seem to do much at all" (Washington Post, 5th October 2017).

The characteristic of religion is another prominent feature in this debate. A TIME article (3rd October 2017) detailing the ten deadliest mass shootings note that the second and ninth incidents on the list, Orlando (2016) and San Bernardino (2015) respectively, had perpetrators who were Muslims and were both classified as "terrorism." Similarly, a New York Times (3rd October 2017) article had the headline "If Only Stephen Paddock Were a Muslim." The opening paragraph goes on to state the following:

If only Stephen Paddock had been a Muslim...If only he had shouted 'Allahu akbar' before he opened fire on all those concertgoers in Las Vegas...If only he had been a member of ISIS...If only we had a picture of him posing with a Quran in one hand and his semiautomatic rifle in another...

This is another of "obligation" in meta-discourse, whereby the writer is stating that participation in a proposition (in this case, a terrorist attack) ought to perform this action (Fowler, 1991, p. 86). The repetition of the phrase "If only" and the ellipses all serve to convey a sense of what might have unfolded in a situation perceived to be lone-wolf terrorism driven by religious ideologies. These are acts of political violence committed by individuals who are operating independently from organized groups (Eby, 2012; McCauley, Mokalenko & Van Son, 2013; Nesset, 2012). The point of this paragraph is to surmise that had the attack met these requirements there would be immediate political action: "If all of that had happened, no one would be telling us not to dishonor the victims and 'politicize' Paddock's mass murder by talking about preventive remedies." The use of scare quotes around the word politicize denotes the writer does not agree with its use (Fairclough, 1992, p. 123). In this case, the word is used to close down debates about gun regulations after mass shootings. The comparison with terrorism in this article serves to make a point about political action being taken in those situations; whereas after mass shootings the incident accused of being politicized if gun regulations are mentioned. The evaluation of social practice here serves to delegitimize those actors (Mayr & Machin, 2012, p. 31), advancing the latter argument that talking about guns after mass shootings is politicizing the situation.

A different article has the headline purporting "If the gunman was Muslim, would we be talking about Las Vegas 'terrorism'?" (The Washington Post, 4th October 2017). Since terms evoke a series of emotions, meanings and associations (Mayr & Machin, 2012), the way in which the incident is defined is based on the religion of the perpetrator. The article reports on the results of a survey experiment carried out with 1400 Americans. Findings indicated that people classify terrorism based on the type of weapon used (bombs tend to be associated with terrorism more so than guns) and characteristics of the perpetrator (whether they were Muslim or not and foreign ties). In a similar vein, an article in the New York Times (1st November 2017) collates the views of readers to determine what they classify as terrorism. This discussion is an example of the news media maintaining the salience of the news story (Chyi & McComb, 2004) almost a month after the incident by reframing the issue to terrorism. Around half believed it was terrorism because it still involved the mass killing of civilians. For instance, one wrote "Because a man shouts 'God is Great' it's terrorism? But when a White man has 43 guns in a Las Vegas hotel room, it's not terrorism?" Other readers maintained that the lack of ideology and/or religious motivation means it does not meet the criteria of terrorism: "Terrorism by definition requires political or religious motivation. The Vegas shooter did not have those motivations so he is a mass murderer." With Eby (2012, p. 72) maintaining that the lone wolf terrorism defines his or her goals based on personal grievances, self-interest and established ideology, it may be the case that both explanations offered by article readers are correct. This indicates how definitions of terrorism, similar to those of mass shootings, are fluid and subject to change based on social and political contexts. Interestingly, in the news media sample, there were no letters to the editor focusing on whether the Las Vegas incident could be classified as terrorism suggesting that this is not an issue prevalent in public debates; despite this being a noticeable theme in news media content.

Risk Perceptions

The term "risk" may be defined as "the probability of damage, injury, illness, death or other misfortune associated with a hazard" (Furedi, 1997, p. 17). In the case of mass shootings, it appears that the perception of risk is overinflated based on the actual probability of being victimized by such an incident. An explanation for this may lie in Slovic's (1987, p. 236) theorization that unexpected and devastating events have a "signal potential" which distorts risk more than a familiar system. This is particularly the case for recent events, with salience having a greater impact on perceptions of risk (Sunstein, 2005, p. 37). The concept of being "at risk" categorizes those individuals who are perceived to be more vulnerable to a hazard; with it, therefore, becoming a part of their identities (Altheide, 2002; Furedi, 1997; Garland, 2001). The implication of this is that the risk faced is something *affecting* the individual, rather than being caused by their actions. Although the risk of the crime may still be low such as in the case of mass shootings, this new perception of potential victimizations makes individuals experience higher levels of fear and anxiety (Garland, 2001, pp. 144, 164). The previous chapter highlighted how rare mass shootings are in the overall spectrum of gun violence. In spite of this, it is suggested here that there are distorted risk perceptions around mass shootings.

Ongoing Trend

One of the themes cementing this notion that there is a distorted risk of mass shootings is the portrayal of mass shootings as an "ongoing trend," whereby lists of incidents convey the sense that this is an epidemic in society. The "ongoing trend" theme is generally two-fold in nature. One part focuses on the general threat of gun violence in the United States; whilst the other part focuses exclusively on mass shootings. The first part is exemplified in news articles listing the numbers of gun violence in the United States:

46, 445 murder victims killed by gunfire in the United States between 2012 and 2016 (The New York Times, 5ᵗʰ October 2017).

From 2005 to 2015, some 300, 000 people were killed by gun violence (The New York Times, 3ʳᵈ October 2017).

The United States has around 30,000 gun-related deaths a year (The Washington Post, 5ᵗʰ October 2017).

This adheres to the requirements of the "problem frame" by portraying the issue as something relevant, i.e. many people in society are affected (Altheide, 1997, p. 655). There are other articles and letters that utilize emotive and expressive language to describe the extent of gun violence in the United States, conveying a speaker with strong opinions and feelings (Fowler, 1991, pp. 210-211). A Washington Post article (3ʳᵈ October 2017) chose the headline "American is at war with itself." Continuing the theme of war, the article goes on to use the comparison of 9/11 and wars to give some indication of the number of deaths caused by gun violence: "We suffer roughly a 9/11 every month thanks to gun violence" and "more Americans have died from firearms in the past 50 years than we have lost in all the wars we have ever fought." The article continues with if this was a foreign enemy causing such death tolls, the country would be "up in arms"; instead when it is caused by other Americans "we let the blood flow." The use of the pronoun "we" invokes a sense of collectiveness, demonstrating that this is a common problem facing the country. Another article from the Washington Post (3ʳᵈ October 2017) lists all the other fatal shootings that occurred the same day as the Las Vegas incident, describing these as the "run-of-the-mill homicides that barely draw any attention." The implication from this is that these shootings are so "commonplace" that they generate very little attention, i.e. they are not considered newsworthy because they are not dramatic or unexpected (Berrington & Jemphrey, 2003, p. 227; Galtung & Ruge, 1965, p. 68).

A different Washington Post (17ᵗʰ November 2017) article has the headline "Gird yourself for more gun rampages" implying that this is an imminent threat. The article goes on to detail that there were a hundred gun-related homicides in Washington, D.C. in one day. This is said to be more than the deaths caused by recent mass shootings in California, Nevada and Texas combined. It also lists the number of children and young people killed every day by guns in the United States. Stating the amount of deaths caused in a day is a means to quantify the extent of the problem, with the daily rate exemplifying that this is a commonplace issue. Portraying gun violence as an ongoing social issue in the United States should increase its importance to readers (Galtung & Ruge, 1965, p. 64). The article also states "America is flooded with firearms," with the verb "flooded" implying that the country is being overwhelmed with guns. The writer advocates passing gun restrictions to deal with this issue, postulating that if this does not happen then the country should "gird itself for more rampages." In this sense, the article portrays a problem and then a solution is set up as the answer. A similar tone was adopted in a TIME (12ᵗʰ October 2017) article that describes America as "swimming in firearms and bathed in blood" and "awash in weaponry, gun violence and senseless gore." The use of evaluative adjectives like "washed," "bathed" and "senseless" dramatizes the article and elucidates strong emotions (Fowler, 1991, pp. 210-211). Moreover, this is an example of fear being conveyed through the use of certain terminology (Altheide, 1997, 2002; Furedi, 1997).

In a similar vein, there are letters to the editor which appropriate similar language to convey the extent of gun violence in the United States. One letter states "Our citizens are being gunned down on a regular basis," with the determiner "our" conveying a collective identity and the term "regular basis" portraying an ongoing problem (The New York Times, 3ʳᵈ October 2017). Another letter (The New York Times, 3ʳᵈ October 2017) is written in a poem format and has a pleading tone repeating "Please Mr President" continuously. The opening paragraph portrays a sense of overwhelming gun violence:

We rise each morning Americans in every city.

The newspapers scream black headlines.

Thousands of letters smashed together forming sentences of horror deaths and injuries numbers.

But these aren't numbers.

These are people.

People we cannot replace.

People we should never have lost.

People with families, friends and jobs.

The reminder that the numbers calculating the amount of gun deaths are not just statistics; rather, they represent people with lives and families is a way to make the issue personal (Gardner, 2008, p. 93). If an issue is framed in a way that can elicit emotion, then it is more likely to have an impact (Aaroe, 2011; Gross, 2008; Iyengar, 1991). This point is reiterated with the closing statement, denoting that these are not just numbers; these are people.

Another facet of the portrayal of general gun violence in the United States is comparisons with other advanced, Western countries. For example, there are Washington Post articles focusing on the gun laws that were passed in Australia after a mass shooting in 1996. One article compares and contrasts the rates of gun ownership and deaths between the two countries: "The United States has a gun ownership rate that is seven times higher than Australia's and a gun death rate that is 11 times higher" (Washington Post, 6ᵗʰ October 2017). A different Washington Post (3ʳᵈ October 2017) article also compares the firearm homicide rate in the United States with other Western countries: "16 times the rate in Germany and six times that of Canada." Another country referenced is Great Britain, which also passed strict gun laws after a mass shooting. In a Washington Post (5ᵗʰ October 2017) article, the point is made that the United States has a rate of gun deaths forty times higher than Great Britain; yet, makes the point that there is not forty times the amount of mental health problems — one of the factors commonly blamed for mass shootings.

Continuing this theme, there is also a letter to the editor that makes the point "the death rate from gun violence in the United States is on average 25 times higher than in high-income nations" (The New York Times, 2ⁿᵈ October 2017). These articles tend to advance the notion that the way to deal with this disparity is for the United States to implement tighter restrictions. This meets another component of the "problem frame," in which there is a known procedure in place to fix the problem requiring the government to act as the repair agent (Altheide, 1997, p. 655). Interestingly, there was an article in the Washington Post (3ʳᵈ October 2017) that was written by a statistician who researched the gun laws in Britain and Australia and concluded that the restrictions had an ambiguous effect on other gun-related crimes or deaths. This article is an anomaly within the wider media sample, for it runs counter to the general theme that the United States has a problem with gun violence. It is important to note that the writer does not have a "pro-gun" mind-set, however, and is merely reporting the results of their research. The solution proposed in the rest of the articles conveying this sentiment advance the idea that tighter gun restrictions will help to resolve this problem. It is also contradicted by a New York Times (2nd October 2017) article that cites research published in the Journal of Public Health Policy that postulates that the gun homicide rate was almost halved in Australia after it passed its strict laws.

More specifically, the "ongoing trend" theme focuses on the issue of mass shootings. The amounts of mass shootings within a specific time period are listed in feature articles:

In the 477 days from June 1, 2016 to Oct. 1, 2017, there were 521 mass shootings (The New York Times, 5th October 2017).

From 1966 to 2015, our database contains 210 mass public shootings (The Washington Post, 3rd October 2017).

511 Days. 555 Mass Shootings (The New York Times, 6th October 2017).

A reliance on statistics to convey the extent of the problem mirrors the findings of other studies looking at mass shootings (Kupchik & Bracy, 2009; Schildkraut, 2014). A further technique used in feature articles to portray this as an ongoing trend is the use of adjectives like "another," "familiar," "each" and "latest" when referring to mass shootings. For instance, a Washington Post article (17th November 2017) has the opening sentence of "Here we go again." This is then followed up with "Another shooting rampage. Another from-out-of-nowhere attack on the public. Another tale of carnage, bloodshed and indiscriminate killing." Evident here is intonation (Fowler, 1991, p. 62), whereby the language used, including the repetition of "another" in three consecutive sentences, and the structures of sentences convey a sense of weariness. This is also evident in a number of articles which claim to be "sick" or "tired" of mass shootings.

Another technique used in feature articles and letters is referencing different mass shooting incidents. This is a form of addition, where elements are added to legitimize a point made (Mayr & Machin, 2012, p. 31). In this case, it is the point that mass shootings are not standalone incidents but part of a trend. For instance, one article references the locations of recent mass shootings, showing that these occur in a variety of venues all over the United States: "This time it's a rural community in California. Last week it was a Baptist church in Texas. Before that, a country music concert in Las Vegas" (The Washington Post, 17th November 2017). Another article (The New York Times, 3rd October 2017) follows a similar pattern listing the titles of well-known mass shootings: "Sandy Hook, Columbine, Orlando and on and on." The use of "on and on" here conveys the sense of this as never-ending. Similarly, a letter (The New York Times, 14th December 2017) references Sandy Hook, the Pulse Nightclub and Las Vegas shootings and is assigned the title "Newtown, Orlando, Las Vegas…" with the use of commas designating a list and the ellipses suggesting there will be more to follow in future. This is an example of a letter being chosen to continue a theme prevalent within the news media content (Ericson, Baranek & Chan, 1989, p. 341). In this case, it is continuing the theme of mass shootings as an ongoing trend and sustaining the news story of the Las Vegas shooting a few months after the incident.

Normalization

The "ongoing trend" theme paves the way for the "normalization" theme," intimating that mass shootings *will* occur again and that this has become part of everyday life in the United States. This theme is particularly conducive to creating an atmosphere of fear, with its inevitability and expectation that the threat is imminent by labelling incidents that are high-profile but atypical as trends (Glassner, 2004). This is fundamental to creating a climate of fear for it portrays mass shootings as a normal part of society. One article has the headline "Columbine Shocked the Nation. Now, Mass Shootings Are Less Surprising" (The New York Times, 10th November 2017). The article goes on to state that after Las Vegas one central emotion seen after Columbine appears to be missing: surprise. The implication from this is that American society has become somewhat desensitized to mass shootings because they occur so frequently. Continuing this theme, another article accuses Americans of being "apathetic" about mass shootings, which have become "ordinary, normal" (The Washington Post, 6th November 2017). Another article (The New York Times, 23rd March 2018) is written by a survivor of the Westside Middle School (1998) shooting. The writer claims that the incident is often forgotten because it took place "so many shootings ago." At the time, the shooting was an "anomaly" — particularly with it occurring over a year before Columbine — and yet now it is said to be the acceptance of a "new norm," particularly with proposals like arming teachers implying that it is an ever-present threat.

Continuing this theme, the inevitability of another mass shooting percolates a number of the feature articles in the sample:

They will continue to happen — different venues, different innocent lives — like clockwork, year after year. (TIME, 3rd October 2017).

It's critical to understand that the Groundhog Day phenomenon of horrific mass shootings is exclusive to the United States (The Washington Post, 2nd October 2017).

Set your clock. I will write this column again — just fill in the blanks as to the number of dead (The Washington Post, 2nd October 2017).

These articles all support the argument that gun control is needed to deal with the issue. The second article is written by Chris Murphy, a Democrat representing Connecticut — a state with the second tightest gun laws in the country — in the Senate. It is clear that the portrayal of mass shootings as something that *will* happen again is part of the argument for why further gun laws are needed. Hilgartner and Bosk (1988, pp. 61-62) advanced the argument that the notions of urgency and drama are pertinent to selecting and maintaining a condition as a "social problem" within the public sphere. In this case, these articles written just after the Las Vegas shooting elucidate that mass shootings are a problem and the inevitability of these occurring again conveys a sense of urgency and drama; thus, setting the need to solve the problem. This adheres to the requirements of the "problem frame," whereby there is a mechanism in place to "fix" an issue that is affecting many people (Altheide, 1997, p. 655).

A similar theme is continued in letters to the editor. One letter writer states "Perhaps the saddest fact about the horrifying mass shooting in Las Vegas is that it won't be the last" (The New York Times, 2nd October 2017). It is followed up with "these mass shootings will continue until there is the political will to enact effective gun control measures." This is a form of evaluation, evaluating social practice and delegitimization of certain actors and actions running counter to this theme (Mayr & Machin, 2012, p. 31), i.e. Congress and the Presidency for failing to pass stricter gun laws.

NARRATIVES AND REACTIONS OF FEAR

At its core, fear is a survival signal anticipating danger (de Becker, 1997). Since humans have the ability to anticipate events that may transpire in future, this paves the way for fear to be experience in anticipation of possible threats (Hill, 2001, p. 454). Within a climate of fear, the emotion of fear is described as being "free-floating" with the ability to attach itself to a variety of phenomena. This culture promotes hesitancy, avoiding risk and anticipates the worst possible outcome. A phenomenon like terrorism is illustrative of this where the worst possible scenario is investigated and actions taken to deal with this fear; despite the actual threat posed being relatively low (Furedi, 2006, pp. 4-5, 9). For the phenomenon of mass shootings, the atypical but horrific nature of these events mean that risks of future attacks are likely to be overestimated. This contributes to a climate of fear, whereby the distorted sense of risk gives the sense that one is likely to be victimized (Ferraro & LaGrange, 1987; Skogan, 1993).

Creating a Climate of Fear

The content in the news media sample about the Las Vegas incident contributes to a culture of fear through a number of techniques. One of these is eyewitness accounts from the shooting. Since the descriptiveness of news articles is said to affect perceptions of risk (Wahlberg & Sjoberg, 2000), this is another contributing factor. Descriptive accounts in feature articles convey the sense of being there, talking about bodies lying on the ground, bullets feeling like they were coming from everywhere and people screaming. Such stories are what Altheide (1997, p. 663) described as "tales of fear" whereby citizens participate in perpetuating the discourse of fear. Moreover, the tone adopted in articles makes use of "poetic" features like metaphors (Fowler, 1991, p. 44). One article, for instance, uses the metaphorical description of "the terror of it closed like a cold hand on their throat" (TIME, 3rd October 2017). With language (re)producing representations of social reality (Mayr & Machin, 2012, p. 7), this kind of terminology serves to add to the perception of what it is like to be victimized by this type of crime (Chermak, 1995; Garland, 2001).

This is further exemplified in the visual images and videos in the news media sample. Since images do not have the same fixed meaning as language, these may be interpreted in a greater number of ways (Mayr & Machin, 2012, p. 29). A series of photographs in the Washington Post (2nd October 2017) were accompanied by a warning about graphic content, serving to add to the sense of fear, anxiety and terror (Altheide, 1997, 2002; Furedi, 1997). The images convey the sense of chaos during the shooting: people running and hiding behind a fence; a man in a wheelchair being helped to safety; people being carried away; the wounded being tended to. There are some images that are particularly striking for their attention to detail. There are pictures of objects lying in the street: one has a pair of cowboy boots; another has a cowboy hat; a different one has a pair of shoes covered with blood. This conveys a sense of abandonment where these personal possessions have been left to allow the people to move to safety. There are some graphic images of people at the Las Vegas concert. One picture commonly used is a woman lying on the ground with a man on top of her, with it being unclear whether they have been hit. Another features two bodies lying on the ground, one of which has blood running down the legs. The use of images in crime reporting give readers a visual insight into what it is like to be a victim (Chermak, 1995, p. 93). This technique further adds to the climate of fear by offering a visualization of what it is like to be personally affected by a mass shooting.

Videos in the sample are similar, with significant amounts of footage taken by people at the concert. There are people running and lying on top of each other; injured people are being carried on stretchers. A clip that appeared frequently in the news media sample is one of a musician playing on stage and upon hearing gunfire, running off the stage and turning off the lights. With these clips being taken on handheld cameras, the shots are shaky and the shot durations are quite short (Newbold, 1998, p. 134). This is the "citizen media component" of news stories where citizens take real-life footage of events as they unfold, e.g. JFK's assassination in 1963 and 9/11 (Gillmor, 2007). This is part of "participatory culture" where media consumers become active producers in the process (Jenkins, 2006, p. 3). There are also videos taken by law enforcement body cameras, which convey a similar sense of chaos and horror. Also featured in the video sample are recordings taken after the shooting with survivors and the medical staff who treated injuries from the attack. Visually, these types of videos are not as unsettling as the previous citizen and police recordings of the incidents; however, these all suggest what it was like to be part of this mass shooting. Eyewitnesses describe trying to help friends, being shot themselves and witnessing others get shot. The medical professionals treating the injured and deceased look visibly upset, describing being covered in blood and how there was a "trail of blood into the hospital." These visualizations contribute to the "affect of fear," whereby the situation is cognitively perceived as threatening or dangerous (Gabriel & Greve, 2003, p. 602).

Another element of the culture of fear was the theme "sounds of terror." This theme is of particular importance to this shooting, given the use of the bump stock device to turn the semi-automatic weapon into automatic firing. The noise effects (Newbold, 1998) are evident in the videos involving footage recorded by eyewitnesses and law enforcement. Rapid and non-stop popping can be heard in the videos. A New York Times (2nd October 2017) video puts together footage from thirty videos to reconstruct what happened. There are twelve bursts of non-stop gunfire heard, with pauses in-between generally lasting seconds affording people the opportunity to flee. A central focus in feature articles is on the gunfire noises heard during the shooting. One article describes it in the following way: "A shattering pop-pa-pop-pop of unique explosions. Like fireworks during a grand finale. Or the crackling of electrical feedback" (TIME, 3rd October 2017). The rhythm of the pop-pa-pop-pop gives a sense of the intensity of the gunfire; whilst the comparisons with fireworks and electrical feedback offer a comparative source for the sound effects (Newbold, 1998, p. 135). Eyewitness described the persistent nature of the gunfire:

It was relentless (The Washington Post, 2nd October 2017).

It seemed like the shots would never end (TIME, 2nd October 2017).

The bullets whistling past you, the cracks when it hits something metal (TIME, 4th October 2017).

This argument was advanced by Mairal (2008, pp. 51, 53) who states that intense memories described by survivors can contribute to the production of "terror." The descriptiveness of experiencing the terror as it unfolds could, therefore, provoke the feeling of fear in audiences, in the sense that this is a survival signal to anticipate death, pain and danger (de Becker 1997; Warr 2000).

Juxtaposed with this is an article about the immediate aftermath of the shooting, where Las Vegas which is usually bustling and busy is described as "dead silent" (TIME, 7th October 2017). Continuing the theme of noise are discussions in the aftermath of Las Vegas about how much worse the shooting could have been if a "silencer" was used in the firearms. This was raised by former presidential candidate, Hillary Clinton, referencing a House bill that would reduce restrictions on gun silencers, who claimed that this would have made the Las Vegas attack even deadlier by removing the audible cue of gunfire (The Washington Post, 2nd October 2017). A similar point was made by Tim Kaine, a Senator for Virginia, who claimed the shooter was only stopped before more damage occurred because he did not have a silencer, with the noise of gunfire alerting law enforcement to his location (The Washington Post, 4th October 2017). This is an example of a frame in communication being defined in relation to a specific issue to influence how people think about this issue (Chong & Druckman, 2007, p. 106). In this sense, politicians are acting as "issue entrepreneurs" turning the personal — in this case, the story of a mass shooting — into a political issue (Goss, 2006, p. 107). Further information will be given on the policy debates pertaining to guns in the aftermath of Las Vegas in Chapter 4.

Fear of Mass Shootings

A consequence of a climate of fear surrounding mass shootings is the fear of this particular crime. Fear of crime has been described as a "rational or irrational state of alarm or anxiety engendered by the belief that one is in danger of criminal victimisation" (McLaughlin, 2001, pp. 118-119). Perceptions of risk affect how vulnerable individuals feel to becoming victims of crime (Ferraro & LaGrange, 1987; Gabriel & Greve, 2003; Lee, 2007). Although fear is an individual emotional reaction, it is also a social phenomenon shaped by cultural norms that prescribe how fear is experienced, expressed and managed by individuals (Furedi, 2007, p.2). In the case of mass shootings, it could be said that the fear of this crime is influenced by constructions of this phenomenon. For instance, Doran (2014) documented how news media coverage about the shooting at Columbine High School created fear amongst parents and students. This fear was at odds with the actual risk of another school shooting taking place. The themes mentioned earlier of portraying mass shootings as an ongoing trend and normalizing them serves to create fear of crime (Glassner, 2004). It could be said that this feeling of fear is sustained via the "fear of crime feedback loop," whereby crime and victim surveys represent the object of fear statistically and convey a sense of fear amongst citizens (Lee, 2007, p. 77).

Following on from this, recent polls indicate that there may be distorted levels of fear in relation to mass shootings. A third of those surveyed were so worried about the prospect of a mass shooting that they avoided certain places or events. Just under a quarter had changed their lives due to this fear. The fear appeared to be gendered with women more likely to report stress at 85% in comparison to 71% for men. Sixty-two percent of parents surveyed were said to "live in fear" of their children being victimized by a mass shooting (Ducharme, 2019). Another study showed that 57% of teenagers were worried about the possibility of a shooting taking place at their school. Moreover, this is shown to be a racialized and gendered issue. Two-thirds of Hispanic and Black teenagers claiming to be at least somewhat worried about this threat compared with 51% of White teenagers. Sixty-four percent of girls claimed to be very or somewhat worried compared to 51% of boys. Even more noteworthy is the fact that parents showed higher levels of anxiety with 63% surveyed expressing worry about a shooting occurring at their child's school (Graf, 2018). As the next chapter will show, reactions can also center on controlling fear by controlling its causes (Warr, 2000, p. 462). The majority of the news media sample advocates for tighter gun regulations as a means to reduce mass shootings, with a number of politicians promoting particular gun legislation. On the other hand, there are also policymakers whose solution to deal with the problem is via other means, such as addressing mental health issues or passing lenient gun laws to allow more citizens to carry guns in more places.

as a method of protection

CONCLUSION

This chapter explored how mass shootings are defined, understood and represented in public discourses. This is the first of two chapters that focus on the 2017 Las Vegas mass shooting incident. It sets the scene for the next chapter which centers on the policy responses to the attack. The news media coverage of the Las Vegas incident was found to reshape definitions of mass shootings. One of the ways it does this is by categorizing mass shootings by death and injury tolls; thus, emphasizing the sensational characteristics of the violent act (Schildkraut, 2014). Categorizing Las Vegas as the "worst mass shooting" and constant references to the death toll has the potential to increase the sense of competition with future attackers, encouraging them to exceed that number of victims (Coleman, 2004; Lankford & Madfis, 2017; Lankford & Tomek, 2017; Towers et al., 2015). It is advised that the news media try to avoid this by refusing to name the perpetrator or use their image/likeness in reporting (Lankford & Madfis, 2017). Another suggestion would be to avoid including the perpetrator, should they commit suicide at the end of the attack, in the death toll to increase the numbers. There are also comparisons to other mass shootings, with articles producing lists of the top five or ten deadliest incidents. An unexpected finding from analyses was that there were limited references to Columbine. This is in direct contrast to it being a constant reference point for mass shootings in other studies (Doran, 2014; Kupchik & Bracy, 2009; Schildkraut, 2014).

Another prolific theme in news media coverage is "terrorism" and whether the Las Vegas incident meets the definition. Articles debate the differences between mass shootings and terrorism, highlighting issues of race and religion as defining features. This adheres to the definition of terrorism as an act motivated by political, religious or ideological goals (Eby, 2012; Meloy, 2016). Articles draw upon intonation (Fowler, 1991) to convey a sarcastic and ironic tone when discussing these issues. The argument is advanced that the Presidency and Congress would take legislative action if it were a terrorist attack; yet it is likely that nothing will be done when it is defined as a mass shooting. This idea is revisited in Chapter 4, when news media articles adopt a defeatist tone that no policy action will be taken in the aftermath of Las Vegas. It is worth considering this point that if the incident had been defined as terrorism, it would have provoked a different policy response.

This chapter also discussed the construction of a climate of fear by the news media coverage of the Las Vegas incident. A distorted sense of risk was evident in the news media coverage via a number of themes. The first was portraying general gun violence in the United States and mass shooting incidents as an "ongoing trend." Exemplifying this is the listing of the numbers of deaths from gun violence and mass shootings within specific time periods, giving readers a benchmark to estimate the extent of the problem. It gives readers a sense that gun violence is a social problem (Galtung & Ruge, 1965). Another facet of this is comparing and contrasting gun violence rates in the United States with those in other Western countries like Australia and Great Britain. As per the "problem frame" (Altheide, 1997), the solution advanced to deal with this is to pass tighter gun laws much like the countries referenced. Further elements of the "ongoing trend" theme are to use evaluative adjectives like "flooded" and "bathed" to convey the sense of the United States being overwhelmed by gun violence; in addition to using adjectives like "another" and "latest" when referencing mass shootings to show Las Vegas is one in a series. The second theme in media content was "normalization," labelling incidents that are atypical as a regular part of everyday life (Glassner, 2004). Within feature articles, arguments are advanced that mass shootings are inevitable in society. These portray mass shootings as a social problem (Hilgartner & Bosk, 1988) and are made to buttress the proposed solution of passing stricter gun laws to reduce the incidences of mass shootings.

These two themes of "ongoing trend" and "normalization" serve to contribute to a culture of fear, the prevalence of fear and anxiety within the public sphere (see Altheide 1997, 2002; Furedi 1997, 2006, 2007; Glassner 1999, 2004). News media coverage of Las Vegas creates a climate of fear via a number of techniques. One of these is "tales of fear" (Altheide, 1997) in the form of descriptive eyewitness accounts from survivors. This is coupled with a focus on sounds heard during the shooting. Since descriptiveness of news affects perceptions of risk (Wahlberg & Sjoberg, 20000), this serves to add to a sense of fear. Another technique is visual representations from the shooting with real-life footage and images. This gives a sense of what it is like to be victimized by a mass shooting (Chermak, 1995).

The climate of fear created is conducive to a fear of crime around mass shootings. This is a perception that one will be personally victimized because of a particular crime (Ferraro & LaGrange, 1987; Gabriel & Greve, 2003; Lee, 2007). Opinion polls indicate those surveyed have fear around mass shootings. Some people report avoiding certain places due to this fear. With fear driving the need to do something about a problem (Altheide, 1997; Warr, 2000), this paves the way for the next chapter which looks at the gun-related policies proposed in response to mass shootings.

REFERENCES

Aaroe, L. (2011). Investigating Frame Strength: The Case of Episodic and Thematic Frames. *Political Communication*, *28*(2), 207–226. doi:10.1080/10584609.2011.568041

Altheide, D. L. (1997). The News Media, The Problem Frame and the Production of Fear. *The Sociological Quarterly*, *38*(4), 647–668. doi:10.1111/j.1533-8525.1997.tb00758.x

Altheide, D. L. (2002). *Creating Fear: News and the Construction of Crisis*. Aldine de Gruyter.

Berrington, E., & Jemphrey, A. (2003). Pressures on the Press: Reflections on Reporting Tragedy. *Journalism*, *4*(2), 225–248. doi:10.1177/146488490342005

Chermak, S. M. (1995). *Victims in the News: Crime and the American News Media*. Westview Press.

Chong, D., & Druckman, J. N. (2007). Framing Theory. *Annual Review of Political Science*, *10*(1), 103–126. doi:10.1146/annurev.polisci.10.072805.103054

de Becker, G. (1997). *The Gift of Fear: Survival Signals that Protect Us from Violence*. Bloomsbury Publishing PLC.

Doran, S. E. M. (2014). *News Media Constructions and Policy Implications of School Shootings in the United States* (Ph.D. Thesis). Glasgow, UK: University of Glasgow.

Duchame, J. (2019, August 15). *A Third of Americans Avoid Certain Places Because They Fear Mass Shootings*. TIME. https://time.com/5653218/mass-shootings-stress/

Ericson, R., Baranek, P., & Chan, J. (1989). *Negotiating Control: A Study of New Sources*. Open University Press.

Ferraro, K. F., & LaGrange, R. (1987). The Measurement of Fear of Crime. *Sociological Inquiry*, *57*(1), 70–101. doi:10.1111/j.1475-682X.1987.tb01181.x

Fowler, R. (1991). *Language in the News: Discourse and Ideology in the Press*. Routledge.

Furedi, F. (1997). *Culture of Fear: Risk-Taking and the Morality of Law Expectation*. Cassell.

Furedi, F. (2006). *The Politics of Fear: Beyond Left and Right*. Continuum International Publishing Group.

Furedi, F. (2007). *Invitation to Terror: The Expanding Empire of the Unknown*. Continuum Press.

Gabriel, U., & Greve, W. (2003). The Psychology of Fear of Crime: Conceptual and Methodological Perspectives. *British Journal of Criminology*, *43*(3), 600–614. doi:10.1093/bjc/43.3.600

Galtung, J., & Ruge, M. H. (1965). Structuring and Selecting News. In S. Cohen & J. Young (Eds.), *The Manufacture of News: Social Problems, Deviance and the Mass Media* (pp. 62–72). Sage.

Gardner, D. (2008). *Risk: The Science and Politics of Fear*. Virgin Books Ltd.

Garland, D. (2001). *The Culture of Control: Crime and Social Order in Contemporary Society*. University of Chicago Press. doi:10.7208/chicago/9780226190174.001.0001

Gillmor, D. (2007, April 17) *Virginia Tech: How Media Are Evolving*. Center for Citizen Media. http://citmedia.org/blog/2007/04/17/virginia-tech-how-media-are-evolving/

Glassner, B. (1999). *Culture of Fear: Why Americans are Afraid of the Wrong Things*. Basic Books.

Glassner, B. (2004). Narrative Techniques of Fear Mongering. *Social Research*, *71*(4), 819–826.

Goss, K. A. (2006). *Disarmed: The Missing Movement for Gun Control in America*. Princeton University Press.

Graf, N. (2018, April 18). *A majority of U.S. teens fear a shooting could happen at their school, and most parents share their concern*. Pew Research Center. https://www.pewresearch.org/fact-tank/2018/04/18/a-majority-of-u-s-teens-fear-a-shooting-could-happen-at-their-school-and-most-parents-share-their-concern/

Gross, K. (2008). Framing Persuasive Appeals: Episodic and Thematic Framing, Emotional Response and Policy Opinion. *Political Psychology*, *29*(2), 169–192. doi:10.1111/j.1467-9221.2008.00622.x

Hilgartner, S., & Bosk, C. L. (1988). The rise and fall of social problems: A public arena model. *American Journal of Sociology*, *94*(1), 53–78. doi:10.1086/228951

Iyengar, S. (1991). *Is anyone responsible? How television frames political issues*. University of Chicago Press. doi:10.7208/chicago/9780226388533.001.0001

Jenkins, H. (2006). *Convergence Culture: where old and new media collide*. New York University Press.

Kupchik, A., & Bracy, N. L. (2009). The News Media on School Crime and Violence: Constructing Dangerousness and Fueling Fear. *Youth Violence and Juvenile Justice, 7*(2), 136–156. doi:10.1177/1541204008328800

Lee, M. (2007). *Inventing Fear of Crime: Criminology and the Politics of Anxiety.* Willan Publishing.

Mairal, G. (2008). Narratives of risk. *Journal of Risk Research, 11*(1-2), 41–54. doi:10.1080/13669870701521321

Mayr, A., & Machin, D. (2012). *The language of crime and deviance: an introduction to critical linguistics analysis in media and popular culture.* Continuum Publishing Group.

McLaughlin, E. (2001). Fear of Crime. In E. McLaughlin & J. Muncie (Eds.), *The Sage Dictionary of Criminology* (pp. 118–119). Sage.

Schildkraut, J. V. (2014). *Mass Murder and the Mass Media: An Examination of the Media Discourse on U.S. rampage shootings, 2000-2012* (PhD dissertation). San Marcos, TX: Texas State University.

Skogan, W. G. (1993). The Various Meanings of Fear. In W. Bilsky, C. Pfeiffer. & P. Wetzels (Eds.), Fear of Crime and Criminal Victimization (pp. 131-140). Hanover, Germany: RFN.

Slovic, P. (1987). Perception of Risk. *Science, 236*(4799), 280–285. doi:10.1126cience.3563507 PMID:3563507

Sunstein, C. R. (2005). *Laws of Fear: Beyond the Precautionary Principle.* Cambridge University Press. doi:10.1017/CBO9780511790850

Wahlberg, A. A. F., & Sjoberg, L. (2000). Risk perception and the media. *Journal of Risk Research, 3*(1), 31–50. doi:10.1080/136698700376699

Warr, M. (2000). Fear of Crime in the United States: Avenues for Research and Policy. *Measurement and Analysis of Crime and Justice. 4.*

ADDITIONAL READING

Altheide, D. L. (1997). The News Media, The Problem Frame and the Production of Fear. *The Sociological Quarterly, 38*(4), 647–668. doi:10.1111/j.1533-8525.1997.tb00758.x

Altheide, D. L. (2002). *Creating Fear: News and the Construction of Crisis.* Aldine de Gruyter.

Furedi, F. (1997). *Culture of Fear: Risk-Taking and the Morality of Law Expectation.* Cassell.

Garland, D. (2001). *The Culture of Control: Crime and Social Order in Contemporary Society.* University of Chicago Press. doi:10.7208/chicago/9780226190174.001.0001

Glassner, B. (1999). *Culture of Fear: Why Americans are Afraid of the Wrong Things.* Basic Books.

KEY TERMS AND DEFINITIONS

Copycat Attacks: Mass shootings following shortly after a high profile incident, thought to have been provoked by the original attack.

Culture of Fear: A specific phenomenon in which feelings of fear and anxiety are present within society.

Fear: An emotional reaction anticipating danger.

Fear of Crime: The feeling that one is likely to be victimized by a certain crime in future.

Normalization: Portraying atypical high-profile incidents as routine so it appears that they will occur again.

Risk: The probability of a harmful action (e.g. damage, injury, death or illness) associated with a hazard.

Tales of Fear: A news media technique whereby citizens report their accounts from a horrifying event.

Terrorism: The showcasing of violence against a particular person(s), group or institution. This tends to be enacted for religious, political, or ideological reasons.

Chapter 4
Policy Reform After a Mass Shooting:
The Case of Las Vegas

ABSTRACT

This chapter focuses on the case study of the Las Vegas mass shooting. Utilizing analyses of news media content and results from interviews with gun violence prevention (GVP) advocates, it explores the policy debates occurring after this shooting. Findings indicate that within the news media coverage the two main targets for policy change were bump stock devices and assault weapons. Bump stock devices had a direct link to the shooting and ended up banned; however, there are some issues with the way this measure was passed. There was also no traction on renewing the assault weapons ban. In the immediate aftermath of the shooting, the news media coverage was shown to adopt a defeatist tone indicating that no policy reform was expected to take place, citing a lack of action after previous incidents and the current political landscape as the reasons why nothing would happen.

INTRODUCTION

This chapter examines the gun-related policy responses to the Las Vegas shooting. Despite the news media pushing the policy proposals of restricting bump stock devices and renewing the assault weapons ban, there was very little action on gun-related legislation. A restrictive measure on bump stocks was eventually passed via Executive Order; yet, there are a number of issues with doing it this way. Throughout the news media coverage, there was a defeatist tone indicating that policy action was unlikely to take place. News media analyses and results from interviewees in the GVP movement are documented here.

The main target of blame after the Las Vegas shooting were bump stocks, device allowing a semiautomatic firearm to fire automatically with a single trigger pull. This is likely because bump stocks had a direct link to the attack. Moreover, political leaders including the Presidency and Republican Congress representatives seemed tentatively open to the idea of discussing restrictions on these. In the end, a ban was passed via Executive Order. Interviewees and news media coverage denote that doing it this way

DOI: 10.4018/978-1-7998-3916-3.ch004

could have been strategic to save Republicans in Congress from having to vote on legislation. Assault weapons were the other main policy target after Las Vegas. Letters to the editor cited these more frequently than bump stocks as a blame factor for this incident and mass shootings generally. News media coverage also centered on renewing the assault weapons ban as a means of policy change. In the end, no action was taken on assault weapons, probably because these had no direct link to Las Vegas. This shows that the news media influence over policy debates can be limited (Kingdon, 1994/2003). The last emerging theme from news media coverage was a defeatist tone in the immediate aftermath of the shooting. It seemed that writers were inured to the idea that no policy action would be taken with the current political make-up. Paralinguistic techniques like evaluative adjectives, meta-opinions, emphasis, broken sentence structure and presenting the alternative argument as the "Other" (Fowler, 1991; Van Dijk, 1998) were used in news media coverage and letters to the editor. These techniques are utilized mainly to discredit the arguments of political leaders who refuse to take policy action after the shooting and advance the idea that there is the need for tighter gun restrictions.

This chapter goes through each of these issues. The first section defines what bump stocks are and what the legislation around these was at the time of the shooting. It then moves on to explore the theme of bump stocks being blamed for the Las Vegas shooting and how a measure was eventually passed on these devices. The second section details the other emerging theme of blaming assault weapons for the shooting. Finally, the chapter finishes by looking at the theme of a lack of action within news media coverage. In this, it was anticipated that despite calls for a policy response, reform will not occur due to the political climate at that time.

BUMP STOCKS

Blaming Bump Stocks

Examining the news media coverage of the Las Vegas shooting found that bump stocks were commonly blamed for the incident. Bump stocks are devices that allow for a semiautomatic firearm to fire automatically with a single pull of the trigger. Their basic purpose is to transform a semiautomatic firearm into a fully automatic one firing all available ammunition when the trigger is depressed, known as a "machine gun" (Giffords Law Center to Prevent Gun Violence, 2018). A ban on machine guns resulted from the rise of organized crime during the Prohibition period. Pictures of the St. Valentine's Massacre appeared in the front pages of newspapers in 1929. This was an incident where Al Capone's hit men killed seven from a competing gang using Thompson submachine guns (known as "Tommy guns"). The widespread publication of images from this massacre caused outrage and culminated in a political movement that eventually led to the 1934 Gun Control Act passed by former President Franklin D. Roosevelt. This legislation restricted access to machine guns and sawed-off shotguns, the common weapons of choice for those involved in organized crime (Dizard, Muth & Andrews, 1999, pp. 6, 10-11; Vizzard, 1999, p. 132; Winkler, 2012). As a result, machine guns are tightly regulated by federal law requiring registration. Moreover, any transfers on these weapons are taxed and have to be approved by the Bureau of Alcohol, Tobacco, Firearms & Explosives (ATF). Newly manufactured machine guns are prohibited; yet, those owned before 1986 are "grandfathered" in that they are still legal to own provided they are registered with the ATF. Recent figures indicated that 638,260 machine guns were still registered in the United States. Fifteen states and the District of Columbia have laws prohibiting the sale, possession and manufacture of machine guns. The remaining states do not have any regulations at this level, relying instead on the federal law (Giffords Law Center to Prevent Gun Violence, 2018). Extrapolating from this, it could be said that the use of bump stocks and devices with similar characteristics are all a way to circumvent the federal law on machine guns by turning a semiautomatic weapon into an automatic one.

News media coverage in the immediate aftermath of the shooting focuses on bump stock devices. A selection of headlines illustrates the tone adopted:

A loophole in our gun laws that all Republicans should want to close. (The Washington Post, 5th October 2017).

All about bump stocks, the deadly gun accessory used in Vegas that Congress might ban. (The Washington Post, 4th October 2017).

Bump stocks Might Be Restricted After Las Vegas Shooting (TIME, 5th October 2017).

Articles in the news media sample directly blame bump stock devices for the shooting, pointing out that one of these was needed to allow the shooter to obtain automatic gunfire. Every article in the sample that makes reference to the devices advocates for regulatory action. For instance, one article states that "opposing the closure of a loophole that was just used to massacre at least 58 Americans and injure hundreds more is the very definition of a losing battle" (The Washington Post, 5th October 2017). In contrast to this, there are only a few mentions of the bump stock ban in the letters sample. One letter published by the New York Times (4th October 2017) questions how one can legally obtain a bump stock, when fully automatic weapons are illegal. The writer's credentials as a professor of law and director of the mediation clinic at Columbia Law School are stated here, bestowing a greater degree of credibility onto their viewpoint. This brings to mind the point made by Ericson, Baranek and Chan (1989, p. 342) that the "quality newspaper depends on those evaluated in the hierarchy of credibility," whereby writers having a certain social status indicates that the newspaper is an influential source. Another letter mentions the bump stock ban, criticizing it for not going far enough. It instead maintains that all assault weapons, including bump stocks, should be completely banned in order to prevent future mass shootings (New York Times, 5th October 2017). As will be discussed shortly, assault weapons were another target for policy reform in news media debates after the Las Vegas incident.

The political reaction immediately after Las Vegas shows a *willingness* at least to discuss these devices. In a press conference, then press secretary, Sarah Sanders, intimated that President Donald Trump would be open to banning bump stocks: "We would like to be part of the conversation about that." She followed it up by reiterating that President Trump is a "strong supporter of the Second Amendment" and "that is not going to change." Other videos in the sample (The Washington Post, 5th October 2017) have other Republicans express willingness to consider such a ban. For instance, there is a video with Senator Tom Cotton (R-Ark.) in which he says he would be "willing to entertain this." News media articles record that Speaker of the House, Paul Ryan, and gun rights group, the National Rifle Association, are all open to having a discussion about bump stocks. It is noted that Senator Dianne Feinstein (D-Calif.) has logged a bill to ban bump stocks and all other devices used to circumvent federal law. This implies all political forces are coalescing around the idea of taking action on bump stocks.

Banning Bump Stocks

Despite the tentative political support indicated for a potential ban on bump stocks, action then appeared to stall on it. This is also in spite of the support shown in the news media; thus, suggesting that whilst the news media may *shape* the policy debate, its overall influence is limited. Kingdon (1994/2003, p. 58) claimed that the news media may have a less-than-anticipated effect on policies, given it has a prominent coverage of stories for a short period of time and then moves onto the next one. In this sense, the issue can fade away; thus, the impact of the news media is diluted. This also feeds into Rood's (2019, pp. 24-25, 45) theory about "public memory," whereby judgments about acts like mass shootings are intertwined with the proposed lessons citizens remember from previous acts of gun violence.

The occurrence of similar events can be another opportunity for the issue to reemerge. In this case, another high-profile mass shooting in Sutherland Springs, Texas, provided the opportunity to once again push for bump stock regulation. A Washington Post (27th November 2017) article published after this incident referenced the Las Vegas shooting once again. It is maintained that "a loophole in federal law allowed the gunman in the Las Vegas shooting to modify his weapons to perform like machine guns." As per the requirements of the "problem frame" (Altheide, 1997), a clear problem is set up with a view in mind of the solution to fix it. The issue is raised once again after the 2018 Parkland shooting. A Washington Post (22nd February 2018) article has the headline "Are you serious about gun control, Mr. Trump? Prove it." This is a direct challenge to President Trump, with the sentence structure here of a question followed by a two-word sentence of "prove it" serving to emphasize this point. The use of questions and incomplete sentences is a paralinguistic technique that can be used to suggest variations of emphasis (Fowler, 1991, p. 39). The article then criticizes the approach the Presidency has taken to deal with bump stocks, by ordering the Justice Department to investigate these devices. The article contended that if President Trump is "genuinely committed to banning bump stocks" he should back legislation raised by Senator Dianne Feinstein (D-Calif.) to ban the devices. As it transpired, it was not until the Parkland shooting in early 2018 when further action was taken on bump stocks. A video in the Washington Post (21st February 2018) features a statement from Trump where he cites the "evil massacre" at Parkland and says he has signed a memorandum ordering the Attorney General to change regulations on bump stocks. Trump stated that the "critical regulation" will be finalized very soon. It appears from this that the Parkland shooting prompted action on bump stocks, even though the devices are not connected to that particular incident.

In the end, an Executive Order banning bump stocks was passed by the Trump administration in December 2018. This ruling mandated that those who possess the devices had a time period of ninety days to destroy or turn them in (Jarrett, 2018). Interviewees pointed to the direct link to the Las Vegas shooting as crucial in giving traction to this law. The first point made was that prior to Las Vegas, there was a lack of awareness about the devices: "People didn't even know these things existed until there was the shooting in Las Vegas."-Jim Kessler (TW). Secondly, the footage captured by survivors of the shooting recorded the sounds made by the weapon firing. These videos were shared by news media and on social media (BBC News, 2017). As noted in the previous chapter, the news media coverage of Las Vegas frequently mentioned the sound of gunfire in its eyewitness accounts from that night. The noises were akin to that from an automatic firearm: "It's absurd because when we hear the videos of the shooting, it sounds like there was a machine gun being used not an adulterated semi-automatic."-Rukmani Bhatia (formerly CAP). Thirdly, it was felt that there was broad support from members of the public following the Las Vegas attack:

The mass casualty was pretty chilling, even for those who support gun rights. – Po Murray, NAA.

I think if Trump hadn't done something, people would have been really upset. – Tom Mauser (CC).

A poll taken a few weeks after the massacre gives credence to this claim. Seventy-two percent of those surveyed supported a bump stock ban. Support was highest amongst Democrats at 79%; although Republicans were still supportive with 68% in favor (Sanger-Katz & Bui, 2017).

Considering all this, the landscape was ripe for the passage of laws on bump stocks. Gun rights groups like the National Rifle Association (NRA) have often spoken out against the passage of gun regulations (see Davidson, 1998; Vizzard, 1999). On this occasion, however, the NRA did endorse tighter restrictions on bump stocks after the massacre, calling for the Bureau of Alcohol, Tobacco and Firearms (ATF) to review whether they comply with federal law. It was lamented that this could actually have been to prevent any action being taken, with the ATF being far less likely to ban them than Congress (Zornick, 2017). As it transpired, the ATF had ruled that bump stocks were not subject to federal regulation since they were merely a gun accessory. This resulted in President Trump passing the measure via Executive Order (Jarrett, 2018). It was postulated that this could have been strategic in nature:

The NRA wanted to stop it [bump stock legislation] going through Congress because they didn't want to set a precedent that Congress would act on the issue. And that's why when the administration decided to do it, they said 'That's okay, we'll let this one go. – Adam Skaggs (GLCPGV).

Taking heed of the fact that the NRA was opposed to the proposals raised in Congress around bump stocks (Jarrett, 2018), this is a credible point.

The news media sample has a handful of articles making similar arguments. One article, for example, has the headline "N.R.A and G.O.P[1], Together Forever" (The New York Times, 7th October 2017). The use of the sentence structure and presenting the "Other" in a negative way (Van Dijk, 1998, p. 39) emphasizes the perceived interlinkage of the NRA with Republicans. The article purports that the NRA's support for restrictions on bump stocks is strategic to prevent further laws being passed. In this sense, it is accused of "substituting accessory control for actual gun control." Another article has the headline "After getting an NRA permission slip, the G.O.P shouldn't be let off the hook" (The Washington Post, 6th October 2017). Strong opinions are expressed in this article, describing it as "pathetic" that policymakers in federal office are waiting to "get instructions from the NRA before suggesting they might be willing to *discuss* a laughably tiny move to regulate bump stocks." The emphasis on "discuss" shows that this is "predicate," where the action is under the control of agents (Fowler, 1991, p. 73). In this case, it is within the control of political officials to pass regulations; yet, their action is just to discuss the matter. The regulation on bump stocks is described as "laughably tiny," with the adverb "laughably" indicating disapproval at the state of affairs communicated by the proposition (Fowler, 1991, p. 87). A different Washington Post (28th November 2017) article stated that the "seeming support" from the NRA on bump stock was a "subterfuge" and that Congress has not acted on the issue. This is an example of a word conveying a value judgment (Van Dijk, 1998, p. 31). In this case, that the NRA is acting duplicitously and Congress is refusing to take action.

In a similar vein, it was also maintained that Trump may have taken this action to relieve Republicans in Congress: "It got Republicans in Congress off the hook because they didn't have to vote for anything."- Jonathan Perloe (CAGV). Moreover, it was maintained that passing legislation through Congress would have been a more robust way to do it: "It took longer as he had to go through a regulatory process and it can still be overturned."-Tom Mauser (CC). The main concern, explained Jonathan Perloe (CAGV), is that the measure can now be subject to legal challenges. From this point of view, it was postulated that Trump's motives for proposing the legislation may have been to "look like he was doing something but not as solid as actually promoting legislation."-Jonathan Perloe (CAGV).

In addition to the federal measure, eleven states and the District of Columbia have laws relating to bump stocks. This is slightly complicated by the fact that states define these devices differently. For instance, California bans "multi-burst trigger activators"; whilst Connecticut refers to "rate of fire enhancements." Giffords Law Center to Prevent Gun Violence (2018) recommended that the definition should be broad enough to encompass all those devices that are intended to increase the rate of fire in a semiautomatic firearm.

BLAMING ASSAULT WEAPONS

Assault weapons are the other main target for policy change after the Las Vegas shooting. It has been said that letter writers can propose new frames for an existing theme within the news source (Ericson, Baranek & Chan, 1989, p. 339). Banning assault weapons gains more attention than bump stocks in the letters to the editor sample, with eight advocating for this. A Washington Post (5th October 2017) letter writer, for example, said they are "absolutely opposed" to civilians owning assault weapons and multi-round magazines, maintaining that "the only reason for these weapons is to kill people, and they belong in law enforcement and the military." The writer explained that they are a gun owner and a strong supporter of the Second Amendment, presumably to demonstrate that they are not "anti-gun." It could be the case that these letters are purposefully chosen because they extend the salience of the issue being promoted by the news media.

Prolific throughout the articles in the sample are calls to ban assault weapons. A Washington Post (4th October 2017) article has the headline "After Las Vegas, let's forget about 'assault weapons' and focus on banning all semiautomatic guns." The opening sentence in the article gives the following explanation "I'm a doctor. I want you to live and thrive. So I want semiautomatic guns banned." The articles goes on to criticize the previous assault weapons ban that was in place, saying it focused too much on cosmetic features. The writer draws a direct link between mass shootings and semi-automatic weapons, describing them as causing a "sheer quantity of terrifying projectiles flying through crowded spaces at thousands of feet per second." The use of the evaluative adjectives (Fowler, 1991) "sheer" and "terrifying" here indicates that these weapons are contributing to the damage caused in mass shootings. Another Washington Post (5th October 2017) article continues this theme, citing doctors who describe what a bullet from an AR-15 rifle does to the body when struck. It also postulates a link between these weapons and mass shootings: "Not only are they capable of firing many rounds of ammunition in a relatively short period of time, but a shooter doesn't have to be particularly adept to do great damage." The article lists some of the previous mass shootings where semi-automatic rifles have been used as a means to back up their statement.

In spite of this being a salient issue in the news media, assault weapons are not an issue considered by political leaders after the Las Vegas attack. These are not mentioned at all in any of the press conferences, nor do any of the articles document statements of support from Republicans like they did with the bump stock ban. The lack of political support on this issue means it mainly fades away, probably because it does not have a direct link to the Las Vegas attack. It then re-emerges in the aftermath of two other high-profile mass shootings that occurred during the year after Las Vegas. The first of these is the Sutherland Springs (2017) mass shooting. A Washington Post article (27th November 2017) uses this shooting to advocate again for a bump stock ban. It is also argued that Congress should reinstate the assault weapons ban, with the point being made that "Military-style semi-automatic guns that have — even without bump stocks — become the weapon of choice of mass killers."

The next opportunity comes with the Parkland shooting in early 2018, which gives salience to the issue of assault weapons. An article that brings up bump stocks again also makes references to assault weapons, citing their use in the recent Parkland shooting. It is maintained that such weapons "pose a risk to public safety" and should be banned or stringently regulated at the very least (The Washington Post, 22nd February 2018). One of the very last articles in the sample is written by a Senator Mark Warner (D-Virginia) and has the headline "I voted against an assault weapons ban. Here's why I changed my mind." In the article, he goes on to explain that recent mass shootings have changed his mind, claiming that assault rifles and high capacity magazines are being used to generate "ever-higher body counts" and "mow down students in school hallways." This is an example of a feature article functioning as a critique to specific groups in society and offering advice (Van Dijk, 1998, p. 62). A qualifying statement is added about the writer being a gun owner, a proud supporter of the Second Amendment and having signed in bills solidifying the rights of law-abiding gun owners to purchase and carry firearms when he was the Governor of Virginia. The purpose of this is likely to demonstrate that ideologically they are in favor of gun rights.

In spite of this, there was no action on assault weapons. Contributing to this is a lack of political leadership on the issue, with this not being raised as a viable issue. Moreover, a poll of public opinion at this time showed that citizens were still divided on the issue, with 50% in favor and 46% opposed. This is even less than the level of support of 51% measured in 2016; it is also markedly lower than the 80% public support shown in 1994 when the ten year ban was first enacted. Support is partisan in nature, with 29% support from Republicans, 45% from Independents and 71% of Democrats (The Washington Post, 20th February 2018). As Chapter 10 will show, it appears unlikely there will be any action on assault weapons in the near future; although large-capacity magazines remain a more viable policy target.

"CONGRESS, SURPRISE US": A LACK OF ACTION

The quote above was the headline in a Washington Post (27th November 2017) article lamenting the lack of action since the Las Vegas shooting. With it being written after the Sutherland Springs shooting, it speculated about whether Congress will enact sensible gun restrictions "this time" or "fold under the pressure of the gun lobby" as it has with previous incidents. The headline of "Congress, Surprise Us" encapsulates another theme in the news media coverage of the Las Vegas shooting: the expectation that there will be no concrete policy action after this and subsequent incidents. This mirrors the findings of Kerr (2018) where there was a similar defeatist tone in news media coverage after the 2012 Sandy Hook school shooting. This sentiment continued throughout the remainder of Obama's time in office. In 2015, after a mass shooting at Umpqua Community College, Obama claimed that this has become "routine," with the reporting of these types of incidents and his response at the White House podium all being routine (Rood, 2019, p. 3). In relation to the Las Vegas incident, this sentiment relating to a "lack of action" was probably exacerbated by the avoidance of discussions about guns in the immediate aftermath of the shooting. A statement made by Trump immediately after the shooting calls for unity, makes religious references and calls the attack "an act of pure evil." It is notable for its omission of comments about guns. In a similar vein, Vice-President Mike Pence describes it as "a tragedy of unimaginable proportions" and calls it the worst mass shooting, citing the death toll. There are, however, no references made to guns.

The majority of the news media sample advocates for tighter gun laws after the Las Vegas shooting. A Washington Post (2nd October 2017) article is written by Congressman Chris Murphy and argues that the response to "regular mass slaughter" has been "un-American," claiming that doing nothing seems to go against the innovative nature of the country. It maintains that "Americans want change" to gun laws and "we know the changes that work." Murphy accuses politicians of being "scared" to take action because of the gun lobby and attempt to "silence voices of change" via accusations of politicizing the tragedy or saying it is impossible to "regulate evil." This is an example of a meta-opinion, where an opinion is expressed about an opinion (Van Dijk, 1998, p. 59). In this case, it is intended to discredit the claims made by opposing politicians. In a video in the sample, Murphy makes a speech with similar points. He accuses America of becoming "regularized" and "normalized" to mass shootings.

Another theme emerging from news media content is that direct blame for mass shootings is assigned to the policy inaction: "Congress has done absolutely nothing and because of that mass shootings continue" (The Washington Post, 2nd October 2017). Similarly, a New York Times (7th October 2017) article accuses Congress of "doing nothing" in the years since Sandy Hook and maintains that it is likely nothing meaningful will happen after Las Vegas: "Republicans will round up all the usual clichés and excuses for inaction." This mindset is even evident in the two cartoons within the sample (Washington Post, 2nd October 2017). One cartoon has a praying man wearing an American-themed hat and a speech bubble denoting "I don't care what anyone says." There is a pool of blood on the ground and written down the bottom is the statement "Now stand up and do something." Another cartoon has three lawmakers standing in a line and one praying. The text denotes "Lawmakers offer 'thoughts and prayers' again for shooting victims." There is a speech bubble with the text "Time to stand up and do something about guns." These are directly referencing the calls for thoughts and prayers after a mass shooting; yet are also referring to a lack of action. Most of the letters to the editor in the sample that mention guns also advocate for tighter gun laws.

Looking back to the 2012 Sandy Hook mass shooting finds it explicated a conflict between whether the aftermath of was an appropriate time to talk about gun laws. The National Rifle Association's Executive President Wayne LaPierre claimed that policies should not be discussed after such a tragedy, accusing those advocating stronger laws of lacking decency and judgment for doing so. This is met with President Barack Obama, who was in favor of tighter laws, claiming that *not* talking about gun policies or taking action is showing a lapse in judgment and decent behavior (Rood, 2019, pp. 92-93). This pattern was mirrored to some degree in the coverage of the Las Vegas incident. News media articles accuse Republicans and the gun lobby of "silencing" the debate after the shooting by saying it is too soon to discuss gun regulations. With agency, responsibility and blame being key components of ideological orientation, whereby good acts are attributed to Ourselves/our allies and bad acts attributed to Others/ their allies (Van Dijk, 1998, p. 43). One article has the headline "More Madness, More Cowardice." It claims that mass shootings will occur again because of the "political cowardice" of Congress (The Washington Post, 2nd October 2017). Another article said that the NRA has Trump and many members of Congress "quivering in fear," implying the group has a strong hold over them. The accusation is made that America may have a defeatist mindset when it comes to passing gun regulations, questioning "why do we bend to the nonsense that immediately after an attack is 'not the time' to have this conversation?"

(The Washington Post, 5th October 2017). Another article is written by a Democratic politician explaining why he boycotted a moment of silence held by Congress for the victims of Las Vegas. It states that Republican leaders do not want to alienate the minority of Americans with strong opinions on guns or the NRA who contribute to their campaigns. It instead contends that "an impotent Congress will hold a moment of silence, and an uninterested president will order flags flown at half-mast and make a show of a somber visit to the scene of the latest crime." The use of "impotent" and "uninterested" here are emotive adjectives (Fowler, 1991), showing the writer's strong feelings on this issue. He explains that he boycotted the moment of silence because he believes that the best way to honor victims is to prevent future mass shootings by enacting of gun laws.

Ten letters to the editor in the sample make similar points, adopting a defeatist and accusatory tone. One letter accuses elected officials in Congress of "cowardly behavior" by avoiding taking action (New York Times, 4th October 2017). Another New York Times (2nd October 2017) letter says that President Trump has done nothing to protect Americans from "homegrown terrorism" like the Las Vegas attack. It states this would involve him "having a face-to-face debate with the National Rifle Association and this president will never do that." The letter finishes with "Shame on him!" where the use of the exclamation mark expresses a strong value judgment (Van Dijk, 1998, p. 29). A different letter speculates about how many people must be killed before the gun lobby and Congress accept "reasonable controls" that "many (if not most) Americans want." The writer laments that "sadly" they will see future death tolls increase; yet do not think they will ever see the gun lobby accept sensible restrictions (The New York Times, 3rd October 2017).

CONCLUSION

Following on from the previous chapter which focused on how the Las Vegas mass shooting was understood and added to a climate of fear around mass shootings, this chapter reviewed the policy reform after this incident. News media analyses and interview results informed the discussion. Findings indicate that despite the news media pushing for action on bump stock devices and renewing the assault weapons ban there was very little in the way of policy change. An Executive Order was passed to restrict bump stock devices; yet this is purported to be weaker than passing a ban via legislation and possibly strategic in nature to avoid Republicans in Congress having to vote on a bill. The defeatist tone in the news media about the perceived lack of action on gun restrictions after Las Vegas showed there was little expectation that this incident would lead to policy change.

Bump stocks were commonly blamed for the Las Vegas incident in news media coverage, likely due to their direct link to the shooting. These are devices that transform a semiautomatic firearm into a fully automatic one known as a "machine gun." As it stands, fully automatic weapons are tightly regulated by federal law, requiring registration, taxes on transfers and approval by the ATF. Fifteen states also have individual laws prohibiting the sale, possession and manufacturing of machine guns (Dizard, Muth & Andrews, 1999; Giffords Law Center to Prevent Gun Violence, 2018; Vizzard, 1999; Winkler, 2012). Bump stocks and similar devices appear to be a way to circumvent federal law allowing for semiautomatic weapons to take on traits of automatic ones.

The news media coverage immediately focused on bump stocks after the shooting. These are directly blamed for the Las Vegas shooting and the need for regulatory action is highlighted. Political leaders show a degree of wiliness to discuss a ban on bump stocks. President Trump is said to be open to the idea by his then press secretary; although she reemphasizes his strong support for the Second Amendment. Other Republicans and the gun rights group, the NRA, also appear to be supportive of having a discussion about bump stocks. An opinion poll showed that this was an issue also gaining public support, with 72% supporting a bump stock ban. This was not particularly partisan in nature, with 68% Republican support and 79% of Democrats favoring it (Sanger-Katz & Bui, 2017). Considering all of this, there are surprisingly only a few mentions of bump stocks in the letters to the editor. One of those criticizes a ban on bump stocks, saying that it does not go far enough and all assault weapons need to also be banned.

In spite of the climate seeming to be conducive to change, action then appears to stall on bump stocks in the months after the Las Vegas shooting. This could be attributed to the coverage of Las Vegas fading away; thus, diluting the impact of news media coverage on the issue (Kingdon, 1994/2003). Further mass shootings in Sutherland Springs in late 2017 and Parkland in early 2018 provide opportunities for the issue to be raised again. Despite them having no direct link to the subsequent incidents, bump stock regulations are pushed again setting up a clear solution to the problem posed by mass shootings (Altheide, 1997). Articles use paralinguistic techniques such as questions and incomplete sentences to emphasize their point (Fowler, 1991). The Presidency's approach to bump stocks of ordering the Justice Department to investigate is criticized. After the Parkland shooting, Trump's statement makes reference to bump stocks, stating the "critical regulation" will soon be finalized. Extrapolating from this, it appears that the Parkland shooting prompted this policy action; although it is probably not the case in reality.

In the end, Trump passed an Executive Order banning bump stocks over a year after the Las Vegas incident. Although policy action was taken, there was still criticism over the approach adopted. The news media sample lamented that the NRA endorsed tighter restrictions on bump stocks via the ATF in order to prevent further laws being passed. Presenting the "Other" in a negative way, using value judgments and emotive adverbs (Fowler, 1991; Van Dijk, 1998), articles criticize the NRA and link the group to Republicans who do not want to pass stronger gun laws. Interviewees, moreover, claimed that Trump may have taken this action to relieve Republicans in Congress from having to vote for legislation and that passing legislation would have been a more robust way to enact policy change.

The other target for policy change after Las Vegas is assault weapons. This is discussed in eight letters to the editor, acting as a means of proposing new frames for an existing news media theme (Ericson, Baranek & Chan, 1989). Evaluative adjectives (Fowler, 1991) are utilized in letters to draw a link between mass shootings generally and assault weapons. News media articles also center on renewing the assault weapons ban, arguing that these firearms cause a greater degree of damage in a mass shooting. These points are reiterated after the Sutherland Springs (2017) and Parkland (2018) mass shootings. In spite of this, assault weapons are not discussed by political leaders like bump stocks were. Furthermore, polling shows that the public is still divided on this issue with 50% in favor and 46% against an assault weapons ban. This is partisan support, with 71% Democrats in favor compared to 29% of Republicans (The Washington Post, 20th February 2018).

Lastly, another theme in the news media coverage of Las Vegas was the expectation that there will be no concrete action. Similar results were indicated in Kerr's (2018) study about coverage after the 2012 Sandy Hook School shooting. The basis for this presumption that there will be a lack of action seems predicated on political leaders avoiding talking about guns in the immediate aftermath of the Las Vegas shooting and their claims about not wanting to politicize the tragedy. Articles and cartoons in the news media sample are critical of this response, accusing politicians of being scared and silenced by the NRA. The use of meta-opinion is used in this case to discredit the claims made by those politicians (Van Dijk,

1998). Letters to the editor make similar claims and advocate for tighter gun laws, thus entrenching the themes raised in news media content (Ericson, Baranek & Chan, 1989).

Overall, looking at the policy reform after Las Vegas finds a mixed picture. Although some action was taken on bump stock devices, there were issues with this and it seems this could have been a strategic move. There was no notable action on other policy areas such as assault weapons. This shows the news media only had a limited impact on policymaking in this case (Kingdon, 1994/2003). Adding to this is the sense of defeat inherent in news media coverage, where the expectation is that no action will be taken.

REFERENCES

Altheide, D. L. (1997). The News Media, The Problem Frame and the Production of Fear. *The Sociological Quarterly, 38*(4), 647–668. doi:10.1111/j.1533-8525.1997.tb00758.x

BBC News. (2017, October 2). *Las Vegas Attack: As It Happened.* https://www.bbc.co.uk/news/live/world-us-canada-41466148#lx-commentary-top

Davidson, O. G. (1998). *Under Fire: The NRA and the Battle for Gun Control.* University of Iowa.

Dizard, J. E., Muth, R. M., & Andrews, S. P. Jr. (1999). The Rise of Gun Culture in America. Introduction: Guns Made US Free – Now What? In J. E. Dizard, R. M. Muth, & S. P. Andrews (Eds.), *Guns in America: A Reader* (pp. 1–15). New York University Press.

Ericson, R., Baranek, P., & Chan, J. (1989). *Negotiating Control: A Study of New Sources.* Open University Press.

Giffords Law Center to Prevent Gun Violence. (2018). *Machine Guns & 50 Caliber.* https://lawcenter.giffords.org/gun-laws/policy-areas/hardware-ammunition/machine-guns-50-caliber/

Jarrett, L. (2018, December 18). *Trump administration officially bans bump stocks.* CNN. https://edition.cnn.com/2018/12/18/politics/bump-stocks-ban/index.html

Kerr, S. E. M. (2018). *Gun Violence Prevention? The Politics Behind Policy Responses to School Shootings in the United States.* Palgrave MacMillan.

Rood, C. (2019). *After Gun Violence: Deliberation and Memory in an Age of Political Gridlock.* The Pennsylvania State University Press. doi:10.5325/j.ctv14gp5h1

Sanger-Katz, M., & Bui, Q. T. (2017, October 12). *A Bump Stock Ban is Popular with the Public, But Experts Have Their Doubts.* New York Times. https://www.nytimes.com/interactive/2017/10/12/upshot/a-bump-stock-ban-is-popular-but-experts-have-their-doubts.html?searchResultPosition=1

Van Dijk, T. A. (1998). Opinions and Ideologies in the Press. In A. Bell & P. Garrett (Eds.), *Approaches to Media Discourse* (pp. 21–63). Blackwell Publishers.

Vizzard, W. J. (1999). The Impact of Agenda Confliction Policy Formulation and Implementation: The Case of Gun Control. In *Guns in America: A Reader* (pp. 131–144). New York University Press.

Winkler, A. (2012, July 13). *Why Don't Mass Shootings Lead to Gun Control?* Daily Beast. https://www. thedailybeast.com/why-dont-mass-shootings-lead-to-gun-control

Zornick, G. (2017, October 5) *Don't Be Fooled: The NRA Doesn't Want to Ban 'Bump Stocks.'* The Nation. https://www.thenation.com/article/archive/dont-be-fooled-the-nra-doesnt-want-to-ban-bump-stocks/

ADDITIONAL READING

Altheide, D. L. (1997). The News Media, The Problem Frame and the Production of Fear. *The Sociological Quarterly, 38*(4), 647–668. doi:10.1111/j.1533-8525.1997.tb00758.x

Kerr, S. E. M. (2018). *Gun Violence Prevention? The Politics Behind Policy Responses to School Shootings in the United States.* Palgrave MacMillan.

Rood, C. (2019). *After Gun Violence: Deliberation and Memory in an Age of Political Gridlock.* The Pennsylvania State University Press. doi:10.5325/j.ctv14gp5h1

Van Dijk, T. A. (1998). Opinions and Ideologies in the Press. In A. Bell & P. Garrett (Eds.), *Approaches to Media Discourse* (pp. 21–63). Blackwell Publishers.

Vizzard, W. J. (1999). The Impact of Agenda Confliction Policy Formulation and Implementation: The Case of Gun Control. In *Guns in America: A Reader* (pp. 131–144). New York University Press.

KEY TERMS AND DEFINITIONS

Assault Weapons: A term commonly used to refer to rifles and pistols that are semi-automatic (i.e., a weapon where a round is discharged with a pull of the trigger) in nature, as well as shotguns.

Automatic Weapons: Firearms that fire automatically (i.e. with a single trigger pull) that are tightly regulated in the United States.

Bump Stocks: Devices that covert a semiautomatic firearm to an automatic one, by allowing it to fire automatically with a single pull of the trigger.

Gun Lobby: An organized group in the United States that seeks to influence policies and laws relating to the ownership and access to firearms.

Other: A way of presenting an argument as in direct opposition to the one being made as theorized by Fowler (1991).

Problem Frame: A hypothesis by Altheide (1997) about a particular frame whereby a clear problem is set up with a view in mind of the solution to fix it.

Public Memory: Judgments about acts like mass shootings are said by Rood (2019) to be interlinked with what people remember about previous acts of gun violence and the lessons to be learned.

ENDNOTE

[1]   G.O.P refers to the "grand old party," another term for the Republican Party.

Section 2
Assessing the Risk of Mass Shootings

The theme of this section is to describe different techniques of assessing the risk of mass shootings.

Chapter 5
The Role of Leakage and Warning Behaviors

ABSTRACT

This chapter considers ways to detect mass shootings before they occur. It focuses on the role of leakage in prevention, whereby the communication of an intention to do harm can be used to assess the nature and viability of a mass shooting occurring. Eleven case studies of mass shootings are used to assess leakage and other warning signs displayed prior to these attacks. Documented are possible types of leakages, audiences for leakages, ways leakages were communicated, and other types of warning behaviors. Findings from interviews with threat assessment experts are also discussed in relation to the role leakage plays. It is hoped this chapter will go some way to informing risk and threat assessment procedures, which will be discussed in more detail in the subsequent chapters.

INTRODUCTION

One of the key warning behaviors preceding and, in certain cases, predicting an act of mass violence is "leakage." This phenomenon may be defined as the "communication to a third party [another person] of an intent to do harm to a target" (Meloy & O'Toole, 2011, p. 2). It is more subtle than making a direct threat against a target; yet, it still conveys an intent to cause harm. Coupled with any other available evidence, leakage can be used to assess the nature of the threat. "Leakage of their plans to third parties" was one of the eight warning behaviors theorized in Meloy and O'Toole's (2011) typology model[1], which was devised as part of their review of school shooters in the United States and Germany. Aside from this warning behavior, the other proposed activities in the typology are the following: *Pathway Warning Behavior*, i.e. actions that signal the commencement of preparations for an attack; *Fixation* on the idea of carrying out an attack; *Identification* with other school shooters; *Novel Aggression* relating to violence other than the shooting; *Energy Burst* in the form of increased frequency of activities relating to the attack; *Last Resort* signaling desperation or distress and offering one final chance for things to change; *Direct Threat* of an attack. This chapter will firstly address the warning behavior of leakage in the typology. A sample of case studies will be examined, looking at the leakage displayed, which format

DOI: 10.4018/978-1-7998-3916-3.ch005

it was in and to whom it was communicated. The chapter will then assess whether the remaining warning behaviors in Meloy and O'Toole's (2011) typology were present in the same sample. Also discussed are the thoughts and experiences of interviewees working in the threat assessment field. These insights are useful for detailing real life experiences of leakage and other warning behaviors.

Eleven case studies were selected to assess leakage and the other warning behaviors in Meloy and O'Toole's (2011) typology. The eleven incidents took place from 1986 through to 2019, giving a broad indication of the forms leakage took prior to and after the growth of the internet. These were selected from the list of worst mass shootings in the United States (CNN, 2020), whereby worst is defined in this context as the ones with the greatest death toll. A caveat to this is the original intention was to include the ten worst mass shootings on the list. The tenth case was the University of Texas shooting which resulted in sixteen deaths in 1966. The decision was reached to drop this incident, however, for several reasons. Firstly, due to it occurring over fifty years ago, it was difficult to locate relevant news media articles. Secondly, the presence of a brain tumor found in the perpetrator post-mortem may have played a part in his actions to a degree. The post-mortem was specifically requested by the perpetrator within his suicide note, presumably to explain why he was driven to act this way. Whilst it cannot be determined to what degree this influenced him, the worry was it may distort the overall results of the leakage inquiry. To that end, the decision was reached to include the next deadliest shooting on this list (CNN, 2020). Both the San Bernadino (2015) and Edmond Post Office (1986) attacks came joint eleventh on this list, with a death toll[2] of fourteen people. Both of these shootings are included in the final collection of case studies.

Four participants were interviewed for this chapter, selected for their experience and knowledge of the threat assessment process:

- Heilit Biehl, a threat assessment coordinator in Adams 12 Five Star Schools, a K-12[3] school district. This role which requires her to travel between schools in the region;
- John-Nicolletti, one of the founders of Nicolletti-Flater Associates, which is a threat assessment and emergency management consultancy firm;
- Stephen Brock and Melissa Reeves, the lead authors of the Prevent, Reaffirm, Evaluate, Provide and Respond, Examine (PREPaRE) School Crisis Prevention and Intervention curriculum. Melissa Reeves is also a Senior Consultant with SIGMA Threat Management Associates (SIGMATMA) and Associate Professor at Winthrop University; whilst Stephen Brock is currently affiliated to California State University (CSU), Sacramento, where he is a professor and school psychology program coordinator.

Interviewees were questioned about the role of leakage and other warning behaviors prior to mass shootings.

This chapter starts with an overview of previous research studies about leakage in mass shooting incidents. It will then provide a synthesis of results from eleven mass shooting incidents, documenting when, how and to whom leakage occurred. Patterns relating to leakage will be traced across these results. Finally, the thoughts of the four participants about the role leakage plays will be presented. Aside from leakage, other warning behaviors indicate that a mass shooting may be about to transpire. The chapter then goes on to detail the warning behaviors, aside from leakage, evident in the eleven mass shooting case studies. This sets up the context for the next two chapters which look at ways to deal with leakage and warning behaviors to determine whether a threat is credible.

LEAKAGE AND MASS SHOOTINGS

Leaking is defined as offences being announced prior to them being carried out (Bondu & Schithauer, 2015, p. 278). It can vary in its specifics about when, how and where the act will occur and what the target will be (Meloy & O'Toole, 2011, p. 2). As well as direct threats, leakage may also take the form of the documentation of thoughts, feelings and fantasies, indicating that an act of violence is going to take place (O'Toole, 2000, p. 16). Participants explained that leakage is prolific in relation to planned acts of mass violence. John Nicolletti (Nicolletti-Flater Associates) noted that most active shooters — an individual killing or attempting to kill as many people as possible in a confined area — will broadcast some form of leakage. Similarly, Melissa Reeves (SIGMATMA), explained that in incidents of mass violence taking place in K-12 schools, the majority of perpetrators elicited concerns from others and communicated their intentions to attack. Considering this, leakage can be a useful resource in the threat assessment process. Heilit Biehl, Adams 12, explained that in her role as a threat assessment coordinator within a school district, incidences of leakage have identified students in need; thus, allowing for earlier interventions with them.

Scholars have found that "leakage" was a trend present in a number of mass violence incidents. A review of forty-three attacks against federal governmental targets found that a third had made threats or veiled references about harming their targets. Threats were directly conveyed to the target themselves for three of the incidents (National Threat Assessment Center, 2015, p. iv). Similarly, a report by the National Threat Assessment Center (2019a) of twenty-seven mass violence attacks in public spaces found that 93% of them had engaged in communications that were threatening or concerning in nature (e.g. expressing an intense interest in previous attackers). A study comparing German case studies with nine school shooters and thirty-nine students of concern found that leakage was high in both groups, with 100% of school shooters and 90% of students of concern displaying this. Interestingly, there was a negative correlation with direct threats, with this being displayed by 39% of students of concern compared to 11% of school shooters (Meloy, Hoffmann, Roshdi & Guldimann, 2014, pp. 207-208). Inferring from this, it is possible that school shooters are more likely to communicate their intentions via leakage rather than direct threats to targets. This mirrors what was found by the *Safe School Initiative* study that most attackers did not threaten their target directly; despite engaging in pre-attack behavior signaling a potential threat (Fein, Vossekuil, Pollack, Borum, Modzeleski & Reddy, 2002, p. 20). In 2018, Silver, Horgan and Gill looked at a sample of public mass attackers (n=67). Leakage was found to be present in 58.3% of cases, with some displaying more than one type of leakage. In 2000, the Federal Bureau of Investigation (FBI) carried out a study into the characteristics of school shooters. Findings indicated that the majority of perpetrators made threats or communicated their intentions prior to the attack (O'Toole, 2000). Similarly, in a sample of 278 mass public shooters, 40% were found to have leaked clues to their intentions, thoughts and feelings prior to the incident (Capellan & Lewanowski, 2018). Bondu and Schithauer (2015) reviewed seven school attacks and also found that every attacker displayed leakage, with there being an average of 12.4 leakings per offender. A recent study by Lankford, Adkins and Madfis (2019) found that in the fifteen deadliest mass shootings incidents in the United States occurring from 1998-2018, the perpetrator had expressed violent thoughts or intentions to others in 87% of these cases. Moreover, 80% of the incidents had leakage specifically relating to an interest in mass killings.

Studies also found there were variations in how and when leakage was displayed. After studying the leakage of public mass perpetrators who killed four or more victims in their attacks, Silver and colleagues (2018, p.97) found it was expressed in three types: written statements (n=14); verbal statements to family or friends (n=38) or other members of the public (n=35). Capellan and Lewanonski's (2018, pp. 7-8) study of 278 mass public shooters found that 60% made a threat beforehand. Forty-three percent communicated the threat directly to at least one of the potential victims; whilst 37% relayed their threats to friends and family members and 20% posted them in online communication platforms such as social media sites. With there being leakage in 111 of the incidents included in their sample, this varied in format: 53% of this was in a verbal form (e.g. conversations), 27% was written (e.g. diaries) and 20% was in another form (e.g. drawing). In comparing single victim (SV) attacks with those that harmed multiple victims (MV), it was found that MV-offenders showed more leaking over a longer period of time (generally 3 to 6 months); although leaking never occurred on the day of the offence or the one preceding it. Only the SV-offenders made detailed statements in their leakings about the planned offence, making the particulars of their intended attack (time, place, victim and so forth) easier to determine (Bondu & Schithauer, 2015, pp. 287-288, 292-293). Interestingly, a parallel was discovered between the most severe form of leakage in the form of signaling specific interest in mass killings and the deadliest mass shooters (i.e. those who killed and wounded the greatest number of victims). In 47% of incidents, law enforcement had been informed about the attacker's interests (Lankford, Adkins & Madfis, 2019, pp. 9, 16).

CHALLENGES WITH LEAKAGE

Extrapolating from all of this, whilst leakage can be a valuable resource in threat assessment, it comes with challenges. For instance, in the case of K-12 schools, there is the issue of the wider community in which it is situated: "The community who report it [the leakage] to us want to know what we're doing and what we know."-Heilit Biehl, Adams 12. This, therefore, presents a tricky nuance of the need to protect and safeguard students; whilst also trying to be as transparent as possible with the community in question. Another issue is prior to most mass shooting incidents it is likely that leakage will be communicated to those around the attacker, e.g. family, friends, colleagues or other members of the public. Those within that group experiencing leakage are known as "bystanders." After carrying out research with bystanders, Pollack and colleagues (2008) found they fell into two groups: those who had prior knowledge of an attack but failed to report it; and those who did share their knowledge and helped avert an attack. For those in the first group, the lack of action was attributed to a number of factors including their relationship with the attacker, disbelieving the threat, or parents or figures of authority discouraging reporting it. To prevent targeted violence, it is pertinent to encourage bystanders to be part of the second group of reporting knowledge.

Participants explained that a potential problem with this is the tendency of leakage to now be posted online. Concurrently, a high percentage of individuals who are planning an attack tend to post a warning of some kind on social media beforehand. The implications of this are that the recipients of this leakage tend to be other children who are on those platforms rather than adults. Considering this, it is important that students feel they are able to share their concerns: "We need to help kids understand the difference between tattling and keeping other people alive and then letting them know that the adults will take it seriously and with confidentiality."-Stephen Brock, CSU. This mirrors the advice of Spearman (2019, p. 2) that the "bystander effect" of noticing concerns but not reporting them needs to be negated by awareness training of what, when and how to report concerns; as well as for those reported to be taken seriously and kept confidential. Doing so could help turn "bystanders" into "upstanders" who report concerns and help avert attacks (Amman et al., 2017).

For threats taking place outside of schools, "upstanders" could be created by reminding members of the public that they are "the first line of defense" against mass shootings, since they are more likely to witness leakage and threats than law enforcement officials (Lankford, Adkins & Madfis, 2019, p. 18). Creating a culture of shared responsibility would help with this, so it is not presumed that someone else will bear the burden of reporting what they know (Amman et al., 2017, pp. 11-12). It would also be worth reminding people that the calls to "see something, say something" does not just refer to the suspicious behavior of strangers. Furthermore, people have to feel that their report will be taken seriously (Lankford, Adkins & Madfis, 2019, p. 4). One of the other challenges is that even if people report their concerns to law enforcement, they may not be able to arrest the individual because no laws have actually been broken. To negate this, it is suggested that a "knock and talk" visit from law enforcement could act as a barrier to an incident transpiring:

Just by the fact that they go and talk to the person lets them know we're on their radar. We've disrupted a lot of them [incidents] just by simple knocks and talks. – John Nicolletti, Nicolletti-Flater Associates.

LEAKAGE – CASE STUDIES

In order to explore the issue of leakage in more detail, eleven case studies were critically assessed from the list of the worst — in terms of death toll — mass shootings in the United States (CNN, 2020). For each of the case studies, it was explored whether leakage was displayed and, if it was, to whom and in what format. This was carried out by reviewing relevant news articles about the eleven incidents. Table 1 provides an overall indication of the results.

Findings were similar to that of previous research in this area. Eighty-two percent of the attackers (n=9) displayed some form of leakage prior to the incident. The most common audience for this leak-

Table 1. Leakage Displayed Prior to Incidents

Case Study	Type of Leakage Displayed Pre-Attack	To Whom Was It Displayed
San Ysido (1984)	Verbal	Wife and former colleagues.
Edmond Post Office (1985)	Verbal	Colleagues
Luby's Cafeteria (1991)	Written (non online) and verbal	Neighbor's daughters, colleagues and former roommate.
Virginia Tech (2007)	Written (online and non-online).	Classmates, teachers and suitemates at university.
Sandy Hook (2012)	Written (online and non-online).	Classmates, teacher, online community interested in mass murders and acquaintance from community.
San Bernardino (2015)	Written (online).	Social media audience.
Pulse (2016)	Verbal and written (online).	Colleagues and social media audience.
Las Vegas (2017)	None	N/A
Sutherland Springs (2017)	Verbal, written (online and non-online).	Colleagues, former colleague and mother-in-law.
Parkland (2018)	Verbal, written (online and non-online).	Classmates, online audience and acquaintance.
El Paso (2019)	None	N/A

age were colleagues, classmates and teachers, with 73% "leaking" to them (n=8). Forty-five percent of leakage (n=5) occurred to an online audience. Leaking took place with family members in 18% (n=2) of cases. Neighbors and roommates and friends/other acquaintances received leakage in 27% (n=3) and 18% (n=2) of cases respectively. These totals add up to greater than a hundred percent because perpetrators tended to leak to more than one type of audience. Occurring in 45% of incidents (n=5) was written leakage in a format that was not online: e.g. class assignments, papers and text messages. Written leakage that was displayed online occurred in 64% of cases (n=7). Unsurprisingly, given the increased popularity and availability of internet access, these incidences of online written leakage took place in the fairly recent case studies from 2012 through to 2019. On the contrary, verbal communications were the main form of leakage in the incidents occurring prior to the advent of the internet, i.e. those occurring in 1984, 1986 and 1991.

Cross-referencing the audience to whom leakage was communicated with the different forms found that the perpetrators who expressed this verbally tended to be communicated to colleagues, teachers and classmates (n=6). This occurred in the earliest of the case studies, the shooting at the McDonald's in San Ysido (1984). When the perpetrator was made redundant at his welding job, he made a comment about committing suicide and "taking everyone with him". The Luby's Cafeteria (1991) perpetrator used to postulate in work about what would happen if he killed someone. Other incidents were the Pulse Nightclub (2016) shooter who alluded to having links to terrorist networks to his work colleagues. The Sutherland Springs (2017) attacker made death threats to his superiors when he was in the air force.

The clearest examples are the Edmond Post Office (1986) and Parkland (2018) shootings, whereby the leakage was conveyed to colleagues, teachers and classmates and the attacks took place in their workplace and school respectively. In advance of his actions, the Edmond Post Office (1986) shooter approached a female colleague who had been kind to him and told her she should stay home from work the next day. Moreover, he also made a comment to a colleague a week before the attack that people at work would be sorry and everyone would know why. The Parkland (2018) perpetrator introduced himself as a "school shooter" to his classmates and talked about "shooting up" public establishments. He also talked about the Pulse massacre and how he was glad homosexual people were killed in this attack. This is perhaps the reason why an unidentified source close to him reported him to the FBI, arguing his potential to become a school shooter.

Verbal communications were leaked to neighbors/roommates in 18% of incidents (n =2). Interestingly, verbal leakage to this category was for suicidal ideation only. The Virginia Tech (2007) and Luby's Cafeteria (1991) shooters both threatened to kill themselves around their roommates. Inferring from this, it is plausible that perhaps they threatened to do so in order to receive intervention from those in closest proximity to them at this time. Family members and friends/other acquaintances were jointly the next categories for verbal leakage in 9% of cases (n=1 for each category). The San Ysido (1984) perpetrator leaked almost exclusively to his wife. On the day of the shooting, he made the following verbal statements: "Society had its chance" and "I'm going to hunt humans."

Pre-attack written leakage that was not relayed online took the form of class assignments, letters and text messages (n=5). The colleagues, teachers and classmates category was the main audience, with forty percent of the incidents displaying this type of leakage (n=2). The Sandy Hook (2012) school shooter wrote a class assignment when he was ten that contained disturbing themes, such as cannibalism and child murder. Perhaps a more illustrative form of leakage was the Virginia Tech (2007) perpetrator who consistently wrote papers with homicidal and suicidal intents for his creative writing class at university. This was particularly evident in a play he wrote about a student who hates the other students at his school and goes onto kill them. The other three incidents where non-online written leakage was present are split equally across the categories of neighbors/roommates, friends/other acquaintances and family members. Firstly, the Luby's Cafeteria (1991) shooter wrote letters to his neighbor's young daughters that were threatening in nature, including content such as "There is no place to run or hide." Leakage in the friends/other acquaintances category was present in the Parkland (2018) shooting, whereby the perpetrator sent a text message to a girl he had been harassing saying he felt like killing people. The family members' category was covered by the Sutherland Springs (2017) shooter who sent a threatening text message to his mother-in-law.

Six incidents involved online written communication. For most of these cases, the intended audiences tended to be mixed, including people they knew as well as a general online audience. The Virginia Tech shooter's (2007) pre-attack leakage only included suicidal ideation, which was communicated via instant message to his suitemates. The Sutherland Springs attacker (2017) sent a former colleague Facebook messages, where he showed an obsession with mass murders and joked about committing one himself. The Sandy Hook (2012) shooter sent an email debating potential weapons for committing a mass act of violence to an acquaintance he knew from an online community interested in mass murders. He also made posts within the online community forum about mass murderers and killers; as well as editing Wikipedia articles about mass murders. San Bernardino (2015) and Pulse Nightclub (2016), the two incidents in the sample motivated by terrorist ideologies, both included online leakage via posts about ISIS which were uploaded to social media. The Parkland (2018) shooter was reported over an Instagram post he left, seen by a neighbor's son, intimating he would "shoot up" his school. Furthermore, he left a comment on YouTube saying he intended to become a "professional school shooter." This was reported by the video's owner to the FBI but dropped due to a lack of further evidence.

Interestingly, there were also instances of leakage after attacks where perpetrators set out to ensure that their "message" was relayed, even after their deaths. Twenty-seven percent of the sample had some form of leakage after the attack. Table 2 illustrates in which incidents this occurred.

Table 2. Leakage Displayed Following Incidents

Case Study	Type of Leakage Displayed Following the Attack	To Whom Was It Displayed
Virginia Tech (2007)	Verbal, written (non-online) and physical.	Broadcast on NBC news station. Covered in other news media sources.
Parkland (2018)	Verbal.	Left on cell phone and displayed on news media sources.
El Paso (2019)	Written (online).	Posted on a website for extremists and covered in news media articles.

Two-thirds of this leakage was communicated verbally in the form of recorded videos. An example of this is the Parkland (2018) perpetrator who recorded videos on his cellphone declaring his intentions to be the next school shooter. One-third of leakings were in a physical format (e.g. staged photographs). For instance, the Virginia Tech (2007) shooter posed for photographs holding a hammer and gun and included these images in the manifesto that he mailed to the broadcast news station National Broadcasting Corporation (NBC) just before commencing the second half of his attack. Two-thirds were written in the format of manifestos. An example of this is the El Paso (2019) shooter, who wrote a manifesto stating he was motivated by the mass shooting at a mosque in Christchurch, New Zealand. He also referred to Great Replacement theory, which is a conspiracy ideology about Indigenous Europeans being replaced by Arab, African and Muslim populations. Additionally, his manifesto mentioned environmental degradation and how he believed Hispanics would put the Democrats into power in America. The percentages of post-attack leakage add up to greater than one whole, since most perpetrators used more than one type of format.

Perhaps the most perplexing case of all is the Las Vegas (2017) mass shooting. Although the perpetrator *did* display warning behaviors — these will be discussed in the section below — there was no leakage prior to the shooting. Likewise, there was no suicide note or other kind of manifesto left. This has meant that despite presently being the worst mass shooting in the United States, the incident has no identifiable motive attached to it. This highlights that whilst leakage is important due to its prominence in most mass shooting attacks, it is also important to consider other possible factors that may be indicative of an attack. The next section will go on to consider these in further detail.

WARNING BEHAVIORS

Aside from leakage of threats, there are other warning behaviors that have occurred in previous mass shootings. Warning signs may be described as the "verbalization of behaviors, emotions and physical presentation" (Brock & Louvar Reeves, 2017, p. 4). One of the conditions for targeted violence to occur is the preparation stage, whereby attackers must research, consider, plan and prepare for an attack (Bondu & Schithauer, 2015; Fein, Vossekuil & Holden, 1995; Hollister & Scalora, 2015). A report looking at attacks on federal government premises found that the behaviors of change included:

- Disturbing communications referencing grievances, threats (included those that are veiled in nature), socio-political or ideological issues, depression and bizarre or delusional beliefs.
- Changes in behavior that may be both subtle and dramatic as they pertain to social, interpersonal and occupation functioning, as well as physical appearance.
- Interpersonal problems, which could be in the form of withdrawing from those closest to them and increased conflicts with others.
- Behaviors that are stalking or harassing in nature, e.g. following people, making threatening comments.
- Final acts such as leaving goodbye messages, giving away belongings and emptying out bank accounts.

In this sample, all but one of the offenders exhibited concerning behaviors. Moreover, almost two-thirds elicited concern from others about their own safety or the safety of others (National Threat Assessment Center, 2015, pp. ii, 5-6). Similarly, a study about mass shootings in public locations found that the following pre-attack behaviors elicited concern: expressions of suicidal ideation and/or increased levels of depression; purchasing weapons; erratic behavior and/or acting paranoid; inappropriate behavior towards females; writing about violence or weapons and/or social media posts with alarming content. Seventy percent of the attacks in the sample elicited concern from others to the extent where they feared for the safety of the individual themselves or others. Moreover, 41% of the attackers exhibited a fixation, which is an intense or obsessive preoccupation with a person, activity or belief to the extent that it negatively impacted aspects of their lives (National Threat Assessment Center, 2019a, pp. 8, 10-11).

Another study by the National Threat Assessment Center (2019b, pp. 20, 28) looking at targeted school violence yielded similar findings. Half the attackers were found to have an interest in violent topics, without an appropriate explanation. In addition to this, fifty percent had prior contact with law enforcement and school disciplinary procedures. Further, all of them exhibited behaviors that elicited concern from others and had stated their intention to attack. In 23% of cases, the attackers displayed a fascination with the Columbine massacre, i.e. they had photos of the perpetrators, paraphrased their diaries, consumed movies and music that they liked. Fifty-one percent of them engaged in attack-planning behaviors that went beyond making statements of intent.

As mentioned earlier, social media has cemented itself as one of the most significant locations for leakage to be communicated. The online presence of an individual requires consideration when investigating warning behaviors. This is particularly the case for young children, whose social media usage may be unknown by their parents. Heilit Biehl, Adams 12, has come across this in her role as threat assessment coordinator for K-12 schools: "Even for children in primary school we are seeing that they have access, they have profiles — sometimes known by parents; often not." Another facet of an individual's engagement with the internet is this also has the potential to encourage an attack:

If you have an individual that's thinking about doing this, they get additional ideas. They research it, so it's actually contributing to the development to a lot of these plans. – Melissa Reeves, SIGMATMA.

An example of this was cited by Adams 12's Heilit Biehl about a student who was researching "how to rent a van" following the mass violence attack in Bastallie where a van was used as the weapon of harm. Furthermore, individuals may also become part of a community that could encourage them to perpetrate an attack. This is probably exacerbated by the "cluster effect" of increased reporting of threats on anniversaries of mass shootings and shortly after the most recent highly-publicized incident.

The reasons for this are two-fold in nature. Firstly, the number of threats increases exponentially after a mass shooting incident and the anniversaries of infamous shootings such as Columbine and Parkland. John Nicoletti, Nicolletti-Flater Associates, whose premises are located near Columbine High School, said there were around eighty threats made around the time of the twenty year anniversary. It is worth noting that not all of these threats come to fruition. For instance, Calhoun and Weston (2009) postulated that there are two types of people that make threats: howlers and hunters. The more common type "howlers" make threats that tend to be emotionally charged and ominous in nature. Upon experiencing a "final straw incident," a "howler" may then become a "hunter." As the less common but more dangerous type, "hunters" may not overtly communicate threats; but they tend to engage in quiet preparation. Extrapolating from this, there may be individuals who make threats out of frustration, anger or a need for attention rather than intent to cause harm. According to Heilit Biehl, Adams 12, the increased presence of threats following a mass shooting or on the anniversary of one also results in an increase in the reporting of threats made by others. Whilst this is positive in the sense of allowing threats to be assessed, it can also have a contagion effect, whereby "it increases threat perceptions, it scares people. Legitimate threats and school shootings are rarer than what people feel."-Melissa Reeves, SIGMATMA. The challenge lies in determining which of the threats have some degree of credibility and intent and which are motivated by other factors. That is where threat assessment comes in, allowing for a consideration of the threat within a wider context. Threat assessment is considered in depth in Chapter 7.

WARNING BEHAVIORS – CASE STUDIES

The eight-point typology model proposed by Meloy and O'Toole (2011) was tested on nine school shooters and thirty-nine students of concern. Findings indicated that school shooters were distinguished from the students of concern by the warning behaviors of pathway (100% versus 6%), fixation (100% versus 16%), identification (100% versus 10%), novel aggression (56% versus 3%), last resort (78% versus 0%) and, to a lesser degree, energy burst (22% versus 0%) (Meloy, Hoffmann, Roshdi & Guldimann, 2014). Utilizing this typology, Table 3 below gives an overview of the presence of warning signs across all the case studies.

The *Pathway Warning Behavior* relates to actions that signal the commencement of preparing for an attack. For all eleven case studies, the perpetrators would have needed to procure weapons to use in the attack; thus, making that 100% of all incidents. In terms of other pathway warning behaviors, this was evident in 72% of the case studies (n=8). For example, the San Ysido (1985) perpetrator scoped out the supermarket and the post office before deciding on McDonald's as a target. The Virginia Tech (2007) shooter invested a lot of time into his manifesto, by hiring a van and renting a hotel room so he could record videos supporting it. He also ordered additional supplies such as chains to allow him to secure the doors when he carried out his attack. The Sandy Hook (2012) attacker visited the school's website beforehand to view their security procedures. The two shooters of the San Bernardino (2015) incident spent twelve months preparing for it. Preparation included target practice and leaving explosive devices in their homes. After initially targeting Disney World, the Pulse Nightclub (2016) shooter changed his mind after visiting its shopping complex and seeing the armed security present. To find an alternative location, he Googled "nightclubs in Orlando" and selected what would become his final target. The Las Vegas (2017) shooter searched for open air festivals and investigated the SWAT tactics of law enforcement in Las Vegas. Further to this, his girlfriend reported he was acting strangely when they stayed at Las Vegas the previous month by constantly looking out windows at the Las Vegas Village Venue from different angles. As evidenced within the videos he recorded on his cellphone, the Parkland (2018) attacker planned the logistics of his attack such as getting an Uber ride to his school. The El Paso (2019) attacker wrote his manifesto entitled "The Inconvenient Truth" and posted it online just prior to committing his massacre. This manifesto detailed his motivations, citing the Christchurch mosque mass shooting in New Zealand, which had occurred earlier that year, as an inspiration for his attack.

Becoming increasingly obsessed with the idea of carrying out an attack is known as *Fixation*. Thirty-six percent of the incidents evidenced this (n=4). The Virginia Tech (2007) shooter appeared to be fascinated with the Columbine shooting, writing an essay about the perpetrators for school coursework and referring to them in his manifesto. Fixation with mass shootings was taken to another level with the Sandy Hook (2012) perpetrator, whose interest was described by law enforcement as "unprecedented." This interest was initially sparked by the Virginia Tech incident five years earlier. The Sutherland Springs (2017) attacker was obsessed with mass murders, especially the Charleston massacre which took place in a church. Similarly, the perpetrator of the Parkland (2018) attack had an obsession with mass shootings, as well as knives and guns.

Similar to the previous warning behavior, *Identification* refers to an individual identifying with school shooters (in this case, mass shooters in general), weapons or viewing themselves as agents to advance a particular cause. This warning behavior was evident in eighty-two percent of the attackers (n=9). The San Ysido (1985) attacker was a conspiracy theorist who believed the breakdown of society was imminent. Extrapolating from this, it is possible he believed he was advancing a particular cause. Moreover, guns were described as the one thing he liked. In a similar vein, the Luby's Cafeteria (1991) perpetrator showed misogynistic tendencies and hated minority groups like gay people and Hispanics; thus, suggesting identification with a particular cause based on this belief system. The class assignments written by the Virginia Tech (2007) perpetrator showed an interest in school shooters and violence in general. Similarly, the Sandy Hook (2012) attacker was part of an online community fascinated with mass murder and serial killers. Additionally, he was a gun enthusiast who owned at least a dozen firearms. The San Bernadino (2015) and Pulse Nightclub (2016) attackers both had radical ideologies based on ideas about martyrdom. Although his family said he was not an "avid gun guy," the Las Vegas (2017) perpetrator was found to possess forty-seven firearms, thousands of rounds of ammunition and explosives at two properties he had. The Parkland (2018) shooter identified with school shooters and talked frequently about the Pulse Nightclub incident.

The next warning sign is *Novel Aggression* in the form of violence not related to the shooting. Sixty-four percent of the attackers in this sample showed indications of violence or aggression (n=7). The San Ysido (1985) attacker had a history of domestic violence and had previously been arrested for disorderly conduct at a gas station. The Edmond Post Office (1986) and Luby's Cafeteria (1991) shooters had no reported history of violence; however, both engaged in passive aggressive behaviors such as flying into a rage and jumping out in front of cars respectively. Stabbing a carpet with a knife at a party attended by other university students was an example of the Virginia Tech (2007) shooter showing novel aggression. The Pulse Nightclub (2016) and Sutherland Springs (2017) perpetrators both had histories of domestic abuse in their marriages. The Sutherland Springs shooter also display cruelty to animals (e.g. punching a dog). The perpetrator of the Parkland (2018) massacre used violence against his family members, committed self-harm and killed and mutilated animals.

Energy Burst behaviors are those pertaining to an increased frequency or variety in the types of activities relating to the attack; these were evident in five of the case studies. Ammunition and magazines were bought on five separate occasions by the Virginia Tech (2007) attacker. He was also seen two days before the day of the shooting at the site where the majority of his massacre took place and had chained the doors closed, presumably in preparation. Plans were made for the child and mother of the male perpetrator to be taken care of in the run-up to the San Bernadino (2015) attack. The male perpetrator also attended his work's Christmas party just before the attack. Similarly, the Pulse Nightclub (2016) perpetrator visited the nightclub just prior to the attack, left and later returned to carry out the shooting. The Las Vegas (2017) shooter prepared the hotel rooms a few days before with everything he would need for the attack and put "Do Not Disturb" signs up on the doors. The perpetrator of the El Paso (2019) shooting moved out his family home a few weeks prior to the attack, perhaps to allow him to plan his attack undisturbed.

The final two warning signs of *Last Resort* and *Direct Threat* were present in 18% and 9% of the incidents respectively (n=2; n=1). The *Last Resort* behavior signals a degree of desperation and offers a final chance for things to change. It could be said this was happening with the San Ysido (1985) attacker giving his wife explicit hints like "I'm going to hunt humans" and "Society had its chance" right before the shooting. Similarly, the Sutherland Springs (2017) perpetrator tied his wife to the bed before going off to enact his massacre. The presence of a *Direct Threat* behavior was also in this case study, with him making a direct threat to his mother-in-law who attended the church he targeted.

There were also a number of warning signs in addition to the eight stages proposed by Meloy and O'Toole (2011). Grouping these additional signs into categories gives the following: stalking/harassment

Table 3. Warning Signs from Meloy and O'Toole (2011) typology

Case Study	Warning Signs Present
San Ysido (1984)	Pathway; Identification; Novel Aggression; Leakage; Last Resort.
Edmond Post Office (1985)	Novel Aggression; Leakage.
Luby's Cafeteria (1991)	Identification; Novel Aggression; Leakage.
Virginia Tech (2007)	Pathway; Fixation; Identification; Energy Burst; Novel Aggression; Leakage.
Sandy Hook (2012)	Pathway; Fixation; Identification; Leakage.
San Bernardino (2015)	Pathway; Identification; Energy Burst; Leakage.
Pulse (2016)	Pathway; Identification; Novel Aggression; Energy Burst; Leakage.
Las Vegas (2017)	Fixation; Identification; Energy Burst.
Sutherland Springs (2017)	Fixation; Novel Aggression; Leakage; Last Resort; Direct Threat.
Parkland (2018)	Pathway; Fixation; Identification; Novel Aggression; Leakage.
El Paso	Pathway; Energy Burst.

of women; behavioral issues/antisociality; mental health issues; perceived as a loner/strange by others. These have been documented in Table 4.

Five of the perpetrators engaged in the stalking/harassment of women: Edmond Post Office (1986), where allegations of sexual harassment and an obscene phone call were made; Luby's Cafeteria (1991), where female neighbors were followed and received unwanted phone calls and letters; Virginia Tech (2007), where instant messages and other unwanted communications were made to three female students; Sutherland Springs (2017), the perpetrator previously stalked his ex-girlfriends; and Parkland (2018), where a girl he knew was harassed by him.

Behavioral issues/antisociality indicators were present in seven of the case studies. By being arrested for disorderly conduct, the San Ysido (1985) attacker falls into this category. The Edmond Post Office (1986) attacker used to display strange behavior in his community and was called "Crazy Pat" by chil-

Table 4. Additional Warning Sign Categories

Case Study	Warning Signs Present
San Ysido (1984)	Behavioral/antisociality.
Edmond Post Office (1985)	Stalking/harassment; behavioral/antisociality; strange/loner.
Luby's Cafeteria (1991)	Stalking/harassment; behavioral/antisociality.
Virginia Tech (2007)	Stalking/harassment; behavioral/antisociality; mental health issues; strange/loner.
Sandy Hook (2012)	Mental health issues; strange/loner.
San Bernardino (2015)	No additional categories.
Pulse (2016)	Behavioral/antisociality.
Las Vegas (2017)	Mental health issues.
Sutherland Springs (2017)	Stalking/harassment; behavioral/antisociality; mental health issues.
Parkland (2018)	Stalking/harassment; behavioral/antisociality.
El Paso (2019)	Strange/loner.

dren, which used to provoke him into a rage. The perpetrator of the Luby's Cafeteria (1991) massacre exhibited bizarre behaviors in the neighborhood, such as jumping in front of cars, to the extent that people reported being scared of him. The Virginia Tech (2007) shooter displayed strange behavior in class, such as taking photos of classmates and wearing a hood and sunglasses indoors. When attendance began to decline at the class, the teacher asked one of the students why and the response was "It's that boy. Everyone is afraid of him." The Pulse Nightclub (2016) perpetrator had behavioral problems as a child. The Sutherland Springs (2017) attacker was discharged from the military for bad conduct. The Parkland (2018) shooter was expelled from school for disciplinary reasons.

Mental health issues were particularly evident in four of the cases. The Virginia Tech (2007) shooter had selective mutism and appeared to have other mental health issues. The perpetrator of the Sandy Hook (2012) incident had Asperger's Syndrome, Autism and OCD which caused him to engage in behaviors like only communicating with his mother via email, despite her living in the same house, and change his socks twenty times a day. The Sutherland Springs (2017) shooter had ADHD, adjustment disorder and depressed mood. The perpetrator of the Las Vegas (2017) incident had mental health issues, including narcissism. There should be caution, however, in linking mass shootings with mental health issues. The National Threat Assessment Center (2019) argued that mental illness is not a risk factor in violence, with most violent acts being committed by individuals who are not mentally ill. Moreover, a recent controversy was raised about this when President Donald Trump attributed two mass shootings, including the El Paso one, to mental health problems. Experts in the field condemned this, arguing that his statement overstated the correlation and risked stigmatizing people with mental health issues (Thomas, 2019).

Lastly, the category of being perceived as strange/loner applied to four of the incidents. The Edmond Post Office (1986) attacker was described as a "quiet loner." The Virginia Tech (2007) shooter was seen as strange by classmates and did not appear to have any friends at university. The Sandy Hook (2012) attacker seemed to have no close friends and was home-schooled, so had a lack of face-to-face contact with people. The perpetrator of the El Paso (2019) massacre was described as "strange and off," due to his tendency to ask people strange questions and only giving closed answers when asked questions himself.

CONCLUSION

This chapter examined the role of leakage in addition to other warning behaviors prior to mass shooting incidents. Since leakage is defined as the communication of intent to cause harm prior to an attack, it is broad in its scope and can include the expression of thoughts, feelings and fantasies as well as direct threats (see Bondu & Schithauer, 2015; Meloy 7 O'Toole, 2011; O'Toole, 2000). It is well-documented within the field that leakage was present in a high number of mass violence incidents (see, for instance, Bondu & Schithauer, 2015; Capellan & Lewanowski, 2018; Lankford, Adkins & Madfis, 2019; Meloy et al., 2014; National Threat Assessment Center, 2015, 2019a; Silver, Horgan & Gill, 2018). Findings from interviews with threat assessment experts indicated that leakage is a valuable resource in determining the level of seriousness of a threat. With the advent of social media, leakage is more likely to be posted online and seen by children rather than adults. This then leads to challenges in the form of trying to encourage bystanders to report concerns.

In order to explore the occurrence of leakage in real-life mass shooting incidents that have taken place in the United States, a case study approach was utilized. Eleven mass shootings with the highest death tolls were selected. For each of the incidents, it was reviewed whether leakage was present and, if so, the form it took and to whom it was communicated. Results indicated that nine of the eleven incidents displayed leakage prior to the attacks. The audience was cross-referenced with the form of leakage, showing that verbal and non-online written leakage was most commonly relayed to colleagues, classmates and teachers. Online written leakage was a mixture of acquaintances and friends, as well as a general online audience. There was also leakage following incidents, with three of the incidents involving the relaying of a message post-attack. Only two of the case studies did not involve any form of leakage either before or after the attack. One of those was the Las Vegas (2017) mass shooting, which is considered to be the worst incident due to its high death and injury toll.

Also examined in this chapter were the warning behaviors that were present aside from leakage. For instance, a National Threat Assessment Center (2015) report found that in the run-up to incidents the following trends were present: unsettling behaviors such as stalking or harassing; suffering from interpersonal issues, e.g. withdrawing or conflict with others; changes in physical appearance; disturbing communications; final acts such as emptying out bank accounts. Those interviewed for this book also indicated that the online presence of an individual is another consideration when investigating warning behaviors. In particular, looking at whether an individual is researching how to perpetrate an attack or receiving encouragement from others. In order to examine the eleven case studies, the typology of eight warning signs theorized by Meloy and O'Toole (2011) was used. There were also additional warning signs outside the typology: stalking/harassment of women; behavioral issues/antisociality; mental health issues; perceived as a loner/strange.

REFERENCES

Amman, M., Bowlin, M., Buckles, L., Burton, K. C., Brunell, K. F., Gibson, K. A., Griffin, S. H., Kennedy, K. & Robins, C. J. (2017). Making Prevention a Reality: Identifying, Assessing and Managing the Threat of Targeted Attacks. Washington, DC: U.S. Department of Justice, Federal Bureau of Investigation.

Bondu, R., & Schithauer, H. (2015). Kill one or kill them all? Differences between single and multiple victim school attacks. *European Journal of Criminology*, *12*(3), 277–299. doi:10.1177/1477370814525904

Brock, S. E., & Louvar Reeves, M. A. (2017). School Suicide Risk Assessment. *Contemporary School Psychology*, *18*(1).

Calhoun, F., & Weston, S. (2009). *Threat Assessment and Management Strategies: Identifying the Howlers and the Hunters*. CRC Press.

Capellan, J. A., & Lewanowski, C. (2018). Can threat assessment help police prevent mass shootings? Testing an intelligence-led policing tool. *Policing*, *42*(1), 16–30. doi:10.1108/PIJPSM-07-2018-0089

CNN. (2020, May 3). *Mass Shootings in the US. Fast Facts*. https://edition.cnn.com/2019/08/19/us/mass-shootings-fast-facts/index.html

Fein, R. A., Vossekuil, B., & Holden, G. A. (1995). *An Approach to Prevent Targeted Violence*. National Institute of Justice.

Fein, R. A., Vossekuil, B., Pollock, W. S., Borum, R., Modzeleski, W., & Reddy, M. (2002). *Threat Assessment in Schools: A Guide to Managing Threatening Situations and to Creating Safe School Climate*. United States Secret Service and United States Department of Education.

Hollister, B. A. & Scalora, M. J. (2015). Broadening campus threat assessment beyond mass shootings. *Aggression and Violent Behaviour, 25*(A), 43-53.

Lankford, A., Adkins, K. G., & Madfis, E. (2019). Are the Deadliest Mass Shootings Preventable? An Assessment of Leakage, Information Reported to Law Enforcement and Firearms Acquisition Prior to Attacks in the United States. *Journal of Contemporary Criminal Justice, 35*(3), 315–341. doi:10.1177/1043986219840231

Meloy, J. R., Hoffmann, J., Roshdi, K., & Guldimann, A. (2014). Some warning behaviors discriminate between school shooters and other students of concern. *Journal of Threat Assessment and Management, 1*(3), 203–211. doi:10.1037/tam0000020

Meloy, J. R., & O'Toole, M. E. (2011). The Concept of Leakage in Threat Assessment. *Behavioral Sciences & the Law, 29*(4), 513–527. doi:10.1002/bsl.986 PMID:21710573

National Threat Assessment Center. (2015). *Attacks on federal government 2001-2013: threat assessment considerations*. U.S. Secret Service, Department of Homeland Security.

National Threat Assessment Center. (2019a). *Attacks in Public Spaces – 2018*. U.S. Secret Service, Department of Homeland Security.

National Threat Assessment Center. (2019b). *Protecting America's Schools: A U.S. Secret Service Analysis of Targeted School Violence*. U.S. Secret Service, Department of Homeland Security.

O'Toole, M. E. (2000). *The School Shooter: A Threat Assessment Perspective*. U.S. Department of Justice, Federal Bureau of Investigation.

Silver, J., Horgan, J., & Gill, P. (2018). Foreshadowing targeted violence; Assessing leakage of intent by public mass murderers. *Aggression and Violent Behavior, 38*(Jan-Feb), 94–100. doi:10.1016/j. avb.2017.12.002

Spearman, M. M. (2019). School Based Behavioral Threat Assessment and Management: Best Practices Guide for South Carolina. Columbia, SC: States of South Carolina, Department of Education.

Thomas, E. (2019, August 23). *Trump's claims and what experts say about mental illness and mass shootings*. ABC News. https://abcnews.go.com/Politics/trumps-claims-experts-mental-illness-mass-shootings/story?id=65101823

ADDITIONAL READING

Calhoun, F., & Weston, S. (2009). *Threat Assessment and Management Strategies: Identifying the Howlers and the Hunters*. CRC Press.

Lankford, A., Adkins, K. G., & Madfis, E. (2019). Are the Deadliest Mass Shootings Preventable? An Assessment of Leakage, Information Reported to Law Enforcement and Firearms Acquisition Prior to Attacks in the United States. *Journal of Contemporary Criminal Justice, 35*(3), 315–341. doi:10.1177/1043986219840231

Meloy, J. R., Hoffmann, J., Roshdi, K., & Guldimann, A. (2014). Some warning behaviors discriminate between school shooters and other students of concern. *Journal of Threat Assessment and Management, 1*(3), 203–211. doi:10.1037/tam0000020

Meloy, J. R., & O'Toole, M. E. (2011). The Concept of Leakage in Threat Assessment. *Behavioral Sciences & the Law, 29*(4), 513–527. doi:10.1002/bsl.986 PMID:21710573

Pollack, W. S., Modzeleski, W., & Rooney, G. (2008). *Prior Knowledge of Potential School-Based Violence: Information Students Learn May Prevent a Targeted Attack*. United States Department of Education.

KEY TERMS AND DEFINITIONS

Bystanders: Those who are the audience of the leakage communicated by the attacker (e.g., friends, family members, colleague, classmates, neighbors, an online community or acquaintances).

Contagion Effect: This is the phenomenon whereby a high-profile act of violence can result in many more threats and acts of violence.

Leakage: The communication of an intention to carry out harm to a target to others, which may be written, verbal, or some other form of expression (e.g., drawing).

Leakings: Instances where offences are announced prior to them being carried out.

Typology: This is a way to categorize and organize potential indicators of violence, listing those behaviors that may make an individual more susceptible to an increased or accelerated risk of violence.

Upstanders: Those who are in receipt of leakage reporting what they have been told to authorities or someone else in a position to take action.

Warning Behaviors: These are potential behavioral indicators of an attack, such as making preparations to carry out a mass shooting.

ENDNOTES

1 The leakage displayed to his former roommate was for suicidal ideation only, with him threatening to kill himself.
2 This was for suicidal ideation only with him sending an instant message online to his suitemates stating 'I may as well kill myself.'

[1]   It has been postulated that this typology could allow law enforcement to narrow the focus of an investigation, plan interventions and prioritize cases. It is cautioned, however, that it does not predict violence and should not be used as a risk assessment tool (Meloy, 2016, p.2).

[2]   The author consciously never includes in the perpetrators in the overall death toll. Firstly, it is felt that the news media includes the deaths of the perpetrators to report a higher death toll and make the incident more "newsworthy." Secondly, the deaths of victims who were murdered as they went about their everyday lives are different to those of the perpetrators who either commit suicide or are shot dead by the police. If the incidents were ranked this way, the San Bernardino shooting would have a higher death toll since it resulted in the deaths of the two perpetrators; whereas the Edmond Post Office attack only had one shooter.

[3]   This refers to Kindergarten through to Grade 12 schooling, which generally takes students through to the end of High School.

Chapter 6
Risk Assessment of Mass Shootings

ABSTRACT

This chapter turns its focus to ways to assess the risk of mass shootings. Risk assessment is used for the prevention and initial identification of violence. The usefulness of risk assessment instruments in this process is debated. Also discussed is the viability of criminal profiling, looking at characteristics associated with a particular type of offender. To add to the discussion, the motives of previous mass shooters selected as case studies are detailed. This goes some way to showing that the varied motivations of perpetrators make it difficult to adequately assess the risk posed. The next chapter will illustrate that threat assessment is a more useful approach to determine whether an individual intends to perpetrate a mass shooting.

INTRODUCTION

This chapter explores ways to assess the risk of mass shootings through the techniques of risk assessment instruments and profiling. Also detailed are the motives and pathways to violence of a selection of mass shooters, highlighting that these are varied in nature. The conclusion is reached that whilst there is value in applying risk assessment instruments to some degree, criminal profiling should be avoided for assessing the risk of mass shootings.

The use of instruments that identify relevant risk factors for a particular type of offending is a way to conduct risk assessment. These can be used for a variety of purposes: predicting reoffending risk; decision making about treatment, sentencing and post-sentencing detention; case management within institutional settings (Douglas, Pugh, Singh & Savulescu, 2017; Fazel & Wolf, 2018). There are a number of risk assessment instruments designed to assess targeted violence, including the Terrorist Radicalization Assessment Protocol (TRAP-18) (Meloy, 2016), Violent Extremism Risk Assessment, version 2-revised (VERA-2R) (Pressman, Rinne, Duits & Flockton, 2016) and Workplace Assessment of Violence Risk (WAVR-21) (White & Meloy, 2007). Critiqued here will be the usefulness of risk assessment tools in general, as well as in relation to assessing the risk of a mass shooting occurring.

DOI: 10.4018/978-1-7998-3916-3.ch006

Also examined will be criminal profiling, which focuses on identifying likely perpetrators through a set of characteristics hypothesized to represent this type of offender (Cornell, 2009). The theory is predicated on the notion that offenders will display similar behaviors in their crimes and other aspects of their lives (Snook, Cullen, Bennell, Taylor & Gendreau, 2008, p. 1260). Although there are commonalities between mass shootings, there does not appear to be a clear "profile" of this type of attacker (see O'Toole, 2000; National Threat Assessment Center, 2019b; Silver, Horgan & Gill, 2018). Other potential pitfalls with using profiling will also be detailed.

Participants who are experienced in risk assessment were interviewed: Heilit Biehl, a threat assessment coordinator at Adams 12 County School District; John-Nicolletti, a founders of a threat assessment and emergency management consultancy firm; Stephen Brock, one of the lead authors of the Prevent, Reaffirm, Evaluate, Provide and Respond, Examine (PREPaRE) School Crisis Prevention and Intervention Curriculum; Melissa Reeves, who is another lead author of the PREPaRE guidance and Senior Consultant with SIGMA Threat Management Associates (SIGMATMA). Interviews centered on their experiences of using risk assessment instruments and criminal profiling.

Also included were analyses of the eleven mass shooting case studies cited in the previous chapter. These were taken from the list of the worst mass shootings (in terms of death toll) prepared by CNN (2020). Although the original intention was to include the top ten, one of those case studies (the 1966 University of Texas shooting) was excluded due to concerns about the perpetrator's mental capacity and a lack of information available about it. Additionally, two of the incidents were joint eleventh on the list in terms of their death tolls (the 2015 San Bernardino and 1986 Edmond Post Office attacks), so both of those were included in the final collection of case studies. To add a final layer to the analysis, the motivations for the eleven case studies are then examined. The categories used in the National Threat Assessment Center's (2019a) study were utilized: mental health symptoms, grievances, ideological beliefs, fame/notoriety and unknown reasons. Also examined are the pathways to violence types (Cornell, 2009): conflict, antisocial and psychotic.

This chapter firstly outlines the purpose of risk assessment tools. Those that can be used for targeted violence acts will be outlined. Next, the discussion will center on profiling, with the results from interviewees and the literature all indicating that this is not an appropriate response. The motives for mass shootings, including the eleven case studies, are then discussed. It is shown that the most common motivation category for the case studies is grievances, with six of the incidents seemingly provoked by them.

RISK ASSESSMENT INSTRUMENTS

Risk assessment instruments are used by criminal justice practitioners to assess recidivism risk, as well as to assist with sentencing and treatment decisions. They can also be used by law enforcement to prioritize cases and narrow the focus of an investigation. For that reason, instruments should be grounded in empirical evidence relevant to the risk being measured, e.g. risk of committing violent acts. They should also be validated in the population being assessed, showing predictive accuracy (i.e. they accurately measure the risk of reoffending) and inter-rater reliability (i.e. different users using the tool will reach the same results) (Douglas, Pugh, Singh & Savulescu, 2017; Fazel & Wolf, 2018; Meloy, 2016). Historically, instruments were actuarial in nature based on static risk factors to assess risk using a quantified score. These have since evolved to include dynamic risk factors that may be used to inform decisions about treatment and individualized management plans. These types of instruments forego the quantified score and rely on the judgment of assessors to make the final decision about risk levels; hence, are appropriately named "structured professional judgment" (SPJ) tools (Hart & Logan, 2011; Lloyd, 2019; Logan, 2016). These types of tools tend to encompass both static and dynamic risk factors. Static factors are those which are historical, will not change over time or through interventions, e.g. history of criminal behavior. Dynamic factors, by contrast, are situational and tend to change at a rapid pace: for instance, weapons possession (Amman et al., 2017, p. 29).

There are a number of SPJ tools designed to specifically measure the risk of targeted violence. The TRAP-18 is intended to be used to assess an individual's potential risk of engaging in lone-actor terrorism. The focus is on patterns of behavior captured in eight dynamic risk factors in the form of proximal warning behaviors, such as leakage and directly communicated threat, and ten static items containing distal characteristics like mental disorder and history of criminal violence. Assessment is carried out by interviewing the individual and those acquainted with them who are aware of their behavior and the records from law enforcement and national security. The results can be used to determine whether an individual requires monitoring in situations where only distal characteristics are present, or active management in situations where one or more warning behaviors are present (Meloy & Genzman, 2016; Meloy, 2018, 2019; Meloy et al., 2019).

Similarly, the VERA-2R is an SPJ tool which assesses the risk of violence motivated by social, religious or political ideologies. Items cover factors pertaining to beliefs and attitudes, context and intent, history and capacity, commitment and motivation; in addition to protective and risk-mitigating items. A final rating of low, medium or high is assigned based on rankings of all items, with any protective and risk-mitigating factors being scored in reverse order. The tool can be used in both pre-crime and post-incident situations to assess the risk of violence (Lloyd, 2019). Lastly, there is the WAVR-21, which centers on the risk of targeted violence in workplaces and campuses. Although the primary focus is on homicide, it may also be used to assess other forms of violent aggression like stalking. Consisting of twenty-one items, the instrument looks at violent motives, ideation, weapons skills, pre-attack planning, negative personality traits, mental disorders, situational and protective factors. The focused questions included in the coding sheet allow for issues pertaining to threat assessment to be explored. Generally, threat assessment teams or security consultants in workplaces or campus settings would be the intended users of this tool (Brunt, 2013; Meloy, White & Hart, 2013).

For acts of mass violence, traditional risk factors for violence such as criminal history and substance abuse tend not to apply. This is because targeted violence is distinct from other types, such as impulsive and reactive violent acts (Meloy, 2016, p. 1). Notably, targeted violence is the product of three factors interacting: the perpetrator, a stimulus or triggering condition causing them to view violence as a solution to their problem(s) and environmental characteristics that facilitate the perpetration of the act (Fein, Vossekuil & Holden, 1995). More notably, the presence of violent ideation developmental failures, and experiences of frustration and isolation may all contribute to the pathway to targeted violence (White, Meloy, Mohandie & Kienlen, 2017, p. 159). A study of targeted violence in schools found that most of the perpetrators experienced social stressors in their lives, such as relationships with peers or romantic partners, a negative home life and bullying at school. Additionally, they tended to suffer from psychological (e.g. suicidal ideation), behavioral (e.g. ADHD) and developmental (e.g. cognitive difficulties) symptoms (National Threat Assessment Center, 2019b, p. 14). Another study found that suicidal ideation was even greater in attackers of targeted violence at institutes of higher education, with them being three to four times more likely to commit suicide than perpetrators in K-12 schools (Preti, 2008). A different study found that over half of perpetrators of targeted violence attacks on government targets had mental health symptoms (National Threat Assessment Center, 2015, p. ii).

In terms of personality disorders, there are risk assessment tools that specifically examine these, such as the International Personality Disorder Examination (IDPE) (Loranger, 1994) for a generic assessment of disorders, as well as specific instruments like the Psychology Checklist-Revised (PCL-R) (Hare, 2003) and the Comprehensive Assessment of Psychopathic Personality Symptom Rating Scale (CAPP SRS) (Cooke, Hart, Logan & Michie, 2004) for psychopathy. Looking at seventy-three incidents of active shooters, strong evidence and some indication of traits of Autistic Spectrum Disorder (ASD) were prevalent in 8% and 21% of the sample respectively. Comparing this to a prevalence of less than 1% of ASD in the general population, these results indicate that this could possibly be a risk factor for these incidents (Allely, Minnis, Thompson, Wilson & Gillberg, 2014). The features of ASD that may increase the risk of violence are emotional dysregulation, intensely restricted interests and difficulty interpreting social and non-verbal cues. In terms of those who commit mass shootings, comorbidity of disorders such as ASD and psychopathy can have very serious implications for risk. This was prevalent in some mass shooters such as the Virginia Tech University (2007) and Isla Vista (2014) perpetrators. The intense fixations that are characteristic of ASD could act as a catalyst for an individual's preparation for violence; with psychopathic and antisocial traits possibly motivating them to commit violence (White, Meloy, Mohandie & Kienlen, 2017, pp. 154, 157-159).

Interviewees reported mixed experiences with risk assessment tools. Heilit Biehl, who works at Adams 12, is trained in the Structured Interview for Violence Risk Assessment (SIVRA-35) (Brunt, 2012), a guided structured interview to allow risks to be classified as low, medium or high, and the Violence Risk Assessment of the Written Word (VRAW-2) (Brunt, 2015) for written concerns. She also has access to the risk assessment tools, TRAP-18 and WAVR-21. Melissa Reeves, SIGMATMA said the Structured Assessment of Violence Risk in Youth (SAVRY) (Bartel, Borum & Forth, 2006) risk assessment tool could be used as one of the data points within the wider assessment process. She further explained that the SAVRY is a tool that has been validated and normed in the adolescent population. The important point, she said, is that risk assessment tools such as SAVRY should be used as "part of your toolkit," i.e. in conjunction with other forms of assessment. To that end, SIGMATMA's Melissa Reeves gives the following recommendation regarding tools: "There's nothing wrong with using that kind of assessment tool but it doesn't replace the threat assessment process. It doesn't mean you ignore all the other data you get from interviews, daily work assignments, records review, internet searches, etc." Stephen Brock, CSU, emphasized that clinical judgment from competent professionals is how risk assessment instruments should be used, whereby reliance is not placed on the score generated: "Every psychometric measure is an estimate with error. So we never really know for sure what the true score is."

Taking that into account, caution should be heeded upon being too reliant on risk assessment tools. Whilst they are a useful starting point for beginning to assess the individual's proclivity to violence, risk assessment tools may not fully capture the risk and protective factors pertaining to an individual's risk (Douglas, Pugh, Singh & Savulescu, 2017; Fazel & Wolf, 2018). Extrapolating from this, risk assessment tools should be used to inform rather than replace professional judgment of practitioners. To assist with this process, practitioners should refer to guides documenting the strengths and weaknesses of the instrument (e.g. Lloyd, 2019). Doing so should help practitioners decide whether an instrument is suitable to be used within a particular population. Also useful for carrying out risk assessments is formulation, which organizes information into an explanation for why the violence occurred and the circumstances in which it could happen again (Logan, 2016). Another consideration relates to "responsivity," which are individual attributes that could contribute to the effectiveness of interventions. In order to reduce risk, intervention strategies should be informed by responsivity issues (Beaver & Schwartz, 2016; Hubbard & Pealer, 2009).

CRIMINAL PROFILING

Another technique that has been used to identify likely perpetrators of this type of violence is criminal profiling, which focuses on a "checklist" of assigned characteristics to detect this type of offender (Cornell, 2009). This is typically assembled through a process of police officers collecting crime scene information, which then goes to a profiler for analysis. The profiler then makes a number of qualitative judgments and devises a criminal profile, making predictions about the offender's characteristics (Snook, Haines, Taylor & Bennell, 2007, p. 170). This technique has been most commonly used by the Federal Bureau of Investigation (FBI) in the United States. For instance, there is an organized-disorganized dichotomy predicated on the notion that based on the characteristics of the offender, crimes can be organized (i.e. well-planned) or disorganized (i.e. more reactive) (Snook et al., 2008, pp. 1260-1261). In a study involving 51 Canadian police officers, most believed that criminal profiling was a valuable investigator tool; although they did have reservations about using it as evidence in court and its ability to misdirect investigations (Snook et al., 2007).

Looking at targeted violence, there are commonalities between perpetrators. One of those is perpetrators almost always engage in planning and pre-attack behaviors, such as procuring weapons and researching targets (National Threat Assessment Center, 2015, p. ii-iii). Fein and Vossekuil (1998, p. 16) postulated that attackers may deliberate about which target to choose and transfer their interest across targets. Once a target has been selected, attackers may become consumed by planning activities like the weapon to use, materials to leave, the practicalities of carrying out the attack and so forth. In terms of socio-demographics, mass shooting attackers are predominantly male and White (O'Toole, 2000; National Threat Assessment Center, 2019b, p. 14).

Despite these commonalities, research has shown that there does not appear to be a clear "profile" of this type of attacker (see Fein & Vossekuil, 1998; O'Toole, 2000; National Threat Assessment Center, 2019b; Silver, Horgan & Gill, 2018). Interviewee, Stephen Brock, CSU, explained that there are probably as many pathways to violence as there are perpetrators. This means that "in every case, we're talking about a unique set of variables...I don't think it's something we can standardize to a substantial extent." A similar claim was made by Snook and colleagues (2008, pp. 1261-1262) that trait-based models are flawed, since situational factors can also contribute to behaviors. In addition to this, the predictors of criminal behavior used in risk assessment tools (e.g. antisocial attitudes) are quite distinct from those used in criminal profiles, which tend to center on crime scene behaviors and offender demographics.

Further, given profiling is the act of standardizing it can result in short-sightedness. This can result in failure to deal with potential threats because they do not fit the profile or are deemed to be low risk (Cornell, 2013, p. 396; O'Toole, 2000, p. 2; Schneier, 2006, pp. 134, 136). For instance, a study by the National Threat Assessment Center (2019b) found that 17% of attacks were perpetrated by females; whilst African American and Hispanic attackers made up 15% and 5% of cases respectively. A similar point was made by Heilit Biehl, Adams 12, that these attacks are perpetrated by individuals across different socio-economic statuses, race/ethnicities, religions and sexual orientations. These thoughts were echoed by SIGMA Threat Management Associates (2020) that profiles can result in certain individuals being missed, such as females, Hispanic, Asian, older or younger adults.

Another potential consequence of profiling is the trend of "false positives" whereby innocent individuals are wrongly labelled as fitting the profile because they possess certain traits (Meloy, 2016). John Nicolletti, Nicolletti-Flater Associates, cautioned that this can result in racial and gendered profiling. Moreover, he argued, focusing on traits that one may associate with active shooters such as mental illness and social isolation can result in discrimination against those types of people:

If you do a Venn diagram and look at all the people who have mental illness, 99% of them don't become active attackers...If you do a Venn diagram the majority of socially isolated people don't become active killers. So now you become discriminating against introverts.

A similar point was made by Fein and Vossekuil (1998) when discussing assassinations on prominent people (e.g. politicians). One of the myths they debunked as that "assassination is a product of mental illness or derangement" with the argument being made that mental illness only rarely plays a key role in these types of attacks. Stephen Brock, CSU, advanced the argument that falsely identifying perpetrators is dangerous because "that kind of stigmatization and labelling could really alter someone's life." This is probably the reason that Canadian police officers who were interviewed for a study believed that criminal profiling should not be used as evidence in court nor for all types of criminal investigations, given its ability for causing misdirection (Snook et al., 2007, p. 186).

Profiling can also be a form of confirmation bias, i.e. if one school shooter is bullied it leads to the presumption that bullying must be the cause of future school attacks. Another assumption can be that those who make direct threats are more likely to carry out attacks, when those who pose threats do not always make threats (Fein & Vossekuil, 1998, p. 14). A more effective approach is to focus on a range of factors, changes in behavior and how they interact in order to accurately predict future attacks (Mears, Moon & Thielo, 2017, pp. 950, 956). Compiling a large-scale database of behavior patterns and the details about the lives of attackers could be a way to inform future investigations (Fein & Vossekuil, 1998, p. 31). Investigations triggered by threatening behaviors or reported concerns ensures that those individuals who may pose a threat — even those deemed to be "low risk" — are properly assessed (Cornell, 2013, p. 396). A threat assessment approach may be the best way to do this and the next chapter will focus on the benefits and challenges associated with such a method.

MOTIVATIONS

Interrogating the motivations of mass attackers can be indicative of the warning behaviors displayed. The argument has been advanced that three factors interact to produce targeted violence: an individual willing to take violent action; a stimulus or triggering condition causing the individual to view violence as an option; a setting in which the violence is able to occur (Fein, Vossekuil & Holden, 1995, p. 3). Three main pathways to violence have been proposed:

- Antisocial pathway, where violence is used for predatory or instrumental purposes, including rape, robbery and extortion. Individuals in this pathway tend to have a history of antisocial behavior and links to antisocial peers.

- Conflict pathway, in which individuals are motivated by revenge or the perceived mistreatment of others. Although this individual may not have a history of violent or antisocial behavior, they could have violent fantasies and a preoccupation with violence.
- Psychotic pathway, involving individuals with a severe mental illness. They may have delusions or hallucinations that motivate their behavior (Cornell, 2009, pp. 15-16).

The majority of the time targeted violence tends to fall under the "conflict pathway" in that it is often triggered by a grievance against a person or entity which the individual seeks to address via violence (Silver, Horgan & Gill, 2018, pp. 99-100). In this vein, their massacres can be "statement attacks" in which their motivations mainly make little sense to others (Schneier, 2006, p. 64). Studies by the National Threat Assessment Center (2015, 2017, 2019a) have found that perpetrators were frequently motivated by grievances relating to a domestic, workplace or personal issue. For instance, a report into mass attacks in public spaces found that 52% (n=14) were motivated by perceived wrongs. This perhaps explains why in 41% of cases the perpetrators appeared to have pre-selected their targets prior to attack. Eighty-one percent of the attackers experienced at least one significant stressor in the past five years; thus, indicating a trigger point (National Threat Assessment Center, 2019a, pp. 7-9). In comparing and contrasting single victim offenders (SV) with those who harmed multiple victims (MV), Bondu and Schithauer (2015) found there were more pronounced stressors in MV-offenders' lives, with them seeming to suffer from a greater number of humiliations and failures. Additionally, MV-offenders had a longer and more intense preoccupation with their attack and related topics like the perpetrators of previous mass shootings. Further to this, there appeared to be differences between the age groups of public mass shooters with younger ones (under 25 years) being more likely to attack their school, procure their weapons illegally, have a history of animal abuse and be inspired by previous attackers (Lankford & Hoover, 2019).

With relation to the psychotic pathway, a study of mass shootings in public spaces found that two-thirds had histories of mental health symptoms including depression, suicide and psychotic symptoms. Moreover, 19% of the sample case studies of public mass shooters were motivated by mental health symptoms (National Threat Assessment Center, 2019a, p.2). Whilst the proposed pathways are a useful starting point for thinking about an individual's journey to violence, it should be noted that the pathway to violence and combination of risk factors is highly individual (Bondu & Schithauer, 2015, p. 292). The National Threat Assessment Center's (2019a, pp. 7-9) study, for instance, indicated that aside from mental health symptoms and grievances, other motivations were ideological beliefs (n=2, 7%), fame/notoriety (4%, n=1) and unknown reasons (22%, n=6).

Case Studies

The eleven case studies selected for analysis were taken from CNN's (2020) list of the worst mass shootings in modern American history: San Ysido (1984), a shooting at a McDonald's in California; Edmond Post Office (1985), perpetrated by an employee at the post office; Luby's Cafeteria (1991), a diner in Texas; Virginia Tech (2007), a shooting by a student at the university; Sandy Hook (2012), an attack at an elementary school by an outside perpetrator; San Bernardino (2015), a shooting at an office Christmas party perpetrated by a husband and wife; Pulse (2016), a mass shooting in a gay nightclub in Florida; Las Vegas (2017), an attack at a country music festival; Sutherland Springs (2017), a shooting at a church in Texas; Parkland (2018), a high school attack perpetrated by an expelled student; El Paso

(2019), an attack at Walmart in Texas. These attacks were selected on the basis of their death tolls, with the 2017 Las Vegas incident having the highest.

Applied to the eleven case studies were the categories used in the National Threat Assessment Center's (2019) study: *grievances, mental health symptoms, ideological beliefs, fame/notoriety* and *unknown*. Table 1 gives an indication of the possible motivations for each case study.

Table 1. Motivations for Case Studies

Case Study	Motivations
San Ysido (1984)	Grievances.
Edmond Post Office (1985)	Grievances.
Luby's Cafeteria (1991)	Grievances.
Virginia Tech (2007)	Grievances; Mental Health Symptoms.
Sandy Hook (2012)	Unknown; possibly Mental Health Symptoms.
San Bernardino (2015)	Ideological.
Pulse (2016)	Ideological.
Las Vegas (2017)	Unknown; possibly Fame/Notoriety.
Sutherland Springs (2017)	Grievances.
Parkland (2018)	Grievances; possibly Fame/Notoriety.
El Paso (2019)	Ideological.

It appeared that six of the incidents were provoked by *grievances* held by the perpetrators. The Parkland (2018) perpetrator sought revenge against the school that had expelled him. The Sutherland Springs (2017) incident appeared to be an attack against his mother-in-law who attended the church; however, she was not in attendance that day. The Virginia Tech (2007) shooter seemed to possess hatred for his classmates, calling them "sadistic charlatans" in his manifesto. He had also stalked a number of female students on campus who complained about him, perhaps causing him to become angry about their rejection. The San Ysido (1984) and Luby's Cafeteria (1991) perpetrators both seemed to hold grudges against the places they attacked, despite these taking place in restaurants with members of the public. The San Ysido (1984) attacker shouted at victims before shooting them, implying anger. The Luby's Cafeteria (1991) perpetrator announced "This is payback day!" prior to commencing his attack. Additionally, he evidently had a problem with women as he would shout "bitch" at females before shooting them. Surprisingly, perhaps, he did let a woman with a child escape unscathed.

Three of the incidents were provoked by *ideological* reasons. The El Paso (2019) shooter wrote a manifesto, outlining his beliefs in the Great Replacement Theory, an ideological belief that White Europeans are being replaced by other races and ethnic groups (Schwartzburg, 2019). Documented in his manifesto was a comment about the "Hispanic invasion of Texas" and a fear that an increase in the Hispanic population would put the Democrats into government. He also claimed in this document that he was inspired by a mass shooting that occurred at a mosque in Christchurch, New Zealand earlier that year. The San Bernardino (2015) and Pulse Nightclub (2016) attacks were acts of terrorism, motivated by radical ideologies.

There was also some overlap between categories for a handful of the incidents. Whilst the Parkland (2018) shooter seemed to be provoked by a grievance, there also seemed to be a desire for *fame/notoriety* with him describing himself as the "next school shooter." Similarly, the Virginia Tech (2007) shooter had some serious *mental health symptoms*, with him exhibiting strange behavior such as identifying himself as "Question Mark," pretending to be his twin brother and stabbing a carpet with a knife when attending a party.

For two incidents, it was difficult to definitively say which categories the motivations fell into. For instance, the Las Vegas (2017) attacker did not leave a suicide note or manifesto explaining his motive(s). It may be inferred that this attack was to gain *fame/notoriety*, with him ensuring that he surpassed the death toll of the previous worst mass shooting. He was also said to have some mental health issues, indicating that *mental health symptoms* may also be applicable to this case. The motivations of the Sandy Hook (2012) shooter are also less than clear. Given he did suffer from a number of mental health conditions and had an obsession with mass shootings that law enforcement described as "unprecedented," it may be theorized that his attack was related to *mental health symptoms*.

Table 2. Pathway to Violence Types

Case Study	Pathway to Violence Types
San Ysido (1984)	Conflict; antisociality displayed
Edmond Post Office (1985)	Conflict; antisociality displayed
Luby's Cafeteria (1991)	Conflict; antisociality displayed
Virginia Tech (2007)	Conflict; possibly Psychotic; antisociality displayed
Sandy Hook (2012)	Possibly Psychotic.
San Bernardino (2015)	Possibly Antisocial.
Pulse (2016)	Possibly Antisocial.
Las Vegas (2017)	Unknown; antisociality displayed.
Sutherland Springs (2017)	Conflict; antisociality displayed.
Parkland (2018)	Conflict; antisociality displayed.
El Paso (2019)	Possibly Antisocial.

Table 2 provides a breakdown of possible pathway to violence types for each case study. The "antisocial" pathway is cases where individuals use violence for predatory or instrumental purposes. The "conflict" pathway relates to those motivated by perceived mistreatment or revenge. The "psychotic" pathway involves those with severe mental illness, such as paranoid schizophrenia (Cornell, 2009, pp. 15-16).

Relating these eleven incidents to the three pathways of violence proposed by Cornell (2009) finds 55% (n=6) fell into the *conflict pathway* since they were provoked by perceived grievances. It is possible that the three incidents motivated by ideological beliefs could fall into the *antisocial pathway*, as these attacks serve the instrumental purpose of trying to propagate their ideologies to a wider audience. In addition to this, some of the perpetrators did show indicators of antisociality prior to their attacks. For instance, the Virginia Tech (2007) shooter stalked a number of females at the university. Another example is the Sutherland Springs (2017) perpetrator who stalked ex-girlfriends, committed domestic abuse and made death threats against his superior officers in the air force. The Luby's Cafeteria (1991) attacker stalked two young girls in his neighborhood, behaviors including turning up at their workplace and staring at them, writing them letters and making phone calls to them. The Edmond Post Office (1986) perpetrator was known as a "peeping tom" in his neighborhood, staring in people's windows. Indecent images of children were found on the laptop of the Las Vegas (2017) shooter. The *psychotic pathway* could perhaps be said to include the Virginia Tech (2007) and Sandy Hook (2012) shootings, for both of these perpetrators suffered from serious mental health issues.

CONCLUSION

This chapter examined the different possible methods that can be used to assess and manage risk and threats of violence. Risk assessment tools may be used as one data point within a larger assessment; although judgments should not rest exclusively on them. Interviewees recommended that criminal profiling is avoided. The motivations and pathways to violence of the eleven mass shooting case studies show that these are varied in nature. The implication from this is that a more nuanced approach is required to adequately assess the risk posed by an individual. The next chapter will recommend that threat assessment is used as part of this approach; although risk assessment instruments can also be used in conjunction with this.

Discussed were risk assessment tools, which may be used to predict the risk of recidivism for certain types of offences (see Douglas, Pugh, Singh & Savulescu, 2017; Fazel & Wolf, 2018). Mass shootings are distinct from other types of violence, with attackers tending to experience different psychological, behavioral and developmental symptoms to more commonplace violent offenders (Meloy, 2016; National Threat Assessment Center, 2015, 2019b; Preti, 2008). There are tools containing risk factors specific to mass shootings and other types of targeted violence: TRAP-18, VERA-2R and WAVR-21. Risk may be exaggerated in those mass shooters who suffer from personality disorders like ASD, which could encourage their intense fixation with attack-planning (White, Meloy, Mohandie & Kienlen, 2017). In those cases, personality disorder tools, e.g. CAPP, IDPE, PCL-R, could be used in conjunction with those measuring violence. Since the aforementioned targeted violence tools are normed with adults only, an adolescent-specific tool like the SAVRY should be used when assessing this population. Referencing guides that document the strengths and weakness of tools (for instance, Lloyd, 2019) can help assessors decide which one is most appropriate to use. Practitioners assessing an individual's risk of committing a mass shooting or other acts of targeted violence should not rely solely on risk assessment tools (Douglas, Pugh, Singh & Savulescu, 2017; Fazel & Wolf, 2018). These instruments can only be used to inform the process aided by techniques like formulation detailing the circumstances in which violence could occur (Logan, 2016).

Criminal profiling was another approach discussed, concluding that there are too many issues with this method for it to be a viable option to assess threats of violence. First and foremost, as a method it is said to lack scientific support (Snook et al., 2008). Secondly, there is not a clear "profile" in terms of a prescribed set of key characteristics for mass shooters (O'Toole, 2000; National Threat Assessment Center, 2019b; Silver, Horgan & Gill, 2018). Profiling can result in certain individuals who pose a threat getting missed or "false positives" where people are wrongly labelled as a threat because they have certain characteristics (Cornell, 2013; Meloy, 2016; O'Toole, 2000; Schneier, 2006). Interviewees backed up these sentiments and also highlighted that profiling can result in discrimination against certain types of people, such as those with mental illness.

The motivations of a selection of mass shooters were examined, showing that these are varied. Appropriating the categories used in the National Threat Assessment Center's (2019a) study of mental health symptoms, grievances, ideological beliefs, fame/notoriety and unknown finds that the majority of incidents appeared to be the grievances motivation. Also utilized were the three pathways of violence proposed by Cornell (2009) of antisocial, conflict and psychotic. Findings indicated that most mass shooters appear to be following the conflict pathway of violence; although there were also elements of antisociality displayed by the perpetrators. This adds to the idea that assessing the risk of violence posed by potential mass shooters requires a more intensive approach than can be offered by risk assessment instruments and criminal profiling. This paves the way for the next chapter which looks at threat assessment as a way to assess threats made and the potential for violence.

REFERENCES

Allely, C. S., Minnis, H., Thompson, L., Wilson, P., & Gillberg, C. (2014). Neurodevelopmental and psychosocial risk factors in serial killers and mass murderers. *Aggression and Violent Behavior, 19*(3), 288–301. doi:10.1016/j.avb.2014.04.004

Amman, M., Bowlin, M., Buckles, L., Burton, K. C., Brunell, K. F., Gibson, K. A., Griffin, S. H., Kennedy, K., & Robins, C. J. (2017). *Making Prevention a Reality: Identifying, Assessing and Managing the Threat of Targeted Attacks*. U.S. Department of Justice, Federal Bureau of Investigation.

Beaver, K. M., & Schwartz, J. A. (2016). The utility of findings from biosocial research for public policy. In J. M. Blomberg, K. M. Brancale, & W. D. Bales (Eds.), *Advancing criminology & criminal justice policy* (pp. 452–460). Routledge.

Bondu, R., & Schithauer, H. (2015). Kill one or kill them all? Differences between single and multiple victim school attacks. *European Journal of Criminology, 12*(3), 277–299. doi:10.1177/1477370814525904

Brookman, F. (2010). Homicide. In F. Brookman, M. Maguire, H. Pierpoint, & T. Bennett (Eds.), *Handbook on Crime* (pp. 217–244). Willan. doi:10.4324/9781843929680

Brunt, B. V. (2013). A Comparative Analysis of Threat and Risk Assessment Measures. *The Journal of Campus Behavioral Interventions, 1*, 111–151. doi:10.17732/JBIT2013/7

CNN. (2020, May 3). *Mass Shootings in the US: Fast Facts*. https://edition.cnn.com/2019/08/19/us/mass-shootings-fast-facts/index.html

Connell, R. W. (2000). *The Men and the Boys*. University of California Press.

Cornell, D. (2009). *Recommended Practices for Virginia College Threat Assessment: Prepared for the Virginia Department of Criminal Justice Services' School Safety Center by Dewer Cornell, Ph.D., of the University of Virginia*. https://rems.ed.gov/docs/resources/VA_Recommendations_College_Threat_Assessment.pdf

Cornell, D. (2013). The Virginia Student Threat Assessment Guidelines: An Empirically Supported Violence Prevention Strategy. In N. Böckler, S. Nils, S. Thorsten, P. Sitzer, & W. Heitmeyer (Eds.), *School Shootings: International Research, Case Studies and Concepts for Prevention* (pp. 379–400). Springer Science-Business Media. doi:10.1007/978-1-4614-5526-4_17

Douglas, T., Pugh, S., Ilina, J., Savulescu, J., & Fazel, S. (2017). Risk assessment tools in criminal justice and forensic psychiatry: The need for better data. *European Psychiatry, 42*, 134–137. doi:10.1016/j.eurpsy.2016.12.009 PMID:28371726

Douglas, T., Pugh, S., Ilina, J., Savulescu, J., & Fazel, S. (2017). Risk assessment tools in criminal justice and forensic psychiatry: The need for better data. *European Psychiatry, 42*, 134–137. doi:10.1016/j.eurpsy.2016.12.009 PMID:28371726

Fazel, S., & Wolf, A. (2018). Selecting a risk assessment tool to use in practice: A 10 point guide. *Evidence-Based Mental Health, 21*(2), 41–43. doi:10.1136/eb-2017-102861 PMID:29269440

Fein, R. A., & Vossekuil, B. (1998). *Protective Intelligence and Threat Assessment Investigations: A Guide for State and Local Law Enforcement Officials.* U.S. Department of Justice.

Fein, R. A., Vossekuil, B., & Holden, G. A. (1995). *An Approach to Prevent Targeted Violence.* National Institute of Justice.

Gadd, D., & Jefferson, T. (2007). *Psychosocial Criminology.* Sage.

Hart, S. D., & Logan, C. (2011). Formulation of violence risk using evidence-based assessments: The structured professional judgment approach. In P. Sturmey & M. McMurran (Eds.), *Forensic case formulation* (pp. 83–106). Wiley-Blackwell. doi:10.1002/9781119977018.ch4

Hubbard, D. J., & Pealer, J. (2009). The Importance of Reponsivity Factors in Predicting Reductions in Antisocial attitudes and cognitive distortion among adult male offenders. *The Prison Journal, 89*(1), 79–98. doi:10.1177/0032885508329987

Lankford, A., & Hoover, K. B. (2019). Do the Ages of Mass Shooters Matter? Analysing the Differences between Young and Older Offenders. *Violence and Gender, 6*(1), 11–15. doi:10.1089/vio.2018.0021

Lloyd, M. (2019). *Extremism Risk Assessment: A Directory.* Centre for Research and Evidence on Security Threats.

Logan, C. (2016). Structured professional judgment: applications to sexual offender risk assessment and management. In A. Phenix & H. M. Hoberman (Eds.), *Sexual Offenders: Diagnosis, Risk Assessment and Management* (pp. 571–588). Springer.

Mears, D. P., Moon, M., & Thielo, A. J. (2017). Columbine Revisited: Myths and Realities about the Bullying-School Shootings Connection. *Victims & Offenders, 12*(6), 939–955. doi:10.1080/15564886.2017.1307295

Meloy, J. R. (2016, Apr.). Identifying Warning Behaviors of the Individual Terrorist. *FBI Law Enforcement Bulletin.*

Meloy, J. R. (2018). The Operational Development and Empirical Testing of the Terrorist Radicalization Assessment Protocol (TRAP–18). *Journal of Personality Assessment, 100*(5), 483–492. doi:10.1080/0 0223891.2018.1481077 PMID:29927673

Meloy, J. R. (2019). Terrorist Radicalization Assessment Protocol (TRAP-18). In M. Lloyd (Ed.), *Extremism Risk Assessment: A Directory* (pp. 33–37). Centre for Research and Evidence on Security Threats.

Meloy, J. R., & Genzman, J. (2016). The clinical threat assessment of the lone actor terrorist. *The Psychiatric Clinics of North America, 39*(4), 649–662. doi:10.1016/j.psc.2016.07.004 PMID:27836158

Meloy, J. R., Goodwill, A. M., Meloy, M. J., Amat, G., Martinez, M., & Morgan, M. (2019). Some TRAP-18 indicators discriminate between terrorist attackers and other subjects of national security concern. *Journal of Threat Assessment and Management, 6*(2), 93–110. doi:10.1037/tam0000119

Meloy, J. R., Hoffmann, J., Roshdi, K., & Guldimann, A. (2014). Some warning behaviors discriminate between school shooters and other students of concern. *Journal of Threat Assessment and Management, 1*(3), 203–211. doi:10.1037/tam0000020

Meloy, J. R., & O'Toole, M. E. (2011). The Concept of Leakage in Threat Assessment. *Behavioral Sciences & the Law, 29*(4), 513–527. doi:10.1002/bsl.986 PMID:21710573

Meloy, J. R., White, S., & Hart, S. (2013). Workplace Assessment of Targeted Violence Risk: The Development and Reliability of the WAVR-21. *Journal of Forensic Sciences, 58*(5), 1353–1358. doi:10.1111/1556-4029.12196 PMID:23865721

National Threat Assessment Center. (2015). *Attacks on federal government 2001-2013: threat assessment considerations.* U.S. Secret Service, Department of Homeland Security.

National Threat Assessment Center. (2019a). *Attacks in Public Spaces – 2018.* U.S. Secret Service, Department of Homeland Security.

National Threat Assessment Center. (2019b). *Protecting America's Schools: A U.S. Secret Service Analysis of Targeted School Violence.* Washington, DC: U.S. Secret Service, Department of Homeland Security.

O'Toole, M. E. (2000). The School Shooter: A Threat Assessment Perspective. Washington, DC: F.B.I., U.S. Department of Justice.

Preti, A. (2008). School Shooting as a Culturally Enforced Way of Expressing Suicidal Hostile Intentions. *The Journal of the American Academy of Psychiatry and the Law, 36*(4), 544–550. PMID:19092074

Schneier, B. (2006). *Beyond Fear: Thinking Sensibly About Security in an Uncertain World.* Springer.

Schwartzburg, R. (2019, August 5). *The 'white replacement theory' motivates alt-right killers the world over.* The Guardian. https://www.theguardian.com/commentisfree/2019/aug/05/great-replacement-theory-alt-right-killers-el-paso

Silver, J., Horgan, J., & Gill, P. (2018). Foreshadowing targeted violence; Assessing leakage of intent by public mass murderers. *Aggression and Violent Behavior, 38*(Jan-Feb), 94–100. doi:10.1016/j.avb.2017.12.002

Snook, B., Cullen, R. M., Bennell, C., Taylor, P. J., & Gendreau, P. (2008). The Criminal Profiling Illusion: What's Behind the Smoke and Mirrors? *Criminal Justice and Behavior*, *35*(10), 1257–1276. doi:10.1177/0093854808321528

Snook, B., Haines, A., Taylor, P. J., & Bennell, C. (2007). Criminal profiling belief and use: A survey of Canadian police officer opinion. *The Canadian Journal of Police & Security Services*, *5*(3), 169–179.

White, S. G., Meloy, J. R., Mohandie, K., & Kienlen, K. (2017). Autism Spectrum Disorder and Violence: Threat Assessment Issues. *Journal of Threat Assessment and Management*, *4*(3), 144–163. doi:10.1037/tam0000089

ADDITIONAL READING

Cornell, D. (2009). *Recommended Practices for Virginia College Threat Assessment: Prepared for the Virginia Department of Criminal Justice Services' School Safety Center by Dewey Cornell, Ph.D., of the University of Virginia.* https://rems.ed.gov/docs/resources/VA_Recommendations_College_Threat_Assessment.pdf

Douglas, T., Pugh, S., Ilina, J., Savulescu, J., & Fazel, S. (2017). Risk assessment tools in criminal justice and forensic psychiatry: The need for better data. *European Psychiatry*, *42*, 134–137. doi:10.1016/j.eurpsy.2016.12.009 PMID:28371726

Fazel, S., & Wolf, A. (2018). Selecting a risk assessment tool to use in practice: A 10 point guide. *Evidence-Based Mental Health*, *21*(2), 41–43. doi:10.1136/eb-2017-102861 PMID:29269440

Hart, S. D., & Logan, C. (2011). Formulation of violence risk using evidence-based assessments: The structured professional judgment approach. In P. Sturmey & M. McMurran (Eds.), *Forensic case formulation* (pp. 83–106). Wiley-Blackwell. doi:10.1002/9781119977018.ch4

Snook, B., Cullen, R. M., Bennell, C., Taylor, P. J., & Gendreau, P. (2008). The Criminal Profiling Illusion: What's Behind the Smoke and Mirrors? *Criminal Justice and Behavior*, *35*(10), 1257–1276. doi:10.1177/0093854808321528

KEY TERMS AND DEFINITIONS

Actuarial Instruments: Risk assessment tools based on static risk factors that result in a quantified score.

Dynamic Risk Factors: Those which are situational and tend to change quite rapidly (e.g., possession of a weapon).

Motivations: This may be defined as the reason(s) why an attacker would carry out a mass shooting attack.

Pathways to Violence: The journey of an individual that leads to them committing a violent act, particularly in the case of targeted violence which is planned in advance.

Profiling: This technique focuses on identifying the likelihood of someone being a perpetrator of a criminal act by comparing them against a list of characteristics.

Risk Assessment: This refers to the assessment of an individual's potential for violence looking at relevant risk factors.

Risk Assessment Instruments: Tools that identify relevant risk factors for a particular type of offending that may be used to make decisions about treatment, manage cases and predict recidivism.

Static Risk Factors: Those which are historical and fixed and cannot be changed through interventions (e.g., having a history of criminal behavior).

Stressors: These are situations that can make them more susceptible to committing harm against themselves or others (e.g., the breakdown of a relationship, failing at school, etc.).

Structured Professional Judgment Instruments: Risk assessment tools including static and dynamic risk factors and which rely on the judgment of assessors to make the final decision about risk levels.

Chapter 7
Threat Assessment of Mass Shootings

ABSTRACT

This chapter builds upon discussions in the previous ones about leakage of threats and other warning signs prior to mass shootings. The discussion here centers on assessing and managing threats in order to try to prevent mass shootings from occurring. The argument will be put forward that threat assessment allows for the seriousness of threats to be ascertained. This approach is two-fold in nature involving the assessment of the threat, as well as the individual who made the threat to determine whether they pose a danger to themselves or others. Moreover, it generally involves a follow-up plan for the threatening individual to be managed. Interviews with experts in this field provide advice relating to the process of carrying out threat assessment and management.

INTRODUCTION

As documented in the previous chapters, leakage and other warning signs are prevalent indicators of mass shootings. More specifically, the worst mass shooters exhibited more warning signs (e.g. unnatural interest in homicide) and were reported to law enforcement more frequently than other active shooters (Lankford, Adkins, Krista & Madfis, 2019). This chapter intends to build upon this by looking at "threat assessment," the process used when a concern has been reported and needs to be managed (Reeves & Brock, 2017, p. 2). First of all, this method identifies individuals of concern based on a threat made or other concerns raised. The next step is to gather and thereafter evaluate information about the individual and the threat made to determine whether they pose a threat to themselves or others. Once this has been completed, interventions are delineated to manage the situation and reduce the risk of violence (Cornell, 2013, p. 380).

This chapter discusses threat assessment, its purpose and how this can be used to prevent mass shootings from occurring. Advice will be given on how to utilize threat assessment in order to manage the threat of mass shootings. Literature in this field, interviews with experts in this field and material from

DOI: 10.4018/978-1-7998-3916-3.ch007

a threat assessment training course were used to inform the discussion in this chapter. Interviews were carried out with the following participants:

- Heilit Biehl, a threat assessment coordinator in Adams 12 Five Star Schools, a K-12 school district;
- John-Nicolletti, one of the founders of Nicolletti-Flater Associates, a threat assessment and emergency management consultancy firm;
- Stephen Brock and Melissa Reeves, the lead authors of the PREPaRE emergency management guidance and past Presidents of the National Association of School Psychologists. Brock is also a professor and school psychology program coordinator at California State University (CSU), Sacramento; whilst Reeves is a Senior Consultant with SIGMA Threat Management Associates (SIGMATMA) and Associate Professor at Winthrop University.

Discussions in interviews focused on methods to report threats, the purpose of threat assessment, potential benefits and downfalls of using this approach, and the role of leakage in the process.

ABOUT THREAT ASSESSMENT

Threat assessment is one of the ways to try to prevent an attack occurring. Interviewee, Heilit Biehl, Adams 12, cautioned organizations against the mindset of "it can't happen here." Instead, the mindset should be one of being prepared, meaning that policies and procedures pertaining to threat assessment should be implemented to allow for threats and concerns to be dealt with. As a method, threat assessment is the process of evaluating the credibility and seriousness of a threat and the context in which it was made. Also assessed are the resources, intentions and motivations of the individual who made the threat in order to ascertain the likelihood of it being carried out (O'Toole, 2000, pp. 5-6). This includes looking at factors such as detailed planning, procurement of weapons, practicing for the attack and possibly attempts to secure assistance for the attack (Spearman, 2019, p. 15). Assessing all these factors is likely to provide a more accurate indication of the threat posed; whereas "the evaluation of a single example of leakage will likely result in an inaccurate and incomplete threat assessment" (Meloy & O'Toole, 2011, p. 12). In contrast to a technique like profiling which focuses on demographic and personal features of an individual, threat assessment is a reactive method triggered by threatening or concerning behavior of some kind (Cornell, 2019, p. 2). To that end, threats should *not* be dismissed on the basis that the individual does not have a history of violence (Spearman, 2019, p. 15). In addition to including violence or harm against others, the risk of suicide or self-harm should also be a primary consideration when carrying out threat assessments (Cacialli, 2019, p. 39).

A threat may be defined as "an expression of intent to do harm or act violently against someone or something" (O'Toole, 2000, p. 6). Threats may be "transient" in nature in that they do not contain a genuine intention of harm to oneself or others and may just be provoked by emotions such as anger. For example, if one person yells that they are going to kill the other during a physical fight. By contrast, "substantive" threats are those which reflect serious intent, including planning and preparing to enact harm. An example would be a written note specifying a time and place to meet and mentioning violence. A very serious substantive threat would be an individual telling a friend that they were going to bring a gun to school and make bullies pay (Burnette, Datta & Cornell, 2017, p. 4; Cornell, 2019, p. 3; Cornell

& Williams, 2012, pp. 509-510). Of key importance in evaluating a threat is whether it contains specific and plausible details, as well as the emotional context in which it was made (O'Toole, 2000, pp. 7-8).

Threats may also vary in their delivery. Some of them are specific individual threats where the individual making the threat and possibly the intended victim(s) are able to be clearly identified. This comes with the challenges of victim-safety planning and conflicting legal requirements around privacy to the individual who made the threat, coupled with the one to ensure a safe environment for all. Another delivery method can be mass threats made online by an anonymous person. This comes with the difficulties of not having information about who made the threat and dealing with possible fear and media attention resulting from the sharing of the threat (Regehr, Glancy, Carter & Rawshaw, 2017). In certain situations, a threat may not even have been made; yet threat assessment can still go ahead based on communications that could indicate a potential threat in the form of leakage (Capellan & Lewanowski, 2018, p. 2). What is important is not whether an individual has made a threat; rather, it is whether they pose a threat. Some individuals who make threats never pose them; whilst others who pose threats may never make threats (Fein, Vossekuil & Holden, 1995, p. 2).

What is critical is that any concerns, including threats and other warning behaviors, are correctly reported to the appropriate authority. In the case of a mass shooting, law enforcement should make members of the public aware of the warning signs and reassure them that any information submitted will be dealt with in a constructive way. What this means is that information gathered about individuals should be evaluated through a two-stage process. The first stage involves examining information for evidence of behaviors and attributes that would be consistent with an attack. The next stage is to ascertain whether the individual appears to be moving towards or away from carrying out an attack. For cases where the conclusion is reached that an individual does not pose a threat, the reported concerns should not affect their lives in a negative way (Capellan & Lewanowski, 2018, pp. 11-12; Fein, Vossekuil & Holden, 1995. p.5).

The remainder of cases where a potential threat is posed should be managed. Intervention plans designed to reduce the risk of the individual committing violence should be formulated. Included in those should be what actions will be taken to address the safety of potential victim(s). Ongoing follow-up and support should be built into case management plans to ensure the threat is effectively dealt with (Cornell, 2013, p. 380; National Threat Assessment Center, 2018, p. 17; Reeves & Brock, 2017, p. 12). An anecdote was shared by Heilit Biehl, Adams 12, about a student in a high school who underwent three threat assessments over a two year period and was subject to constant monitoring: "Because we couldn't feel confident that his risk factors were being reduced externally, we maintained an ongoing intervention strategy of check-in, random person checks." As it transpired, the student did eventually go on to attempt to stab other students with a makeshift weapon and because of the intervention mechanisms in place this was prevented.

In addition to dealing with threats of violence to others, threat assessment also needs to take heed of those relating to self-harm which interviewees claim are far greater in number. Stephen Brock, CSU, said that whilst school shootings receive the most attention "its impact pales in comparison to suicide — it takes far more lives." Heilit Biehl, Adams 12, made a similar point that the majority of reports that come through their reporting hotline Safe2Tell are for suicide concerns. She explained that this can become part of the threat assessment by incorporating this into the initial screening stage, whereby a suicide risk assessment is conducted to determine whether the individual is unsafe to themselves before then assessing if there is any potential harm posed to others. The predictors of suicidal behavior include: individual factors like psychopathology, depression and behavioral disorders; family factors, e.g. poor communication and history of depression; social factors such as being bullied, problems at school; historical factors, e.g. child abuse and previous suicide attempts. Ideally, all members of a threat assessment team should be able to identify the warning signs of suicide (Brock & Reeves, 2017, pp. 3, 10). Suicide risk can also turn into homicidal ideation, explained Melissa Reeves, SIGMATMA, so it is something to be mindful of when carrying out threat assessment.

PUTTING THIS INTO PRACTICE

Gathering the views of experts in this area, coupled with findings from literature, provides an insight about how to put threat assessment into practice. Reporting threats is an important component, as is proper investigation of them. There are also the more practical aspects, such as the composition of the threat assessment team. Learning from past mistakes is also something which can be of value.

Reporting Threats

The first step in the threat assessment process is getting the Intelligence (Intel) about threats and other related concerns. John Nicolletti, Nicolletti-Flater Associates, described the threat assessment team as the "vortex": "They're only as good as the Intel they get from everybody else." To facilitate the process, methods of reporting threats should be accessible and understandable. Some individuals may report threats to the Federal Bureau of Investigation (FBI) or their local law enforcement agency; others may go through specific reporting programs.

Heilit Biehl, Adams 12, shared that in Colorado, the state in which she lives, there is a tip-line called Safe2Tell, which is accessible via telephone, smartphone applications and website. The program also endorses having a trusted adult for school students to report their concerns to. Individuals reporting concerns via Safe2Tell are able to send screenshots or just provide a written or verbal account of their concerns. Over the last year, the Safe2Tell program has changed allowing for information goes to an active dispatch team who are able to have a two-day conversation with individuals. This is said to have had a noticeable impact with reporting having increased: "I think it's made a difference in just people knowing that it's taken seriously, that action is happening."-Heilit Biehl, Adams 12.

Gathering Information

Once a concern or threat has been reported, the next step is to screen/triage it to decide whether the case needs to go to someone else, e.g. community mental health team. Information needs to be collected in order to assess the threat. To help facilitate data collection, the TOADS acronym can be used: *time* to execute their plan; *opportunity* to carry out their plan; *ability* in terms of the capabilities to execute their plan; *desire* to carry out plan; *stimulus* relating to whether any stressors are impacting upon their lives and decision-making (Nicoletti & Spencer-Thomas, 2002). Trying to stop a threat from escalating is generally more successful when an individual is at the beginning of the pathway to violence: "Ideally, we're hearing about it early on when we're seeing the warning signs and we can activate the process for those intervention points."-Heilit Biehl, Adams 12.

The process of gathering information can be made challenging due to social media. SIGMATMA's Melissa Reeves and CSU's Stephen Brock described it as dually being a resource and a problem. Social media can help the threat assessment process with it being a "huge source of information that can be an indicator that something is about to happen."-Melissa Reeves, SIGMATMA. In a school context, she explained, it would be the students who would be more likely to see content on social media than the adults; hence, underlining the importance of training them to report these concerns. A similar point was made by Heilit Biehl, Adams 12, that parents and other adults may not be as knowledgeable about the apps and websites students use. In some cases, parents may not even be aware that their child has a social media presence. It becomes pivotal for the school and wider district to address these gaps in knowledge via education without it coming across as a judgment on parenting. Another challenge relates to privacy requirements. Although it is fine for individuals to share screenshots during the reporting process, the subsequent investigation can be complicated when social media is involved. Heilit Biehl, Adams 12, provides an example of a practice that would be considered rather dubious: "If someone doesn't have an online profile but pretends to be a student and then befriend students around the district to get in on what's happening." A further complication of social media is its reach which "can potentially be so widespread that it can really exacerbate things"-Stephen Brock, CSU.

As part of the process of gathering information, the person of concern should be assessed. With re-gards to the questioning of the individual being assessed, John Nicolletti, Nicolletti-Flater Associates, explained that this process is more straightforward when dealing with an "insider threat," i.e. someone inside the organization. This allows them to meet with the individual to interview and question them; whereas an "external threat" will be an outsider that will require indirect threat assessment.

Assessing Threats

Putting this into practice, information should be gathered from multiple sources to ensure as thorough a picture as possible of the threat and the individual of concern is created. Documentation should be maintained to track when information comes in and from which sources, including online social media pages (National Threat Assessment Center, 2018, p. 7). Once the information has been gathered, the next stage is to perform an assessment. John Nicolletti, Nicolletti-Flater Associates, mentioned that in cases where the threat is "external" — the organization does not have control over the individual making the threat — an indirect threat assessment should be conducted. He explained that for his organization this would involve a trend analysis on their behavior and carry out three ratings based on the following: pro-attack behaviors, e.g. pre-meditated ones relating to weapon of choice; reactive attack behaviors, whereby the individual uses weapons of opportunity during a triggering event; behaviors causing social and psychological disruption, making others feel concerned, fearful and intimidated. The next step is to look at an individual's responsiveness to countermeasures and the effect this has had on risk trajectories, i.e. whether these have went down or remained static. In other words, "pretty much, we just do a strict behavioral trend analysis."-John Nicolletti, Nicolletti-Flater Associates. The National Threat Assessment Center (2018, pp. 9-16) provided a list of the issues that should be assessed:

- Motives, which can give an insight into the student's goals.
- Communications that are bizarre, threatening or violent in nature.
- Inappropriate interests, e.g. an intense interest in previous mass shootings.
- Stressors that the individual is experiencing and how they are coping.
- Emotional and developmental issues like suicidal ideation and depression.
- Whether the individual feels desperate and/or feels violence is the only way to solve a problem.

- Any concerning behaviors raised by others and whether statements made by the individual are consistent with what others say about them.
- Capacity to carry out an attack in terms of resources.
- Whether the individual has made any specific plans.
- Protective factors that may restore hope to the individual.

Ideally, this information should thereafter be assessed using an appropriate tool. A screening tool could be used for a direct threat assessment to gauge whether there is a credible threat. If this is indeed the case then a more detailed tool should be utilized (National Threat Assessment Center, 2018, p. 7). For direct threat assessments, tools can be used to facilitate the assessment process. Heilit Biehl, Adams 12, said that the eleven questions devised by the United States Secret Service are used as the initial screening tool to determine potential for violence. This initial screening could also flag suicidal ideation meaning a suicide risk assessment would be carried out. In cases where the screening does not find a credible threat, the strategy within her organization is still to speak to the student and their parents and then follow-up with them to check how their situation is at a later date. If required, the screening would be followed by a more in-depth structured professional judgment tool, such as the Adams County one, which goes through student and family history, potential for violence, protective factors and so forth. Using this in conjunction with the SIVRA-35 allows for the severity of threats to be cross-checked "It allows us to quantify a bit; it's numerically ranked levels of concern."-Heilit Biehl, Adams 12. The focus on risk and protective factors in the tool can help inform interventions — more will be said on them momentarily.

A tool which encompasses both risk and protective factors will be more effective in determining the level of risk/concern posed (Spearman, 2019, p. 14). It is also pertinent to take heed of the advice provided by Melissa Reeves, SIGMATMA, that "in a good threat assessment, we never base any decision on one data point." To clarify, she explained that the tool could return a rating of low concern; yet it may not capture social media posts or the gun collection that the individual has shown to their friends. Extrapolating from this, whilst tools should inform the threat assessment process, assessors should not rely solely on them to make decisions about the risk posed and appropriate ways to manage risk.

Managing Threats

The final stage in the threat assessment process is to manage the threat. Tools used in the threat assessment process can facilitate with this by identifying risk and protective factors. It is advised by Spearman (2019, p. 14) that "the higher the level of concern, the more directive and intensive supports must be." Intervention strategies are always followed, explained Heilit Biehl, Adams 12, after screening or a full threat assessment as part of a "response management support plan." Interventions should be incorporated into individualized management plans, with strategies to negate violence and appropriate resources allocated to support the individual (e.g. counselling) (National Threat Assessment Center, 2018, p. 17).

According to John Nicolletti, Nicolletti-Flater Associates, the process of managing threats is three-fold in nature. The first part is keeping track of the individual of concern to see if the intervention is working or whether they are continuing or escalating. Secondly, there is target-hardening to keep the affected community safe. The third part is countermeasures, i.e. what can be done to disrupt the individual and how can law enforcement or community members help with this. For the first part of tracking an individual, the challenge comes with "false positives" in cases where "the individual is never intent on doing it but you don't know that so you have to take action anyway."-John Nicolletti, Nicolletti-Flater Associates.

Another element to be mindful of is target switching, as individuals may change their minds about where to target based on what is accessible to them. For instance, the Pulse Nightclub (2016) shooter had initially selected Disney World's shopping complex as a target but switched targets after witnessing the security provisions there (Kerr & Markey, 2020). Another more recent example was during the COVID-19 pandemic, where a man switched his target for a planned bomb attack to a hospital. His previous targets of a school with a large population of Black students, a mosque and synagogue were all closed at the time due to the lockdown imposed to prevent the spread of COVID-19. Had it not been prevented, an attack on a hospital during a public health crisis would have allowed him to kill and injure a large number of targets (New York Times, 2020; TIME, 2020).

Keeping the affected community safe should be addressed and documented in management plans (National Threat Assessment Center, 2018, p. 17). In the case of an entire school community being targeted, explained SIGMATMA's Melissa Reeves, there would need to be visible security and safety measures put in place to try to negate fear. When law enforcement conducts a threat assessment they are responsible for determining if a law has been broken and whether immediate containment is needed. When mental health professionals (e.g. clinical, forensic psychologists) conduct a threat assessment, they can only hospitalize an individual in cases of imminent risk. If there is not an imminent safety concern, therefore, they cannot force an individual into treatment.

Schools, however, are held to a higher standard when it comes to threat assessment: "Law enforcement and mental health providers in the community — they're not responsible for the intervention, but schools are."-Melissa Reeves, SIGMATMA. In cases that occur within institutions like public schools, the organization becomes responsible for also providing the intervention as they must provide educational services. In order to implement effective and appropriate intervention strategies, it must be considered "how do we help them off the pathway to violence."-Melissa Reeves, SIGMATMA. Including individuals as active participants in an intervention helps ensure its effectiveness: "We want to be including them in some kind of appropriate intervention. Excluding only increases the threat."-Stephen Brock, CSU.

For schools, explained SIGMATMA's Melissa Reeves, expelling the individual of concern is "one of the worst things they can do," for this removes the ability to support, supervise and monitor them. This point is backed up by the National Threat Assessment Center's (2018, p. 17) list of recommendations, which maintains that "removing a student from the school does not eliminate the risk to the school community." The study cites instances where attacks were carried out by former students who had been expelled from the school. One of the reasons for this is likely to be the fact that expelling them also runs the risk of disgruntling the individual further: "I say to school administrators all the time 'You've expelled them? You've just potentially made them madder.'"-Melissa Reeves, SIGMATMA. If the threat is legitimate and there must be some punishment, there needs to be "consequences with care" to prevent escalating grievances. There must also always be supports to help them off the pathway to violence.

Once the three parts of managing threats have been enacted, the next part is to follow-up to monitor and re-evaluate the effectiveness of interventions (Cornell, 2009). Follow-up should be holistically included in threat assessment and management, maintained CSU's Stephen Brock. To that end, follow-up should be built into the threat management plan: "You need to establish goals and collect data to show them improving."-Melissa Reeves, SIGMATMA. Since stressors could derail the interventions implemented, these should be recognized and efforts to reduce these should be enacted (National Threat Assessment Center, 2015, p. ii; National Threat Assessment Center, 2018, p. 18). Accordingly, the plan should be revised in cases where there is a continuing threat or an increased risk of violence (Cornell, 2009, p. 13).

Only when there is no longer any concern about the individuals' risk for violence should a management plan cease to exist (National Threat Assessment Center, 2018, p. 17).

Threat Assessment Team

Putting these recommendations into practice firstly requires putting together an effective threat assessment team. As Melissa Reeves, SIGMATMA, explained "The core team is responsible for making a lot of decisions about the level of concern and how are we going to address and mitigate those concerns." The first step should be deciding who should establish threat assessment teams within an organization/collection of organizations (e.g. school district). The next question is around the required expertise of the professionals serving on the team (Spearman, 2019, p. 1). Scholars in this field maintain that administrative, mental health and law enforcement expertise should be part of the team (Cornell & Williams, 2012; Cornell, 2013; National Threat Assessment Center, 2018; Reeves & Brock, 2017). There should also be a designated leader to guide the team, with substitutes in place for instances where the leader is unavailable. The team leader or designee should aim to achieve consensus in decisions reached by the team; however, they will retain sole decision-making authority for cases requiring immediate or decisive action (Cornell, 2009, p. 10).

From her own experience in school threat assessment, Heilit Biehl, Adams 12, explained the roles and disciplines involved. Her own role as a threat assessment coordinator involves overseeing and providing training to threat assessment teams across the entire school district. This role also involves reviewing administrative threat assessments, monitoring patterns relating to threats, schools, etc., and looking out for any gaps in intervention strategies across the entire district. It sits within the discipline known as "case management" or "student engagement." Other disciplines involved in threat assessment include crisis prevention (e.g. mental health and suicide risk representations); student support services to account for behavioral special needs and disabilities; a case manager to assist with human services and resources; law enforcement, usually from a youth division; safety and security services, such as school resource officers or security personnel; administrative support to assist with note-taking and follow-up; a representative from student discipline/conduct to address student code infractions. Reeves and Brock (2017, p. 2) noted that other faculty members familiar with a student of concern such as teachers and counsellors can also be included on a case-by-case basis. There may also be the need for legal counsel (Kloeker-Webster, 2019, p. 66).

It is recommended that threat assessment teams are a distinct group from others that meet to deal with judiciary issues. The frequency of meetings should be dependent upon the caseload to be managed (Cornell, 2009, p. 10). At the screening stage, Heilit Biehl, Adams 12, explained that a minimum of two individuals are required, generally a school district and mental health representative. It is advised that mental health representatives should be exempt from information-sharing limitations, given they are best-placed to watch for mental health issues and flag risk (Cacialli, 2019, pp. 38-39). If this becomes a full threat assessment, law enforcement representation needs to be involved. This is backed up by Reeves and Brock's (2017, p. 2) recommendation that law enforcement professionals should be included for moderate to serious risks.

A challenge involved is the requirement to have these professional disciplines serves on a threat assessment team without any additional funding or resources; hence, schools are "having to do this on top of everything else and pretty much have to try to find a way to do it."-Melissa Reeves, SIGMATMA. Stephen Brock, CSU, explained that training in threat assessment has become a required credential in the school psychology field. Some states have passed laws mandating that K-12 schools establish threat assessment teams; thus school professionals have to be trained in how to conduct the behavioral threat assessment and management process. In some states, whilst this is not written into law, the "ethical expectation is that you [school psychologist] need to have this kind of training now."-Melissa Reeves, SIGMATMA. Exemplifying this is Cacialli's (2019, p. 39) point that due to their expertise and knowledge, mental health professionals may be the most approachable member of the threat assessment team. Moreover, Kloeker-Webster (2019) spoke to chairs from threat assessment teams from various universities in North Carolina to determine the key competencies required. Thirteen competencies were identified: assessment and evaluation, communication, cultural humility and social justice, ethics and professional integrity, information gathering, interpretation of information, knowledge of laws and mandates, knowledge of mental health factors, knowledge of policies and procedures, literacy across disciplines, relationship building, use of technology and use of threat assessment tools and models. It is recommended that more attention is paid to the skills and knowledge development of threat assessment teams to ensure the presence of these competencies.

Challenges

The practical application of threat assessment comes with a host of challenges. The initial challenge comes in convincing people to come forward with any concerns they may have. This requires a "bystander" defined as someone who knows information but takes no action into an "upstander" which is "someone who is doing something and sharing that concern so we can take action"-Heilit Biehl, Adams 12. This may be challenging due to concerns about peer pressure, getting the individual into trouble unnecessarily or not knowing if their reporting will get taken seriously (Weisenbach Keller, Hughes & Hertz, 2011, p. 81). This is particularly the case in a school environment: "Kids don't want to get their friends into trouble or be the one responsible if they're wrong and this kid gets kicked out of school."-Melissa Reeves, SIGMATMA. In the case of Columbine High School (1999), for instance, a "code of silence" was said to have existed, in which students did not want to be seen as "tattling" on their peers (Elliott, 2009, p. 54). A campaign similar to "If you see something, say something" — originally developed by the New York City Metropolitan Transport Authority to encourage reporting of suspicious behaviors — could encourage people to come forward with their concerns (National Threat Assessment Center, 2019, p. 13). In the case of schools, Stephen Brock, CSU, advised that there are "consequences with care." To clarify, if students are suspended or expelled for making a threat without a proper investigation as to whether they actually *pose* a threat, then this will prevent others from reporting concerns as they do not want to feel responsible for another student being removed from school.

On the other side of the coin are "false reports," whereby people misreport in order to defame another individual. Potential cases of "false positives" elucidate the importance of threat assessment investigations being kept confidential to protect the individual under investigation, as well as any potential victims (Cornell, 2009, p. 10). Although these are rare occurrences, Heilit Biehl, Adams 12, explained that discussions are currently taking place within system frameworks on how to deal with a false report. Since false reporting is atypical, however, the focus is primarily on encouraging genuine concerns to be reported even where they turn out to be innocuous.

There is also the question of how to report concerns and to whom. Although at least ten students had concerns about the perpetrator of the Arapahoe High School shooting, only one reported their concerns beforehand to a counsellor. This may have been due to a lack of awareness of where to report information to, since no training was offered on the tip-line Safe2Tell to students or staff members (Williams & Goodrum, 2016, p. 9). It has been recommended that an institution should have multiple ways to report threats to the appropriate team, e.g. online forms, telephone numbers, smartphone apps, in person submissions and letters. This reporting system should be centralized to allow for all reports to be held in the one place, regardless of how they were submitted (Cornell, 2009, pp. 5, 12; Weisenbach Keller, Hughes & Hertz, 2011, pp. 81, 86-87). Something like the Safe2Tell tip-line is a constant resource, because it is funded and run by the state law enforcement agency. In North Carolina, where Melissa Reeves, SIGMATMA, works, a problem has arisen in that state law mandates that every school has a mechanism in place to report threats; yet, the resources are not in place to support it. The consequences of this can be that school psychologists and administrators are expected to take on additional work out of hours, e.g. take a call at 2am on a Saturday. In reality, these types of concerns should be going to law enforcement and/or if suicidal ideation is present community mental health when they occur out-of-school hours. Stephen Brock, CSU, explained that any kind of reporting system has to be a "twenty-four/seven entity" to deal with "twenty-four/seven concerns." Whilst school professionals are well placed to deal with concerns, "our weakness is we work five days a week, eight hours a day. We don't work weekends or holidays."-Stephen Brock, CSU. Proactive monitoring is also important to encourage the reporting of threats to allow those doing so to "feel confident that team members will be responsive to their concerns" (Cornell, 2009, p. 5).

Another issue in a school context is that students frequently make statements or engage in behaviors that could be deemed threatening. Determining which ones actually pose a threat can be testing (Cornell, 2013, p. 380). Erroneous information arising during the threat assessment process can complicate this, either by inflating the seriousness of a transient threat or resulting in complacency around a serious threat. This highlights the need to pay particular attention to patterns of escalation, intensity of effort and focus, evidence of motive, justifications for violence and potential leakage of harm during the assessment process. Another recommendation is to look at whether past or present tense is used in any leakage with post-tense suggesting that the individual considers the attack to be a foregone conclusion (Amman et al., 2017, pp. 8, 18, 35). Additionally, the threat assessment model in place should adequately assess the individual's potential for violence, taking into consideration potential stressors and situations that could provoke this. In the case of the Arapahoe High School attack, the threat assessment tool and process were never validated; hence, there was no way of knowing if it predicted violence. Due to this, follow-up and safety planning were not properly executed (Williams & Goodrum, 2016, pp. 10-11).

As mentioned earlier, intervention strategies and plans devised following a threat assessment process should be individualized. There is a responsibility to the individual making the threat, in addition to legal requirements around maintaining a safety environment for everyone (Regehr, Glancy, Carter & Rawshaw, 2017). There are also civil rights laws and policies to comply with, such as the "Americans with Disabilities" Act (1990). Heilit Biehl, Adams 12, explained that intervention strategies and plans need to take into account learning and emotional disabilities. She explained that if there was a student behaving in a particular way such as blurting out statements and being physically aggressive: "We're more inclined to be cognizant of that and the intervention strategies come from supporting their disability and behavior or disability and condition." This does not mean, however, that there is a right for the student to engage in unsafe behavior that may frighten or injure another student or staff member. The main difference is the approach taken in managing that student: "A disability does not excuse a student from harming others or even that potential; it just has us work in a different manner to understand what the source of this was."-Heilit Biehl, Adams 12.

Protecting individual victims of threats is also a priority (Cornell, 2009, p. 10). This can be made challenging by the information that may be distributed to them under privacy law requirements (SIGMA Threat Management Associates, 2020). Moreover, if threats become known within the affected population — whether these are credible or not — this could result in fear contagion, which could be further exacerbated by social media and possibly media attention (Regehr, Glancy, Carter & Rawshaw, 2017). Inferring from this, demands to maintain a safe environment should be met whilst ensuring the reaction to the threat is proportionate. This is particularly the case in higher education institutes and other environments which are open and accessible to everyone (Weisenbach Keller, Hughes & Hertz, 2011, p. 82).

Learning from past mistakes can be a way to prevent challenges arising in future. Melissa Reeves, SIGMATMA, explained "We're making changes in our approach with every large-scale incident." An incident response evaluation will highlight any failures occurring from the current procedure or how it was implemented (Weisenbach Keller, Hughes & Hertz, 2011, p. 89). A prime example of this was the Columbine school shooting where a post-incident evaluation was carried out: "We looked out what was done wrong and from there modified how do we track these different things."-John Nicolletti, Nicolletti-Flater Associates. Reviews of the Columbine High School (1999) shooting found that a disruption in information flow meant that only a fragmented profile of student behavior was put together. If there had been a clear flow of information through the school, this could have resulted in signs been spotted and dealt with earlier (Elliott, 2009; Fox & Harding, 2005).

A debrief should be held after every mass shooting to assess what was missed. In cases such as the Arapahoe High School and Stoneman Douglas (Parkland) school shootings, "those individuals had a threat assessment done but according to the reports, it was not done well", explained Melissa Reeves SIGMATMA. Additionally, sometimes official reports are conducted after large-scale incidents to determine what was done well and mistakes that were made. Woodward and Goodrum (2016) carried out a report into what happened in the Arapahoe High School attack and concluded there were three major failures relating to internal and inter-agency information sharing and a lack of training relating to anonymous reporting systems like Safe2Tell. There were also issues with the threat assessment model used, whereby only five out of twenty-five possible risk factors were checked. Further to this, the nature of subsequent safety planning and follow-up were inadequate.

CONCLUSION

Findings from the literature and interviews indicate that threat assessment and management is the most effective and holistic approach to deal with mass shooting threats. Recommendations were given about the practical aspects and challenges associated with threat assessment and management. It is hoped this may be useful to those looking to implement such a system within their organization.

Threat assessment and management is reactive, taking place after an intention to do harm or act violently towards oneself or others is expressed. Threat assessment evaluates the credibility and seriousness of a threat. It also considers the resources, intentions and motivations of the individual who made the threat (see Cacialli, 2019; Cornell, 2019; O'Toole, 2000; Spearman, 2019). In cases where it is determined that a potential threat is posed, intervention plans should be drawn up to avert and negate the risk of violence (Cornell, 2013; National Threat Assessment Center, 2018; Reeves & Brock, 2017). Importantly, threat assessment should also consider threats relating to self-harm, which interviewees noted are far greater in number than threats of violence against others. Another aspect to be mindful of is the fact that suicide risk can turn into homicidal ideation, important in the context of mass shootings which tend to be homicide-suicide incidents.

Practical guidance was offered by interviewees and retrieved from the literature around how best to undertake this approach. The first piece of advice centered on ensuring the necessary intelligence reaches the threat assessment team. This requires an easily accessible way to report threats, ideally through multiple channels: telephone, website, smartphone apps and in-person. Something like the Safe2Tell tip-line available in Colorado is ideal as this has multiple methods of reporting and is constantly monitored by state law enforcement. Additionally, individuals within an organization and the wider community need to be encouraged to come forward with any concerns they may have.

Once the initial concern has been documented, information should be gathered from multiple sources, including the individual of concern and those familiar with them, as well as the person(s) who reported the concern. Intelligence can also be retrieved from social media; although this brings challenges in the form of privacy requirements and issues being amplified. The type of information gathered should adhere to the TOADS acronym devised by Nicoletti and Spencer-Thomas (2002): does the individual have *time* and *opportunity* to carry out their plan; do they have the *ability* in terms of the resources to do so; how strong is their *desire* to execute their plan; are there any *stimulus* in the form of whether stressors are affecting their lives and decision-making This process can be facilitated by the use of screening and assessment instruments assessing risk and protective factors.

Results from the assessment stage will inform how to manage the individual to reduce the risk of violence, with those interviewed advising on how best to do this. Firstly, intervention strategies such as counselling should be incorporated into individualized management plans. Potential stressors for the individual should be identified; if these are triggered, the plan should be modified accordingly. Also documented in these plans should be ways to keep the affected community safe (Cornell, 2009; National Threat Assessment Center, 2015, 2018). The individual should be monitored to determine whether the intervention/countermeasures are working and/or whether there is an escalating threat or change in attack planning (e.g. target-switching). Importantly, individuals should be included as active participants in the intervention process and followed-up to ensure the threat has been effectively dealt with. Expelling them from the organization should also be resisted unless absolutely necessary, as it removes the ability to support, supervise and monitor the individual.

To carry out all these tasks, a threat assessment team needs to be in place. Interviewees and scholars (e.g. Cornell & Williams, 2012; Cornell, 2013; Kloeker-Webster, 2019; National Threat Assessment Center, 2018; Reeves & Brock, 2017) note there should be presence from administrative support, mental health, law enforcement, safety and security, and crisis prevention on the team. Support may sometimes be needed from legal counsel, counselling and personnel familiar with the individual of concern. A designated leader should manage the team and have the final decision-making authority. The frequency of team meetings should be dependent upon caseload.

Putting threat assessment into practice comes with a number of challenges. The initial one is convincing "bystanders" with concerns to become "upstanders" who report their concerns. People need to be aware of how to share their concerns and what will happen with them once reported (Weisenbach Keller, Hughes & Hertz, 2011). Interviewees highlighted that any kind of reporting system needs to be a "twenty-four/seven entity," since concerns can arise at any time not just within business hours. Once information is reported, challenges can arise in the form of "false reports" made to defame an individual and erroneous information reported in error. To try to deal with this, particular attention during the threat assessment process should be paid to: patterns of escalation, intensity of effort and focus, stressors, evidence of motive, justifications for violence and potential leakage of harm (Amman et al., 2017). Managing individuals of concern and protecting potential victims may also be testing. Civil rights laws such as the "Americans with Disabilities" Act (1990) and privacy requirements must be adhered to. In terms of the victims of threats, there is the possibility for fear contagion exacerbated by social media (Regehr, Glancy, Carter & Rawshaw, 2017).

In order to deal with potential challenges and make improvements, the threat assessment process should be continuously reviewed. Mistakes from past incidents can be identified and thereafter corrected. For instance, Williams and Goodrum (2016) published a study into what went wrong in the Araphoe High School incident. Threat assessment models and risk assessment tools should be periodically checked to ensure they are fulfilling the necessary purpose. Members in threat assessment teams should be trained on a regular basis to maintain their expertise.

REFERENCES

Amman, M., Bowlin, M., Buckles, L., Burton, K. C., Brunell, K. F., Gibson, K. A., Griffin, S. H., Kennedy, K., & Robins, C. J. (2017). *Making Prevention a Reality: Identifying, Assessing and Managing the Threat of Targeted Attacks*. U.S. Department of Justice, Federal Bureau of Investigation.

Brock, S. E., & Louvar Reeves, M. A. (2017). School Suicide Risk Assessment. *Contemporary School Psychology*, *18*(1).

Burnette, A. G., Datta, P., & Cornell, D. (2017). The Distinction between Transient and Substantive Student Threats. *Journal of Threat Assessment and Management*. Advance online publication.

Cacialli, D. O. (2019). The unique role of and special considerations of the mental health professionals on threat assessment teams at institutions of higher education. *International Journal of Law and Psychiatry*, *62*, 32–44. doi:10.1016/j.ijlp.2018.10.005 PMID:30616852

Capellan, J. A., & Lewanowski, C. (2018). Can threat assessment help police prevent mass shootings? Testing an intelligence-led policing tool. *Policing*, *42*(1), 16–30. doi:10.1108/PIJPSM-07-2018-0089

Cornell, D. (2009). *Recommended Practices for Virginia College Threat Assessment: Prepared for the Virginia Department of Criminal Justice Services' School Safety Center by Dewey Cornell, Ph.D., of the University of Virginia*. https://rems.ed.gov/docs/resources/VA_Recommendations_College_Threat_Assessment.pdf

Cornell, D. (2013). The Virginia Student Threat Assessment Guidelines: An Empirically Supported Violence Prevention Strategy. In N. Böckler, T. Seeger, P. Sitzer, & W. Heitmeyer (Eds.), *School Shootings: International Research, Case Studies and Concepts for Prevention* (pp. 379–400). Springer Science-Business Media. doi:10.1007/978-1-4614-5526-4_17

Cornell, D. (2019). *Overview of the Comprehensive School Threat Assessment Guide (CSTAG)*. Technical report. https://www.curry.virginia.edu/sites/default/files/images/YVP/Comprehensive%20School%20Threat%20Assessment%20Guidelines%20overview%20paper%205-10-19.pdf

Cornell, D., & Williams, F. (2012). Student Threat Assessment as a Strategy to Reduce School Violence. In S. R. Jimerson, A. B. Nickerson, M. J. Mayer, & M. J. Furlong (Eds.), *Handbook of School Violence and School Safety* (pp. 503–514). Routledge.

Elliott, D. (2009). Lessons from Columbine: Effective school-based violence prevention strategies and programmes. *Journal of Children's Services, 4*(4), 53–62. doi:10.5042/jcs.2010.0021

Fein, R. A., Vossekuil, B., & Holden, G. A. (1995). *An Approach to Prevent Targeted Violence*. National Institute of Justice.

Fox, C., & Harding, D. J. (2005). School Shootings as Organizational Deviance. *Sociology of Education, 78*(1), 69–97. doi:10.1177/003804070507800104

Kerr, S. E. M., & Markey, M. A. (2020). Exploring the Phenomenon of Mass Shootings in Public Locations. In G. Crews (Ed.), *Handbook of Research on Mass Shootings and Multiple Victim Violence* (pp. 122–155). IGI Global. doi:10.4018/978-1-7998-0113-9.ch008

Lankford, A., Adkins, K. G., & Madfis, E. (2019). Are the Deadliest Mass Shootings Preventable? An Assessment of Leakage Information Reported to Law Enforcement and Firearms Acquisition Prior to Attacks in the United States. *Journal of Contemporary Criminal Justice, 35*(3), 315–341. doi:10.1177/1043986219840231

Meloy, J. R., & O'Toole, M. E. (2011). The Concept of Leakage in Threat Assessment. *Behavioral Sciences & the Law, 29*(4), 513–527. doi:10.1002/bsl.986 PMID:21710573

National Threat Assessment Center. (2015). *Attacks on federal government 2001-2013: threat assessment considerations*. U.S. Secret Service, Department of Homeland Security.

National Threat Assessment Center. (2018). *Enhancing School Safety Using a threat assessment model: an operational guide for preventing targeted school violence*. U.S. Secret Service, Department of Homeland Security.

National Threat Assessment Center. (2019). *Attacks in Public Spaces – 2018*. U.S. Secret Service, Department of Homeland Security.

New York Times. (2020, March 25). *Man Suspected of Planning Attack on Missouri Hospital Is Killed, Officials Say*. https://www.nytimes.com/2020/03/25/us/politics/coronavirus-fbi-shooting.html

O'Toole, M. E. (2000). The School Shooter: A Threat Assessment Perspective. Washington, DC: F.B.I., U.S. Department of Justice.

Reeves Louvar, M. A., & Brock, S. E. (2017). School Behavioral Threat Assessment and Management. *Contemporary School Psychology, 22*(2), 148–162. doi:10.100740688-017-0158-6

Regehr, C., Glancy, G. D., Carter, A., & Rawshaw, L. (2017). A Comprehensive approach to managing threats of violence on a university or college campus. *International Journal of Law and Psychiatry, 54*, 140–147. doi:10.1016/j.ijlp.2017.06.009 PMID:28687175

Spearman, M. M. (2019). School Based Behavioural Threat Assessment and Management: Best Practices Guide for South Carolina. Columbia, SC: States of South Carolina, Department of Education.

TIME. (2020, March 26). *FBI: Man 'Fatally Injured' During Domestic Terrorism Arrest, Had Plotted Attack on Hospital Amid Coronavirus Pandemic.* https://time.com/5810734/fbi-terrorist-bomb-corona-virus-hospital/

Weisenbach Keller, E., Hughes, S., & Hertz, G. (2011). A model for assessment and mitigation of threats on the college campus. *Journal of Educational Administration, 49*(1), 76–94. doi:10.1108/09578231111102072

Woodward, W., & Goodrum, S. (2016). *Report on the Arapahoe High School Shootings: Lessons Learned on Information Sharing, Threat Assessment and Systems Integrity.* Presented to The Denver Foundation and Colorado SB-15-214: Committee on School Safety and Youth in Crisis.

ADDITIONAL READING

Cornell, D., & Williams, F. (2012). Student Threat Assessment as a Strategy to Reduce School Violence. In S. R. Jimerson, A. B. Nickerson, M. J. Mayer, & M. J. Furlong (Eds.), *Handbook of School Violence and School Safety* (pp. 503–514). Routledge.

National Threat Assessment Center. (2018). *Enhancing School Safety Using a threat assessment model: an operational guide for preventing targeted school violence.* U.S. Secret Service, Department of Homeland Security.

O'Toole, M. E. (2000). The School Shooter: A Threat Assessment Perspective. Washington, DC: F.B.I., U.S. Department of Justice.

Reeves Louvar, M. A., & Brock, S. E. (2017). School Behavioral Threat Assessment and Management. *Contemporary School Psychology, 22*(2), 148–162. doi:10.100740688-017-0158-6

Weisenbach Keller, E., Hughes, S., & Hertz, G. (2011). A model for assessment and mitigation of threats on the college campus. *Journal of Educational Administration, 49*(1), 76–94. doi:10.1108/09578231111102072

KEY TERMS AND DEFINITIONS

False Positives: Individuals who never intend to enact harm to themselves or others but are erroneously identified as a risk anyway.

Follow-Up: The last part of threat management involving monitoring and reevaluating the effectiveness of interventions to ensure risk has been reduced.

Interventions: Strategies to prevent violence and resources to support the individual that should be included in individual management plans.

Substantive Threat: A threat that reflects a serious intention to act violently.

Target Switching: Individuals changing their target of harm based on availability or other reasons.

Threat Assessment: A method to identify individuals of concern on the basis of a threat being made or other concerns being flagged.

Threat Management: This should be coupled with threat assessment to deal with the potential threat.

Threats: This is an expression of an intention to cause harm against someone or something.

Transient Threat: A threat generally provoked by emotion which has no real basis of threat behind it.

Section 3
Responding to Mass Shootings

The theme of this section is to introduce the processes and procedures to prepare for, respond to, and recover from mass shooting scenarios.

Chapter 8
Preparing for a Mass Shooting

ABSTRACT

This chapter discusses ways to prepare for a mass shooting incident. In terms of planning, these types of incidents are referred to as "active shooter situations" in which a shooting is unfolding and the outcome can potentially be affected by the responses to it. Discussed here are the drafting of emergency management plans and which factors should be considered in the planning process. The chapter then moves onto look at the use of drills and other exercises to help prepare for mass shootings. The views of emergency management experts and activists campaigning against active shooter drills are captured. This paves the way for the next chapter, which discusses how to respond and recover from a mass shooting incident.

INTRODUCTION

With their potential to cause a high casualty rate, mass shootings are one of the most dangerous threats an organization can face (Doss & Shephard, 2015, p. 43). It is, therefore, of utmost importance to adequately prepare for such events. For the purposes of planning, an incident of this nature would generally be described as an "active shooter situation." This references a scenario in which a shooting is unfolding and law enforcement and, to a lesser degree, citizens have the potential to affect the outcome with their responses (Blair & Schweit, 2014, p. 4).

The United States Departments of Education and Homeland Security prescribes that a crisis can be successfully managed via the following principles:

1. Prevention, referring to the activities to prevent violent incidents from occurring, e.g. those pertaining to leakage, risk assessment and threat assessment discussed in the previous three chapters;
2. Preparedness, ensuring an organization is ready for crises that are not prevented;
3. Response, including actions to minimize damage when a crisis does transpire;
4. Recovery, referencing activities to repair the long-term damage caused by the crisis (Brock, Jimerson, Hart & Nickerson, 2012, p. 464).

DOI: 10.4018/978-1-7998-3916-3.ch008

Whilst the previous section spoke about activities pertaining to *prevention* of an incident, this and the subsequent chapter examine the remaining three principles. The first principle of *preparedness* refers to the creation and practicing of response plans to ensure the organization is equipped to deal with an active shooter scenario. Particular emphasis should be placed on minimizing loss and lessening the impact of such an event. The next chapter focuses on *response* and *recovery*. Response refers to ways to respond quickly and neutralize the attacker. Recovery is allowing a community to recover from an active shooter event (Northern Illinois University Police Department, 2010, pp. 143-144). Notably, these phases are not distinct; with there being some element of overlap in each. For instance, recovery from a mass shooting may inform future planning efforts (Lindsay, 2012, p. 2). Similarly, the elements are not necessarily sequential nor should equal weighing be given to each (Cronstedt, 2002, p. 12).

Throughout this discussion, results from empirical research with emergency management experts are cited:

- John-Michael Keyes and Ellen Stoddard-Keyes, the co-founders and Executive Director and Operations Director respectively of the I Love U Guys (ILUG) Foundation, which provides emergency management training to schools and other organizations.
- John Nicoletti, one of the founding partners in Nicoletti-Flater Associates, which provides threat assessment and emergency management guidance and training. It works with the I Love U Guys Foundation and security personnel from Columbine High School to provide emergency management training for active shooter situations.
- Stephen Brock and Melissa Reeves, lead authors of the PREPaRE crisis prevention and intervention model used to respond to school violence. Brock is a Professor and School Psychology Program Coordinator at California State University (CSU), Sacramento. Reeves is a Senior Consultant with SIGMA Threat Management Associates (SIGMATMA) and an Associate Professor at Winthrop University.

Also included are extracts from interviews with two of the gun violence prevention groups who expressed views on active shooter drills in schools:

- Brian Malte, executive director of the Hope and Heal Fund (H&HF).
- Shaun Dakin, founder of Parents Against School Shooter Drills (PASSD).

The chapter begins by discussing what the principles of emergency management planning in terms of preparedness, risk management and target-hardening. Next, the considerations when drafting an emergency management plan are discussed. Ways to plan specifically for active shooter incidents are then documented. Training for incidents is thereafter discussed, looking at drills to prepare for active shooter incidents. This discussion sets up the next chapter looking at how response agencies should deal with active shooter incidents and ways in which organizations recover from them.

PREPAREDNESS – GETTING READY TO MANAGE CRISES

Preparedness, as a principle, assumes the occurrence of crises and enhances the capacity of an organization to respond to a variety of incidents (Lindsay, 2012; McEntire, 2020). With its consideration of multiple hazards and threats, emergency management planning is a form of risk management. In this sense, threats determine the risks involved and, thus, the measures to be taken to negate these. The goal of this risk management process "is not to eliminate the risks but to reduce them to manageable levels" (Schneier, 2006, p. 21). Assessing risk tends to be aligned with "possibilistic thinking," entrenched in speculation about what could possibly go wrong. Probabilities can be calculated and managed to ensure adverse outcomes are minimized (Furedi, 2008, pp. 653-654). Part of this process is identifying vulnerabilities that could affect its ability to respond to identified threats and hazards (U.S. Department of Education, 2013, p. 8). To deal with the threat from vulnerabilities, an integrated approach to planning should be adopted. The capabilities of the organization to negate potential risks are fundamental to this (U.S. Department of Homeland Security, 2011, p. 5).

Generally, target-hardening is used to improve the security of an organization to make it more difficult for an attacker to enter and thereafter reach targets. John Nicoletti, Nicoletti-Flater Associates, explained that there is a distinction between "hard" and "soft" targets in both physics and psychology. Something like a military base is a "hard target" with it being well-equipped to detect and deal with threats both physically and in mind-set. By contrast, a grocery store is one of the softest targets:

"From a physics standpoint, grocery stores have one entrance and one exit and they're generally right next to each other. The psychology is the attitude folks go grocery shopping with: you're going in there to get what you need, so you're oblivious and are not going to pick up any signals."-John Nicoletti, Nicoletti-Flater Associates.

Challenges can come with trying to target-harden a location which has already suffered a high-profile mass shooting. Since its inception the Briefings, the bi-annual conference held by the I Love U Guys Foundation, has mainly been held at Columbine High School. From 2019 onwards, however, the decision was reached to shift the conference to an alternative location; this was due to safety concerns arising from an exponential increase in threats to the school around the time of the twentieth anniversary of the attack. Operations Director, Ellen Stoddard-Keyes, explained "it's a visitor attraction," with people walking on to the property and driving by it. The school district has reached the decision not to tear the school down, but further security modifications are going to be made. It is important to note that whilst security systems are put in place to mitigate risks, these are not impervious to exploitation by attackers. An example of this was when the Westside Middle School attackers activated the fire alarm to lure students outside and then began shooting them. Further to this, security systems may also fail to take action when needed (Schneier, 2006, pp. 52, 54).

EMERGENCY MANAGEMENT PLANNING

As part of the planning process, a written document should be drafted detailing what should be done and who is responsible when dealing with crisis situations (McEntire, 2020). Some of the scenarios organizations have to consider are fires, explosions, weather disasters, chemical spills, terrorist attacks and active shooter events. The language varies across organization as to what this is called, ranging from "safety plan" to "crisis plan" or "emergency plan" (Pagliocca & Nickerson, 2001, p. 388). Regardless of what this is called, the content of the plan should be uniform across the board containing: a) leaders designated to manage the crisis; b) a description of the plan itself; c) training and drills that will be undertaken to practice the plan; d) prevention activities; e) intervention methods such as evacuation; f) ways to facilitate recovery (Brock, Jimerson, Hart & Nickerson, 2012, p. 467).

Communicating During a Crisis

Importantly, the description of the plan should list multiple means of crisis communication for both during and after an incident. As John Nicoletti of Nicoletti-Flater Associates explained, this process of crisis communication is three-fold in nature in terms of *how* you let people know what is going on, *what* is actually said and *who* is in charge of making sure this message is relayed. In terms of *how*, this should be done in a timely manner led ideally by an organization's communications department (Cassidy, 2021). Internal notification systems (e.g. loudspeakers, text message alerts) should be used to alert the affected population. In addition to these, communication methods should ideally include the organization's website and social media channels to ensure that updates are received by external persons, e.g. parents whose children are at a school where a shooting has taken place (Coombs, 2012, p. 5; Goodrum & Woodward, 2019, p. 63).

A useful guide for this may be the emergency notification system installed at Virginia Tech University following the shooting there in 2007. There was controversy regarding the institution failing to meet the requirements of the Jeanne Clery Disclosure of Campus Security Policy and Campus Statistics Act, mandating that all colleges and universities participating in federal financial aid programs provide "timely warnings" in emergency situations involving an immediate threat to students and faculty members. The institution was fined for failing to meet these requirements on the day of the shooting and the Clery Act was revised to clarify the meaning of "timely warning" (see Kerr, 2019). At Virginia Tech University, digital signs were installed throughout classrooms and facilities; outdoor sirens and a public address system were installed in six locations throughout the campus, with an "All Clear Signal" once the threat has passed. Notifications are also sent through posts to the university website homepage, university email addresses, and the university hotline. A phone alert system was also rolled out to allow those outside the institution to "opt-in," allowing them to be notified in the case of an emergency. This consists of text messages to mobile devices, phone calls to external cell phones and landlines and emails to non-university addresses (Virginia Polytechnic Institute and State University Office of Emergency Management, 2011, pp. 5-6).

For *what* is said during crisis communication, information should be relayed in a way that is simple and clear (Schwerin, Roggiero, Thurman & Goldstein, 2020; Zhu, Lucas, Bercerik-Gerber & Southers, 2020). Virginia Tech University was also criticized for failing to be specific or urgent in its warning messages sent on the day of the shooting, so this is another consideration for crisis communication (Kerr, 2019). A common problem with emergency communication, such as in the case of fires, can be people thinking they are false alarms and ignoring them (Zhu, Lucas, Bercerik-Gerber & Southers, 2020). Notifications should relay the ongoing status of the incident and let people know when it has ended (U.S. Department of Health and Human Services, 2014, p. 13). Furthermore, it is recommended that codes such as "code blue" are avoided, because they will not be understood by external persons visiting an organization or a public location like a shopping mall: "You'd rather have shots fired, because then tactically you know what to do"-John Nicoletti, Nicoletti-Flater Associates. The only exception to this would be in cases where it is prudent to prevent panic. For instance, in a hospital situation where there are patients and visitors, it would be best to stick with codes to avoid escalating panic.

Lastly, *who* is responsible for relaying this message is important to ensure it is carried out promptly. Rapid notification of a threat during a crisis can help keep people out the site of danger. Emergency notification systems should alert local law enforcement, hospitals and other first responders of the need to respond (U.S. Department of Homeland Security, 2008, p. 6). It is imperative that multiple first responder agencies are then able to communicate with each other during a crisis and are aware of who is responsible for relaying information under which circumstances (U.S. Department of Education, 2007, p. 10). The emergency management plan should detail the responsibilities of individuals involved and their contact information, as well as information for hospitals in the local area (U.S. Department of Homeland Security, 2008, p. 6).

Drafting the Plan

In terms of the drafting of an emergency management plan, there are numerous considerations. First and foremost planning should represent the entire affected population and all of its needs (U.S. Department of Homeland Security, 2010, p. 1-1). The core planning team should include representatives from a range of groups:

- those with disabilities and/or access and functional needs, ensuring none are left behind;
- racial minorities and religious groups;
- the core population likely to be affected by an incident (e.g. students, parents and teachers in a school context);
- local, regional and national first responders;
- mental health and public officials;
- local emergency management team members.

Including all those groups should ensure a plan is as comprehensive as possible and contains the following facets: customized to the type of building(s) involved; consideration of all threats and hazards in different settings and times; provision of the access and functional needs of the entire community, e.g. non-English speaking persons, those with physical disabilities; places to shelter if appropriate and alternatives in case those locations are not available. The finished plan should detail the building schematics, including door and window locations, access codes if needed, escape routes, floor plans, and advance notice of where those who may face a challenge evacuating (e.g. those with physical disabilities, pregnant women) are likely to be located (Mincin, 2019; U.S. Department of Education, 2013, pp. 5-6, 58; U.S. Department of Health and Human Services, 2014, p. 11; U.S. Department of Homeland Security, 2008, p. 6).

It is recommended by the U.S. Department of Education (2013, pp. 29-35) that the plan be divided into multiple sections. A Basic Plan section can provide an overview of the approach that will be taken to deal with crises. There could also be a Functional Annexes section, detailing goals, objectives and operational functions that apply depending on the threat or hazard faced. Threat and hazard specific annexes could provide further details about the actions that will be taken pertaining to different types of threats and hazards. There could also be annexes for the following functions: Communications and Warnings, detailing communication and coordination during crises; Security, detailing ways to secure the organization from internal and external threats. In terms of specific actions to take during an event, there could be annexes for the various actions that could be taken: lockdown, securing the building(s) during an incident; lockout, when the affected population remain indoors because the threat is outside; evacuate in cases where there is greater safety outside the building; shelter, tending to be used for weather and other natural disasters (Goodrum & Woodward, 2019, pp. 60-61). Another possible annex could be accounting for all persons, used for determining the whereabouts of the population following the crisis. For recovering following a crisis, there could be a number of annexes: Public Health, Medical and Mental Health, focusing on physical and mental recoveries; Continuity of Operations, detailing how to ensure functions continue during a crisis and its aftermath; Recovery, focusing specifically on the recovery of the organization and wider community following an incident. The plan should be written in a way that is understandable to a broad audience, i.e. using plain language, making use of visual aids, and avoiding abbreviations and jargon. To ensure compliance with the "Americans with Disabilities Act," accessible formats such as Braille and audio should also be available (U.S. Department of Education, 2013, pp. 17-19).

Once the plan is finalized, it should be shared with community partners, stakeholders, first responders and designated staff members at the organization. Roles for first responders and staff members should be clearly outlined and contact details should be up-to-date. Response agencies should be included in practicing the plan via drills and exercises. There should be integration with the facility and incident commander to ensure a common language across all response agencies and compatibility with communication systems (e.g. radios) (Doss & Shephard, 2015, p. 42; U.S. Department of Education, 2013, pp. 16, 58; U.S. Department of Education, 2007, p. 10; U.S. Department of Health and Human Services, 2014, p. 10). Generally, the Incident Command System is used to centralize, organize and coordinate emergency response (Brock, Jimerson, Hart & Nickerson, 2012, p. 466). The emergency management plan should continually be reviewed and updated (U.S. Department of Health and Human Services, 2014, p. 10). Although not quite a "live document," it is important to record any changes to the building, population, and so forth; as well as to ensure new and changing hazards are taken into consideration. Importantly, as Greenberg (2007, p. S58) cautions, it should not be presumed that the plan is clearly understood by the organization's population or that one-off training will prepare them for an active shooter situation.

PREPARING FOR ACTIVE SHOOTER INCIDENTS

Active shooter events are one of the scenarios that should be considered when putting together an emergency management plan. This is a scenario in which the perpetrator(s)'s activity is immediately causing death or injury. A dynamic situation would be one that is evolving rapidly; whereas a static one suggests the actions of the perpetrator(s) appear to be contained (McGinty, 2011). Given the mass casualty potential of these incidents, there are further considerations when planning for them. Firstly, these have the potential to take place in a variety of locations. Out of a hundred and sixty mass shootings occurring from 2000 to 2013, 45.6% took place in commerce (businesses, malls), 24.4% in educational environments, 10% in governmental properties, 9.45% in open spaces, 4.9% in residences, 2.5% in healthcare facilities and 3.8% in places of worship (Blair & Schweit, 2014, p. 13). Emergency management plans, where possible, should be adapted for the type of location: for instance, an educational institution has a very different population and requirements to those of a place of worship. Linking in with this, any security systems put in place for an organization should extend beyond its buildings. For instance, the National Threat Assessment Center's (2015) report on attacks on federal government buildings recorded that almost three-quarters of perpetrators commenced their attacks outside of a facility. Similarly, Blair and Schweit's (2013, p. 12) review of a hundred and sixty mass shootings found that 15% of incidents involved more than one location. Further to this, three incidents occurred at the security checkpoints inside the building. Given the amount of patients it deals with and the numbers of different departments it houses, hospitals and other healthcare institutions have particular challenges in planning and response, (Schwerin, Roggiero, Thurman & Goldstein, 2020, p. 1). Trying to plan for open spaces such as public parks is also tricky; although local response agencies should have a plan in place to ensure their response to such an attack is coordinated.

A more unsettling aspect of emergency management planning for active shooter incidents is considering the potential of an internal attacker. This individual would, therefore, know about the layout of the building, the procedures to be undertaken in response to an attack and so forth. It also means that they could pretend to be another frightened victim of the attack in order to lure people into a certain place (Doss & Shepherd 2015, p. 53; Northern Illinois University Police Department, 2010, p. 64). That is why it is pertinent for emergency management plans to also include a degree of prevention, i.e. what actions will be taken to identify individuals within the organization who may have the capacity to carry out a violent attack (U.S. Department of Health and Human Services, 2014, p. 11).

An additional consideration for emergency management planning pertaining to active shooter incidents is the unpredictability and speed of such an event. Lessons learned from previous incidents show these take place in target-rich environments and involve unpredictable behavior from perpetrators (McGinty, 2011). In terms of unpredictability, this can also affect how people react. John Nicoletti, Nicoletti-Flater Associates, explained that in the mass shooting at the Aurora Theater (2012) "decoding error" occurred in people who were there: "It [what was happening] didn't make sense and the brain didn't register." He further explained that this could be related to the dynamics of where it was taking place, for the opening nights of movies can sometimes feature patrons wearing costumes. Moreover, the attack started during a scene of the film where there was shooting, so people might have theorized that it was a 4D film and that the person in the gas mask shooting could have been part of the experience. There are also a variety of scenarios for how a shooting might end:

- Mobile crisis, where the shooter continues to fire whilst on the move.
- Fleeing suspect, whereby the shooter has left the scene but remains in close proximity.
- Suicidal intent, in situations where the shooter either threatens suicide or actually commits suicide.
- Investigation, for scenarios where the shooter has been captured and arrested (Greenberg, 2007, p. S60).

These are only some of the potential scenarios, emergency management planning should consider others ones which could take place.

With regards to the speed of active shooter attacks, out of sixty-three incidents where duration could be determined 69.8% of these ended in five minutes or less. In 23.1% of incidents, the shooter committed suicide before the police could arrive (Blair & Schweit, 2014, pp. 8, 10). The worst mass shooting in modern United States history lasted approximately eleven minutes and resulted in the deaths of 58 and more than 700 people being injured (Las Vegas Metropolitan Police Department, 2018). The implications of this are although law enforcement response should be swift and efficient, the individuals affected may have to deal with the incident to some degree (U.S. Department of Health and Human Services, 2014, p. 18). This notion is furthering the ideas about expanding the concealed carry of firearms to public locations, including universities, as a means to deal with potential attacks (see Morse, Sisneros, Perez &

Sponsler, 2016; Rizzi, 2015; Stroud, 2015 for further information). Interviewee, Stephen Brock, CSU, argued that this is rooted in a disproportionate perception of risk:

You are more likely to be the victim of a homicide in a restaurant than you are in a school. When was the last time you heard an argument about the need to arm waiters and waitresses? The logic just befuddles.

In Blair and Schweit's (2014, p. 10) study, it was found that any shooting was generally done by law enforcement. Only 3.1% of incidents involved an armed citizen exchanging gunfire with the attacker. Off-duty law enforcement officers engaged and killed the perpetrator in 1.3% of cases.

It is instead far more likely that any citizens would need to help with more practical aspects such as reunification and medical response. An example of this was the Las Vegas mass shooting (2017), which took place at an open air concert. Due to the size of the event, the response task force struggled to reach the victims. Interviewee, Ellen Stoddard-Keyes, ILUG, explained that because a lot of the crowd were trained in medical techniques like "stop the bleed and transport" this helped treat victims in the interim: "There could have been more causalities, if it had been a different audience." In organizations like schools and businesses, there should be staff members who are trained in a range of medical techniques who those with responsibility for managing the situation may be able to assist if required. With active shooter events being so unpredictable, there may be times when impromptu action is required; the best way to ensure this is successful is to prepare for the unexpected by building a degree of flexibility into planning. Furthermore, greater emphasis should be placed on countermeasures to stall shooters before law enforcement arrives (Zhu, Lucas, Bercerik-Gerber & Southers, 2020, p. 6).

EXERCISING PLANS

Once an emergency management plan is in place, the next stage could be the possible execution of parts of it depending on what scenario actually transpires. This is two-fold in nature: mitigation in order to eliminate or reduce injuries during an incident as well as its impact; response, which is carrying out the appropriate actions during a situation (Goodrum & Woodward, 2019, pp. 54, 59). For the mitigation part, this has to be reactive to a certain degree, for it is impossible to foresee every possible risk and plan for it (Sjoberg, Peterson, Froom, Boholm & Hanson, 2005, p. 614). Moreover, security systems put in place to negate risk have the possibility to fail or be exploited (Schneier, 2006, pp. 52, 54). An emergency management plan has the potential to provide a false sense of security unless it is realized that: a) not every risk can be predicted; b) security systems will not protect against every potential threat. As highlighted in the previous sections, the plan should be adaptable to some degree to cope with the unfolding situation (Coombs, 2012, p. 106). An example of this is an active shooter situation changed into a hostage one, meaning it required a different response, e.g. the presence of bomb squads and hostage negotiators (U.S. Department of Education, 2007, p. 7). In terms of the response part to carry out the appropriate actions, this can also be vulnerable to pitfalls. For instance, if response agencies are fixated on receiving "complete information" this could slow down operations. There may be breakdowns in communication, perhaps arising from a lack of channels and routines, a lack of trust or narrow definitions of what is unfolding. Additionally, too much reliance on command and control could be detrimental, with responses needing a degree of flexibility built into them (Boin & t'Hart, 2010, pp. 360-361).

One of the ways to ensure that response is as effective as it can be is to *exercise* the emergency management plan. In their research with participants who have expertise in emergency preparedness, Zhu and colleagues (2020) found that training and drills were the factors most recommended to enhance response to incidents. That will ensure it "takes into account all aspects of the process" (Doss & Shepherd, 2015, p. 50). In the example cited in the U.S. Department of Education's (2007, p. 12) study, it was found that students in wheelchairs and other mobility devices had difficulty navigating to the outdoor evacuation location which was in a field with rough terrain. There are a variety of ways to exercise the plan to ensure it meets all needs:

- Table-top exercises, which are small group discussions talking through a scenario and the actions needed.
- Drills, whereby the buildings are used to practice responding to a situation.
- Functional exercises, which are drills involving multiple partners and involve realistic, simulated events.
- Full scale exercises, whereby a drill is conducted among various agencies and partners using equipment and communications systems (U.S. Department of Education, 2013, p. 21).

In the United States, one of the frameworks that used to carry out specific actions during a crisis is the "Standard Response Protocol." The purpose of it is to "simplify and standardize the actions and language used by stakeholders facing a safety emergency" (Goodrum & Woodward, 2019, p. 49). The specific actions in the SRP are Hold, Secure, Lockdown, Evacuate and Shelter. Depending on the context, the directives can serve both as nouns, e.g. "We are in a lockdown" and verbs, e.g. "lockdown." The lockdown directive is used in cases where there is a threat or hazard inside the building and contains the verbal command "Lockdown! Locks, lights, out of sight!" The secure directive, by contrast, is for scenarios in which there is a threat or hazard outside the building, with the verbal command: "Secure. Get inside. Lock outside doors." When evacuation from one location to another is needed, the evacuate directive is used. Its verbal command is "Evacuate to…" with the name of the new location being announced. The shelter directive is for cases where shelter is required, e.g. when there is a hurricane. A "train-the-trainer" model is available for the SRP. This is useful in allowing for more people to be able to train others within their organization in the program (Goodrum & Woodward, 2019, p. 49; Schildkraut, 2019, pp. 3, 29). The Executive Director of the I Love U Guys Foundation, John-Michael Keyes, explained that there is now an adult version of the SRP, which is used in all city and county buildings in Denver. Training videos and other materials are being formulated for this municipal version.

In 2017, the SRP became the SRP-X, adding a fifth element of "Hold" to the model. When questioned about why the fifth element was introduced to the SRP, it was explained by John-Michael Keyes, ILUG, that this was initially trialed in 2015 as an optional fifth action and based on feedback the organization received about it they decided to integrate it into the SRP. Furthermore, the "Hold" directive is "probably the one used most often because when stuff happens we need to keep kids out of the hallways."-John-Michael Keyes, ILUG. There were also some further changes made to the terminology in the SRP, with the "lockout" directive being replaced by "Secure." Essentially, it is the same directive of getting inside the building and locking the outside doors just with a different term. The reasoning behind this was due to the confusion between lockout and lockdown: "When they heard the word 'lock' they immediately went into 'down.'"-John-Michael Keyes, ILUG. Moreover, the "Secure" directive also allows for evolution of the action, whereby it could be changed to monitoring entry in terms of controlling who comes into the building. Ellen Stoddard-Keyes, ILUG, explained that people can feel that they cannot veer from the absolute directive, probably due to a fear of litigation; therefore, this shift in the "Secure" directive "relaxes that and lets it [the directive] evolve as a potential situation is evolving." This comes back to the argument made earlier that emergency management plans should have a degree of flexibility built into them to account for the situation that is unfolding. John-Michael Keyes, ILUG, highlighted that people should have greater latitude in their options in order to "introduce some flexibility that's situationally appropriate."

The SRP may become more widespread throughout the United States. The Foundation is expanding its partnerships throughout the country, e.g. a recent one being the Texas School Safety Center. I Love U Guys Foundation have joined forces with Partnered with Love, which allows it to offer organizations various ways to become a partner. The implications of this are building sustainability and another layer of accountability. Additionally, I Love U Guys is also expanding internationally. Occasional training takes place in Canada and a partnership has been forged with Smoothwall, a British company expanding into the United States. John-Michael Keyes, ILUG, shared that this presents opportunities for training the SRP internationally: I think the partnership with Smoothwall is an opportunity to look at other English-speaking countries initially and go from there."

ACTIVE SHOOTER DRILLS IN SCHOOLS - TRAUMATIZING CHILDREN?

Recently, there has been criticism of drills and exercises, with the argument being made that these traumatize children. For instance, the President of the National Education Association said that realistic drills "can frighten, terrorize and traumatize" both staff and students at the school. The NEA has advocated that drills in which weapons are drawn, and actors and fake blood are used should be abolished. It also maintained that students and parents should be informed ahead of drills (CBS News, 2020). A couple of the gun violence prevention groups interviewed also provided critical commentary on school shooter drills. One of the organizations is called Parents Against School Shooter Drills and its mission is to "change the dynamic around the endless drilling in American schools."-Shaun Dakin, PASSD. It is claimed by Shaun Dakin, PASSD, that drills traumatize children, so ending these would "let kids become kids again." The other argument advanced is that because most school shooters are internal attackers, going through active shooter drills means "we're actually teaching the potential shooter exactly what the protocol is."-Shaun Dakin, PASSD. The alternative suggestion advanced by Shaun Dakin, PASSD, is for staff members at the school to be trained in active shooter drills and for students to only receive fire drills. In a similar vein, Brian Malte, H&HF, wrote a blog post making similar points about active shooter drills traumatizing children (Malte, 2019). When I asked him about this in our interview, he said this came from listening to people and receiving their emails detailing how scared their children are going through these drills: "I've talked to parents who don't even want to send their kids to school if there is an active shooter drill."-Brian Malte, H&HF. Moreover, he argued that schools are taking drills to the extremes by using fake blood and making children stand on toilets so the attackers cannot see their feet. It was also argued that in ethnic minority communities having a police presence in the school could be counterproductive: "Depending on where you live, it's a different view of how to handle school shootings."-Brian Malte, H&HF.

With I Love U Guys offering training in the SRP and advocating drilling this procedure, their response to criticisms of active shooter drills in schools was sought. ILUG's Executive Director, John-Michael Keyes, explained that there has been confusion about the different between a drill and an exercise:

With a drill, you want to create muscle memory. You want to practice the action but we don't recreate or simulate events during a drill. It's an exercise where we might simulate an event in order to test capacity.

With this distinction, exercises might involve fake blood and other frightening aspects since they are simulations of an event. Due to this, "we advise being very deliberate in the decision of whether or not to engage students and staff in an exercise."-John-Michael Keyes, ILUG. Turning to empirical research in this area finds mixed results. One study explored whether crisis drills improved children's knowledge and skills, in addition to whether it increased anxiety and skewed perceptions of school safety. Seventy-four children participated in a training session and intruder drill or a placebo control condition and thereafter completed measures to record their feelings. It was found that the children who participated in drills had higher levels of knowledge and their feelings of anxiety and school safety were similar to those who were in the control group (Zhe & Nickerson, 2007). Likewise, a study by Schildkraut and Nickerson (2020) found that students, faculty and staff members noted greater feelings of preparedness following lockdown training. Scoring particularly highly were the elements of locking doors (89%), turning lights off (85%) and not responding to door knocks (91%). Another study by Schildkraut (2019) tested the SRP in the Syracuse City School district. A marked improvement in lockdown effectiveness after training in the SRP was found for all schools that took part in the research. The post-training survey following the second lockdown drill, however, indicated that students were less likely to document feeling safe than students who had not engaged in drills. It is theorized that the continual drilling throughout the school year highlighted perceived vulnerabilities for the students, making them feel less safe at school (Schildkraut, 2019, p. 10).

Further to this, some of the training for active shooter events in schools and other organizations focuses on the "Run, Hide, Fight" technique. This operates on a continuum, with fight being the last resort. The first advised course of action is to *run* to somewhere safe. In cases where this is not possible, the next recommendation is to *hide* in a safe location. When neither of these is possible, the next option is to *fight* the attacker, possibly using nearby items (U.S. Department of Health and Human Services, 2014, p. 21). It was found this transpired in 13.1% of incidents, whereby unarmed citizens restrained the shooter in some way (Blair & Schweit, 2014, p. 10). Similarly, ALERRT have a protocol they teach called "Avoid, deny, defend." This consists of avoiding the attacker where possible, denying them access and the last option is defending oneself (Martaindale & Blair, 2019, p. 352). There have been some criticisms of these kinds of techniques. Although there have been incidents where unarmed citizens have physically restrained the attacker, this is extremely dangerous and could result in a higher death toll. With regards to the *run* option, ILUG's Ellen Stoddard-Keyes, pointed out that if people do not know the shooter's whereabouts then this will likely cause a higher casualty rate. This scenario actually transpired in the case of the Parkland (2018) school shooting. Furthermore, this point was also backed up by a study carried out by Lee and Oietz (2018) which found that when an automated door lock system is used for a lecture hall this increases the shooter's time in the hallway; resulting in fewer causalities within the locked lecture hall but an increased number of deaths for individuals attempting to evacuate via the hallway. A further point was made by John-Michael Keyes, ILUG, that this RHF technique is not child-friendly nor is it compliant with the Americans with Disabilities Act.

CONCLUSION

This chapter went through the last three principles of crisis management as prescribed by the United States Department of Education and Department of Homeland Security: preparedness, response and recovery. The component of preparedness is ensuring an organization is prepared should an event transpire. Entrenched within preparedness is risk management, looking at the capacity of an organization to deal with potential vulnerabilities (U.S. Department of Education, 2013; U.S. Department of Homeland Security, 2011; Schneier, 2006). One component of this can be target-hardening to turn an organization into a "hard target," which makes it difficult for an attacker to enter and reach potential targets due to heightened security, awareness and security measures such as metal detectors. By contrast, a "soft target" could be one in which there is a lack of security and the population is unaware of any threats. In spite of this, an organization should not become too reliant on target-hardening to negate risks, because these have the potential to fail when needed or be exploited by potential attackers (Schneier, 2006).

This raises the other facet of preparedness in the form of an emergency management plan. This plan should be drafted, shared with relevant partners, revised, practiced and enacted if the situation calls for it. The first stage of drafting the plan requires careful consideration of various elements: how to prevent violent incidents from occurring; numerous scenarios that might arise; who will manage the crisis, including within the organization and externally with first responders; ways to practice the plan and frequency of doing so; methods of communication during and after a crisis; how the organization will help its affected population and wider community recover following an incident (see Brock, Jimerson, Hart & Nickerson, 2012; Coombs, 2012; Goodrum & Woodward, 2019; U.S. Department of Education, 2013; U.S. Department of Health and Human Services, 2014). To draft this plan, it is important to have input from a variety of groups: those with disabilities and functional needs, ethnic minorities, community partners, first responders, emergency managers, internal spokespersons from various roles within the organization, and mental health practitioners. This will allow for a fuller consideration of needs and requirements: for instance, making sure there is an evacuation plan for those who may face physical challenges. Once a draft of the plan is available, this should be shared with relevant partners, such as first responders, community members and designated staff members at the organization. The plan should never be considered "complete"; instead it should be periodically reviewed and updated to take stock of new challenges, changes to the organization and record lessons learned from any incidents or near misses that have occurred. Moreover, the plan should have a degree of reactivity built into it to match the situation unfolding. As theorists in this area (see, for example, Coombs, 2012; Sjoberg, Peterson, Froom, Boholm & Hanson, 2005) note, it is not possible to foresee every potential risk; henceforth, believing that an emergency management plan does this has the potential to create a false sense of security. To that end, planning for crises should never be considered complete (McEntire, 2020).

One of the scenarios that should be considered for organizations in the United States is "active shooter events," where a shooter(s) is attacking people with the intention to harm. Integral to planning for these types of scenarios is trying to consider how to deal with the following components. Active shooting incidents could be perpetrated by an internal attacker with knowledge of the building(s), security procedures and so forth. These events may take place in a variety of locations, including outside buildings. Furthermore, active shooter events tend to be over very quickly, sometimes before law enforcement has the time to arrive (Blair & Schweit, 2014; Doss & Shepherd, 2015; National Threat Assessment Center, 2015; Northern Illinois University Police Department, 2010; U.S. Department of Education, 2013; U.S. Department of Health and Human Services, 2014). Considering all of this, planning should take into account these potential issues and suggest ways to deal with them. For instance, if an active shooter event takes place over multiple locations then there should be mechanisms in place to deal with affected populations at each site, such as exit points, hiding places, reunification locations, and first responders should visit each targeted area.

In order to effectively execute the next principle of crisis planning of "response," the emergency management plan needs to be practiced. This can be via methods like drills and exercises and can be assisted via the use of a designated framework. A framework that is used in a number of schools and other organizations such as workplaces in the United States is the "standard response protocol" (SRP). This protocol was designed by the I Love U Guys, a non-profit organization that seeks to improve school safety. The protocol was updated to the SRP-X in 2017, consisting of five elements: lockdown (securing the building during an incident); secure (previously known as lockout, where the threat is outside the building); evacuate (leave the building); shelter (go to a designated shelter point); and hold (remain static as the threat may be in the hallway). These five elements are practiced in drills.

Interestingly, there has been some debate recently about the potential harmful effect of active shooter drills in schools. Two of those interviewed claimed that these traumatize children, with one even noting that it teaches students the procedure which could be exploited by them if they were to become a school attacker. Responding to this criticism, the director of the I Love U Guys Foundation maintained there is a distinction between drills and exercises, with the former being about training "muscle memory" and the latter employing the more frightening elements such as fake blood. The interviewees from the I Love U Guys Foundation were critical of the "run, hide, fight" technique sometimes taught in training for active shooter situations. They maintained that it could be counterproductive in cases where the attacker is in the hallway and someone attempts to "run." It is also argued that this technique — particularly the fight element — is not really suitable for children or for those with disabilities. Empirical research in this area gives mixed results. Zhe and Nickerson (2007) found that children who participated in school drills possessed higher levels of knowledge; but no increase in feelings of school safety or anxiety. In 2019, Schildkraut found that students who participated in numerous drills were surveyed as feeling less safe; yet there was an improvement in lockdown effectiveness for schools that took part in the research. Considering all of this, it is difficult to draw definitive conclusions about whether active shooter drills are harmful to children in schools. There is definitely value in practicing scenarios within an emergency management plan, however, so it likely that this type of training will continue in schools and other organizations across the United States.

REFERENCES

Blair, J. P., & Schweit, K. W. (2014). A study of active shooter incidents, 2000-2013. Washington, DC: Texas State University and F.B.I., U.S. Department of Justice.

Boin, A., & 't Hart, P. (2010). Organising for effective emergency management: Lessons from research. *Australian Journal of Public Administration*, 69(4), 357–371. doi:10.1111/j.1467-8500.2010.00694.x

Brock, S. E., Jimerson, S. R., Hart, S. R., & Nickerson, A. B. (2012). Preventing, Preparing for and Responding to School Violence with the PREPaRE Model. In S. R. Jimerson, A. B. Nickerson, M. J. Mayer, & M. J. Firlong (Eds.), *Handbook of School Violence and School Safety: International Research and Practice* (2nd ed., pp. 463–474). Routledge.

CBS News. (2020, February 14). *Schools' active shooter drills face criticism for causing "trauma and fear."* https://www.cbsnews.com/news/active-shooter-drills-at-public-schools-face-criticism-two-years-after-marjory-stoneman-douglas-shooting/

Coombs, T. W. (2012). *Ongoing Crisis Communication: Planning, Managing and Responding* (3rd ed.). Sage.

Doss, K., & Shepherd, C. (2015). *Active Shooter: Preparing for and Responding to a Growing Threat.* Butterworth-Heinemann.

Furedi, F. (2008). Fear and Security: A Vulnerability-led Policy Response. *Social Policy and Administration, 42*(6), 645–661. doi:10.1111/j.1467-9515.2008.00629.x

Goodrum, S., & Woodward, W. (2019). *Colorado School Safety Guide.* Attorney General's Office.

Greenberg, S. F. (2007). Active shooters on college campuses: Conflicting advice, role of the individual and the need to maintain perspective. *Disaster Medicine and Public Health Preparedness, 1*(5), 557–561. doi:10.1097/DMP.0b013e318149f492

Kerr, S. E. M. (2019). Emergency Management and Communication Improvements: Changing the Landscape of School Safety. In G. Crews (Ed.), *Handbook of Research on School Violence in American K-12 Education* (pp. 474–493). IGI Global. doi:10.4018/978-1-5225-6246-7.ch024

Las Vegas Metropolitan Police Department. (2018). *LVMPD Preliminary Investigative Report: 1 October. Mass Casualty Incident.* LVMPD. https://assets.documentcloud.org/documents/4356142/Las-Vegas-Police-Report-on-Oct-1.pdf

Lee, J. Y., & Oietz, J. E. (2018). Assessing the Effectiveness of Automatic Door Lock System by Discharge Detection to Lower Casualty during an Academic Active Shooter Incident. *Proceedings of the 2018 AJC International Conference.*

Lindsay, B. R. (2012). *Federal Emergency Management: A Brief Introduction.* Congressional Research Service.

Martaindale, M. H., & Blair, J. P. (2019). The Evolution of Active Shooter Response Training Protocols Since Columbine: Lessons from the Advanced Law Enforcement. *Journal of Contemporary Criminal Justice, 35*(3), 342–356. doi:10.1177/1043986219840237

McEntire, D. A. (2020). Emergency Management: Preparedness and Planning. In L. R. Shapiro & M. H. Maros (Eds.), Encyclopedia of Security and Emergency Management. Springer Nature.

McGinty, J. (2011). Active Shooter Awareness Virtual Roundtable Webinar. Washington, DC: Homeland Security: National Protection and Programs Directorate Office of Infrastructure Protection.

Mincin, J. (2019). Emergency Management: Working with Vulnerable Populations. In L. R. Shapiro & M. H. Maros (Eds.), Encyclopedia of Security and Emergency Management. Springer Nature.

Morse, A., Sisneros, L., Perez, Z., & Sponsler, B. A. (2016). Guns on Campus: The Architecture and Momentum of State Policy Action. Washington DC: NASPA (Student Affairs Administration in Higher Education.

National Threat Assessment Center. (2015). *Attacks on federal government 2001-2013: Threat assessment considerations*. Washington, DC: U.S. Secret Service, Department of Homeland Security.

Northern Illinois University Police and Public Safety Department. (2010). *Lessons learned in response and recovery: Northern Illinois University*. Northern Illinois University Police and Public Safety Department.

Pagliocca, P. M., & Nickerson, A. B. (2001). Legislating School Crisis Response: Good Policy or Just Good politics? *Law & Policy*, *23*(3), 373–407. doi:10.1111/1467-9930.00117

Rizzi, C. (2015). A duty to protect: Why gun-free zones create a special relationship between the government and victims of school shootings. *Cornell Journal of Law and Public Policy*, *25*(2), 499–526.

Schildkraut, J. (2019). *Implementing and Testing the Standard Response Protocol: Final Report*. New York: A Report presented to the Syracuse City School District.

Schildkraut, J., & Nickerson, A. B. (2020). Ready to Respond: Effects of Lockdown Drills and Training on School Emergency Preparedness. *An International Journal of Evidence-Based Research. Policy & Practice*, *15*(5), 619–638.

Schneier, B. (2006). *Beyond Fear: Thinking Sensibly About Security in an Uncertain World*. Springer.

Schwerin, D. L., Roggiero, C., Thurman, J., & Goldstein, S. (2020). *Active Shooter Response*. Stat Pearls Publishing.

Sjoberg, L., Peterson, M., Fromm, J., Boholm, A., & Hanson, S.-O. (2005). Neglected and overemphasized risks: The opinions of risk professionals. *Journal of Risk Research*, *8*(7-8), 599–616. doi:10.1080/13669870500062576

Stroud, A. (2015). *Good Guys with Guns: The Appeal and Consequences of Concealed Carry*. Chapel Hill, NC: University of North Carolina Press.

U.S. Department of Education. (2007). Responding to and recovering from an active shooter incident that runs into a hostage situation. *Lessons Learned from School Crises and Emergencies*, *2*(6), 1–16.

U.S. Department of Education. (2013). *Guide for Developing High-Quality School Emergency Operations Plans*. Washington, DC: Office of Elementary and Secondary Education, Office of Safe and Healthy Students.

U.S. Department of Education. (2013). *Guide for Developing High-Quality School Emergency Operations Plans*. Office of Elementary and Secondary Education, Office of Safe and Healthy Students, U.S. Department of Education.

U.S. Department of Health and Human Services. (2014). *Incorporating Active Shooter Incident Planning into Healthcare Facility Emergency Operations Plans*. Office of the Assistant Secretary for Preparedness and Response, U.S. Department of Health and Human Services.

U.S. Department of Homeland Security. (2008). *Active Shooter – How to Respond*. U.S. Department of Homeland Security.

U.S. Department of Homeland Security. (2010). *Developing and Maintaining Emergency Operations Plans' Comprehensive Preparedness Guide (CPG) 101. Version 2.0*. U.S. Department of Homeland Security.

U.S. Department of Homeland Security. (2011). *National Preparedness System*. U.S. Department of Homeland Security.

Virginia Polytechnic Institute and State University Office of Emergency Management. (2011). *Virginia Tech. Emergency Notification System Protocols. Annex B to Crisis and Emergency Management Plan. Revision 2.0*. Virginia Polytechnic Institute and State University Office of Emergency Management.

Zhe, E. J., & Nickerson, A. B. (2007). Effects of an Intruder Crisis Drill on Children's Knowledge, Anxiety and Perceptions of School Safety. *School Psychology Review*, *36*(3), 501–508. doi:10.1080/02 796015.2007.12087936

Zhu, R., Lucas, G. M., Bercerik-Gerber, B., & Southers, E. G. (2020). Building preparedness in response to active shooter incidents: Results of focus group interviews. *International Journal of Disaster Risk Reduction*, *48*, m101617. doi:10.1016/j.ijdrr.2020.101617

ADDITIONAL READING

Coombs, T. W. (2012). *Ongoing Crisis Communication: Planning, Managing and Responding* (3rd ed.). Sage.

Doss, K., & Shepherd, C. (2015). *Active Shooter: Preparing for and Responding to a Growing Threat*. Butterworth-Heinemann.

Kerr, S. E. M. (2019). Emergency Management and Communication Improvements: Changing the Landscape of School Safety. In G. Crews (Ed.), *Handbook of Research on School Violence in American K-12 Education* (pp. 474–493). IGI Global. doi:10.4018/978-1-5225-6246-7.ch024

U.S. Department of Education. (2013). *Guide for Developing High-Quality School Emergency Operations Plans*. Office of Elementary and Secondary Education, Office of Safe and Healthy Students, U.S. Department of Education.

U.S. Department of Health and Human Services. (2014). *Incorporating Active Shooter Incident Planning into Healthcare Facility Emergency Operations Plans*. Office of the Assistant Secretary for Preparedness and Response, U.S. Department of Health and Human Services.

KEY TERMS AND DEFINITIONS

Active Shooter: A scenario in which a shooting is actively unfolding.

Drills: Practicing responding to a scenario by making use of the buildings within an organization.

Emergency Management Planning: Preparing for a variety of emergency situations, which involves drafting a plan(s) and exercising it.

Full Scale Exercises: Drills practiced amongst various agencies and partners, whereby equipment and communication systems are used.

Functional Exercises: A simulation of particular scenarios, involving multiple partners (e.g., response agencies).

Possibilistic Thinking: A particular mindset rooted in probabilities, surmising about what could transpire and how to manage those situations.

Preparedness: A principle intended to improve the capacity of an organization to deal with a variety of possible incidents.

Table-Top Exercises: Small group discussions working through a particular scenario and the actions required to deal with it.

Target-Hardening: Measures implemented to try to improve the security of an organization, such as making it difficult for an attacker to enter buildings and reach targets.

Chapter 9
Responding to a Mass Shooting

ABSTRACT

This chapter documents ways to respond to and recover from a mass shooting situation. Response is two-fold in nature: dealing with a scenario when it unfolds and reuniting the affected population with their families once the crisis has been resolved. The chapter then moves on to look at ways to recover from a mass shooting to repair the long-term damage caused. Recovery centers on dealing with the psychological impact on the affected community, physical damage caused, and the reputational damage on the organization. Another part of recovery is learning lessons from previous mass shootings. Captured throughout this chapter are the recommendations from emergency management experts, citing their knowledge and experience in dealing with active shooter incidents and other types of crises.

INTRODUCTION

The previous chapter outlined the preparedness principle of emergency management, looking at the ways in which to effectively prepare for a mass shooting incident before it occurs. Moving on from this, discussion in this chapter centers on *response* and *recovery*. Alongside prevention and preparation, these principles are part of the National Incident Management System (NIMS) designed by the Federal Emergency Management Agency (FEMA) (Lindsay, 2012; Salzman & Fuentes, 2020). Response and recovery relate to preparedness, since they are thought to improve operations following crises (McEntire, 2020).

Response refers to the ways in which an incident can be dealt with in a timely and effective manner. Response agencies such as law enforcement, fire and medical services should be actively involved in this stage. As per the discussion in the previous chapter, these response agencies should be included in planning and practice the roles assigned to them (Brock, Jimerson, Hart & Nickerson, 2012, p. 464). Facilitating an interoperable approach across different types of response agencies is the "Incident Command System" (ICS), organizing procedures, communications, personnel and facilities (Salzman & Fuentes, 2020; Schulz, 2019).

The *recovery* principle references those activities that take place to allow the affected community to recover from an active shooter event. This includes repairing physical damage and restoring services, as well as managing psychological damage and stress to those affected by it (Doss & Shepherd, 2015;

DOI: 10.4018/978-1-7998-3916-3.ch009

Goodrum & Woodward, 2019 Lindsay, 2012). Activities related to recovery typically begin once the response part of an incident is considered "over" (Cavaliere, 2019).

Similar to the previous chapter, results from interviews with emergency management experts are cited. Interviews focused on ways to respond effectively when a crisis occurs, as well as what should be prioritized in the recovery process. The following representatives were consulted for their expertise:

- The co-founders of the non-profit Foundation I Love U Guys (ILUG), John-Michael Keyes (Executive Director) and Ellen Stoddard-Keyes (Operations Director). This organization focuses on school safety and provides training in emergency management procedures to schools and some businesses.
- One of the founding partners of Nicoletti-Flater Associates, John Nicoletti. This organization specializes in emergency management planning and training and works alongside the I Love U Guys Foundation to provide training for active shooter scenarios.
- Stephen Brock and Melissa Reeves, the lead authors of the PREPaRE crisis prevention and intervention model used to respond to school violence.

The chapter firstly discusses ways to respond to mass shootings. Outlined are the roles of response agencies such as law enforcement, fire and medical. Next, the importance of reunification of the affected population with their families after an incident is discussed, looking at the method used by the ILUG Foundation. The chapter then moves on to discuss how to recover following mass shootings. Possible ways to repair psychological and reputational damage caused to the affected population and the organization itself are outlined. Lastly, the value in learning lessons from previous mass shooting incidents is detailed.

RESPONDING TO A CRISIS

Response Agencies: A Unified Approach

As detailed by the United States Departments of Education (2013) and Homeland Security (2011), one of the key principles of crisis planning is "response." This is denoted as the actions taken during and immediately after a crisis when it does actually transpire (Edwards, 2009, p. 20). A pivotal part of managing a crisis is the ability for the effective coordination of first responders: law enforcement, firefighters, paramedics, emergency medical staff and public health representatives (Doss & Shepherd, 2015, pp. 43, 55). Informing this is the National Incident Management System, an emergency preparedness and response model authorized by Homeland Security Presidential Directive 5 (Lindsay, 2012, p. 2). Whilst the NIMS model is applicable to all agencies who may respond to an incident, it is based on the principle that responses should be local in nature (Salzman & Fuentes, 2020).

Pertinent to an effective response is sharing a common language across the different response agencies (Doss & Shephard, 2015). Facilitating this is the Incident Command System, frequently utilized in training exercises and crises. The purpose of this is to provide a common set of procedures for organizing communication, equipment, systems and personnel during an incident. It is rooted in the idea of unified command meaning that responders should work as a team under the same command organization, rather than the structures within their own agencies (Billings, 2014, p. 20; Salzman & Fuentes, 2020; Schulz, 2019). The U.S. Department of Education (2007, pp. 10-11) recommended that there should be an Incident

Command Post during emergencies and all communications and procedures should be incorporated into emergency management plans and training. The Incident Commander (IC) is in charge and coordinates all activities for staff members. Assisting the IC are the following command staff members: the "Safety Officer" who ensures safety, health and environmental hazards are assessed; the "Public Information Officer" who deals with release of information to the media; the "Liaison Officer" who supports the IC in contacting all agencies involved in the response (Schulz, 2019).

Whilst training for active shooter incidents should focus on the affected population (e.g. students and teachers, workplace staff members, etc.), it is equally important to ensure response agencies are well-versed and thoroughly prepared to enact their part of the emergency management plan (U.S. Department of Education, 2013; U.S. Department of Health and Human Services, 2014). The I Love U Guys Foundation provides training using the "standard response protocol" (SRP). Based on the NIMS model, the intention of the SRP is to simplify and standardize the actions and vocabulary of emergency response. This model was updated to SRP-X in 2017 and consists of five elements to deal with a variety of scenarios: lockdown, whereby a building is secured; secure, in situations where the threat is outside the building; evacuate, requiring the affected population to leave the building; shelter, involving travelling to a designated shelter area; hold, mandating that the affected population remain static (Goodrum & Woodward, 2019, p. 49; Schildkraut, 2019, p. 4). Additionally, some NIMS training courses are available for free on the website of the Federal Emergency Management Agency: ICS-100, for the NIMS Incident Command System; IC-800 of the National Response Framework. Further training like the ICS-200 may also be taken to build upon knowledge in this area (Salzman & Fuentes, 2020).

Active Shooter Response

In terms of preparing for active shooter incidents, it is important to note that these are generally over in less than five minutes (see Blair & Schweit, 2014). The Advanced Law Enforcement Rapid Response Training (ALERRT) refers to this first phase as the "stop killing" portion of the active shooter situation. For law enforcement, this part could involve performing building searches and entering rooms to determine the location of the attacker (Martaindale & Blair, 2019, p. 348). Research has indicated that law enforcement can face a disadvantage when carrying out these actions, due to delays in reaction times (i.e. the attacker will be aware of them coming because of the noise generated). Blair and Martaindale (2017) explored the notion of whether law enforcement throwing a chair during this process could distract the suspect's attention away from the doorway. An experimental design with a sample size of 113 was used to explore this. Findings showed that this technique did work by slowing the suspect's reaction time by an average of 0.5 seconds, which could be enough time to allow law enforcement to fire. Conversely, in a third of the assignments, the suspect fired at the chair before law enforcement entered the room; thus, demonstrating how dangerous entering rooms are to law enforcement officers. Further complicating matters are "access control" countermeasures such as locked doors. Concern was expressed by participants with expertise in emergency management that locking doors could lead to a large concentration of people, which may delay evacuation efforts and create an easy target for shooters (Zhu, Lucas, Bercerik-Gerber & Southers, 2020, pp. 4-5). On the other side of the spectrum are organizations with a large number of entrances and exits who may not be able to lock doors, such as hospitals. For this reason, access, security and exits should be at the forefront of emergency management planning for healthcare institutions (Schwerin, 2020, p. 1).

Once the attacker has been dealt with, the situation moves onto the next stage described as "stop the dying" by responding to those who need immediate medical assistance. The provision of pre-planned first aid kits to provide oxygen and warmth, stop bleeding and treat fractures within the organization can facilitate this (Schwerin, Roggiero, Thurman & Goldstein, 2020. P. 11). Providing medical care in a high casualty incident like a mass shooting goes beyond the normal remit, with an increased need for resources; as well as added stress and vulnerabilities given the danger faced (U.S. Department of Health and Human Services, 2014, p. 9). Medical providers must have an understanding of triage, treatment, transport and morgue sections of the Incident Command System (Salzman & Fuentes, 2020).

Pertinent to emergency medical responders being able to treat injuries is effective coordination with partners in the organization affected, as well as external response agencies like fire, law enforcement and emergency managers. The role of law enforcement in this situation is to safeguard medical first responders. Whilst it is useful to have law enforcement officers trained in medical techniques, it is preferable to have medical or fire professionals provide the care to those who have been injured (Martaindale & Blair, 2019, p. 349). To this end, fire and medical personnel need to wait for law enforcement to secure the scene in what is called the "hot zone" where an immediate threat or hazard exists. Law enforcement officers have been trained to deal with such environments and have personal ballistic injury protection equipment. Until that point, emergency medical services and fire responders generally wait in the "cold zone" in which there is little or no threat. The "warm zone" is one in which they may enter; although it cannot be considered risk-free because it has not been secured (Billings, 2014, pp. 8, 14, 22).

There are models that can be used to ensure medical and fire response agencies are able to locate and treat the injured. The "protected island" is the creation of a secure location within the site of attack, allowing for casualities to be collected and treated. "Secure task force" involves law enforcement providing security for law enforcement and fire agents whilst they travel throughout the attack site. A "secure corridor" is a similar idea, whereby law enforcement provide security at key points (e.g. intersections in a hallway) to allow medical and fire services to be able to transport patients and provide care (Martaindale & Blair, 2019, p. 349). This performance and collaboration was tested in a study by Bachman and colleagues (2019) using four hundred and sixty-eight law enforcement officers (LEO) and three hundred and eighty-eight emergency medical services (EMS) to sixty-nine simulated active shooter incidents. Seventy percent of the time there was appropriate communication to ensure EMS was safe to treat patients. The appropriate casualty collection point was selected 84% of the time. There were also some incorrect operational actions, including inappropriate single patient evacuation and failure to maintain a protective LEO-EMS formation 20% and 49% of the time respectively.

Reunification Following an Incident

Another part of the response is reunification of the affected population with their families. It was noted that procedures should be implemented into emergency management plans and training. In the case of schools, details should be provided and practiced the purposes of organizing students and transporting them to evacuation sites. Moreover, parents of students should be given specific information about the reunification location and procedures following an incident (U.S. Department of Education, 2007, p. 12). This is particularly important in cases where students cannot return to the classroom or even the school grounds. The I Love U Guys Foundation has a "Standard Reunification Method" to facilitate this process. The actions involved in this are:

- Establishing a check-in location for parents/guardians;
- Students to be delivered to the staging area;
- Once students are in place, notify parents/guardians of their location and direct them to the parent check-in location to go through the process with them;
- Parents/guardians complete reunification cards, allowing them to self-sort during check in;
- The person in charge of reunification retrieves students from the staging areas and takes them to the parents.

The use of reunification cards in this method allow for streamlining and, therefore, an orderly and speedy process. Moreover, the parents and students are dealt with in separate areas until the time is right to reunite them; thus, hopefully reducing anxiety and panic (Goodrum & Woodward, 2019, pp. 51-52). During their interview, the representatives from the I Love U Guys Foundation said they shared their reunification method with the Homeland Security Advisory Council of Massachusetts and this was thereafter used to create a model for regional family reunification.

Further to this, the Foundation is in the beginning phases of developing a software application allowing people to create their own reunification job action sheets. Alongside this process, a small reunification kit would be used "where it's just a greeter and checker and a principal to do some training on the way to the full-scale reunification."-John-Michael Keyes, ILUG. Moreover, this application is said to be expandable beyond schools: "It can also be used for family reunification in communities… weather disasters and so forth."-Ellen Stoddard-Keyes, ILUG. The expansion and development of the SRM means that it could possibly be used to facilitate response in other types of scenarios outside of schools. Reunification should be considered and documented in emergency management planning and having a structured method in place like the SRM could assist with this.

RECUPERATION AFTER A CRISIS

Dealing With the Aftermath

Recovery refers to the short to long term phase of restoring a community following an incident (Edwards, 2009, p. 20). Recovering from a crisis like an active shooter incident is two-fold in nature. First is the restoration of physical facilities and services that may have been damaged in the attack. This is in addition to trying to heal the psychological damage to the affected population (Doss & Shepherd, 2015, p. 43; Goodrum & Woodward, 2019, p. 66; Lindsay, 2012, p. 3). It differs from the response part of an operation in that recovery does not occur at a specific time; rather, it occurs over stages as required. The recovery aspect should be considered during emergency management preparation and thereafter detailed into plans (Cavaliere, 2019).

For the first part, restoring facilities and services will likely take a lengthy period of time, so there needs to be contingency plans in place to deal with it. For instance, businesses need to consider issues such as whether employees can work remotely, how to retrieve important documents from the building if needed, reassuring customers that their needs will still be met, and so forth (Cassidy, 2021). In the case of schools, there needs to be a place for the affected population to relocate whilst recovery takes place. An example of this is after the 1999 Columbine school shooting, students were repatriated to a nearby school whilst repairs and remodeling took place (Doran, 2014). Municipalities are mainly responsible for managing recovery efforts and state and federal agencies can provide support as required (Cavaliere, 2019).

Important in this stage will be post-crisis public relations to frame public perceptions of the event in order to reduce harm for the organization and its partners (Reynolds & Seeger, 2005, p. 46). As Coombs (2007, p. 164) explains, crises can be a threat to organizational reputations because they provide an opportunity for people to form negative opinions about the organization. The first step for post-crisis public relations is to address the physical and psychological concerns of those directly affected by the event. Once this has been completed, the next stage is to try to maintain reputational assets (Coombs, 2007, p. 165). A public information officer (PIO) should serve as a liaison with the media during and following the incident, with regular briefings scheduled to avoid misinformation (U.S. Department of Education, 2007, p. 11). To this end, first responders should not interact with the media and should instead refer to the PIO. In situations with a high number of victims, there may be more than one PIO and it is imperative that they coordinate their responses before they are released to the media (Schulz, 2019).

It is important to note that stakeholders can learn about a crisis and its response from a variety of sources, including social media (Coombs, 2007, p. 164). Fiore (2018) carried out dissertation research on crisis messaging on social media, looking at how organizations can reach Twitter users before and after a situation. From this study, a number of recommendations were made for public relations practitioners within organizations: fear tweets to maximize the saturation of the message; empathy tweets to reach a wider audience and inform members of the public quickly; advocacy tweets to maximize engagement; tweet frequently during the situation; engage in communications with members of the public. Specifically, post-crisis public relations involve relaying messages to "prevent or lessen the negative outcomes of a crisis and thereby protect the organization, stakeholders or industry from damage" (Coombs, 1999, p. 4). "Image repair" theory can inform the design of these messages, whereby the response is proportionate to the severity of the incident and the damage caused to the organization's reputation (Beniot, 1997, p. 182). These messages can involve statements to detail a full account of the crisis: actions taken, causes of it, and assignments of blame and responsibility. In cases where there has been wrongdoing on the part of the organization, particularly in how they responded to the situation, a full apology accepting responsibility should be issued (Coombs, 2012, pp. 154, 156; Reynolds & Seeger, 2005, p. 50). Pertinent here will be maintaining or repairing "reputation," described as "an evaluation stakeholders make about an organization" (Coombs, 2012, p. 35).

An example of this was the "Discussion Agenda" devised by Virginia Tech University following the 2007 mass shooting. Mirroring Beniot's (1997) "image repair" strategy, the document mandated "own the messages" emerging relating to the shooting. This strategy consists of framing the context and expression of messages; in addition to controlling the language and outlet of messages. To assist with this, staff members are provided with a list of topics to avoid: the shooter's interaction with the faculty; how the university screens for mental health problems and provides counselling; improving emergency communication systems. It is recommended that staff members deflect this line of questioning by saying something to the effect that the reviews of the incident will seek to understand these areas. Acceptable topics for discussion are listed: the poise and character of students; the university's strong academic reputation; how the university has helped the community cope. This elucidates the fact that the "reputation" of an organization is a rational and self-interested risk management asset which can be threatened by the occurrence of a crisis (Heath, Lee & Ni, 2009, p. 125).

More importantly, recovery involves dealing with the psychological impact on the affected population. Mental health needs should be incorporated into emergency management planning. Immediate, intermediate and long-term support needs to be provided to the affected population, as well as the caregivers (e.g. first responders, mental health partners) who may also experience trauma (U.S. Department of Education, 2007, pp. 7, 13-14). In addition to those who were present at the scene of the mass shooting, there can also have secondary and tertiary victims in the form of the communities where the incident occurred and beyond this (Cowan, Blum, Zirony & Cicchetti, 2020, p. 171). John Nicoletti, Nicoletti-Flater Associates, described the irreversible shift in perception following an incident like a mass shooting as the "new normal," whereby "people realize a space they believed was safe no longer is." Once this change has happened, people have to find a way to deal with it. For something like the Aurora movie theatre (2012) shooting, explained John Nicoletti, this has resulted in either of two scenarios: avoidance whereby they have never returned to a theater or denial in which they claim it was just an isolated incident. The ideal solution is for a more proactive mindset: "What we try and do is the 'new normal' when you go to a movie theater you look for the exits."-John Nicoletti, Nicoletti-Flater Associates.

As part of the recovery process, staff members can be trained in psychological first aid to assist with the distress caused. This could be facilitated by determining what social support networks (e.g. ministers, friends, family) victims had in place prior to the incident and ensuring they are connected with those people. Victims should be also made aware of what support services are in place, so they can decide on the type of assistance that would be the most beneficial to them (Cowan, Blum, Zirony & Cicchetti, 2020, pp. 172-173; U.S. Department of Health and Human Services, 2014, p. 12). Another consideration is to be circumspect when planning any memorials and tributes for victim(s), which may have the potential to reintroduce trauma (U.S. Department of Education, 2007, p. 15). By attending such events, counsellors can assist with collective healing in the affected community. A different type of trigger for victims could be when further mass shootings occur. Ways to deal with this should be built into the longer term recovery process (Cowan, Blum, Zirony & Cicchetti, 2020, pp. 173-174).

A further consideration for the recovery process is recognizing the social differences between victims. Economic, gender and race issues affect those who are most at risk in the recovery process. Moreover, religion and culture can also affect mourning and how emotions are dealt with in the aftermath of an incident (Cavaliere, 2019; Mincin, 2019). Additionally, there should be provisions in place to deal with language barriers. For instance, in the 2019 El Paso mass shooting, a great deal of the affected community spoke Spanish (Cowan, Blum, Zirony & Cicchetti, 2020, p. 174). Translated materials and interpreters can facilitate this process (Mincin, 2019).

Learning Lessons

Recovery following a crisis situation involves analyzing the response, noting any strengths and weaknesses in order to learn lessons from this (Doss & Shepherd, 2015, p. 57; Heath, Lee & Ni, 2009, p. 125). Specifically, the NIMS model denotes that lessons learned should be passed forward in an attempt to improve response efforts and reduce the levels of mortality and morbidity (Salzman & Fuentes, 2020). An example of this is the attack at Columbine High School (1999), which has been used as a case study to improve response (Martaindale & Hunter, 2019, p. 344). There were numerous criticisms, for instance, levelled at law enforcement for their response to Columbine, including not allowing medical response to enter the building where a teacher ultimately bled to death without treatment. After the mass shooting at Columbine High School, one of the recommendations made was that staff members in schools should be trained with community partners and first responders to ensure all are aware of their roles and responsibilities. This recommendation was incorporated into the amended Colorado "Safe Schools Act"

(2008). John Michael Keyes, I Love U Guys Foundation, found that the legislative change did have a positive effect, allowing for fire, medical and law enforcement responders to use a shared language (Kerr, 2019). The University of Texas shooting (1969) influenced the establishment of SWAT units in campus security and metropolitan police departments; whilst the Parkland school shooting (2018) highlighted the need for law enforcement to neutralize active shooters (Davis, 2020).

Weaknesses can also be highlighted in other areas after a mass shooting attack. The shooting at Virginia Tech University (2007) highlighted deficiencies in the internal communication system. This meant that the notification about the potential threat faced was relayed too late, for the majority of students were already in class. Following this, significant changes about "timely notifications" were made to the internal university system, as well as at the state and federal levels (Kerr, 2019).

In addition to any weaknesses highlighted, the review should also include what worked well. The review of the shooting at Northern Illinois University (2008) noted the strengths in the response to this attack. Collaborative planning amongst the various response organizations was said to have assisted with the rapid treatment of victims. Furthermore, the emergency communication plan was said to have worked well, providing clear and descriptive messages that told people what to do (Northern Illinois University Police and Public Safety Department, 2010, p. 58). In the case of the Columbine High School shooting, communications were kept separate between the different response agencies of law enforcement, fire and emergency response of which there were forty-six in total. Each agency used its own dispatch center and/ or an agency representative at the incident command post. This minimized the potential confusion and system overload that could have occurred if they had all used a single channel (Jefferson County, 2015).

Similar review processes were described by those interviewed. The I Love U Guys Foundation is working on the Aftermath Project to capture stories from survivors of events like school shootings in order to find out what the lessons from these incidents were. Once this is completed, it should result in some tangible outputs: "We're crafting advice for what to do after something happens and where some mistakes have been made and what to expect."-John-Michael Keyes, ILUG. Further to this, the Foundation is also involved in the Bold Impact project to evaluate the effectiveness of programs to create a safer climate within organizations: "One of the key indicators in the Collective Impact model is constant evaluation: let's make sure what we're doing is right."-John-Michael Keyes, ILUG. In a similar vein, interviewees Stephen Brock, CSU, and Melissa Reeves, SIGMATMA, are the lead authors of the PREPaRE school crisis prevention curriculum. This initially arose from the expert panel of the National Association of School Psychologists, which was set up to respond to large-scale crisis, such as school shootings, natural disasters, and so forth. The PREPaRE guidance is evidence-informed, using findings from literature and drawing upon real-life experiences.

Importantly, once the lessons learned have been ascertained, these should be incorporated into emergency management plans. As mentioned earlier, plans should be constantly reviewed based on new information and after the advent of an incident (U.S. Department of Education, 2013, p. 22; U.S. Department of Health and Human Services, 2014, p. 5). For aspects that have shown to work well in previous crisis scenarios (e.g. partnerships between response agencies), these should still be reviewed to ensure these can be maintained and strengthened even further if possible.

CONCLUSION

The preparedness principles prescribed by the United States Departments of Education and Homeland Security for crisis planning include attempting to prevent and prepare for an incident, as well as reacting when one does occur. In Chapter 8, the ways to prepare for mass shootings were outlined. This chapter followed up on this looking at ways to respond when an incident does occur to minimize damage caused and also how to recover from such events. Planning, practice, effective response and post-incident reflection are all integral to giving an organization the best chance possible to reduce the harm caused in a mass shooting incident. This chapter marks the end of the book section on responding to mass shootings.

Discussed first of all was "response," denoted as the actions taken when a crisis does actually occur. Responding to an incident effectively requires the emergency management plan to be practiced. This can be via methods like drills and exercises and can be assisted via the use of a designated framework. The other element of response is what actually transpires during a situation. First responders like medical, fire and law enforcement need to effectively work together to manage the incident. Pertinent to this is sharing a common language across the different agencies (Doss & Shephard, 2015; U.S. Department of Education, 2013; U.S. Department of Health and Human Services, 2014; Schulz, 2019). The SRP-X framework conceptualized by the I Love U Guys Foundation aims to standardize the actions and language used by response agencies during a situation.

In terms of response agencies performing different roles during an incident, it is important to note the different stages of an active shooter event. The first part is generally known as the "stop the killing" portion, which primarily falls to law enforcement to deal with. The second portion is the "stop the dying" whereby medical response and fire are able to transport and treat the wounded, something which may require law enforcement to provide protection to them (Martaindale & Blair, 2019). It is important to note that due to the speed of active shooter incidents, there is the potential for the first part of "stop the killing" to be over before law enforcement arrives. This is probably one of the motivating factors behind movements like arming teachers and concealed carry of firearms for university students; thus, putting the onus on armed citizens to stop the attacker. There are a number of potential issues with this, covered in more detail in Kerr (2018). Consequently, citizens would be better-placed to help with practical elements such as assisting with medical response if adequately trained and reunification of the affected population with their families.

The final component of crisis management as prescribed by federal guidance is "recovery," actions that may contribute to repairing the psychological and organizational damage caused. In terms of organizational damage, this will probably require the repair of physical facilities. More importantly, perhaps, the reputation of the organization will likely be harmed. For that reason, post-incident public relation messages and strategies should be incorporated into emergency management plans (Coombs 1999, 2007, 2012; Reynolds & Seeger, 2005). For the psychological damage, interviewee, John Nicoletti, Nicoletti-Flater Associates, spoke about the shift to a "new normal" following a mass shooting, a shift in perceptions where a space that was previously believed to be safe is no longer considered in that way. Strategies should be built into emergency management plans to deal with the psychological damage caused to survivors of the attack, as well as the wider community and beyond (Cowan, Blum, Zirony & Cicchetti, 2020; Goodrum & Woodward, 2019; Lindsay, 2012). Cowan and colleagues (2020) highlighted a lack of guidance on how to support survivors of mass shootings within the current body of literature, meaning further research in this area is required.

The other element of the recovery process is critiquing an event after it has transpired and noting what worked well and any pitfalls in the response. Any weaknesses highlighted (e.g. emergency communication system) should be addressed and updates built into the emergency management plan (Doss & Shepherd, 2015; Heath, Lee & Ni, 2009). There were examples of changes being made to processes and systems after the shootings at Columbine High School, Virginia Tech University, the University of Texas and Stoneman Douglas High School (more commonly known as the "Parkland" shooting) (Davis, 2020; Kerr, 2019; Northern Illinois University, 2008). It is also pivotal to document what worked well during an incident: for instance, the rapid treatment of victims facilitated by response agencies working well together (Northern Illinois University, 2008).

REFERENCES

Bachman, M. W., Anzalone, B. C., Williams, J. G., DeLuca, M. B., Garner, D. G. Jr, Preddy, J. E., Cabanas, J. G., & Myers, J. B. (2019). Evaluation of an Integrated Rescue Task Force Model for Active Threat Response. *Prehospital Emergency Care*, *23*(3), 309–318. doi:10.1080/10903127.2018.152148 7 PMID:30204511

Billings, D. C. (2014). *EMS under Fire: Developing an Active Shooter Incident Response Plan*. Manchester Fire-Rescue-EMS Dept.

Blair, J. P., & Martaindale, M. H. (2017). Throwing a chair could save officers' lives during room entries. *International Journal of Police Science & Management*, *19*(2), 110–119. doi:10.1177/1461355717711452

Brock, S. E., Jimerson, S. R., Hart, S. R., & Nickerson, A. B. (2012). Preventing, Preparing for and Responding to School Violence with the PREPaRE Model. In S. R. Jimerson, A. B. Nickerson, M. J. Mayer, & M. J. Firlong (Eds.), *Handbook of School Violence and School Safety: International Research and Practice* (2nd ed., pp. 463–474). Routledge.

Cassidy, K. A. (2019). Criminals: Active Shooters. In L. R. Shapiro & M. H. Maros (Eds.), Encyclopedia of Security and Emergency Management. Springer Nature.

Coombs, T. W. (2007). Protecting Organization Reputations During a Crisis: The Development and Application of Situational Crisis Communication Theory. *Corporate Reputation Review*, *10*(3), 163–176. doi:10.1057/palgrave.crr.1550049

Coombs, T. W. (2012). *Ongoing Crisis Communication: Planning, Managing and Responding* (3rd ed.). Sage.

Cowan, R. G., Blum, C. R., Mihalyi, G., Zirony, S., & Cicchetti, R. (2020). Supporting Survivors of Public Mass Shootings. *Journal of Social, Behavioral and Health Sciences*, *14*(1), 169–182. doi:10.5590/JSBHS.2020.14.1.12

Davis, J. (2020). *American School Shooting: The Growing Problem of Mass Shooting for Homeland Security*. James Davis.

Doss, K., & Shepherd, C. (2015). *Active Shooter: Preparing for and Responding to a Growing Threat*. Butterworth-Heinemann.

Fiore, G. J., III. (2018). Emotional Tweeters: What Causes Individuals to React During a Crisis? A Mixed Methodological Analysis Examining Crisis Response Tweets to the 2018 Stoneman Douglas High School Shooting. Seton Hall University Dissertations and Theses (ETDS 2612). South Orange, New Jersey.

Goodrum, S., & Woodward, W. (2019). *Colorado School Safety Guide*. Attorney General's Office.

Heath, R. L., Lee, J., & Ni, L. (2009). Crisis and Risk Approaches to Emergency Management Planning and Communication: The Role of Similarity and Sensitivity. *Journal of Public Relations Research*, *21*(2), 123–141. doi:10.1080/10627260802557415

Jefferson County. (2015) *Communication Problems*. The Denver Post. https://extras.denverpost.com/news/colreport/Columbinerep/Pages/COMM_TEXT.htm

Kerr, S. E. M. (2019). Emergency Management and Communication Improvements: Changing the Landscape of School Safety. In G. Crews (Ed.), *Handbook of Research on School Violence in American K-12 Education* (pp. 474–493). IGI Global. doi:10.4018/978-1-5225-6246-7.ch024

Lindsay, B. R. (2012). *Federal Emergency Management: A Brief Introduction*. Congressional Research Service.

Martaindale, M. H., & Blair, J. P. (2019). The Evolution of Active Shooter Response Training Protocols Since Columbine: Lessons from the Advanced Law Enforcement. *Journal of Contemporary Criminal Justice*, *35*(3), 342–356. doi:10.1177/1043986219840237

McEntire, D. A. (2020). Emergency Management: Preparedness and Planning. In L. R. Shapiro & M. H. Maros (Eds.), Encyclopedia of Security and Emergency Management. Springer Nature.

Mincin, J. (2019). Emergency Management: Working with Vulnerable Populations. In L. R. Shapiro & M. H. Maros (Eds.), Encyclopedia of Security and Emergency Management. Springer Nature.

Northern Illinois University Police and Public Safety Department. (2010). *Lessons learned in response and recovery: Northern Illinois University*. Northern Illinois University Police and Public Safety Department.

Reynolds, B., & Seeger, M. W. (2005). Crisis and Emergency Risk Communication as an Integrative Model. *Journal of Health Communication*, *10*(1), 43–55. doi:10.1080/10810730590904571 PMID:15764443

Salzman, S. M., & Clemente Fuentes, R. W. (2020). *EMS National Incident Management System*. StatPearls Publishing.

Schildkraut, J. (2019). *Implementing and Testing the Standard Response Protocol: Final Report*. New York: A Report presented to the Syracuse City School District.

Schulz, D. M. (2019). Emergency Management: Incident Command System. In Encyclopaedia of Security and Emergency Management. Springer Nature.

Schwerin, D. L., Roggiero, C., Thurman, J., & Goldstein, S. (2020). *Active Shooter Response*. Stat Pearls Publishing.

U.S. Department of Education. (2007). Responding to and recovering from an active shooter incident that runs into a hostage situation. *Lessons Learned from School Crises and Emergencies*, *2*(6), 1–16.

U.S. Department of Education, Office of Elementary and Secondary Education, Office of Safe and Healthy Students. (2013). *Guide for Developing High-Quality School Emergency Operations Plans.* U.S. Department of Education.

U.S. Department of Health and Human Services, Office of the Assistant Secretary for Preparedness and Response. (2014). *Incorporating Active Shooter Incident Planning into Healthcare Facility Emergency Operations Plans.* U.S. Department of Health and Human Services.

U.S. Department of Homeland Security. (2011). *National Preparedness System.* U.S. Department of Homeland Security.

ADDITIONAL READING

Cavaliere, P. (2019). Emergency Management: Recovery. In L. R. Shapiro & M. H. Maros (Eds.), Encyclopedia of Security and Emergency Management. Springer Nature.

Coombs, T. W. (2012). *Ongoing Crisis Communication: Planning, Managing and Responding* (3rd ed.). Sage.

Doss, K., & Shepherd, C. (2015). *Active Shooter: Preparing for and Responding to a Growing Threat.* Butterworth-Heinemann.

Kerr, S. E. M. (2019). Emergency Management and Communication Improvements: Changing the Landscape of School Safety. In G. Crews (Ed.), *Handbook of Research on School Violence in American K-12 Education* (pp. 474–493). IGI Global. doi:10.4018/978-1-5225-6246-7.ch024

Martaindale, M. H., & Blair, J. P. (2019). The Evolution of Active Shooter Response Training Protocols Since Columbine: Lessons from the Advanced Law Enforcement. *Journal of Contemporary Criminal Justice, 35*(3), 342–356. doi:10.1177/1043986219840237

KEY TERMS AND DEFINITIONS

Emergency Communication: How an organization communicates with the affected population during an incident.

Incident Command System: An organizational structure to provide a common set of procedures for equipment, communication, personnel, and systems across different response agencies.

National Incident Management System: A model of emergency preparedness and response to prevent, prepare for, respond to and recover from crises.

Post-Crisis Public Relations: Messaging to the public following an incident intended to reduce damage to an organization's reputation.

Protected Island: The creation of a secure location within the site of an attack to allow for casualties to be collected by fire and medical responders.

Recovery: Actions to repair the long-term damage caused by a crisis occurs.

Response: Actions to manage a crisis and minimize damage when it does transpire.

Reunification: Reuniting the affected population with their families following an incident.

Secure Corridor: The provision of security by law enforcement at key points throughout a site to allow medical and fire responders to transport and treat casualities.

Secure Task Force: A response model whereby law enforcement provides security for law enforcement and fire responders to allow them to travel through the site of the incident.

Section 4
Gun Policies and Mass Shootings

The theme of this section is to discuss the impact of mass shootings on the gun policymaking landscape in the United States.

Chapter 10
Gun Regulations to Reduce Harm Caused

ABSTRACT

This chapter marks the start of the final section of the book, which focuses on the landscape of gun policymaking in the United States. The intention of this chapter is to examine gun policy proposals believed to reduce incidences of mass shootings and gun violence as a whole. Gun violence prevention advocates provide policy suggestions and deliberate about their chances of gaining traction, considering estimated levels of public support and the current political climate. Discussed first of all are proposals centering on restricting the lethality of weapons (e.g., those focused on ammunition, large capacity magazines, and assault weapons). Policies centered on reducing firearm access to restricted persons are then discussed: extreme risk protection orders, safe storage laws, and universal background checks. Lastly, other miscellaneous proposals are deliberated: age restrictions, ghost guns, funding for research pertaining to guns, a licensing system for firearms, and smart gun technology.

INTRODUCTION

Gun policies are a common discussion point following a mass shooting (see Fleming, Rutledge, Dixon & Peralton, 2016; Goss, 2006; Kerr, 2018). This is likely linked to firearms being the most commonly used weapon in large-scale acts of targeted violence. A study of attacks in public spaces found 89% were carried out using a firearm; whist 61% of targeted violence attacks in schools involved firearms (National Threat Assessment Center, 2019a, 2019b). To that end, these types of incidents act as "focusing events" (Fleming, Rutledge, Dixon & Peralton, 2016), putting the issue of firearms onto the policy agenda. Interest groups can then play an instrumental role in advancing or challenging these issues (Fleming, Rutledge, Dixon & Peralton, 2016; Grossman, 2012; Hrebenar & Scott, 1982; Spitzer, 2004). This raises a question whether the policies advanced after a mass shooting are directly linked to the incident or if they are unrelated but given policy traction by the attack.

The intention of this chapter is to examine the policy proposals advanced by gun violence prevention advocates. Specifically, suggestions center on which gun regulations could prevent firearms being

DOI: 10.4018/978-1-7998-3916-3.ch010

procured prior to attacks, as well as reduce harm when mass shootings do transpire. Sixteen interviewees with gun violence prevention (GVP) knowledge, e.g. representatives from interest groups and other related organizations, were questioned about this. Interwoven into the chapter are opinion poll results to elucidate how much support there is for specific policy measures. The chapter will firstly go through each of the categories of policy proposals raised by interviewees, detailing their reasoning. What will be discussed firstly are proposals centering on ammunition and the lethality of weapons in terms of issuing restrictions on large capacity magazines and assault weapons. Part of this will also be a discussion about whether shifting the debate to focus on "bullet control" rather than "gun control" would make the debate less contentious. Secondly, the discussion will center on policies that reduce access to guns to those who are prohibited. Those proposals extend to: extreme risk protection orders (sometimes known as "red flag laws"), where access is temporarily removed from individuals considered a danger to themselves or others; safe storage laws, requiring firearms to be securely locked away to prevent them being accessed by children or other restricted persons living in the same household; universal background checks, mandating that any purchase or transfer of a firearm involves a background check into an individual's criminal history. The last part compiles miscellaneous proposals that could potentially prevent mass shootings in addition to gun violence more generally. These include age restrictions, eradicating "ghost guns" (those which are untraceable), funding to carry out gun-related research, a licensing system for firearms and smart gun technology to restrict access to authorized users. The viability of all these proposals becoming law will be discussed throughout.

AMMUNITION

A possible avenue of gun legislation to pursue is one centering on ammunition (see Dailard, 1998; Healey, 1998; Kerr, 2019). In 1998, Healey (p. 1) described ammunition control as "the next frontier in gun control policy." In spite of this, it has never really gained proper traction in the policy sphere. The Gun Control Act (1968) required a log of ammunition sales; however, this law ceased with 1986 Firearm Owners' Protection Act (Vizzard, 1999, p. 134). In theory, focusing gun policies on ammunition could afford certain advantages to reducing gun violence. Specifically, these could serve to prevent or reduce the harm caused in mass shooting incidents.

One of those advantages would be the requirement to undergo a background check for ammunition in addition to one for firearms as per the Brady Law requirements. This would act as another barrier for those who are prohibited (Healey, 1998, p. 23). Such a requirement already exists in a number of states. Connecticut, Illinois, Massachusetts and New Jersey all require a license to purchase or possess ammunition. New York requires a background check for commercial transfers of ammunition and logs are taken so police can be informed if someone is stockpiling bullets; whilst California requires background checks on all ammunition sales (Giffords Law Center to Prevent Gun Violence, n.d.; Henderson & Trotta, 2013). A federal bill "Ammunition Background Checks" was introduced in 2018, mandating sales for ammunition to go through the National Instant Background Checks System. The bill was reintroduced in 2019 and named "Jamie's law" in honor of one of the victims of the Parkland High School (2018) shooting. Representative Debbie Wasserman Schultz, one of the policymakers who introduced the bill, maintained that by closing the "ammunition loophole," the illegal purchase of ammunition by prohibited individuals could be prevented (Wasserman Schultz, 2019). It remains to be seen what will transpire with this bill.

Interviewees agreed that background checks for ammunition seem like a wise strategy to pursue. Adam Skaggs (GLCPGV) said if such a system could be implemented effectively and smoothly then it could boost public safety. Buttressing this argument, he made the point that at the moment "if you fail a background check and you can't buy a gun, you can buy as much ammunition as you want." In line with this, Tom Mauser (CC) believed there should be limits on how many bullets can be purchased at the one time. This could be particularly important in cases of mass shootings, whereby large quantities of bullets tend to be used to afford the perpetrator with more opportunities to kill and injure people (see Kerr 2018; Kerr 2019). An exception could be made to those who are purchasing large quantities of ammunition for sporting purposes (Healey, 1998, p. 24).

Another potential area of regulation could be on the type of bullets used. Currently, California, the District of Columbia, Maryland, Massachusetts, Minnesota, New York, New Jersey and Washington all have restrictions pertaining to specific types of ammunition (Law Center to Prevent Gun Violence, 2012). Harm-inducing bullets, such as hollow points, incendiary and armor-piercing ones, have the potential to cause a greater degree of injuries when fired. These have been used in previous mass shootings, including Sandy Hook (2012), Charleston (2015) and Parkland (2018) (Giffords Law Center to Prevent Gun Violence, n.d.; Kerr, 2019). Andrew Goddard (VCPS) argued that the velocity of the bullet is extremely important since the speed at which it travels directly affects how it impacts the body: "The shockwave that goes through your body from a tiny, high-velocity bullet is much worse than being hit by a pointed bigger bullet that's going much slower." Policies focusing on regulating certain types of ammunition, e.g. hollow points, incendiary and armor-piercing bullets, have the potential to reduce the severity of injuries caused in a mass shooting situation. They could also center on ways to regulate homemade bullets which could be equally as dangerous and produced in large quantities (Healey, 1998, p. 27). This is particularly the case with the advent of 3D printers.

Part of the reason for focusing on ammunition is the idea that it could possibly be less contentious than "gun control" in wider policy debates (see Healey, 1998; Kerr, 2019). Interviewees were skeptical, however, about whether this would be the case in reality. Brian Malte (H & HF) made the point that the Second Amendment does not actually document a right to ammunition as it does with firearms. A similar point was made by the former chairman of the United States Consumer Product Safety Commission, who highlighted that the Constitution does not circumscribe any right to ammunition like it does with guns (Brown, 2018). In spite of this, firearms and ammunition seem to go hand-in-hand when discussing rights. In line with this, Tom Mauser (CC) said the whole topic of guns, including ammunition, is "too politically charged a subject." Additionally, Adam Skaggs (GLCPGV) explained that a lot of sports shooters and hunters find it frustrating that there is another layer of regulation, leading to pushback against ammunition regulations. An additional point advanced was that ammunition is not at the forefront of the debate on gun regulation: "Unless it is in the public's mind, I don't think there's a chance of it passing at this moment in time."-Marvin Lim (KGOC). Considering the important role public opinion plays in shaping policy debates (see Burns & Crawford, 1999; Spitzer, 2004), this is a valid point. Whilst banning the possession of armor-piercing bullets polls highly at 67% (Gallup, 2016), it may not be an issue that necessarily concerns the public. In order to be persuasive to members of the public and policymakers, frames utilized in public debates pertaining to ammunition would need to be consistent and resonant (Woodly, 2015, p. 28).

Until such time when there is a concerted and focused effort on regulations pertaining to ammunition, policy proposals relating to them are unlikely to gain any policy traction. Additionally, Dailard (1998,

p. 34) argued that regulations centering on ammunition should be coupled with those relating to guns, as "implemented in isolation, neither approach is likely to succeed."

ASSAULT WEAPONS BAN

Following on from the previous section, the one element relating to ammunition which may have a chance of gaining traction is what is known as "high" or "large capacity magazines." These were previously regulated at the federal level as part of the 1994-2004 Assault Weapon Ban, where the size of large capacity magazines was restricted to a set number of rounds (see Koper, 2013). Krouse and Richardson (2015, p. 29) advanced the argument that a comprehensive dataset of mass shootings should be put together which establishes the types of firearms, number of shots fired and reloads used in incidents. Doing so would, therefore, allow policymakers to assess the capacity of detachable magazines and semiautomatic firearms, and make a case for passing policies based on these restrictions. Interviewees were in agreement that limiting the size of large capacity magazines was a priority to reducing the harm caused in mass shootings. For instance, Andrew Goddard (VCPS) argued that "high-capacity magazines give them more chances to shoot before they have to reload so there's less time for people to escape and all that kind of stuff." A number of interviewees even maintained that limiting large capacity magazines should be a higher priority than regulating assault weapons themselves:

If you have to pick banning large capacity magazines or banning assault style weapons, it's actually the magazines that would be more effective. There's definitely at least circumstantial evidence that demonstrates that without large capacity magazines the deaths and injuries in a mass shooting are fewer. – Jonathan Perloe (CAGV).

If you are talking about firepower and military style weapons the bullets or the magazines that hold the bullets are almost more important than the gun. It's not always necessarily the weapon; it's the firepower in the weapon. – Brian Malte (H & HF).

The point was made by Rukmani Bhatia (formerly CAP) that the gun industry has sought to improve the functionality of large capacity magazines, which has meant that "you're now seeing forty, fifty, sixty, hundred round magazines functioning and shooting out all of those bullets." She compares the 2012 Aurora Theater shooting during which the hundred round magazine drum jammed with the 2019 Dayton shooting where the shooter was able to successfully use a hundred round drum to fire off forty-one rounds in a very short period of time. This was attributable, Rukmani Bhatia (formerly CAP) argued, to "the industry being very effective at recognizing flaws in the accessories and working to fix them."

Limits on large capacity magazines currently exist in a number of states, including Colorado, Connecticut and New York. In spite of this, Tom Mauser (CC) explained that in Colorado some gun shops are flouting the state law limiting large capacity magazines to fifteen rounds. In some cases, they are selling a kit to build a large capacity magazine of greater than fifteen rounds; with the circumvention inherent in the fact that "because it's not complete, they think they're not selling a high capacity magazine." Additionally, there are shops who are just selling magazines that hold more rounds and there is no enforcement of the law because police officers are not getting involved. This highlights the importance of properly implementing and thereafter fully monitoring a law in order for it to be effective. At the federal level, the "Keep Americans Safe" bill was reintroduced in 2019 to limit large capacity magazines to ten rounds. One of the policymakers who reintroduced the bill, Congressman Ted Deutch (Fl-22), represents the district where the Parkland High School (2018) shooting took place. He referred to Parkland and other mass shootings as his motivation for reintroducing the bill, maintaining that large capacity magazines are almost universally used in mass shootings due to their ability to maximize the number of casualties (Deutch, 2019). It is uncertain what will happen with this bill in future. It should be noted that the Supreme Court case, *Heller V. District of Columbia*, ruled that ammunition magazines should be limited to offer a "critical benefit" to law enforcement and bystanders in a mass shooting (Rosenthal & Winkler, 2013, p. 233). This means that such a policy would be considered constitutional under the current parameters.

Interviewees also advocated restrictions on assault weapons as a policy to reduce harm in mass shootings. Rukmani Bhatia (formerly CAP) explained what type of weapon would fall under this definition: "A semi-automatic firearm with a detachable magazine and a military-style accessory, e.g. a pistol grip, a folding stock" The advocacy group, NAA, formed after the Sandy Hook shooting has made campaigning against assault weapons a priority issue, since an AR-15 was used in that incident. This law was subsequently passed in Connecticut, the state where the shooting took place. Like the federal assault weapons ban that was in place from 1994-2004, existing assault weapons were grandfathered, meaning those who owned them prior to the ban were allowed to keep them. More recently, NAA has focused on a new piece of legislation, HR-1296, which is an updated and improved assault weapons ban with additions that includes a gun buyback provision and a ban on bump stocks. As it stands, Po Murray (NAA) believes they have the votes to pass the bill in Congress with 216 cosponsors for the bill; although leadership is "not completely comfortable pushing for a vote at this time to protect the frontline Democratic House Representatives in red districts."

Examining public opinion polls finds that there is some public support for reinstating the assault weapons ban and limiting the number of rounds that can be fired in large capacity magazines. Sixty-one percent of adults believed that banning assault-style weapons would be very or somewhat effective in preventing school shootings (Graf, 2018). Another survey, which oversampled gun owners and non-gun owners living in households with guns, found that circa 65% of overall respondents supported banning military-style semi-automatic weapons and large capacity magazines. Breaking this down into gun owners and non-gun owners found there were significant differences in levels of support. Policies banning the sale of semiautomatic assault weapons were supported by 77% of non-gun owners compared to 46% of gun owners. For large capacity magazines, levels of support were 76% and 48% for non-gun owners and gun owners respectively (Barry, McGinty, Vernick & Webster, 2013, pp. 1077, 1080).

There were also other social characteristics influencing support for an assault weapons ban. A survey of 13-17 year olds found that 59% of White teenagers said this would be somewhat or very effective at preventing school shootings, compared to 80% and 79% of Black and Hispanic teenagers (Graf, 2018). Similarly, a study of 419 university students found that differences in support was gendered, with females being 1.9 times more likely to believe assault weapons and large capacity magazines should be banned than male respondents (Lewis et al., 2016, p. 484). Another study found that support for an assault weapons ban was partisan in nature, with 81% of Democrats maintaining that banning assault weapons would be at least somewhat effective compared to 35% of Republicans (Graf, 2018).

The "Gun Violence Prevention and Community Safety Act of 2020, H. R. 5717" bill, introduced by former Presidential candidate, Senator Elizabeth Warren (D-Mass.), includes a restriction on semiautomatic weapons and limits large capacity ammunition feeding devices to ten rounds or less. This bill is still to be voted on. Whether an assault weapons ban is a viable policy option was said by interviewees to depend on the outcome of the 2020 Presidential Election, which was unknown at the time of interviews. Jim Kessler (TW) purported that President Donald Trump is not going to take any action on it: "I think if he went as far as the assault weapons ban there would be people who would be really upset." Similar points were made by Marvin Lim (KGOC) and Rukmani Bhatia (formerly CAP) who described an assault weapons ban as "very ambitious at this stage" and "a more challenging policy to advance" respectively. Even with the Democratic candidate, Joe Biden, winning the Presidency (BBC News, 2020), there is still only a slim possibility of such a policy being pursued. and it is likely that for a Democratic president other policies would be the priority. Jim Kessler (TW) explained the prioritization of policies should a Democrat become President: "My view is let's get universal background checks first and then go for assault weapons ban next."

RED FLAG LAWS

Another policy proposed by interviewees was "Extreme Risk Protection Orders" which are sometimes known as "red flag laws." This prescribes a written order or warrant issued by a State, Tribal or local county to do one or more of the following: prohibit a named individual from owning, purchasing, possessing or receiving a firearm; having a firearm removed or surrendered by a named individual; this being in effect for a set period of time or until an order terminating or superseding the original one is issued (United States House of Representatives, 2020, Title IV, Section 401). Eileen McCarron (CC) describes what these laws entail:

If someone is going off the rails behaviorally and they're threatening to hurt someone else or themselves, their families or law enforcement can go to court and get a protection order that will have their firearms removed from them and put them on the no-buy list for firearms.

Proposals for these kinds of bills first arose from discussions after the 2012 Sandy Hook school shootings, explained Adelyn Allchin (CSGV). Her organization convened with public health researchers, as well as mental health and legal experts, to formulate policies based on risk of violence rather than a diagnosis of mental illness. This group of experts is now formally known as the Consortium for Risk-Based Firearm Policy and is managed by her organization. She explained the purpose of this order: "It was meant to be a civil order so it wouldn't be criminalizing individuals but as a tool to help temporarily separate guns from the individual at risk during that risky period." A similar point was made by Rachel Graber (NCADV) that the intention is not to stigmatize but to reduce the risk of harm during a particular period: "We're talking about people in crisis— in most cases a temporary crisis." To that end, it is based on risk factors for violence, e.g. alcohol misuse, history of violence and so forth, rather than mental illness. There are two types of orders: a short-term one lasting fourteen to twenty-one days in length; a longer final order tending to last a year. The type issued is dependent upon whether the risk is continuing or just a short respite is needed. Its intention is to "reduce mass shootings, suicides and other interpersonal violence."-Adelyn Allchin (CSGV). Mirroring this, Giffords Law Center to Prevent Gun Violence (2018a) found that properly implemented and utilized extreme risk orders have been shown to prevent firearm suicides and may also help prevent mass shootings and gun homicides. Adelyn Allchin's organization, CSGV, is concentrating on passing these laws and helping implement them at different levels, including state, cities and counties.

Currently, these laws have been passed in seventeen states and the District of Columbia (Paterson, 2019). Eileen McCarron (CC) explained that following the ambush murder of Sherriff's Deputy Zackari Parrish III, her group worked to have the bill introduced in 2018; however, it passed in the House and died in the Senate. In spite of this, the red flag bill became a central issue in the state elections where candidates were asked about it when out campaigning on people's doorsteps. In those elections, Democrats regained control of the State Legislature. In the end, the bill was reintroduced and sponsored by newly-elected Representative, Tom Sullivan, whose son, Alex, was killed in the Aurora Theater massacre (2012). The bill passed in the 2019 legislative session in Colorado with all but three Democrats voting in favor of it and every Republican voting against it. The 2018 Parkland shooting could also have contributed to this. Jonathan Perloe (CAGV) said that prior to this incident, only four or five states had red flag laws and that "the number of states that have adopted those laws since is in response to Parkland." Connecticut was the first state to pass such a law, explained Jonathan Perloe (CAGV), in response to a workplace mass shooting, where people thought the shooter was dangerous, had access to firearms and had been threatening people; yet nothing could be done about it.

In terms of federal-level progress, Bill H.R. 1235 "Extreme Risk Protection Order of 2019" was introduced to the House. Interviewees tentatively agreed that this could gain enough support to pass. Jonathan Perloe (CAGV) maintained that out of all possible policies this one has the greatest chance of passing, particularly since a number of Republican Senators have signaled support for it. Similarly, Marvin Lim (KGOC) pointed to the fact that these laws have "had some measure of bipartisan support, not just at the federal level but at the states that have tried to pass that." This is particularly the case since the El Paso shooting in 2019 could potentially have been prevented with such a law. The law has gained greater attention since then:

Red flag is now a term that is much more in circulation among the general public compared to a year ago when even after Parkland that was something that a lot of GVP advocates knew about but if you asked an average American that cares about gun violence, they weren't focused on that. – Marvin Lim (KGOC)

Backing this up, a recent poll of 1009 American citizens found that red flag laws do have broad support at 77% for family-initiated orders and 70% for those initiated by law enforcement. Two-thirds and 70% of Republicans supported orders initiated by law enforcement and family members respectively. For gun owners, levels of support stood at 60% for law enforcement-initiated orders and 67% for family ones. This support was gendered, however, with females more in favor of red flag laws than men (Paterson, 2019).

Interviewee, Adam Skaggs (GLCPGV), was a bit more skeptical about the red flag law's potential for success at the federal level, questioning whether it would get enough Republican support. In contrast, he believed that the law could center on assisting states to effectively implement those laws: "I think it's more likely we would see federal funding for states to implement more effective red flag laws." In line with this, Jonathan Perloe (CAGV) argued that red flag laws are something that needs to be implemented at the state level: "It requires local law enforcement as they are the ones that actually go and remove the guns, so it's not really something that a federal law could practically address." There is also opposition to contend with in states which have red flag laws. A gun rights group in Colorado describes the recent red flag law as a "gun confiscation scheme." Moreover, local sheriffs have said they will refuse to endorse it on the grounds that the law violates the Second Amendment (Paterson, 2019). It is worth noting that there have been legal challenges to extreme risk laws in Connecticut, Florida and Indiana on the basis that they are unconstitutional under the Second Amendment and/or violate the due process rights of individuals. Despite this, none of these legal challenges have been upheld in court (Giffords Law Center to Prevent Gun Violence, 2018a).

SAFE STORAGE LAWS

Another policy proposal interviewees believed would reduce mass shootings is laws relating to "safe storage." These are laws that mandate gun owners should store their firearms safely and unloaded when left unattended (Giffords Law Center to Prevent Gun Violence, 2018b). Rukmani Bhatia (formerly CAP) explained why this law could make a difference: "When there is a gun at home, there is an increased likelihood of firearm injury and death in that home; whether it be from unintentional shootings, youth suicide or, in some cases, homicide committed by a family member." This was backed up by a study by which found that between 6-32% of youth firearms deaths by suicide and unintentional injury could be prevented by an intervention requiring adults to lock up guns in their home (Monuteaux, Azrael & Miller, 2019).

In the case of mass shootings, safe storage is particularly relevant when one is committed by an individual unable to buy a gun because they are prohibited. A National Threat Assessment Center (2019b) report into school violence found that 45% acquired a firearm from the home of a parent or another relative. In 29% of those cases, the firearms were readily accessible or not stored securely. In line with this, one of the main messaging aims of Shaun Dakin's group, PAASD, is to ensure that the school community educates parents and community members regarding this issue: "It's about educating parents to store their guns safely in the home and just making sure that parents really understand that." Brian Malte (H & HF) made a similar point that to reduce school shootings and youth suicides: "There needs to be an awareness of parents and neighbors about guns in the home."

Eleven states have laws relating to safe storage. Massachusetts mandates that all firearms should be stored with a lock in place; whilst other states like California, Connecticut and New York require it for certain situations, e.g. if there is a domestic abuser in the home. A number of states also set standards for the locking devices used. This is one of the Executive Orders that were passed by former President Barack Obama in 2013, mandating that the Consumer Product Safety Commission were to review the effectiveness of gun locks and safes since a number of them had been subject to recall due to design failures (Bandlamudi, 2019; Giffords Law Center to Prevent Gun Violence, 2018b). The law in Connecticut recently changed due to an incident with a boy who played at a friend's house and accidently shot and killed himself with the gun of his friend's father. At the time, the law was that only loaded firearms needed to be stored securely. The father had stored his handgun together with ammunition in the closet, allowing the boys to load the gun. This resulted in a law passing where the home storage requirement applies to both loaded and unloaded guns if there is a child aged under eighteen years in the home. Jonathan Perloe (CAGV) noted the high levels of support for that bill: "It passed with more votes than any bill has ever passed the legislature and more Republican support than ever before." In spite of this, it was separated from a bill that required safe storage in a car if it was unattended: "The idea that a gun owner should lock up their gun in a car when they're not in it was too much for some legislators."-Jonathan Perloe (CAGV). Safe storage of guns in cars could probably help to reduce thefts of guns. Furthermore, explained Eileen McCarron (CC), required reporting of any lost or stolen firearms would prevent them flowing into the secondary market of guns. A similar recommendation was made by Vizzard (2015, p. 894) to reduce trafficking of firearms from the primary or legal market to the secondary or unlicensed market.

In terms of public opinion, a survey of more than 1000 Americans found that almost eight in ten supported safe storage laws. There were a few variations based on social characteristics. Nine in ten Democrats supported this compared to almost seven in ten Republicans. A greater number of women supported it at 83% compared to 74% of men. Two in ten gun owners were opposed to the laws, something which is important since they are the group that will be directly responsible for following the requirements of the law (Bandlamudi, 2019). It may be the case that incidents like the one in Connecticut are what persuaded more people to support safe storage laws.

UNIVERSAL BACKGROUND CHECKS

Universal background checks is a policy that was mentioned by all interviewees as a desirable law to pass. Rukmani Bhatia (formerly CAP) explained why such a law is so important: "Currently, we don't have universal background checks, so it is possible for prohibited persons who are legally not allowed to buy or possess guns to easily purchase and possess guns from private sellers." Similarly, Vizzard (2015, p. 893) recommended that future policy objectives should center on reducing access to firearms by prohibited and high-risk individuals. A universal background checks law would require checks to be conducted via the National Instant Criminal Background System (NICS) for all gun purchases and transfers, including private ones and straw purchases. The Bureau of Alcohol, Tobacco and Firearms (ATF) could offer assistance to local and state law enforcement agencies to trace firearms. If it transpired that firearms from unlicensed persons were commonly used in homicides, then that could strengthen the argument for universal background checks (Krouse & Richardson, 2015, p. 29). Heather Ross (TGS) highlighted that the only problem with this is that criminal history will not show up on the NICS record for individuals that are underage. Fox and Fridel (2016, p. 16) made a similar point that restricting guns from dangerous individuals is a challenge in cases where there is no official record of criminality or psychological impairment.

Following the Sandy Hook school shooting in 2012, passing such a law at the federal level was something that the gun violence prevention movement seemed to be coalescing around (Kerr, 2018). A bill was introduced into Congress to expand background checks; however, this fell short of the sixty votes needed due to the filibuster role (Jones & Stone, 2015, p. 170). There was some progress at the state-level. For instance, in Connecticut, the state in which the Sandy Hook shooting took place, background checks were one of many laws passed. Po Murray (NAA) said that members of the public were supportive of these laws and her group worked to ensure the Governor, Dannel Malloy, was re-elected because of his strong support for gun violence prevention. Currently, the District of Columbia, California, Colorado, Connecticut, Delaware, New York, Oregon, Rhode Island and Washington mandate universal background checks for all gun transfers. Eighteen states in total require background checks for private transfers (Lott, 2016, p. 6).

Reviewing opinion polls indicates that universal background checks is one of the bills that gains high levels of public support. Eighty-five percent of all adults and 86% of those aged 13-17 supported preventing individuals with mental illnesses from buying guns as a way to prevent school shootings (Graf, 2018). Likewise, a survey by Barry, McGinty, Vernick and Webster (2015) found background checks were supported by 84% of respondents; although this was a slight decrease from an earlier survey that found overall levels of support stood at 89%. Surprisingly, perhaps, the slight decline in support was in the non-gun owners group; whilst levels of support remain static amongst gun owners. Universal background checks was agreed by all interviewees to be one of the gun policies that gun owners and National Rifle Association (NRA) members tend to support. Sheila Islong's group, Giffords, is currently building a coalition of gun violence prevention activists and gun owners to focus on "reasonable policy positions" such as background checks. She explained how this works:

There are people who essentially call me and say 'Hey, I hear you guys built a gun owners coalition in Texas and I'm a gun owner and I support better laws on background checks. How do I get involved?'

Rukmani Bhatia (formerly CAP) maintained that educating people about the purpose of a universal background check could help build support at the grassroots level. She explained that talking through any issues they have with a universal background checks system, as well as explaining that there is no registry involved could help convince people that such a system is not "gun grabbing."

In addition to criminal history, background checks should also regulate for serious mental health impairment. Eighty-five percent of those surveyed by Barry and colleagues (2013) supported the specific requirement for those individuals who have been involuntarily committed or declared mentally incompetent to be submitted to the national background checks system. It has been cautioned by Fox and Fridel (2016, p. 16), however, that any law focusing on background checks for mental illness does not limit access to those with moderate issues. There is the possibility that this could dissuade people with moderate mental health issues from seeking treatment for fear of losing access. Following on from this, Heather Ross (TGS) explained that any strategy for curbing gun violence needs to center on providing comprehensive mental health care in addition to gun laws. Increased spending on mental health care as a strategy for reducing gun violence received support from 61% of respondents in the study by Barry, McGinty, Vernick and Webster (2013).

Currently, there is some federal progress in this area. The House of Representatives passed H.R. 8 to require background checks on all gun sales and H.R. 1112 to attempt to close the so-called "Charleston loophole" where the waiting period for the background check is extended to ten days from its current limit of three days. The bills have been stalled in the U.S. Senate. Po Murray (NAA) described it in the following way: "They're [the bills] sitting on Mitch McConnell's desk in the Senate graveyard." Interviewees postulated that the results of the 2020 Presidential election would determine whether or not the bills pass the Senate and are signed into law. Marvin Lim (KGOC) said that if Democrats had control of the Senate from Republicans and the Presidency, then there was a chance of this happening. Jim Kessler (TW) believed that President Trump could "get away with" supporting universal background checks, because it is a popular policy even amongst gun owners. He speculated that Trump might support such a policy if he was looking to pick up votes in the suburbs. In the end, however, Jim Kessler (TW) predicted that Trump would "back off" in order to avoid challenging his base on guns. As it transpired, the Presidency was called for the Democratic candidate, Joe Biden; whilst the situation in Congress remained unchanged, with the Democrats retaining control of the House and the Republicans keeping a majority in the Senate (BBC News, 2020).

OTHER PROPOSALS

Interviewees also made a number of other recommendations for policies intended to reduce mass shootings and gun violence more generally. One of the proposals focused on expanding the research relating to guns undertaken. Rachel Graber (NCADV) explained it in the following way: "Gun violence is a very uniquely American problem and it's not well-understood so we need to invest in research." In particular, she explained, funding for public health research by the Center for Disease Control and Prevention (CDC) would be welcomed. A public health approach aims to prevent gun violence through identification of risk factors and devising solutions (see Butts, Roman, Bostwick, Porter, 2015; Mercy, Rosenberg, Powell, Broome & Koper, 1993; Mercy, Krug, Dahlberg & Zui, 2003). In 1996, the Dickey Amendment was passed forbidding the CDC to "advocate or promote gun control." Although this did not specifically ban gun-related research, funds were cut and the agency was dissuaded from pursuing such projects. This situation changed in 2018 when the restrictions on gun violence research were lifted. The following year, Congress approved twenty-five million dollars in federal funding to study gun safety. The money will be split between the CDC and the National Institutes of Health (Hauck, Ellis & Filby, 2020). Additionally, Sheila Islong (Giffords) said funding for gun research should be extended to states to "try to come up with some answers about why this is becoming an epidemic." The language used here of "epidemic" is in line with a public health approach. In this sense, gun violence is treated as another health issue and uses deaths and injuries to quantify the extent of that violence (Mercy, Rosenberg, Powell, Broome & Koper, 1993, p. 8). As the frontline staff dealing with the injuries caused by gun violence, physicians have recently come out in support of a public health approach to gun violence (Hauck, Ellis & Filby, 2020). Although there has been some resistance from the NRA, gun-related research is a relatively uncontroversial measure that should be welcomed by members of the public.

Another proposal made by interviewees was to have a gun licensing and registration system. Adelyn Allchin (CSGV) explained the motivation behind such a policy: "The licensing would ensure that everyone has had a background check and you'd need to go through law enforcement to get that license." Further to this, Jonathan Perloe (CAGV) believed this could reduce criminal usage of guns, in that "if you have to show up at law enforcement and give your fingerprints and sometimes be questioned or whatever, it's less likely that a criminal or someone with criminal intent is going to go and register a gun." Stoebe (2015) and Vizzard (2015) made similar claims that a comprehensive system of licensing and registration would allow for individual transfers to be tracked and removed from prohibited persons. Moreover, it would allow controls on the secondary or illegal market of guns to be enforced. It is suggested that the information repository is managed centrally by the federal government, with states taking on the primary responsibility of registering firearms akin to state motor vehicle departments (Vizzard, 2015, p. 900). The main barrier to such a system would appear to be resistance to it. Jonathan Perloe (CAGV) argued that one of the positions advanced by gun rights advocates is that "we can't have registration because then the government will know who has guns and they are going to come and seize our guns." He described this as "absurd" in the present-day context. In order to shift levels of public support, it may be that a cultural change in attitudes towards guns is needed (Stoebe, 2015, p. 23). In line with this, it seems unlikely there will be political action in this area in the near future. Jonathan Perloe (CAGV) maintained that the only way a licensing proposal would pass at the federal level would be if Democrats took control of the Senate — this would have to be at least sixty Democrats due to the filibuster rule — held the House and won the Presidency. Considering the results of the election left Republicans in control of the Senate (BBC News, 2020), it seems unlikely licensing will become law anytime in the future. Having said that, the fact that Democratic candidates are talking about it is a positive sign: "I think it's really helpful that the candidates have been talking about licensing. This issue has become more mainstream; whereas previously people were shying away from measures like this."-Jonathan Perloe (CAGV).

In line with a public health approach, there was also a proposal to make greater use of smart gun technology to reduce accidental shootings. This would also prevent people stealing and using guns for gun crime, including mass shootings. Using radio frequency or biometric identifications, this kind of technology would make guns operate only for authorized users (Wolfson, Teret, Fraltardi, Miller & Azral, 2016, p. 411). Rukmani Bhatia (formerly CAP) noted, however, that there was some skepticism around digitized trigger locks because of current flaws in fingerprint technology: for instance, sometimes users' smartphones do not work properly. In order for the industry to innovate, she argued, there would need to be a demand for it. Andrew Goddard (VCPS) believed that there is a market for it and that "a lot of people would buy it if it was proven that it was going to fire when they wanted it to." Findings from a survey of 3949 individuals by Wolfson and colleagues (2015) backed up this notion. Fifty-nine percent indicated that they would be willing to purchase a gun that fires only for authorized users; whilst 23% were undecided and 18% unwilling. The highest levels of interest were from those who consider themselves to be politically liberal at 71%; although conservatives and moderates also showed some support at 56% and 36% respectively. It is surmised that based on these results a substantial market exists amongst potential purchasers of new guns (Wolfson et al., 2015, pp. 411-412).

The last miscellaneous proposal centered on "ghost" and other types of untraceable guns such as ones made using a 3D printer. There are loopholes in federal law that are allowing individuals to circumvent the restrictions by creating a mostly plastic firearm with metal parts that can be removed prior to metal detector screenings (Giffords Law Center to Prevent Gun Violence, 2018c). As they are not technically firearms, explained Jonathan Perloe (CAGV), the kits for these kinds of weapons do not require a background check to purchase and the lack of serial numbers makes them untraceable. There are kits online that allow people to make guns at home. A homemade weapon made using a kit like this was recently used in a high school shooting in Santa Clarita, California (Bates, 2019). Po Murray's group, NAA, is actively running a campaign to stop blueprints for 3D guns from being released after the Trump administration settled the lawsuit with Defense Distributed. Her group worked with Attorney Generals across the country who filed a lawsuit to try to stop the release of these blueprints. A federal judge has issued a temporary restraining order to block the 3D weapon blueprints being published online, halting the issue for the moment (Brown, 2020). Laws pursuant to dealing with undetectable and untraceable guns have been passed in California, Connecticut, New Jersey, New York and Washington (Giffords Law Center to Prevent Gun Violence, 2018c). The law in Connecticut passed after a number of cases in which "ghost guns" were being sold to, or in the possession of criminals. Jonathan Perloe (CAGV) noted that the bill regulating ghost guns "passed with more Republican support than ever before. That is a sign of how things are changing."

CONCLUSION

This chapter has presented an overview of policy proposals pertaining to firearms that are believed to reduce the incidence of mass shootings, as well as gun violence more generally. Mass shootings can act as "focusing events," positioning firearms onto the policy agenda. A short "window of opportunity" to pass legislation is afforded by the public debate prompted by a mass shooting incident, particularly if it is covered extensively in the news media. During this time period, more restrictive gun proposals tend to be advanced (Fleming et al., 2016). In spite of this, there tends to be little in the way of progress — particularly in relation to federal laws — following a mass shooting (Kerr, 2018).

Outlined by interviewees were proposals that may help reduce the incidence of and harm caused by mass shootings. Regulations centering on ammunition rather than firearms were one of the proposals raised by interviewees. This would involve individuals looking to purchase ammunition having to undergo a background check; in addition to limitations on the quantities of bullets that could be purchased at the one time. Additionally, there could also be bans placed on harm-inducing bullets that cause greater injuries when fired. These ideas are particularly relevant to mass shootings, in which large quantities of bullets tend to be used and harm-inducing bullets have sometimes been used (Kerr, 2019). Although several scholars have raised the idea that focusing on ammunition could be less contentious than focusing on firearms (e.g. Healey, 1998; Kerr, 2019), interviewees believed it would still be as politically-charged a topic. Moreover, it was felt that proposals would be unlikely to pass since ammunition is neither at the forefront of citizens' minds nor part of the gun violence debate. What could have a better chance of passing are restrictions on the amount of bullets that can be fired at any one time, by limiting what are known as "large" or "high capacity magazines." Interviewees maintained this should be a high priority, particularly since large capacity magazines tend to be used in mass shootings. Public opinion polls show there is a good degree of support for limiting large capacity magazines. Due to the current political make-up in Congress, however, interviewees were skeptical about whether such a proposal would gain traction at the federal level. It is far more likely that any proposals would pass at the state level.

Other proposals advanced by interviewees centered on restricting access to guns from those most at risk. One of those policies was "extreme risk protection orders," which temporarily remove the firearm during a risky period in an individual's life. Interviewees were cautiously confident that this law would pass at the federal level, particularly given bipartisan levels of support for it. Another proposal is to pass "safe storage laws," mandating that firearms have to be stored safely and left unloaded to prevent children and other unauthorized persons from accessing them. Public levels of support for safe storage laws are reasonable high, so this is another potential proposal that could pass. Universal background checks are another policy intended to restrict access to firearms to those who are prohibited by requiring a background check for all sales and transfers via the NICS. This is one of the proposals that continuously receive high levels of support from citizens, even gun owners and NRA members. The results of the 2020 Presidential Election are said to determine whether or not universal background checks get signed into law at the federal-level. Interviewees were optimistic about the chances should the Democrats gain control of the Senate and the Presidency. Since the interviews, the election results have now been called with Democrats winning the Presidency but not gaining control of the Senate (BBC News, 2020). This will make the chances of passing legislation more challenging.

Ideas were also suggested for other policies intended to reduce mass shootings and gun violence in general. One of these was to expand research relating to gun violence, which seems likely given the recent increase in funding for this purpose. Another was to have a gun licensing and registration system; although it was acknowledged by interviewees that this is unlikely to become law anytime soon. There was a proposal to make use of smart gun technology to prevent gun thefts and accidental shootings. Further innovation and design is likely needed; however, this becoming law is a possibility in future. The final proposal focused on "ghost guns" and those made using 3D printers, which are untraceable and can be made at home. Whilst there was an ongoing dispute with the Trump administration in 2020 over these types of weapons, there may be some action on this at the federal level.

This chapter has documented the ideas from gun violence prevention interviewees about proposals that may reduce mass shootings, as well as overall gun violence rates. As demonstrated, public support and backing from policymakers are fundamental to whether a proposal passes and becomes law. The proposals with the best chances of doing so at the present time are extreme risk protection orders and safe storage laws. Moreover, with Democrats winning the 2020 Presidential election, there is also the possibility of universal background checks and limits of large capacity magazines passing; although the Republican-controlled Senate may pose some barriers to this. The involvement of interest groups to frame the issue of gun violence in a way that is persuasive to members of the public and policymakers is crucial. The final two chapters will build upon this by summarizing what happened with the 2020 election; in addition to outlining ways to frame the issue to make it important and future strategies that could be used.

REFERENCES

Bandlamudi, A. (2019, October 2). *Most Americans Support Safe Gun Storage Laws, Polls Finds.* WANU University Public Radio. https://wamu.org/story/19/10/02/most-americans-support-safe-storage-laws-according-to-new-poll/

Barry, C. L., McGinty, E. E., Vernick, J. S., & Webster, D. W. (2013). After Newtown – Public Opinion on Gun Policy and Mental Illness. *The New England Journal of Medicine, 368*(12), 1077–1081. doi:10.1056/NEJMp1300512 PMID:23356490

Bates, J. (2019, November 23). *The Saugus High School Shooter Used an Illegal 'Ghost Gun.' Authorities Warn More Criminals Are Using Untraceable Weapons to Get Around Gun Laws.* TIME. https://time.com/5737227/saugus-shooter-ghost-gun/

BBC News. (2020). *US Election 2020.* https://www.bbc.co.uk/news/election/us2020/results

Brown, A. (2018, January 6). *America should regulate bullets.* The Washington Post (Opinion). https://www.washingtonpost.com/opinions/we-should-regulate-bullets/2016/01/06/62de9322-b3dc-11e5-a76a-0b5145e8679a_story.html?utm_term=.290b5ec41469

Brown, K. (2020, March 9). *Judge Blocks White House Bid for Online 3D Printed Gun Blueprints.* Courthouse News Service. https://www.courthousenews.com/judge-blocks-white-house-bid-to-put-3d-printed-gun-blueprints-online/

Burns, R., & Crawford, C. (1999). School shootings, the media and public fear: Ingredients for a moral panic. *Crime, Law, and Social Change, 32*(2), 147–168. doi:10.1023/A:1008338323953

Butts, J. A., Roman, C. G., Bostwick, L., & Porter, J. R. (2015). Cure Violence: A Public Health Model to Reduce Gun Violence. *Annual Review of Public Health, 36*(1), 39–53. doi:10.1146/annurev-publhealth-031914-122509 PMID:25581151

Chong, D., & Druckman, J. N. (2007). Framing Theory. *Annual Review of Political Science, 10*(1), 103–126. doi:10.1146/annurev.polisci.10.072805.103054

Dailard, S. D. (1998). The Role of Ammunition in a Balanced Program of Gun Control: A Critique of Moynihan Bullet Bills. *Journal of Legislation, 20*(1), 3.

Deutch, T. (2019, February 12). *Press Release: Deutch, Mendendez Lead Bill to Ban Large Capacity Magazines*. Congressman Ted Deutch's website. https://teddeutch.house.gov/news/documentsingle. aspx?DocumentID=399504

Fleming, A. K., Rutledge, P. E., Dixon, G. C., & Peralton, S. (2016). When the smoke clears: Focusing events, issue definition, strategic framing and the politics of gun control. *Social Science Quarterly, 97*(5), 1144–1156. doi:10.1111squ.12269

Fox, J. A., & Fridel, E. E. (2016). The Tenuous Connections Involving Mass Shootings, Mental Illness and Gun Laws. *Violence and Gender, 3*(1), 14–19. doi:10.1089/vio.2015.0054

Giffords Law Center to Prevent Gun Violence. (2018a). *Extreme Risk Protection Orders*. https://lawcenter. giffords.org/gun-laws/policy-areas/who-can-have-a-gun/extreme-risk-protection-orders/

Giffords Law Center to Prevent Gun Violence. (2018b). *Safe Storage*. https://lawcenter.giffords.org/ gun-laws/policy-areas/child-consumer-safety/safe-storage/

Giffords Law Center to Prevent Gun Violence. (2018c). *Ghost Guns*. https://lawcenter.giffords.org/gun-laws/policy-areas/hardware-ammunition/ghost-guns/

Giffords Law Center to Prevent Gun Violence. (n.d.). *Ammunition Regulation*. https://lawcenter.giffords. org/gun-laws/policy-areas/hardware-ammunition/ammunition-regulation/#state

Goss, K. A. (2006). *Disarmed: The Missing Movement for Gun Control in America*. Princeton University Press.

Graf, N. (2018, April 18). *A majority of U.S. teens fear a shooting could happen at their school, and most parents share their concern*. Pew Research Center. https://www.pewresearch.org/fact-tank/2018/04/18/a-majority-of-u-s-teens-fear-a-shooting-could-happen-at-their-school-and-most-parents-share-their-concern/

Grossman, M. (2012). *The Not-So-Special Interests: Interest Groups, Public Representation and American Governance*. Stanford University Press. doi:10.1515/9780804781343

Hauck, G., Ellis, N. T., & Filby, M. (2020, February 10). *Congress approved $25M in funding for gun safety research. Now what?* USA Today. https://eu.usatoday.com/story/news/nation/2020/02/09/gun-violence-how-researchers-spend-25-m-gun-safety-funding/4464121002/

Healey, B. J. (1998). Plugging the Bullet Holes in U.S. Gun Law: An Ammunition-Based Proposal for Tightening Gun Control. *The John Marshall Law Review, 32*(1), 2.

Henderson, P., & Trotta, D. (2013, January 20). *Gun Control Debate Neglects to Address Bullets*. Huffington Post. https://www.huffingtonpost.com/2013/01/20/gun-control-debate_n_2514918.html

House of Representatives. (2020). *Gun Control Plan: Gun Violence Prevention and Community Safety Act of 2020. H. R. 5717. 116th Congress, 2nd session*. Thirteen Colony Press.

Hrebenar, R. J., & Scott, R. K. (1982). *Interest Group Politics in America*. Prentice-Hall Inc.

Jacobs, L. R., & Shapiro, R. Y. (2000). *Politicians don't pander: political manipulation and the loss of Democratic responsiveness.* University of Chicago Press.

Jones, M. A., & Stone, G. W. (2015). The U.S. Gun Control Paradox: Gun Buyer Response to Congressional Gun Control Initiatives. *Journal of Business and Economics, 13*(4), 167–174.

Jordan, G., & Maloney, W. A. (2007). *Democracy and Interest Groups: Enhancing Participation.* Palgrave Macmillan. doi:10.1057/9780230223240

Kerr, S. E. M. (2018). *Gun Violence Prevention? The Politics Behind Policy Responses to School Shootings in the United States.* Palgrave MacMillan.

Kerr, S. E. M. (2019). What We Need is Bullet Control: Could regulation of bullets reduce mass shootings? In G. Crews (Ed.), *Handbook of Research on Mass Shootings and Multiple Victim Violence* (pp. 432–446). IGI Global.

Krouse, W. J., & Richardson, D. J. (2015). *Mass Murder with Firearms: Incidents and Victims, 1999-2013.* Congressional Research Service.

Law Center to Prevent Gun Violence. (2012). *Ammunition Regulation Policy Summary.* http://smartgunlaws.org/ammunition-regulationpolicy-summary/

Lewis, R. K., LoCurto, J., Brown, K., Stowell, D., Maryman, J. V., Dean, A., McNair, T., Ojeda, D., & Siwierka, J. (2016). College Students Opinions on Gun Violence. *Journal of Community Health, 41*(3), 482–487. doi:10.100710900-015-0118-x PMID:26516018

McCarthy, J. (2019, November 4). *64% of Americans Want Stricter Laws on Gun Sales.* Gallup. https://news.gallup.com/poll/268016/americans-stricter-laws-gun-sales.aspx

Mercy, J. A., Krug, E. G., Dahlberg, L. L., & Zui, A. B. (2003). Violence and Health: The United States in a Global Perspective. *American Journal of Public Health, 92*(12), 256–261. doi:10.2105/AJPH.93.2.256 PMID:12554579

Mercy, J. A., Rosenberg, M. L., Powell, K. E., Broome, C. V., & Koper, W. L. (1993). Public Health Policy for Preventing Violence. *Health Affairs, 12*(4), 7–29. doi:10.1377/hlthaff.12.4.7 PMID:8125450

Monuteaux, M. C., Azrael, D., & Miller, M. (2019). Association of Increased Safe Household Firearm Storage With Firearm Suicide and Unintentional Death Among US Youths. *JAMA Pediatrics, 173*(7), 657–662. doi:10.1001/jamapediatrics.2019.1078 PMID:31081861

National Threat Assessment Center. (2019a). *Attacks in Public Spaces – 2018.* U.S. Secret Service, Department of Homeland Security.

National Threat Assessment Center. (2019b). *Protecting America's Schools: A U.S. Secret Service Analysis of Targeted School Violence.* U.S. Secret Service, Department of Homeland Security.

Paterson, L. (2019, August 20). *Poll: Americans, Including Republicans And Gun Owners, Broadly Support Red Flag Laws.* National Public Radio. https://www.npr.org/2019/08/20/752427922/poll-americans-including-republicans-and-gun-owners-broadly-support-red-flag-law?t=1588502583435

Rosenthal, L. E., & Winkler, A. (2013). The Scope of Regulatory Authority under the Second Amendment. In D. W. Webster & J. S. Vernick (Eds.), *Reducing Gun Violence in America: Informing Policy with Evidence and Analysis* (pp. 225–236). The John Hopkins University Press.

Spitzer, R. J. (2004). The Politics of Gun Control (3rd ed.). Washington, DC: Congressional Quarterly (CQ) Press.

Stoebe, W. (2015). Firearm Availability and Violent Death: The Need for a Culture Change in Attitudes towards Guns.'. *Analyses of Social Issues and Public Policy (ASAP)*, *16*(1), 1–29.

Truman, D. B. (1951/1993). *The Governmental Process: Political Interests and Public Opinion* (2nd ed.). University of California.

Vizzard, W. J. (1999). The Impact of Agenda Confliction Policy Formulation and Implementation: The Case of Gun Control. In *Guns in America: A Reader* (pp. 131–144). New York University Press.

Vizzard, W. J. (2015). The current and future state of gun policy in the United States. *The Journal of Criminal Law & Criminology*, *104*, 5.

Wasserman Schultz, D. (2019, March 13). *Press Release: Wasserman Schultz & Blumenthal Introduce Jaime's Law*. Congresswoman Debbie Wasserman Schultz's Website. https://wassermanschultz.house.gov/news/documentsingle.aspx?DocumentID=1309

Wolfson, J.A., Teret, S. P., Fraltardi, S., Miller, M. & Azral, D. (2016). The U.S. Public's Preference for Safer Guns. *American Journal of Public Health, 106*(3), 411-413.

Woodly, D. R. (2015). *The Politics of Common Sense: How Social Movements Use Public Discourse to Change Politics and Win Acceptance*. Oxford University Press. doi:10.1093/acprof:oso/9780190203986.001.0001

Woznidk, K. H. (2015). Public opinion about gun control post Sandy Hook. *Criminal Justice Policy Review*, *28*(3), 255–278. doi:10.1177/0887403415577192

ADDITIONAL READING

Dailard, S. D. (1998). The Role of Ammunition in a Balanced Program of Gun Control: A Critique of Moynihan Bullet Bills. *Journal of Legislation*, *20*(1), 3.

Healey, B. J. (1998). Plugging the Bullet Holes in U.S. Gun Law: An Ammunition-Based Proposal for Tightening Gun Control. *The John Marshall Law Review*, *32*(1), 2.

Kerr, S. E. M. (2019). What We Need is Bullet Control: Could regulation of bullets reduce mass shootings? In G. Crews (Ed.), *Handbook of Research on Mass Shootings and Multiple Victim Violence* (pp. 432–446). IGI Global.

Vizzard, W. J. (2015). The current and future state of gun policy in the United States. *The Journal of Criminal Law & Criminology*, *104*, 5.

Wolfson, J.A., Teret, S. P., Fraltardi, S., Miller, M. & Azral, D. (2016). The U.S. Public's Preference for Safer Guns. *American Journal of Public Health, 106*(3), 411-413.

KEY TERMS AND DEFINITIONS

Bullet Control: This advocates tighter controls on bullets, such as the quantities and types, as well as background checks to purchase ammunition.

Extreme Risk Protection Orders: These refer to orders whereby access is temporarily removed from individuals considered to be a danger to themselves or others. These are also more commonly known in public discourse as "red flag laws."

Framing: This is a technique that sets parameters on a particular issue and has the potential to affect public opinion.

Ghost Guns: These are firearms which are untraceable by law enforcement, including those made by a 3D printer.

Interest Groups: These are organizations motivated by a particular belief system, such as gun violence prevention, which seeks to influence the policy actions of government.

Safe Storage: Laws requiring firearms to be securely locked away in the household (e.g., in a cabinet) to prevent them being accessed by children or other restricted persons.

Universal Background Checks: This extends the current background check system, whereby a universal system would mandate that a background check is required for any purchase or transfer of a firearm, including those at gun shows and in private sales.

Chapter 11
Framing Gun Violence

ABSTRACT

This chapter builds upon the discussion that began in the previous chapter about possible gun-related legislative options to reduce mass shootings. Discussed here are the framing approaches that could be utilized to mobilize the movement. Prior to that, there will be a discussion about the role of mass shootings in prompting debates about gun policies. The role that interest groups play in the process will be detailed. The chapter then moves on to discuss a number of frames centering on gun violence that could persuade people to support tighter gun regulations: an emotional approach predicated on the human interest side of the issue; a public health angle, treating it as an illness; a rights and responsibilities frame, where the right to own a gun is coupled with a responsibility to use it safely.

INTRODUCTION

The main focus of this chapter is to outline the framing approaches that may be used by GVP interest groups to persuade citizens and policymakers to support their cause. Prior to this, discussed will be the ways in which high-profile incidents of gun violence can provoke the policy debate. Fleming and colleagues (2016) maintained that mass shootings act as "focusing events," creating a window of opportunity for policies to be discussed. The various arms of the United States government play varying roles in the process of policy-making. Interest groups have the potential to propagate gun-related legislation within the government. In particular, they work with the Legislature, which is the most effective branch of government for enacting change. Moreover, interest groups may also persuade members of the public to support their proposals (Grossman, 2008; Grossman, 2012; Hrebenar & Scott, 1982; Truman, 1951/1993).

Frames can be a tool to persuade people and change attitudes (Callaghan, 2005, p. 189). For this to occur, it is crucial the public are informed about the reality of gun violence and how it affects society. With an issue like gun violence, framing should be consistent and resonate with people in order to turn it into an issue that they are passionate about (Woodly, 2015, p. 28). Drawing upon the literature on framing (Aaroe, 2011; Chong & Druckman, 2010; Entman, 2010; Gross, 2008; Iyengar, 1991), various possible frames that could be used in the GVP movement are outlined: an emotional slant, centering on the victims of gun violence; a public health approach, viewing and treating gun violence as an illness;

DOI: 10.4018/978-1-7998-3916-3.ch011

a rights and responsibilities approach, working with gun owners to discuss ideas and potentially draft legislation.

The first part of this chapter looks at the landscape for policy change following a mass shooting. This includes a breakdown of the political system in the United States, detailing the role interest groups play. The second half addresses three potential frames for gun violence: an emotional approach, the public health stance, and the rights and responsibilities frame. Discussed throughout is the viability of each of these approaches and their potential to persuade people about the importance of gun violence prevention. Results from interviews with GVP activists pertaining to these issues are documented throughout this chapter. In addition, relevant literature pertaining to framing, social movements and the political landscape relating to guns in America is interwoven throughout to aid contextual understanding.

SETTING THE SCENE FOR POLICY CHANGE

Firearm Focusing Events

The weapon most commonly used in a mass targeted violence attack is a firearm. Eighty-nine percent of attackers in the National Threat Assessment Center's (2019) study of attacks in public spaces used firearms; whilst the remaining 11% used vehicles. Following on from this, references to guns are prevalent in debates in media discourse following a mass shooting. Schildkraut's (2014) study used a sample of news media content from 2000-2012. Findings showed that of the 1026 references to guns, 47.8% referred to gun control, 37.6% to weapons and 14.7% to gun rights. In a similar vein, gun access was found to be one of the two most prominent themes in the news headlines relating to the 2018 Parkland School shooting. Notably, one headline stated the debate relating to guns was renewed after the incident. The implication from the verb "renewed" is that America has already discussed this issue (Lombardi, 2018). Guns are also a prevalent feature in social media debates. Assessing tweets over a year, Benton and colleagues (2016) identified variations in each side of the gun debate following the mass shooting at Sandy Hook Elementary School. Those in favor of gun control were found to be very vocal in the debate in the immediate stages and this disseminated over time. On the other hand, gun rights advocates become more vocal once national legislation for universal background checks failed in Congress. Similarly, Fiore (2018) found that gun control advocacy tweets following the Parkland (2018) shooting yielded the most replies.

With debate taking place within the news and social media arenas, this paves the way for discussions in the policy sphere. Fleming and colleagues (2016) described incidents such as mass shootings as "firearm focusing events" creating the potential for policy solutions to be advanced. The occurrence of a focusing event focuses attention on a problem and this is defined in relation to similar previous events. In the case of a mass shooting, it highlights the issue of gun violence and is compared with the death and destruction caused by past massacres. Policy entrepreneurs, such as politicians and interest groups, have to act very quickly to advance any policy solutions whilst the issue is a prominent topic. Conversely, when there are no focusing events, gun control policy is not an issue of salience. For that reason, punitive and restrictive gun bills tend to be proposed in the year after a mass shooting (Fleming, Rutledge, Dixon & Peralton, 2016, pp. 1-2, 68). In addition to restrictive gun proposals, lenient gun bills are also likely to be introduced following a mass shooting. Policy entrepreneurs such as the National Rifle Association (NRA) also advance policy solutions during the window of opportunity following a firearm focusing event (Fleming et al., 2016, p. 11). This was the case following the shooting at Parkland High School (2018) in which President Donald Trump backed the NRA's position by advocating arming teachers (Mason & Trotta, 2018).

Proposals may come directly from the Executive Branch as was the case in 2012 following the mass shooting at Sandy Hook Elementary School. For instance, former President Barack Obama proposed restrictive gun bills: closing the loophole in background checks allowing this to be circumvented in the sale of firearms at gun shows and other private transfers; banning military-style assault weapons and high capacity magazines (The White House, 2013). Due to the way the political system works in the United States, however, the Presidency has limited policy-making powers. The President has the ability to shape policy agenda by recommending policies and laws to be deliberated. Inferring from this, persuasion and patronage are key to the amount of influence the President can yield in the process (Hrebenar & Scot, 1982, p. 153). The "policy alternatives" to be discussed are defined by White House staff members. The Presidency also has the power to implement a limited number of measures using Executive Orders (Kingdon, 1994/2003, pp. 23-27). These policies do, however, tend to be small in scope. For instance, Executive Orders under President Obama were to give more funding to the Bureau of Alcohol, Tobacco and Firearms (ATF) to enforce existing gun laws, removing legal barriers that hinder states submitting to the National Instant Criminal Background Checks System (NICS) and require any business that sells guns to obtain a federal license and conduct background checks (National Conference of State Legislatures, 2016). Compared to the proposal to pass universal background checks at the national level, these Executive Orders seem considerably smaller in scale and potential impact.

The Legislature has been the primary means of affecting policy change (Truman, 1951/1993, p. 321). Congress, consisting of the House and the Senate, has the scope to control the policy agenda and its alternatives through hearings, the introduction of bills and speeches. Furthermore, Presidential policy proposals are required to pass through Congress. The House is more likely to introduce legislation, because it consists of four hundred and thirty-five members representing districts within states. The Senate, conversely, is less likely to do so because each Senator represents an entire state; thus, meaning citizens from smaller states are overrepresented (Baker, 1989/1995, pp. 16, 101-102; Fleming et al., 2016, p. 4; Hrebenar & Scott, 1982, p. 153). This has been the case recently with the House introducing and passing legislation H.R.8 on universal background checks; yet the Senate has refused to hold a hearing or a vote on this bill for over a year (Neguse & Mauser, 2020).

Considering all of this, it becomes clear that mass shootings are catalysts for debate relating to gun policies, both in terms of further regulations and loosening laws. Despite this, generally there is very little progress in passing laws following a mass shooting, particularly at the federal level (Kerr, 2018). Goss (2006) spoke of there being a "gun control paradox" in the United States, where there is a disparity between public support for stricter gun laws and the failure of the majority of these laws to pass. This is partly attributed to the failure of activists in favor of gun control to become a movement. Further, it is argued that this may be captured in the following measures: lack of discussion of a gun control movement in the news media; lack of scholarship focusing on gun control; low levels of individual participation; supporters of gun control seeming to be more of a latent public than a movement (Goss, 2006, pp. 13-18). Further adding to the gun control paradox are the record numbers of firearm sales following a mass shooting. For instance, following discussions to implement gun control measures after the Sandy Hook school shooting, background checks for firearm purchases increased 60% and there were shortages in ammunition (Jones & Stone, 2015, p. 167, 172).

This is in direct contrast to other Western countries: for instance, the United Kingdom. After a high-profile mass shooting in 1996, an interest group, Gun Control Network, mobilized and lobbied for extremely tight gun control restrictions in Great Britain. With the support of the general public and politicians, these were successfully passed into law (Kerr, 2018). With the main goal of the interest group achieved, it now only focuses on smaller pieces of legislation, such as air gun restrictions. Having said that, the interest group remains ready to scale up its efforts and mobilize again should the need arise. Mick North (GCN) explained the thinking behind this: "We are a bit worried whether the current [Conservative Party] administration is tempted to go backwards…We will keep our eyes and ears open for any warning signs." This fear is predicated on the current Prime Minister, Boris Johnson, who made unsupportive comments following the passage of the gun control legislation years ago. Moreover, upon meeting with Johnson when he was the Mayor of London, Mick North (GCN) felt that "he didn't seem like he could be persuaded by the kind of arguments we were using."

Role of Interest Groups

Whilst the United States is not expected to follow the same pathway on guns that Great Britain has, it does have the potential to overcome the "gun control paradox" Goss (2006) spoke of. In order to do this, interest groups have to mobilize and advance policy proposals. Like the name suggests, interest groups are motived by a particular "belief system," defined as a "configuration of ideas and attitudes in which the elements are bound together by some form of constraint" (Converse, 1974, p. 302). Its membership tends to be voluntary and consisting of private citizens, with leadership tending to be decided by the group's members. The purpose of interest groups is to influence the actions of government and contribute to the drafting of policies (Jordan & Maloney, 2007, pp. 26, 29). Since the Legislature is the primary means of affecting change, more so than the Executive Branch or Judiciary, this arm of government tends to be the main focus for interest groups. The policy demands of interest groups do tend to reach the President, however, if they are influential enough (Hrebenar & Scott, 1982, pp. 3, 154; Truman, 1951/1993, p. 321).

Extrapolating from this, the extent to which interest groups can influence the decisions of policymakers is dependent on their level of "political efficacy" (Grossman, 2008, p. 49). Grossman (2012, pp. 137-139) points to several ways an interest group can try to gain influence and prominence in debates. One of those is to maintain an active membership through local and state chapters. Another is to be actively cited in the news media, particularly with those based in Washington, D.C. The features that increase the likelihood of this are the number of advocacy staff members, the age of the organization and the breadth of its interest agenda. Having an associated political action committee (PAC) also increases prominence in Washington news media reports. In relation to gun policies, interest groups like the National Rifle Association (NRA), focusing on gun rights, and Brady Campaign to Prevent Gun Violence (Brady), centering on gun control, would be considered prominent in the debate. Both center on singular issues and possess large memberships and resources. Due to their histories of advocacy and previous policy success, Brady and the NRA are seen as credible sources and frequently cited by the news media (Steidley & Cohen, 2016, p. 5).

In the policymaking process, interest groups have a number of abilities. In order to secure or overturn a government decision, interest groups have the option to bring cases to court (Hrebenar & Scott, 1982, p. 143). Courts have defined and reshaped the scope of the Second Amendment in cases related to gun laws (Spitzer, 2004, p. 15). For that reason, the appointments of judges in the Supreme Court are crucial to interest groups, because judges tend to be appointed for their lifetimes (Holyoke, 2014, p. 210). Another way to exert influence is by endorsing political candidates and, in some cases, funding their campaigns based on the candidate's stance on a particular issue(s). Interest groups may work with Senators and House Representatives to draft bills or lobby for their support; although they have no control over how the politicians will actually vote on it. Individual groups are also able to coordinate with other interest groups that have similar ideologies in order to advance their shared goals (Baker, 1989/1995, pp. 16, 61; Noel, 2008, pp. 202, 205-206). Another tactic is to eschew government involvement by using ballot initiatives, whereby policy proposals are drafted by interest groups and thereafter submitted to citizens to vote on. In a direct ballot, the proposal is sent directly to the electorate to vote on. An indirect ballot involves sending the ballot to the Legislature first and, if it fails to enact it, submitting this to citizens to vote on (Hrebenar & Scott, 1982, pp. 121-124). It is worth noting that ballot initiatives are only available in twenty-four states, with some of them only allowing the indirect method (National Conference of State Legislatures, 2012).

As well as influencing government, interest groups also have to persuade members of the public. Public opinion is pivotal to policymaking, with the concerns of citizens providing a foundation for the issues to be addressed (Burns & Crawford, 1999, p. 160). For that reason, policymakers track public opinion in an attempt to identify which words, arguments and symbols are most likely to gain public support for a policy issue (Jacobs & Shapiro, 2000, p. 7). The most effective technique to affect public opinion is "framing," defined as "the process by which people develop a particular conceptualization of an issue or reorient their thinking about an issue" (Chong & Druckman, 2007, p. 104). To that end, discourse that is persuasive in nature contains frames which are consistent and resonant with people (Woodley, 2015, p. 27). Chong and Druckman (2007) postulate that if a resonant frame about a particular issue is frequently repeated over time in the media— known as priming — this can crystallize public opinion. Such a shift in public opinion, however, is not automatic or inevitable. Even in cases where priming and framing do not change attitudes, these can still shift people's perceptions of issue salience and potentially cause their policy preferences to shift (Woodly, 2015, p. 148).

In relation to an issue like guns, public support for change should align with the norms and values in society at that time (Spitzer, 2004, p. 15). A recent Gallup poll found that 64% of Americans want laws relating to the sale of firearms to be stricter. This is compared to 28% who believed laws should be kept the same and 7% would prefer laws to be less strict (McCarthy, 2019). A study by Woznidk (2015) found that people's opinions about gun control are political in nature. A public opinion poll found that individuals supportive of the NRA are more likely to say they would not vote for a political candidate with a different stance to their own on guns. Additionally, possessing a gun in one's home, being Republican or holding a conservative or moderate political ideology were all indicators of individuals being more likely to agree with the statement that "gun laws should be kept as they are now." The polarization of beliefs about gun policies was evident in a 2019 Gallup poll which found that 88% of Democrats supported stricter firearm laws in comparison to 64% of Independents and 36% of Republicans (McCarthy, 2019). When it comes to an incident like a mass shooting, this creates a "window of opportunity" to shift public opinion around guns (Fleming et al., 2016, p. 1). In this time period, interest groups have a pivotal role in mobilizing and persuading members of the public (Spitzer, 2004, p. 74). Influence from interest groups can be exerted to vote for particular political candidates, as well as to support the policy aims of the group (Noel, 2008, p. 202).

AN EMOTIONAL FRAME

Previous work in this area (Doran, 2014; Kerr, 2018) has indicated that an emotional approach focusing on the victims and survivors of gun violence could possibly be persuasive. Interviewees were asked about this to determine whether they believed this would constitute an appropriate framing strategy. The broad consensus was that an emotional approach would be a successful approach. Rukmani Bhatia (formerly CAP) maintained that this should be intertwined in gun violence prevention work: "I think it's impossible to talk about this work and not talk about the human impact." Buttressing this argument is the idea that merely citing the extent of gun violence in the United States does not have a discernible impact on the majority of people: "My approach is to look at the statistics but it only seems to work on audiences that are already sympathetic to your ideas. It seems to make no difference whatsoever to others."-Mick North, GCN. Statistics can come across as hollow or meaningless to audiences, as they are not associated with emotion (Gardner, 2008, p. 93). This is backed up by the findings of research on framing, whereby "episodic frames" focusing on individual stories are more engaging and have the potential to elicit emotion. If compelling enough, this may make episodic framing more persuasive than "thematic frames" which use measures like statistics to put issues into context (Aaroe, 2011; Gross, 2008; Iyengar, 1991). In a similar vein, Adelyn Allchin (CSGV) explained that framing gun violence in an emotional way may elucidate to people that the level in the United States is "not normal" and that "we can prevent this" with the right elected officials in place. The invoking of "we" in this sense can contribute to movement building, by legitimizing the involvement of individuals into collective action (Goss, 2006, p. 107).

Another strategy contained within the emotional approach is to highlight the reality of gun violence by holding events specifically to talk about the victims. This has the potential to be successful for it "provides specific characters at which receivers may direct their emotional reactions" (Aaroe, 2011, p. 210). This was something a number of interviewees were already involved in. Heather Ross (TGS) held a "No More Names" event at the NRA Convention Centre, during which she listed the names of people killed by gun violence since the Sandy Hook school shooting. It seems this was a successful strategy for encouraging involvement and focusing attention on the issue: "I inspired some people who hadn't been involved to show up and take action and I got international media attention"-Heather Ross, TGS. Unfortunately, there was some pushback at the NRA Convention, where young people attending the conference with their parents accused Heather and other activists of making up the names. Heather Ross (TGS) pointed out that this shows that "a complete denial exists" amongst some members of the public about the extent of the gun violence problem in the United States.

Similarly, Po Murray's group, NAA, hosts a national vigil service for all victims of gun violence on or near the anniversary of the Sandy Hook school shooting every year. The national vigil service on Capitol Hill in Washington, D.C. anchors hundreds of local vigils and events across the nation. These events are supported by nearly all major national and state gun violence prevention groups and a large number of activists and families impacted by gun violence participate in the vigils across the nation. NAA raises funds and brings together families and survivors who have been impacted by gun violence from across the country to participate in the vigil service in D.C. The day after the vigil, the families, survivors and activists lobby their congressional representatives. An event like the vigil goes some way to gaining public interest and getting policymakers involved. Additionally, they support individuals most impacted by gun violence, unite the disparate groups involved in the gun violence prevention community, gain public interest and help to engage policymakers. All of these are key steps to sustaining an issue in mainstream public discourse and gaining political acceptance, which, in turn, are crucial in sustaining an issue in mainstream public discourse and gaining political acceptance. This needs to be sustained over a lengthy period of time to prompt *policy accommodation*, whereby the political salience of the issue is accepted even by those who disagree with it (Woodly, 2015, p. 155). This is something which could be achieved with continuous events like the ones mentioned by interviewees, if they garner enough public and media attention and generate debate by politicians.

PUBLIC HEALTH APPROACH

Another frame advanced by interviewees was that of a public health approach. This would approach gun violence as a health issue, using injuries and deaths to quantify the impact of this violence (Mercy et al., 1993, p. 8). The United States has very high rates of firearm-related death compared to other Western high-income countries (BBC News, 2019; Grinshteyn & Hemenway, 2016; Mercy et al. 2003). It is estimated there are 32.5 firearm deaths in the United States daily (Wintemute, 2015). The common consensus amongst interviewees was that whilst mass shootings gain all the media attention, gun suicides are actually the highest cause of gun deaths in the United States. In 2016, there were 22, 938 firearm-related suicides in the United States; in contrast to 14, 415 homicides (BBC News, 2019). This provides a reason for focusing on what the evidence is saying about gun violence: "If we really want to save lives, we should focus on where the lives are being lost."-Shaun Dakin (PAASD). Since one of the results of framing is to evoke new beliefs about an issue (Chong & Druckman, 2007; Entman, 2010), talking about more "commonplace" gun deaths like suicides could stimulate people to think about gun violence in a different way.

In terms of a public health approach, Adelyn Allchin (CSGV) detailed what this would involve: "It really starts with the data and understanding where gun violence is occurring, why it is occurring, the different types." Data in this sense could include statistics, interviews with community members and so forth looking at mass shootings, unintentional shootings, suicides, daily gun violence in impacted communities and domestic violence involving firearms. Once that evidence is gathered, Adelyn Allchin (CSGV) explained, risk and protective factors can be identified for gun violence and potential solutions devised, implemented, and evaluated. The main challenge with this approach comes with shifting the focus of analysis of gun violence prevention from individuals to the collective (Vizzard, 1999, p. 139).

Following on from that, Rukmani Bhatia (formerly CAP) maintained that the public health approach should frame gun violence in the following way: "Not so much that it's an illness; but that communities that suffer from gun violence are not healthy." The goal in this sense, explained Rukmani Bhatia (formerly CAP), is to look at what makes a community healthy. This includes access to healthcare, education and nutritional food provisions, in addition to reducing violence and poverty. This is in line with a public health approach, argued Brian Malte (H & HF), looking the broader social factors that can affect change: "You look at tobacco, it wasn't just legislation and tax on cigarettes that caused people to stop smoking; it was changing societal norms, a change in behavior." In line with this, a public health model called Cure Violence aims to change norms relating to gun violence, seeking to shift the attitudes of individuals and the wider community (Butts, Roman, Bostwick & Porter, 2015). Further, the gun violence prevention movement has "for so long only used one hammer in the tool belt, which was legislation."-Brian Malte (H & HF). The public health approach is, therefore, a way to complement this and not solely focus on the reactive approach of drafting legislation. One of the ways to do this is the involvement of other parties that have not commonly been involved in gun violence prevention: for instance, the medical community. They have become more involved in this process in the last few years: "They approach gun violence as a public health crisis, so they are a clear community to advocate for stronger gun regulations."-Jonathan Perloe (CAGV).

A number of interviewees were skeptical about the influence a public health approach would have on convincing members of the public. Shaun Dakin (PAASD) noted that most people do not realize the extent of firearm deaths come from suicide. Similarly, Brian Malte (H & HF) believed that people are not aware of the scale of the problem, with most wanting to get involved after a mass shooting has occurred. Building upon this, he tried to encourage them to help in all situations, particularly with reducing gun suicides which cause the greatest amount of deaths. Interestingly, his organization, H & H F, was formed in response to a mass shooting, the 2015 San Bernardino attack in California; yet approaches the issue of gun violence prevention from a public health angle. The conversations about firearm-related suicide should shift too, explained Andrew Goddard (VCPS), with this being recognized as a form of gun violent in terms of being violence against the self. Moreover, in some states (e.g. Virginia), he explained that suicide is even considered to be a crime.

Interviewees Jonathan Perloe (CAGV) and Adam Skaggs (GLCPGV) lamented, however, that they were uncertain that a public health approach would capture the public's attentions; although it is useful from a policy perspective. Considering Chong and Druckman's (2007, p. 111) argument that strong frames rely on symbols and links to ideology, more so than direct information about a policy, there is some credibility to this point. It does not mean, however, that a public health approach to gun violence prevention should be dismissed. It may be useful to persuade legislators of the importance of GVP efforts, particularly with the input from the medical community about the health impact of gun violence. Iyengar (1991) found that thematic framing in the form of using data to contextualize an issue could increase support for proposals, for people who are already engaged with an issue. Additionally, the public health frame shifts the debate away from one centered on criminal justice and firearms to that of preventing injuries and deaths from firearms (Mercy et al., 1993, p. 18). Moreover, it could be useful in the long-term to try to change social norms and behaviors relating to guns, e.g. persuading gun owners to safely secure firearms to prevent accidental shootings and suicides by others living in the household. The presentation of scientific information on the risks could possibly empower people to take responsibility (Mercy et al., 1993, p. 18). Speaking to members of the public about wider gun violence trends could also be persuasive to those who are already willing to listen. This could motivate individuals to deliberate over alternative considerations (Chong & Druckman, 2007, p. 110). The main gap in public health framing may be in trying to capture the attention of citizens uninterested in the issue and thereafter trying to shape their opinion though a strong framing effect (Chong & Druckman, 2007; Entman, 2010).

RIGHTS AND RESPONSIBILITIES FRAME

What may be a stronger frame than the public health approach to gain attention and persuade citizens is something like the "rights and responsibilities" one. This frame advances the notion that having the right to own a firearm is also a responsibility to ensure people in society remain safe (Kerr, 2018). Chong and Druckman (2007, p. 111) maintained that strong frames tend to be entrenched in symbols, endorsements and ideology; rather than intellectual or morally superior arguments. Interviewees pointed to the success of the gun rights side to frame the issue of ownership through the lens of constitution and liberty. That frame is coupled with a gun culture in the United States conflating gun ownership with other values: "People treat guns like they treat cars— they own them, they modify them; it's a status thing."-Heather Ross (TGS). Since frames can be interpreted in line with pre-existing beliefs, linking gun rights with these types of values can serve to reinforce existing ideas (Entman, 1993; Shen, 2004). By contrast, it was argued by Marvin Lim (KGOC) that "GVP activists haven't so far confirmed a vision of a right of Americans to be secure." A number of interviewees pointed to the fact that there are gun owners who support common-sense firearm restrictions. Additionally, as Brian Malte (H & HF) highlighted, considering the fact that most gun deaths are suicides in the United States, this is an issue that primarily affects gun owners or those living in households with gun owners.

What will be challenging with such a frame is gun violence prevention advocates convincing people that responsibility for protecting others goes hand-in-hand with tighter gun laws. The opposing view advocated by gun rights activists is that this responsibility can be dealt with by allowing greater access to guns in society, something which has a motivational advantage built into it. By contrast, those in favor of gun control need to develop and advance a plan as part of promoting this responsibility and obligation (Rood, 2019, p. 95). A possible way to negate this could be working directly with gun owners who are open to persuasion. This was previously proposed by in the concluding chapter of Kerr (2018) as a way forward for the movement.

A number of those interviewed are already involving gun owners in their advocacy work. Po Murray's organization, NAA, currently has gun owners as members. She shared that this is not entirely unusual: "The majority of gun owners support common sense gun laws, so they are part of the GVP movement already." Likewise, as part of a broader collation, Colorado Ceasefire works with Colorado Gun Owners for Safety and has "always been open to working with reasonable common-sense gun owners."-Eileen McCarron (CC). Probably the most evident example is Sheila Islong's group, Giffords, which has been building a coalition of national gun owners for safety for over a year. This includes a broad range of people motivated by different reasons: some were inspired after a mass shooting; others are retired from the military; there are hunters and sports shooters; some may have lost someone to gun suicide. At the moment, the coalition has been built in Colorado, Texas and Minnesota. There has been interest from gun owners based all over the United States, so the intention is to expand the coalition through a formal launch in summer 2020: "One of the reasons why we're launching nationally to provide people from all pockets of the country with a space and an organization that can help them organize to implement common sense gun laws."-Sheila Islong (Giffords). At the moment, the coalition focuses on advocacy, education and recruitment, with a view to perhaps drafting legislation in future. Commonplace activities involve writing editorials for gun safety legislation, hosting conversations with elected officials and testifying before State Legislatures and Congress.

From discussions with interviewees, the general consensus was this is a way to move the GVP movement forward. Pursuing interest group goals can mean allying or compromising with competing interests (Holyoke, 2014, p. 85). Sheila Islong (Giffords) explained it in the following way: "We can't just tap into the same people that openly agree with us. We need to think about all the different people that essentially are affected by gun violence." Talking about various sides in a debate, Chong and Druckman (2007, p. 114) said "each side has the potential to draw voters away from its opponents using frames for its own position that may appeal to the other side's voters." In the case of gun owners, this would involve framing the issue of gun violence prevention as something that is relevant to them and would not impose on their beliefs about gun usage and ownership. Interviewees pointed out that the movement is not meant to be mutually exclusive:

I don't think this movement is designed to be gun owners versus gun violence prevention advocates. I know that's the NRA's narrative— they say if you support gun ownership you cannot support any legislation on guns; that's a false choice. – Rukmani Bhatia (formerly CAP).

We want people to know that even if you believe in second amendment rights that those values are not at odds with one another. – Sheila Islong (Giffords).

A further proposal from Rukmani Bhatia (formerly CAP) was to look at forming alliances with small gun business owners to see if they would consider policies that could potentially cut into their profit margins but may prevent gun violence in their communities. She pointed to the actions of Dicks Sporting Goods, which stopped the sale of assault weapons after the Parkland (2018) mass shooting.

Central to this idea of working with gun owners is the notion of compromise. Heather Ross (TGS) explained that these discussions had to be approached in a particular way: "Sitting down and presenting people with facts is a hugely important thing. Instead of trying to get them to agree with me on everything, just try to get a few things passed." Similarly, Tom Mauser (CC) agreed that the GVP movement should embrace compromise: "We have to acknowledge their concerns, a different point of view. You may have to make some compromises but it's possible you'll get something like what you want and you try to build on that." This would likely involve pursuing "policy incrementalism" in the form of small policy steps that could shift towards larger political goals (Goss, 2006, p. 145). Mick North (GCN) did caution, however, that this compromise should not be too extreme: "My worry is as with any compromises the whole idea of collaborating is really to pull your opponents a long way in your direction." He explained that whilst attending a debate in Baltimore about the Second Amendment, GVP advocates ended up "talking a bit like the people they thought they were opposed to." To clarify, it appeared that they were espousing similar arguments to the gun rights sides. This mirrors the argument by Berger and Luckman (1967, p. 142) that once ideologies are adopted by an interest group, they are reshaped to fit with particular issues of concern. A balance to ensure that ideologies are considered and partially adopted, but not at the expense of the original ideologies of the group, would be to achieve a sense of collective action through legitimizing the involvement of interested individuals (Goss, 2006, p. 107).

CONCLUSION

This chapter focused on framing strategies that could be used to persuade citizens and politicians of the urgent need to address gun violence. As suggested in previous work in this area (Doran, 2014; Kerr, 2018), an emotional approach focusing on the "human impact" of gun violence could be effective. Interviewees were in agreement that this approach could be useful and some were already engaged in this by holding events specifically to talk about the victims of gun violence. Previous research on framing has found that "episodic frames" focusing on individual stories are more engaging to audiences. If the stories told are compelling enough and elicit emotions, this is a more effective frame to use than a "thematic one" which puts the issue into context using statistics and the like (Aaroe, 2011; Gross, 2008; Iyengar, 1991).

Another potential frame that could be used is a public health approach, in which gun violence is treated like another illness in society (Mercy, Rosenberg, Powell, Broome & Koper, 1993). This frame ties in with the call in the previous chapter to engage in more gun-related research. Collecting such data would allow for the gathering of evidence relating to gun violence, allowing for solutions to be formulated. For instance, greater attention could be paid to suicide which is the highest cause of gun deaths in the United States. In line with public health approaches to other social issues, such as smoking, broader social changes could be advocated: for instance, securing guns in households with children and those who are suffering from severe depression. Moreover, the involvement of groups like the medical community in providing evidence could contribute to "thematic framing" by putting the issue into context (Iyengar, 1991). Whilst a number of interviewees felt that this approach might not capture the attention of citizens, it could be persuasive in trying to make those open to listening to consider gun violence in a different way. Further to this, presenting evidence and potential solutions to policymakers might encourage them to support policy proposals. The main strength in this frame would be making available new beliefs about an issue (Chong & Druckman, 2007; Entman, 2010).

Another frame that could be used to persuade citizens, particularly those who own guns, is one predicated on "rights and responsibilities": the right to own firearms is coupled with a responsibility to ensure people's safety (Kerr, 2018). An important part of this frame would be involving gun owners in the GVP movement. This has previously been advanced by Kerr (2018) as a way to progress the movement. The consensus from interviewees was that this would be a useful approach, widening the scope of participants involved. Moreover, it is felt that the movement was never supposed to be divided into "gun violence prevention" versus "gun owners." To that end, a number of groups are already involving gun owners, particularly Sheila Islong's group, Giffords, which is building a national coalition of gun owners. Whilst this may mean a degree of compromise from GVP groups, working with gun owners could potentially help advance policy via "policy incrementalism" where smaller policy steps can evolve into larger political goals (Goss, 2006).

REFERENCES

Aaroe, L. (2011). Investigating Frame Strength: The Case of Episodic and Thematic Frames. *Political Communication*, 28(2), 207–226. doi:10.1080/10584609.2011.568041

BBC News. (2019, August 5). *America's gun culture in charts*. https://www.bbc.co.uk/news/world-us-canada-41488081

Butts, J. A., Roman, C. G., Bostwick, L., & Porter, J. R. (2015). Cure Violence: A Public Health Model to Reduce Gun Violence. *Annual Review of Public Health*, 36(1), 39–53. doi:10.1146/annurev-publhealth-031914-122509 PMID:25581151

Callaghan, K. (2005). Conclusion: Controversies and New Directions in Framing Research. In K. Callaghan & F. Schnell (Eds.), *Framing American Politics* (pp. 179–189). University of Pittsburgh Press. doi:10.2307/j.ctt6wrbqk.13

Chong, D., & Druckman, J. N. (2007). Framing Theory. *Annual Review of Political Science*, 10(1), 103–126. doi:10.1146/annurev.polisci.10.072805.103054

Doran, S. E. M. (2014). *News Media Constructions and Policy Implications of School Shootings in the United States* (Ph.D Thesis). Glasgow, UK: University of Glasgow.

Entman, R. M. (2010). Media framing biases and political power: Explaining slant in news of campaign 2008. *Journalism*, 11(4), 389–408. doi:10.1177/1464884910367587

Fleming, A. K., Rutledge, P. E., Dixon, G. C., & Peralton, S. (2016). When the smoke clears: Focusing events, issue definition, strategic framing and the politics of gun control. *Social Science Quarterly*, *97*(5), 1144–1156. doi:10.1111squ.12269

Gardner, D. (2008). *Risk: The Science and Politics of Fear*. Virgin Books Ltd.

Goss, K. A. (2006). *Disarmed: The Missing Movement for Gun Control in America*. Princeton University Press.

Grinshteyn, E., & Hemenway, D. (2016). Violent Death Rates: The U.S. Compared with Other High-Income OECD Countries, 2010. *The American Journal of Medicine*, *129*(3), 266–273. doi:10.1016/j.amjmed.2015.10.025 PMID:26551975

Gross, K. (2008). Framing Persuasive Appeals: Episodic and Thematic Framing, Emotional Response and Policy Opinion. *Political Psychology*, *29*(2), 169–192. doi:10.1111/j.1467-9221.2008.00622.x

Holyoke, T. T. (2014). *Interest Groups and Lobbying: pursuing Political Interests*. Westview Press.

Iyengar, S. (1991). *Is anyone responsible? How television frames political issues*. University of Chicago Press. doi:10.7208/chicago/9780226388533.001.0001

Jacobs, L. R., & Shapiro, R. Y. (2000). *Politicians don't pander: political manipulation and the loss of Democratic responsiveness*. University of Chicago Press.

Kerr, S. E. M. (2018). *Gun Violence Prevention? The Politics Behind Policy Responses to School Shootings in the United States*. Palgrave MacMillan.

Mercy, J. A., Krug, E. G., Dahlberg, L. L., & Zui, A. B. (2003). Violence and Health: The United States in a Global Perspective. *American Journal of Public Health*, *92*(12), 256–261. doi:10.2105/AJPH.93.2.256 PMID:12554579

Mercy, J. A., Rosenberg, M. L., Powell, K. E., Broome, C. V., & Koper, W. L. (1993). Public Health Policy for Preventing Violence. *Health Affairs*, *12*(4), 7–29. doi:10.1377/hlthaff.12.4.7 PMID:8125450

Rood, C. (2019). After Gun Violence: Deliberation and Memory in an Age of Political Gridlock. University Park, PA: the Pennsylvania State University Press. doi:10.5325/j.ctv14gp5h1

Steidley, T., & Cohen, C. G. (2016). Framing the Gun Control Debate: Press releases and Framing Strategies of the National Rifle Association and the Brady Campaign. *Social Science Quarterly*, *98*(2), 608–627. doi:10.1111squ.12323

Vizzard, W. J. (1999). The Impact of Agenda Confliction Policy Formulation and Implementation: The Case of Gun Control. In J. E. Dizard, R. Merrill, & S. P. Andrews Jr., (Eds.), *Guns in America: A Reader* (pp. 131–144). New York University Press.

Wintemute, G. J. (2015). The Epidemiology of Firearms Violence in the Twenty-First Century United States. *Annual Review of Public Health*, *36*(1), 5–19. doi:10.1146/annurev-publhealth-031914-122535 PMID:25533263

Woodly, D. R. (2015). *The Politics of Common Sense: How Social Movements Use Public Discourse to Change Politics and Win Acceptance.* Oxford University Press. doi:10.1093/acprof:oso/9780190203986.001.0001

ADDITIONAL READING

Aaroe, L. (2011). Investigating Frame Strength: The Case of Episodic and Thematic Frames. *Political Communication, 28*(2), 207–226. doi:10.1080/10584609.2011.568041

Chong, D., & Druckman, J. N. (2007). Framing Theory. *Annual Review of Political Science, 10*(1), 103–126. doi:10.1146/annurev.polisci.10.072805.103054

Fleming, A. K., Rutledge, P. E., Dixon, G. C., & Peralton, S. (2016). When the smoke clears: Focusing events, issue definition, strategic framing and the politics of gun control. *Social Science Quarterly, 97*(5), 1144–1156. doi:10.1111squ.12269

Holyoke, T. T. (2014). *Interest Groups and Lobbying: pursuing Political Interests.* Westview Press.

Iyengar, S. (1991). *Is anyone responsible? How television frames political issues.* University of Chicago Press. doi:10.7208/chicago/9780226388533.001.0001

KEY TERMS AND DEFINITIONS

Emotional Frame: This is an approach that focuses on the human impact of gun violence, e.g. by discussing the victims and their individual stories.

Focusing Events: Atypical and high-profile incidents that can create opportunities for policy debate.

Frame Amplification: This refers to the process by which values are clarified and associated with a particular issue.

Frames: These set the parameters on an issue and can be a tool to persuade people to change their thinking.

Gun Violence Prevention: This is a term commonly used by interest groups instead of "gun control" and refers to a belief that firearms should be regulated to improve public safety.

Public Health Frame: A frame centering on the idea that gun violence is an illness in society that can be prevented and treated like any other disease.

Rights and Responsibilities Frame: This approach is predicated on the notion that the right to own firearms is intertwined with a responsibility to ensure this is done in a way that does not compromise public safety.

Conclusion

FINAL THOUGHTS ON GUN VIOLENCE PREVENTION

Introduction

The purpose of this chapter is surmise how the direction of the gun violence prevention movement may develop in future. The activism relating to the 2018 Parkland shooting and the results of the midterm elections that year are said to have shaped the political landscape. In line with this, interviewees made predictions about what impact potential results from the 2020 presidential election would have on gun policies in future. The greatest potential for restrictive gun bills was attributed to having a Presidency and Congress that is controlled by the Democratic Party (Fleming, 2012; Fleming, Rutledge, Dixon & Peralton, 2016), a scenario which did not transpire. The weakened status of the gun rights group, the NRA, was also said to be an influencer on the outcome of the election if less funding and grassroots support is offered by them to President Donald Trump.

Another factor which may influence the future direction of the GVP movement is whether there is progress in the individual states, which could have a snowball effect through the country. The other possible influencer is the increased level of public support said to be evident in recent times. In spite of this, it is noted that this does not necessarily lead to involvement in GVP activism or policy change. Other conditions are required to transform support into participation in a social movement, such as sympathizing with the movement, becoming mobilized to take action, overcoming any barriers to participate and so forth (Oegema & Klandermains, 1994; Snow, Rochford, Burke, Worden & Benford, 1986).

To start with, the landscape for policy change provoked by the Parkland (2018) school shooting is outlined. The activism resulting from that incident coupled with the impact on the 2018 midterm elections are discussed. The next section looks at the results of the 2020 presidential election. The role of gun rights groups in the political landscape is then deliberated. State-level progress and then public support for gun violence are the final tenets discussed. These are all brought together in a final thoughts section, which considers the future of this movement and the effect it might have on gun violence in the United States.

Parkland Activism and the 2018 Midterm Elections

One of the factors signaling a shift in the GVP movement is the activism of Parkland students, following the 2018 mass shooting at Douglas Stoneman High School. They organized walkouts, protests and marches via social media. Two of the students, Emma Gonzalez, and, David Hogg, became the primary spokespeople for the activists. They appropriated the hashtag #NeverAgain to push for action on gun reform and #MarchforOurLives to organize a mass protest march in Washington, D.C. Hogg pointed to his generation's familiarity with mass shootings as the reason why change had to be implemented:

Columbine was about 19 years ago. Now that you've had an entire generation of kids growing up around mass shootings, and the fact that they're starting to be able to vote, explains how we're going to have this change. Kids are not going to accept this.

Furthermore, the students took on the National Rifle Association (NRA), criticizing its stance on guns and calling for companies to boycott the gun rights group. The students also had to deal with conspiracy theorists accusing them of being paid actors (Moore, 2018; Wright, Molloy & Lockhart, 2018).

Interviewees pointed to the Parkland shooting as having had more of an impact on the GVP movement than the Las Vegas one, due to the activism of the Parkland students. Interviewees praised the students for their immediate involvement in GVP activism:

Look at the way the Parkland kids came out within minutes almost and they knew the subject and it was very heartening to see that. – Andrew Goddard (VCPS).

There's some who were clearly ready to be leaders at that school because it's quite impressive. – Jonathan Perloe (CAGV).

Although Mick North (GCN) lives in Scotland, he took it upon himself to organize a letter to the students. He has a history of assisting with activism efforts in the United States. In particular, he reached out and supported the Sandy Hook families, with that incident having a lot of parallels to the 1996 Dunblane school shooting in Scotland where Mick North (GCN) lost his daughter, Sophie (Kerr, 2018). The letter to the Parkland students was written by families of survivors and victims from the Dunblane tragedy and showed support for their efforts. An excerpt from it reads "Wherever you march, whenever you protest, however you campaign for a more sensible approach to gun ownership we will be there with you in spirit." The letter also refers to the efforts of the Dunblane families following the 1996 shooting to change the gun laws in Great Britain (Oritz, 2018). When questioned about it, Mick North (GCN) explained why he had the idea to organize the letter: "I thought it was ridiculous not to say something given the circumstances. I was extremely heartened by the Parkland students." The letter was said to be written in a way that required a response and there was some interaction between some of those involved and one of the Parkland students, Jack Blunt.

It is postulated that the Parkland students inspired other young people to get involved in GVP efforts: "Parkland shooting generated a whole new set of activists. Young people who are sick and tired of being victims of gun violence."-Eileen McCarron (CC). Notably, young people are the ones affected by school shootings: "I can't relate to having drills in schools about active shooters but every kid has to go through it now."-Jim Kessler (TW). The normalization of the threat of a school shooting throughout the United States (see Doran, 2014) goes some way to explaining why young people would become frustrated with it. Interestingly, Jonathan Perloe (CAGV) shared that in his home state of Connecticut some of the student survivors of the Sandy Hook tragedy, who are now entering middle school, are starting to become activists. Their efforts have involved visiting the White House to talk about school safety, writing to lawmakers to urge them to pass federal level bills and joining an activist group. A ten year girl, whose brother died in the Sandy Hook tragedy, said she was inspired by the Parkland students and that motivated her to get involved. She has now joined the youth arm of the Newtown Action Alliance, to get involved in activism efforts (Collins, 2019).

In addition to inspiring further young people into activism, the efforts of the Parkland students are said to have encouraged younger people to vote. The greater turnout of young people to vote in the 2018 midterm elections was said by interviewees to be unprecedented. Tom Mauser (CC) explained it in the following way:

There's a historical thing that the young people generally do not vote at the kind of levels older people do. After the Parkland tragedy, you had an energized group of young people stand up. Politicians had to take notice of the new voters participating that might not have done if it hadn't been for Parkland.

Similarly, Jonathan Perloe (CAGV) shared an anecdote about attending a town hall meeting in Connecticut with Senators Blumenthal and Murphy and there being a lot of young people in the audience. One of them said they felt that politicians did not listen to young people and the response was "Politicians listen to people who vote and you guys don't vote." This was illustrative of the fact that younger people generally have lower voter participation rates. Their participation in the election would likely have made a difference, given those aged 18-29 are more likely to favor gun reform than other age groups. Fifty-seven percent felt stricter gun legislation should be an immediate priority for Congress; whilst 17% felt Congress should do so but not urgently. Six out of ten in this age group said they were supportive of efforts to reduce gun violence (Santhanam, 2018).

The efforts of the Parkland students were said to have reframed the way the issue of gun violence is discussed in public debates: "They've made it more of a voting issue, made it more elevated in its role; and giving the candidates the confidence that they must show leadership on this issue."-Adam Skaggs (GLCPGV). A number of the other interviewees noted that they noticed an increase in political candidates, particularly Democratic ones, talking about the issue of gun violence. Andrew Goddard (VCPS) commented that Democrats are "really out of their shell," with those who used to be marginal on the topic "actually speaking out forcefully now." This was said to have a particular impact on the 2018 mid-term elections. Democrats gained forty seats giving them a majority in the House; although the party lost two seats in the Senate, which remained in Republican control. In the 2018 Governor Elections, Democrats gained seven seats; whilst Republicans lost six (The New York Times, 2018). The gains Democrats made in the House were said to be particularly attributable to this:

These were in suburban districts that maybe traditionally voted Republican on an economic basis [but] were sympathetic for calls to stronger regulation of guns. We had a number of candidates running very vocally on the issue in a way that we haven't seen in years past. – Adam Skaggs (GLCPGV).

In the places where Democrats were winning— particularly in the suburbs, where they made a lot of gains— it was helpful. – Jim Kessler (TW).

It is cautioned, however, that too much emphasis should not be placed on gun violence issues and younger voter participation in assessing the 2018 election results: "I think it helped a little, not too much. It was definitely an issue in some of the races but the main issues in 2018 were Donald Trump and healthcare."-Jim Kessler (TW).

Looking to the upcoming elections in 2020 finds the influence of the Parkland students may have waned slightly. Tom Mauser (CC) postulated that the "Parkland effect" may have "cooled off a little bit," with perhaps there not being the same level of enthusiasm as there was in 2018. A similar point was made by Mick North (GCN) that the Parkland student activism seems to have faded since then: "I'm not quite sure what they're doing now. It seemed to peak around the time of the midterm elections but I've not heard anything else since." The reason for this, explained Jonathan Perloe (CAGV), may be the difficulties in trying to harness the activism of university students. In high school, there may be the perceived greater likelihood of a school shooting compared to college and university settings, and perhaps also the greater demands on students' time in university. In spite of this, interviewees still felt that the Parkland students had made a difference in encouraging youth involvement in the GVP issue. Shaun Dakin (PASSD) acknowledged that young people have definitely been participating, which is beneficial since "politicians listen to people who scream the loudest and show up the most." Similarly, Jonathan Perloe (CAGV) noted that more young people were present at rallies and have testified through public hearings. Moreover, Tom Mauser (CC) noted that the issue has become more mainstream as a result: "You have young people who've gotten active in politics and want to vote and were spurred on by this issue."

The involvement of young people in GVP activism encouraged greater voter participation and encouraged political candidates to speak out about gun violence. Increased levels of support were then translated into political results in the November 2018 midterm elections. This backs up a point made by Kingdon (1994/2003) that elections affect policy agendas. Jonathan Perloe (CAGV) intimated that the results of these elections elucidated this shift: "There were Democratic candidates who ran on gun violence prevention and they beat Republicans and that's not the only thing but it was part of that." Rukmani Bhatia (formerly CAP) explained that Democrats have recognized what voters wanted: "Recognising that gun violence prevention was a top five issue for voters in the 2018 midterms, passing H.R.8 in the House in the first ninety days of Congress and continuing to push to get that law for universal background checks passed in the Senate." In a similar vein, all the Democratic candidates in the presidential race in 2020 discussed their plans for gun control (McCarthy, 2019).

United States Presidential Election 2020

The global COVID-19 pandemic raised questions about whether the 2020 United States presidential election would be delayed or whether voting would take place by postal ballots (The Guardian, 2020). As it transpired, the vote did go ahead in November 2020 and there was a greater use of postal ballots. Incumbent President Donald Trump alongside Vice-President Mike Pence ran for the Republican Party; whilst the Democratic Party put forward the candidates Joe Biden, the former vice-president in the Obama administration, for president and Kamala Harris for vice-president. The results of this bestowed the Presidency upon the Democratic Party, with Biden securing the required number of Electoral College seats needed (Ball, 2020). It is difficult to know how much of a role gun violence played in the results. In interviews held before the COVID-19 pandemic, participants indicated that gun violence would be an influencing factor for voters. Adam Skaggs (GLCPGV) hypothesized that it will continue to be at least a top five issue for voters. Further to this, Po Murray (NAA) believed that it is probably one of the top three issues for young voters. In early 2020, the coronavirus COVID-19 spread globally and world leaders including Trump have contracted the virus. With the United States suffering more than two hundred and forty thousand deaths from the virus, it is now theorized that the virus became of one of the most important issues to voters. Furthermore, Trump's response to the virus was described as insensitive and mocking and one of the reasons why he lost the election (Balls, 2020; Bennett & Berenson, 2020).

The results of the election are likely to have an impact on gun policies over the next few years. Even though the Presidency— which includes the president, White House officials and associated offices— is constitutionally limited, it can set the agenda and direction of policy. This may be through the selection of judges to the Supreme Court, issuing executive orders and changing personnel (Brown, 2008, p. 118, 135; Hrebenar & Scott, 1982, p. 153; Kingdon, 1994/2000, p. 27). When speaking about President Trump, interviewees noted that he has a particular pattern following "focusing events" (Kingdon, 1994/2000) like mass shootings:

He'll talk about something, maybe sound reasonable for a couple of days and then he backs away. – Jim Kessler (TW).

In the wake of tragedies, he likes having the talking points that makes it sound like he's going to take action and then does nothing tangible to reduce gun violence. – Rukmani Bhatia (formerly CAP).

The pattern of talking about gun violence prevention after these incidents followed by inaction on gun regulations made interviewees very dubious that anything would have happened with the GVP movement if Trump had been re-elected in 2020. Jonathan Perloe (CAGV) explained this rationale:

The totality of his statements compared to his inaction demonstrates that he clearly favors gun rights over gun regulation. Among his base are some of the most extreme supporters of gun rights of any part of the electorate. Since he has consistently pandered to his base there's virtually no chance that he will embrace stronger gun regulation of any kind.

Similar sentiments were expressed by interviewees in Kerr (2018) when speculating about potential action a Trump administration would take on gun violence prevention. The earlier chapter on the Las Vegas shooting acknowledged that Trump took executive action on bump stocks following this mass shooting; however, there were issues with this making it weaker than it could have potentially been.

Another important facet of influence exercised by the Presidency is the degree of support shown to the gun violence prevention movement. The championing of this issue by Hillary Clinton in the 2016 presidential election was the reason why GVP activists were strongly supportive of her (Kerr, 2018). The Democratic presidential nominee, Biden, has been described as having a lot of credibility on this issue due to his past votes and actions: "He was the author of the Assault Weapons Ban in 1994 and he helped pass the original Brady Law in 1993"-Jonathan Perloe (CAGV); "He led Obama's GVP efforts after Sandy Hook."-Eileen McCarron (CC). Extrapolating from this, the Biden and Harris victory in 2020 will mean the issue of gun violence prevention is at the center of the policy agenda. Considering the economic and health implications of the COVID-19 pandemic for the United States (Hook & Kuchler, 2020), however, it is likely that the economy and responding to the pandemic will be the top priorities for the incoming Biden-Harris administration (Balls, 2020).

Moreover, it has been noted that the period between administrations known as "presidential transi-tion" provides an opening for interest groups to lobby to influence the Executive Branch and shape the direction of policymaking (Brown, 2008, p. 135). With Biden winning the 2020 presidential election, this could afford interest groups an opportunity to act in the transition when the switch begins from the current Trump administration. Nonetheless, the transition of power may not be as seamless as has been the case with previous administrations. Although President Trump has acknowledged that the handover to President-elect Biden must take place, he is still contesting the result with a number of lawsuits against individual states (BBC News, 2020b).

The other consideration is what will happen with Congress in this election. Prior to the election, the Democrats were in the majority in the House; whilst Republicans controlled the Senate. Fundamental to change is the condition that Democrats win the Presidency and take back the Senate: "We will see good laws being passed. We might even get comprehensive national healthcare. I think we'll see comprehensive background checks passed."-Heather Ross (TGS). In line with this, Fleming (2012, p. 71) found that when the Democratic party control both the Presidency and the House part of Congress, the number of restrictive bills proposed after a focusing event is at its highest. Following on from this, skepticism was expressed about whether real change could occur if Democrats did not win back the Senate: "If the Democrat candidate wins the presidency, unless the Senate comes along with fifty-one votes, there's going to be real challenges to making progress on this."-Adam Skaggs (GLCPGV). Another problem, explained Jonathan Perloe (CAGV), is the "filibuster rule" in the Senate that prevents bills from passing without sixty votes. Brian Malte (H & HF) pondered whether this rule would change if Democrats took over the Senate: "Will they go for fifty-one votes instead of trying to get to sixty which the filibuster rule says you need?" The main problem with that is it would be beneficial in the short-term to allow Democrats to pass bills; yet when they are back in the minority in the Senate it would work against them.

As it transpired, the Democrats retained control of the House, albeit losing seven seats, and the Republicans kept their majority in the Senate with the loss of one seat (BBC News, 2020a). Extrapolating from this, the current stalemate in passing legislation will likely continue: "We have hundreds of pieces of legislation that the House has passed that just go to the Senate to die."-Adam Skaggs (GLCPGV). The only factor that may shift things is if Republicans in certain states rethink their positions on guns. Jim Kessler (TW) suggested that Senators in states that are less rural than they once were — for instance, Ohio, Florida and possibly North Carolina and Indiana— could become more "suburban" in their approach and support a policy position like universal background checks. The main point to take away is that the results of the 2020 election will have a significant impact on shaping the GVP movement for years to come.

Gun Rights Groups

Another factor which could affect the momentum of the GVP movement is the degree of opposition they will face from gun rights groups, particularly the National Rifle Association. The power of the NRA has been well-documented (see Halpin, 2014; Patterson, 1998; Wilson, 1981). The group has evolved from its initial set-up where the focus was on gun safety, training and hunting to now pursuing the ideological goal of protecting the right to own firearms. The frames it adopts center on Second Amendment rights and freedoms, particularly using firearms for self-defense purposes; American heritage and culture, of which firearms are an integral part; safety and legal issues relating to responsible gun ownership (Steidley & Cohen, 2016, pp. 5, 8-13). The strength of the organization lies in the fact it has a large membership, is well-funded and offers material incentives to members such as firearms training (Patterson, 1998, pp. 123; Wilson, 1981, p. 105). It also affects political decisions by grading political candidates from A to F based on their stance on the Second Amendment. Those who lead on Second Amendment issues and vote for laws favored by the NRA receive electoral support; whilst challenges are mounted against candidates who vote in favor of stricter gun laws (Patterson, 1998, pp. 135-136). This is a significant form of influence, for it can encourage supporters of the group to vote for particular political candidates (Noel, 2008, p. 206). Moreover, the organization is commonly cited in the news media. Grossman (2012, pp. 62, 76) found the NRA was mentioned more than three hundred times a year; whilst other gun rights groups like Gun Owners of America (GOA) are mentioned far less frequently.

Interviewees highlighted the influence of the NRA, particularly in relation to Trump's approach to guns. In earlier work, GVP activists lamented that the NRA's funding and grassroots support for Trump's campaign helped him get elected in 2016 (Kerr, 2018). A former NRA spokesperson claimed that the NRA did help get Trump elected, with his win being bolstered by the group's support in swing states (Stone, 2019). The previous section discussing the 2020 presidential election had documented frustrations from interviewees regarding Trump's actions after a mass shooting, where he seemed open to taking action of some kind and then reneges on it. Interviewees attributed this to his links with the NRA:

Despite saying he would do some positive things, Trump always fell back to doing what the NRA wanted. – Tom Mauser (CC).

We've seen mass shooting after mass shooting the president saying he's open to doing something meaningful and he's always walked that back when he gets a call from the NRA. – Adam Skaggs (GLCPGV).

The reticence from the NRA to support restrictions on guns is rooted in its ideological foundations and membership expectations, whereby citizens join the group because of their expectation that it will protect their rights (Patterson, 1998, p. 123). Being an NRA member, explained Brian Malte (H & HF), can commonly become a part of gun owner culture similar to hunting. Another interviewee, Marvin Lim (KGOC), attended the NRA Convention in 2017 to obtain his legal education requirement and heard Trump speaking at this event. Trump was newly in office at this time and spoke about keeping America safe from threats more so than gun rights themselves. His rhetoric, thereby, was predicated on "a very vague sort of threat and a very broad idea of gun rights as keeping America safe."-Marvin Lim (KGOC). The conflation of guns and self-defense is one of the frames utilized by the NRA (Steidley & Cohen, 2016). It is also something which is culturally specific to the United States, with many other Western countries not having this "need" for guns to afford them protection (Stoebe, 2015).

In spite of this, there are several gun restrictions which the NRA have not challenged. For instance, an earlier chapter in this book looking at the Las Vegas shooting explained that the organization did not object to the bump stock measure passed by President Trump via Executive Order. It was maintained by interviewees that the Executive Order passed made the law weaker and open to challenge as opposed to the proposals in Congress. Considering this, it could have been the case that the NRA did not speak against this measure to avoid the risk of it being passed in Congress. This also paved the way for Trump to take action on it to be seen to be "doing something" after a mass shooting, without alienating the group who had endorsed him. It has been said that for an electoral threat to be effective, it must be believable that a group can reward or punish a candidate at the polls (Hrebenar & Scott, 1982, p. 99). With the resources, membership and funding of the NRA (Patterson, 1998; Wilson, 1981), their continued endorsement of Trump will likely be enough of a motivating factor for him to comply.

Despite this, it could be the case that the NRA plays a reduced role in the 2020 election. Adam Skaggs (GLCPGV) made the following prediction: "The NRA is going to be a lot more challenged now and weaker going into this election than it was last time around." The reason for this are the legal and financial challenges currently facing the organization, relating to Executive Director, Wayne LaPierre facing accusations of financial impropriety. There are also internal battles predicated on the president of the NRA trying to stage a coup against LaPierre and then being fired (Stone, 2019). In addition to this, the NRA came under criticism from the Parkland activists who ran a Twitter campaign for companies to boycott the NRA (Wright, Molloy & Lockhart, 2018). The use of social media by the Parkland activists to gain support showed that the NRA was "not really prepared for the social media world"-Jim Kessler (TW). Due to all of this, it is felt that the NRA "will never return to its prominence."-Jim Kessler (TW). There may be weight in this claim, with Trump himself tweeting that the NRA had to "stop the internal fighting" and "get back to GREATNESS – FAST." It is speculated that this indicates that Trump has concerns that due to their legal battles the group may not be able to offer the financial and grassroots support in 2020 that they did in 2016 (Stone, 2019).

Several interviewees also noted that NRA members were probably frustrated with the group due to the recent scandals. There are NRA members that do support some gun regulations. For instance, a recent poll found 69% support comprehensive background checks; this rose to 78% for gun owners who are not members of the NRA (Bloomberg, 2018). There is a vulnerability to organizations that pursue political goals, for members may no longer agree with their values or they could lose relevance over time (Halpin, 2014, p. 69). It would be naïve, however, to think that this conflict spells the end for the NRA. In addition to its political influence, the other strength of the group lies in the fact that it is a service organization for gun owners offering firearms training for its members (Patterson, 1998, p. 124). Jim Kessler (TW) pointed out that other gun rights groups like Gun Owners of America (GOA) are not providing any services to gun owners. That means the NRA has a unique selling point, as it were, to retain members: "That's why no one can take its place, because of their services."-Jim Kessler (TW). It may be the case, therefore, that NRA members may retain their membership to access services; yet perhaps be more open to some form of gun regulations. Heather Ross (TGS) previously held a "No More Names" event listing the names of gun violence victims at an NRA convention and said several people came over to talk about it. It seemed they were open to being persuaded: "I brought up some points and they were like 'Oh, I hadn't thought about that' and I was like 'Yeah, that's the problem.'"-Heather Ross (TGS). In a similar vein, Sheila Islong's group Giffords has been building a coalition of gun owners to "provide another space for gun owners to go to." Marvin Lim (KGOC) also noted the potential for trying to persuade people who are "more moderate" on the issue of guns, e.g. gun owners who support some policies: "I think there's some level of influencing them to be able to vote on specific candidate or lobby on certain policies." As discussed earlier, working with gun owners is one tactic proposed by interviewees as a way to move forward with the GVP movement. It may be the case that the GVP movement has to reach out to current and former NRA members to work together to achieve progress.

The main implication to take from all of this is the political sway of the NRA may be diminished, allowing for less opposition to gun regulations proposed. With the possibility of political endorsement or challenge reduced, there may be politicians who are more willing to vote for gun regulatory proposals. Less funding and grassroots support for Trump could also have affected the outcome of the 2020 election. Whilst the GVP movement will still face opposition, particularly from state-level gun rights groups, it appears there may be an opening in the future to act without facing notable opposition.

State Progress

This chapter has deliberated over the possible implications of the 2020 presidential election results for passing gun regulations at the federal level. Whilst national laws are important to set a precedent for the country, making progress in individual states is also important. The power structure in the United States is decentralized, allowing for important decisions to be made at the national, state and local levels (Loomis, 1998, p. 5). Several interviewees pointed to the importance of state laws in influencing policies at the federal level. Jim Kessler (TW) explained that the Manchin-Toomey bill for universal background checks which failed in the Senate in 2013 was able to be raised by Toomey, a Republican from Pennsylvania, because that state already has that law in place. To that end, passing such a law at the federal level would not have affected Pennsylvania, so it was a "safe" political decision to take. Jim Kessler (TW) argued that if laws were already in place in states then it could change the way Senators vote: "They could think 'Oh well, it's not going to change any laws in my state so I'll vote for universal background checks.'" In this sense, "state action precedes the federal action."-Jim Kessler (TW). A similar point was made by Andrew Goddard (VCPS) that the more states that pass a law, the more likely it is that a law becomes normalized: "If you could get thirty-eight or forty states to do something, you perhaps don't need to do much at the federal level because it's easy to put pressure on the hold-out states." He argued that this has been a tactic previously used by the NRA to pass lenient gun laws like the "Castle Doctrine," a legal doctrine mandating that people are able to use any means necessary to protect their home.

Since Democrats have recently regained power in a number of State Legislatures, such as Colorado and Virginia, there is greater potential for gun safety laws to pass at the state-level. Andrew Goddard (VCPS) highlighted that there is now openness amongst politicians to discuss gun violence: "People who have never spoke about gun violence before are speaking about it now. Lots of new candidates are coming out right from the beginning and making bold statements about what they would do." Furthermore, he explained that the NRA ratings for Democrats in the House in Virginia have gone from A ratings ten years ago to almost all having an F rating now. The NRA rates candidates on whether they led on gun rights issues, with those who do being awarded A grades or something similar; whilst those who vote in favor of stricter gun laws tend to receive F grades or other low ratings (Patterson, 1998, pp. 135-136). In Colorado, the Senate and House became Democratic, as well as the Attorney General and Treasurer. Eileen McCarron (CC) conveyed that Tom Sullivan, who lost his son in the Aurora Theater (2012) mass shooting, campaigned on a gun violence prevention platform and won the election by seven points in an area that is typically Republican. Tom Mauser (CC) shared similar stories of the election in Colorado, saying there was a race between an unknown Democrat running on a gun violence prevention platform and the incumbent Republican who tried to distance himself from Trump; in the end, the Democrat won. Similarly, there was another Democrat who was in high school at the time of Columbine (1999) and he also took on the gun issue and won his district. According to Tom Mauser (CC), both of these candidates passed a number of gun reform bills when they got into office; thus, keeping to the promises they made. Moreover, there has also been a shift in which types of regions Democrats are winning in Colorado: "Suburbs are moving more into the Democratic column. Now the Republicans are moving to the further out suburbs."-Eileen McCarron (CC). There is also the possibility, explained Jim Kessler (TW), that staunchly Republican states will pass some meaningful gun safety laws: for instance, Ohio has been discussing universal background checks.

Public Support

Interviewees believed that citizens have gradually moved towards supporting GVP in recent times. Andrew Goddard (VCPS) maintained that people were beginning to realize the impact of "daily shootings" in the United States: "I think people are starting to talk more about [the fact that] for every one person that's killed in a mass shooting there's ninety-nine people killed in a single or double shooting." It appears that it is media coverage of mass shootings that have garnered attention, particularly in recent years: "I think these horrific mass shootings are happening more frequently and with higher death tolls."-Adam Skaggs (GLCPGV). The shift in public support is said to be palpable: "There's always been an outpour— after Columbine, after Sandy Hook— but now it seems much more frequent, seems like it is greater numbers, it seems angrier."-Marvin Lim (KGOC). This is also thought to be evident in opinion polls: "We have seen an uptake in support for strengthening laws and a decreased support for loosening them. I don't want to suggest it's been a massive shift; but it's a slow and steady shift."-Adam Skaggs (GLCPGV). Importantly, it has been said that interest groups are bestowed more legitimacy "when they can show that they are representative of the attitudes and values of a particular segment of the population" (Luttbeg & Zeigler, 1974, p. 208).

Whilst this seems like a positive change for the GVP movement, it is worth remembering that increased public support does not necessarily translate into greater involvement. The "policy capacity" of GVP groups needs to be sufficient enough to allow them to engage in policy work. This includes having resources, abilities and skills to contribute to the formation and implementation of policies (Halpin, 2014, pp. 47, 360-361). Tom Mauser (CC) explained it in the following way: "My movement needs to recruit more people. We especially have to recruit people who are gun owners; people who are more conservative." As mentioned earlier, working with gun owners was a step proposed by interviewees as a way to advance the GVP issue. When a collection of individuals with similar grievances are brought together in a social movement organization, this is known as "frame bridging" (Snow, Rochford, Worden & Benford, 1986, p. 468).

One possible barrier is the perceived division between gun violence prevention and gun rights groups. This could be resolved through frames such as the rights and responsibilities approach, which enforces the idea that the personal right to own firearms comes with a societal responsibility to ensure the public are safe. For further impact, this could be coupled with the emotional approach to gain attention of people, showing them the human impact of gun violence. It is worth remembering that the public is not a blank slate onto which messages can be projected; rather it "picks through this flood of information and selects, rejects and ignores the information and messages" (Jacobs & Shapiro, 2000, p. 221).

What is required is frame amplification in the form of clarifying and associating values with a particular issue. Since this mobilizes support, it is fundamental to encouraging participation in a movement (Snow, Rochford, Worden & Benford, 1986, pp. 464, 469). Willingness to participate, moreover, does not necessarily translate into actual involvement. There are said to be four steps to participation in social movements: becoming a sympathizer; being targeted in mobilization attempts; becoming motivated to participate; overcoming any barriers to participation (Oegema & Klandermains, 1994, pp. 703, 719). Tom Mauser (CC) maintained that further action is needed than just indicating support on an opinion poll:

"Are those people going out in the streets? Are they going to make that a key issue when we go to vote? I don't think we're quite there yet. We've got to get those people willing to do more than just show up in an opinion poll."

Something like signing a petition is a relatively low risk campaign that could appeal to marginal sympathizers, so could be a good place to start in terms of trying to move forward with action (Oegema & Klandermains, 1994, p. 719). Should pursuing smaller policy steps prove worthwhile the focus could perhaps shift towards larger political goals in future (Goss, 2006, p. 145).

Moreover, it is felt that the increased public support has not affected policy change: "So even though there is momentum in terms of the people involved, we haven't seen that translate as much as it reflects the public opinion."-Marvin Lim (KGOC). In line with this, Goss (2006) spoke about the "gun control paradox," where levels of support do not translate into policy success. Part of the issue is the complex nature of the policymaking in the United States, where it is easier to defeat than pass a bill: "In Colorado, a bill has to go through a minimum of six votes to be passed, and it can die in only one vote"-Eileen McCarron (CC). Policy inaction is another barrier to seeing progress in the GVP movement: "I think very slowly we're advancing. It's hard to see it because the legislation hasn't followed yet."-Andrew Goddard (VCPS). The public health frame discussed earlier could be utilized to persuade policymakers of the need to take action. This may be useful in making gun violence prevention a bipartisan issue, something which is needed: "It still comes down to the two political parties taking on this issue and we have to break out of that."-Tom Mauser (CC). Once interest groups are accepted in the political system, they will become legitimate participants in deliberations relating to policy (Holyoke, 2014, p. 70).

Conclusion

It is possible that the results of the 2020 presidential election may shift the landscape on national policy-making. Interviewees felt that for policy change to occur Democrats needed to win the Presidency and control of the Senate. This is backed up by Fleming and colleague's (2012) research, which found that the number of restrictive bills proposed after a focusing event like a mass shooting is at its highest when the Presidency and Congress are Democratic. This did not occur and the current state of play was maintained, whereby the House and Senate retained a majority of Democrats and Republicans respectively. Due to this, it is likely this policy stalemate of the House passing legislation that is then stalling in the Senate will continue. The only way this might change is if Republican Senators rethink their position on guns. With Democrats securing the Presidency, this should also have an impact. Whilst the Presidency is limited in the actions it can take, it does shape the policy agenda and can also make a difference via appointment of judges to the Supreme Court, changing personnel and issuing executive orders (Brown, 2008; Hrebenar & Scott, 1982; Kingdon, 1994/2000). The President-elect, Joe Biden, has substantial experience in gun violence prevention; thus, it is likely to form part of his policy agenda. Moreover, a Biden win should provide an opening for interest groups to shape the direction of policymaking in the "presidential transition" (Brown, 2008) between an outgoing Trump administration and an incoming Biden one.

What could have affected the 2020 election are the reduced funding and resources afforded to Trump by the gun rights group, the NRA. With its resources, membership and funding (Patterson, 1998; Wilson, 1981), the NRA is a powerful force in American politics. Endorsement from powerful interest groups can be a significant form of influence in political campaigns (Noel, 2008). It was said that this support helped Trump's election campaign in 2016 (Kerr, 2018). Interviewees claimed that this is the reason Trump has been reluctant to take policy action after mass shootings, with even the Executive Order Trump passed on bump stocks said to be strategic in nature. It was claimed that the NRA did not speak against this measure to avoid the issue being discussed and possibly passed in Congress, which interviewees said would have made the law stronger. Recent troubles including legal and financial challenges have beleaguered the NRA, leading interviewees to predict that the NRA may be weaker in the 2020 election than it was in 2016.

Another influential factor cited was the progress that might happen in individual states, with a number of the Legislatures recently switching to Democratic control. Interviewees highlighted that what happens in individual states can have a wider influence on the country by setting the standard of what is acceptable. It may be the case that state progress advances ahead of that of federal policymaking in the near future.

Lastly, the support from citizens is another key factor. Interviewees cite a shift in public support for this issue coupled with more of willingness from legislators to talk about it as giving momentum to the GVP movement. Opinion polls show greater levels of support; however, this does not necessarily translate into greater involvement in GVP activism. The "policy capacity" of GVP groups in the form of resources, abilities and skills is needed to successfully engage in policy work (Halpin, 2014). To achieve this, participation in the GVP movement needs to be encouraged. Involvement in any social movement requires the mobilization of support and eradicating any barriers to participating (Oegema & Klandermains, 1994; Snow, Rochford, Worden & Benford, 1986). Smaller steps could be taken with different types of participants, including more conservative voters and gun owners, with the view in mind of pursuing larger goals in future (Goss, 2006; Oegema & Klandermains, 1994). Moreover, interviewees felt that the increased public support has not affected policy change. This mirrors the "gun control paradox" that Goss (2006) spoke of. The political landscape really needs to be conducive to policy change to overcome this paradox, no matter how high the levels of public support for gun violence prevention measures.

Chapter 10 outlined ideas for a number of policy proposals that could be pursued in the short and long term. Universal background checks, red flag laws and other smaller measures such as regulations on ghost guns and funding for gun research appear the most likely of these to gain traction in the future. Vizzard (1999, p. 141) argued that to be effective policies should encourage widespread compliance by members of society. To that end, laws should be easily enforced and avoid unnecessary burdens on those legally entitled to purchase and own firearms. This should be considered when drafting legislative proposals at both the state and federal levels.

Overall, it appears that there is increased public support for gun regulations and interviewees as a whole are quietly optimistic for the future. Despite this, barriers are still faced in the form of the need to translate this support into greater involvement in activism and policy action. The GVP groups interviewed have had a number of successes so far, particularly at the state level; yet there is still blockage in the form of federal level policy action. Further windows of opportunity to discuss and advance policy will likely arise with when future mass shootings occur (Fleming, Rutledge, Dixon & Peralton, 2016, p. 12). Previous work in this area, however, has shown that this alone does not necessarily translate into policy action (Fleming, Rutledge, Dixon & Peralton, 2016; Goss, 2006; Kerr, 2018). Future research should examine the impact of mass shootings on policymaking at the national and state levels. In conclusion, it is worth taking heed of the advice offered by Woodly (2015, p. 5):

"Social movements have their most lasting and permanent effect not through particular policy victories, but instead by changing politics redefining what is at stake and what can and ought to be done about a politicized problem."

REFERENCES

Agiesta, J. (2020, May 13). *CNN Poll: Biden tops Trump nationwide, but battleground tilt Trump*. CNN. https://edition.cnn.com/2020/05/13/politics/cnn-poll-2020/index.html

Ball, M. (2020, November 23). *As Donald Trump Refuses to Concede, America is Caught Between Crisis and Confusion*. TIME. https://time.com/5910875/trump-concede-biden/

BBC News. (2020a). *US Election 2020*. https://www.bbc.co.uk/news/election/us2020/results

BBC News. (2020b, November 24). *Trump accepts US presidency transition to Biden must begin*. https://www.bbc.co.uk/news/election-us-2020-55052640

Bennett, B., & Berenson, T. (2020, November 7). *How Donald Trump Lost the Election*. TIME. https://time.com/5907973/donald-trump-loses-2020-election/

Bloomberg. (2018, March 13). *Most Gun Owners Support Stricter Gun Laws – Even NRA Members*. TIME. https://time.com/5197807/stricter-gun-laws-nra/

Brown, H. (2008). Interest Groups, the White House and the Administration. In M. Grossmann (Ed.), *New Directions in Interest Group Politics* (pp. 118–153). Springer.

Butts, J. A., Roman, C. G., Bostwick, L., Porter, J. R., Hook, L., & Kuchler, H. (2020, April 30). *How coronavirus broke America's healthcare system*. Financial Times. https://www.ft.com/content/3bbb4f7c-890e-11ea-a01c-a28a3e3fbd33

Collins, D. (2019, December 11). *As Newtown students grow up, some turn to activism*. ABC News. https://abcnews.go.com/US/wireStory/newtown-students-grow-turn-activism-67649202

Doran, S. E. M. (2014). *News Media Constructions and Policy Implications of School Shootings in the United States* (Doctoral thesis). Glasgow, UK: University of Glasgow.

Fleming, A. K. (2012). *Gun Policy in the United States and Canada: The Impact of Mass Murders and Assassinations on Gun Control*. Continuum International Publishing Group.

Fleming, A. K., Rutledge, P. E., Dixon, G. C., & Peralton, S. (2016). When the smoke clears: Focusing events, issue definition, strategic framing and the politics of gun control. *Social Science Quarterly*, *97*(5), 1144–1156. doi:10.1111squ.12269

Goss, K. A. (2006). *Disarmed: The Missing Movement for Gun Control in America*. Princeton University Press.

Grossman, M. (2012). *The Not-So-Special Interests: Interest Groups, Public Representation and American Governance*. Stanford University Press. doi:10.1515/9780804781343

Halpin, D. R. (2014). *The Organization of Political Interest Groups*. Taylor and Francis. doi:10.4324/9781315817583

Holyoke, T. T. (2014). *Interest Groups and Lobbying: pursuing Political Interests*. Westview Press.

Hook, L., & Kuchler, H. (2020, April 30). *How coronavirus broke America's healthcare system*. Financial Times. https://www.ft.com/content/3bbb4f7c-890e-11ea-a01c-a28a3e3fbd33

Hrebenar, R. J., & Scott, R. K. (1982). *Interest Group Politics in America*. Prentice-Hall Inc.

Jacobs, L. R., & Shapiro, R. Y. (2000). *Politicians don't pander: political manipulation and the loss of Democratic responsiveness*. University of Chicago Press.

Kerr, S. E. M. (2018). *Gun Violence Prevention? The Politics Behind Policy Responses to School Shootings in the United States*. Palgrave MacMillan.

Kingdon, J. W. (1993/2004). *Agendas, Alternatives and Public Policies* (2nd ed.). Longman.

Loomis, B. A. (1998). Introduction: The Changing Nature of Interest Group Politics. In A. J. Cigler & B. A. Loomis (Eds.), *Interest Group Politics* (5th ed., pp. 1–32). Congressional Quarterly Inc.

Luttbeg, N. R., & Zeigler, H. (1974). Attitude consensus and conflict in an interest group: an assessment of conflict. In N. R. Luttbeg (Ed.), *Public Opinion and Public Policy: Models of Political Linkage* (pp. 208–221). The Dorsey Press.

McCarthy, J. (2019, November 4). *64% of Americans Want Stricter Laws on Gun Sales*. Gallup. https://news.gallup.com/poll/268016/americans-stricter-laws-gun-sales.aspx

Moore, M. (Director). (2018). *Fahrenheit 11/9*. Midwestern Films.

Noel, H. (2008). Political parties and ideology: interest groups in context. In M. Grossmann (Ed.), *New Directions in Interest Group Politics* (pp. 196–229). Routledge.

Oegema, D., & Klandermains, B. (1994, October). Why Social Movement Sympathizers Don't Participate: Erosion and Nonconversion of Support. *American Sociological Review*, *59*(5), 603–722. doi:10.2307/2096444

Oritz, E. (2018, March 13). *Parkland students sent letter of support from Dunblane shooting massacre survivors*. NBC News. https://www.nbcnews.com/news/us-news/parkland-students-sent-letter-support-dunblane-shooting-massacre-survivors-n856076

Patterson, K. (1998). The Political Firepower of the NRA. In A. J. Cigler & B. A. Loomis (Eds.), *Interest Group Politics* (5th ed., pp. 119–142). Congressional Quarterly Inc.

Santhanam, L. (2018, August 7) *Where do young Americans stand on guns?* PBS Nation. https://www.pbs.org/newshour/nation/where-do-young-americans-stand-on-guns

Snow, D. A., Rochford, B. E. Jr, Worden, S. K., & Benford, R. D. (1986). Frame Alignment Process: Micromobilization and movement participation. *American Sociological Review*, *51*(4), 461–481. doi:10.2307/2095581

Steidley, T., & Cohen, C. G. (2016). Framing the Gun Control Debate: Press releases and Framing Strategies of the National Rifle Association and the Brady Campaign. *Social Science Quarterly*, *98*(2), 608–627. doi:10.1111squ.12323

Stoebe, W. (2015). Firearm Availability and Violent Death: The Need for a Culture Change in Attitudes towards Guns.'. *Analyses of Social Issues and Public Policy (ASAP)*, *16*(1), 1–29.

Stone, P. (2019, May 6). *'The NRA is in grave danger': group's troubles are blow to Trump's 2020 bid.* The Guardian. https://www.theguardian.com/us-news/2019/may/06/nra-trump-2020-campaign-new-york-investigation

The Guardian. (2020, April 10). *How will coronavirus change the US presidential campaign?* https://www.theguardian.com/us-news/2020/apr/10/us-election-coronavirus-voting-trump-biden

The New York Times. (2018, November 27). *2018 Midterm Election Results.* https://www.nytimes.com/interactive/2018/us/elections/calendar-primary-results.html

Vizzard, W. J. (1999). The Impact of Agenda Confliction Policy Formulation and Implementation: The Case of Gun Control. In *Guns in America: A Reader* (pp. 131–144). New York University Press.

Wilson, G. K. (1981). *Interest Groups in the United States.* Oxford University Press.

Woodly, D. R. (2015). *The Politics of Common Sense: How Social Movements Use Public Discourse to Change Politics and Win Acceptance.* Oxford University Press. doi:10.1093/acprof:oso/9780190203986.001.0001

Wright, M., Molloyo, M., & Lockharto, K. (2018, February 26). *Parkland students vs the NRA: Has the powerful US gun lobby met its match in Generation Snapchat.* The Telegraph. https://www.telegraph.co.uk/news/2018/02/26/parkland-students-vs-nra-has-powerful-us-gun-lobby-met-match/

About the Author

Selina E. M. Kerr, Ph.D., is a criminologist and researcher working in the United Kingdom. She has recently published a book exploring the gun-related policy responses to school shootings in the United States. Other research areas of interest include solutions to reduce gun violence, threat assessment, emergency management and communication procedures during active shooter incidents and representations of violence in television shows.

Index

V

W

Recommended Reference Books

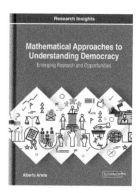

Research Insights

Mathematical Approaches to Understanding Democracy
Emerging Research and Opportunities

Alberto Arteta

ISBN: 978-1-5225-7558-0
© 2019; 148 pp.
List Price: $165

Critical Explorations

Immigration and the Current Social, Political, and Economic Climate
Breakthroughs in Research and Practice

Information Resources Management Association
Volume I

ISBN: 978-1-5225-6918-3
© 2019; 740 pp.
List Price: $495

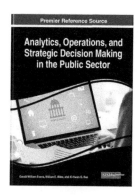

Premier Reference Source

Analytics, Operations, and Strategic Decision Making in the Public Sector

Gerald William Evans, William E. Biles, and Ki-Hwan G. Bae

ISBN: 978-1-5225-7591-7
© 2019; 441 pp.
List Price: $215

Handbook of Research on

Urban and Humanitarian Logistics

Jesus Gonzalez-Feliu, Mario Chong, Jorge Vargas Florez, and Julio Padilla Solis

ISBN: 978-1-5225-8160-4
© 2019; 450 pp.
List Price: $295

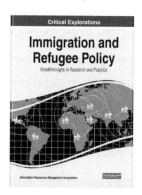

Critical Explorations

Immigration and Refugee Policy
Breakthroughs in Research and Practice

Information Resources Management Association

ISBN: 978-1-5225-8909-9
© 2019; 469 pp.
List Price: $330

Handbook of Research on

Advocacy, Promotion, and Public Programming for Memory Institutions

Patrick Ngulube

ISBN: 978-1-5225-7429-3
© 2019; 453 pp.
List Price: $265

Do you want to stay current on the latest research trends, product announcements, news and special offers?
Join IGI Global's mailing list today and start enjoying exclusive perks sent only to IGI Global members.
Add your name to the list at **www.igi-global.com/newsletters.**

Publisher of Peer-Reviewed, Timely, and Innovative Academic Research

IGI Global
DISSEMINATOR OF KNOWLEDGE

www.igi-global.com Sign up at www.igi-global.com/newsletters f facebook.com/igiglobal t twitter.com/igiglobal in linkedin.com/igiglobal

Ensure Quality Research is Introduced to the Academic Community

Become an IGI Global Reviewer for Authored Book Projects

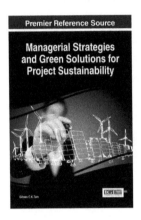

The overall success of an authored book project is dependent on quality and timely reviews.

In this competitive age of scholarly publishing, constructive and timely feedback significantly expedites the turnaround time of manuscripts from submission to acceptance, allowing the publication and discovery of forward-thinking research at a much more expeditious rate. Several IGI Global authored book projects are currently seeking highly-qualified experts in the field to fill vacancies on their respective editorial review boards:

Applications and Inquiries may be sent to:
development@igi-global.com

Applicants must have a doctorate (or an equivalent degree) as well as publishing and reviewing experience. Reviewers are asked to complete the open-ended evaluation questions with as much detail as possible in a timely, collegial, and constructive manner. All reviewers' tenures run for one-year terms on the editorial review boards and are expected to complete at least three reviews per term. Upon successful completion of this term, reviewers can be considered for an additional term.

If you have a colleague that may be interested in this opportunity, we encourage you to share this information with them.

IGI Global Proudly Partners With eContent Pro International

Receive a 25% Discount on all Editorial Services

Editorial Services

IGI Global expects all final manuscripts submitted for publication to be in their final form. This means they must be reviewed, revised, and professionally copy edited prior to their final submission. Not only does this support with accelerating the publication process, but it also ensures that the highest quality scholarly work can be disseminated.

English Language Copy Editing

Let eContent Pro International's expert copy editors perform edits on your manuscript to resolve spelling, punctuaion, grammar, syntax, flow, formatting issues and more.

Scientific and Scholarly Editing

Allow colleagues in your research area to examine the content of your manuscript and provide you with valuable feedback and suggestions before submission.

Figure, Table, Chart & Equation Conversions

Do you have poor quality figures? Do you need visual elements in your manuscript created or converted? A design expert can help!

Translation

Need your documjent translated into English? eContent Pro International's expert translators are fluent in English and more than 40 different languages.

Email: customerservice@econtentpro.com   **www.igi-global.com/editorial-service-partners**

www.igi-global.com

Publisher of Peer-Reviewed, Timely, and
Innovative Academic Research Since 1988

IGI Global's Transformative Open Access (OA) Model:
How to Turn Your University Library's Database Acquisitions Into a Source of OA Funding

In response to the OA movement and well in advance of Plan S, IGI Global, early last year, unveiled their OA Fee Waiver (Read & Publish) Initiative.

Under this initiative, librarians who invest in IGI Global's InfoSci-Books (5,300+ reference books) and/or InfoSci-Journals (185+ scholarly journals) databases will be able to subsidize their patron's OA article processing charges (APC) when their work is submitted and accepted (after the peer review process) into an IGI Global journal. *See website for details.

How Does it Work?

1. When a library subscribes or perpetually purchases IGI Global's InfoSci-Databases and/or their discipline/subject-focused subsets, IGI Global will match the library's investment with a fund of equal value to go toward subsidizing the OA article processing charges (APCs) for their patrons.

   Researchers: **Be sure to recommend the InfoSci-Books and InfoSci-Journals to take advantage of this initiative.**

2. When a student, faculty, or staff member submits a paper and it is accepted (following the peer review) into one of IGI Global's 185+ scholarly journals, the author will have the option to have their paper published under a traditional publishing model or as OA.

3. When the author chooses to have their paper published under OA, IGI Global will notify them of the OA Fee Waiver (Read and Publish) Initiative. If the author decides they would like to take advantage of this initiative, IGI Global will deduct the US$ 2,000 APC from the created fund.

4. This fund will be offered on an annual basis and will renew as the subscription is renewed for each year thereafter. IGI Global will manage the fund and award the APC waivers unless the librarian has a preference as to how the funds should be managed.

Hear From the Experts on This Initiative:

"I'm very happy to have been able to make one of my recent research contributions, "Visualizing the Social Media Conversations of a National Information Technology Professional Association" featured in the *International Journal of Human Capital and Information Technology Professionals*, freely available along with having access to the valuable resources found within IGI Global's InfoSci-Journals database."

– **Prof. Stuart Palmer**,
Deakin University, Australia

For More Information, Visit: www.igi-global.com/publish/contributor-resources/open-access/read-publish-model
or contact IGI Global's Database Team at eresources@igi-global.com.

Lightning Source UK Ltd.
Milton Keynes UK
UKHW050102150122
397188UK00004B/139